Josephus and the Theologies of Ancient Judaism

Josephus and the Theologies of Ancient Judaism

JONATHAN KLAWANS

OXFORD
UNIVERSITY PRESS

OXFORD
UNIVERSITY PRESS

Oxford University Press is a department of the University of Oxford.
It furthers the University's objective of excellence in research, scholarship,
and education by publishing worldwide.

Oxford   New York

Auckland   Cape Town   Dar es Salaam   Hong Kong   Karachi
Kuala Lumpur   Madrid   Melbourne   Mexico City   Nairobi
New Delhi   Shanghai   Taipei   Toronto

With offices in

Argentina   Austria   Brazil   Chile   Czech Republic   France   Greece
Guatemala   Hungary   Italy Japan   Poland Portugal   Singapore
South Korea   Switzerland   Thailand   Turkey   Ukraine   Vietnam

Oxford is a registered trademark of Oxford University Press
in the UK and certain other countries.

Published in the United States of America by
Oxford University Press
198 Madison Avenue, New York, NY 10016

© Oxford University Press 2012

Library of Congress Cataloging-in-Publication Data
Klawans, Jonathan.
Josephus and the theologies of ancient Judaism / Jonathan Klawans.
p. cm.
Includes bibliographical references and index.
ISBN 978-0-19-992861-3
1. Josephus, Flavius.   2. Judaism—History—Post-exilic period, 586 B.C.–210 A.D.
3. Jews—History—168 B.C.–135 A.D.   I. Title.
DS115.9.J6K53 2013
296.309′015—dc23
2012005611

Preface and Acknowledgments

LIKE MOST SCHOLARS of ancient Judaism, I have been engaged with Josephus for as long as I have been studying the second temple period. And like many, if not most, scholars interested primarily in the history of religion (as opposed to social, economic, or political history) my frequent encounters with Josephus's works were mostly selective and secondary. I turned to *Jewish War* and *Antiquities* when directed by other needs—whether to assess the Essenes, measure Herod's temple, or determine which of the Hasmonean rulers could have been *the* Wicked Priest of the *Pesher Habakkuk*. Once that need was met—references checked, data collated—I closed up the Josephus volumes and went back to the matter at hand. There's nothing inherently wrong with this: all scholars must, in the end, center some evidence, and consult the rest as needed, commensurate with its relevance to the text or subject at hand. Many scholars will and should continue doing work on rabbinic literature, the New Testament, and the Dead Sea Scrolls, without being able to spend a few years, as I have recently, living with Josephus. But this book argues that general understandings of ancient Judaism would be improved if more of us religious studies types put Josephus in the center more of the time. We who study ancient Judaism stand to learn more than we might expect about our subject from this ancient historian, for he was a deeply religious thinker. We also stand to contribute something in return to the understanding of Josephus, because this historian's religious thought is frequently downplayed, and too often misunderstood or misconstrued.

A good deal of research and the bulk of the writing of this book occurred during a Sabbatical leave granted by Boston University, which was also supported by an American Philosophical Society Sabbatical Fellowship. I am grateful for the year their support provided, and I hope this book proves worthy of that assistance. The preparation and publication of this book was also made possible by a grant from the Memorial Foundation for Jewish Culture.

In 2007, I assumed the Directorship of Boston University's Division of Religious and Theological Studies, a graduate program that operates largely by combining the resources of the University's Department of Religion and School of Theology. There can be no doubt that this hands-on experience working with colleagues who see themselves as religious studies scholars, theologians, both, or neither has impacted this project productively. Despite having done well enough to be reappointed, I am one of those academics who would prefer to focus more on teaching and research and less on administration. Nevertheless, I am grateful to Dean Virginia Sapiro and Associate Deans Peter Doeringer and Patricia Johnson for finding ways to support my research during these years of service. I also want to thank my current chair, Deeana Klepper, and her predecessor, Stephen Prothero, for their unfailing support and encouragement. I am grateful to John Berthrong for our many helpful and candid conversations about religion, theology, and academic civility. Indeed, I thank all of my colleagues in the Department of Religion and the Division of Religious and Theological Studies for their support, cooperation, and collegiality.

Earlier versions of material relating to this book were presented at various conferences, starting with a symposium held in New York City in honor of the retirement of my teacher Professor David Weiss Halivni from Columbia University (2005). Subsequently, papers relating to this book were presented at meetings of the Society of Biblical Literature (2007, 2008), the World Congress of Jewish Studies (2009), and the New England Region of the Society of Biblical Literature (2011). I thank the organizers of these conferences and panels for the opportunities to share my work. I thank those in attendance for their constructive criticisms and insightful questions. Some portions of the book (dealing with the Sadducees) first appeared in the joint festschrift for my teacher Alan F. Segal (may his memory be a blessing) and his longtime friend Larry Hurtado. This book, *Israel's God and Rebecca's Children*, edited by David B. Capes, April D. DeConick, Helen K. Bond, and Troy A. Miller, was published by Baylor University Press (2007). Other material included here (dealing with the Essenes) first appeared in an essay included in *Rediscovering the Dead Sea Scrolls*, edited by Maxine L. Grossman, and published by Wm. B. Eerdmans (2010). Large portions of chapter 2 appeared as "Josephus on Fate, Free Will, and Ancient Jewish Types of Compatibilism," in

Numen 56 (2009), published by Brill. Significant portions of chapter 5 first appeared as "Josephus, the Rabbis, and Responses to Catastrophes Ancient and Modern," in *Jewish Quarterly Review* 100 (2010), published by the University of Pennsylvania Press. I thank the editors and publishers for their help with the original publications and their more recent permissions to include revised and reworked versions within this volume.

A large number of friends and colleagues have graciously and patiently supported me in my journey through the historical, theological, and even philosophical issues that have been my preoccupations for the last seven years or so. I wish to thank, first of all, David Capes, Helen Bond, Maxine Grossman, John Collins, and Timothy Lim, whose invitations to contribute essays in collected volumes they were editing allowed me, rather safely, to embark on the journey of rethinking ancient Jewish theology and its significance for sectarian disputes. Their generous and helpful comments on the essays they solicited and edited improved this book, too. I also wish to thank the following friends and colleagues who read drafts of articles, essays, chapters, and grant proposals or otherwise offered helpful advice and encouragement along the way: Moshe Bernstein, Susanne Bobzien, Alejandro Botta, David Brakke, Menachem Butler, Marc A. Cohen, Natalie Dohrmann, David Frankfurter, Paula Fredriksen, Adam Gregerman, Christine E. Hayes, Susannah Heschel, Richard Kalmin, Steven T. Katz, Deeana Copeland Klepper, Jennifer Knust, Steve Mason, Nicholas de Lange, Jon D. Levenson, Diana Lobel, John P. Meier, Robert C. Neville, Alan Rosen, Stephen Prothero, Jeffrey L. Rubenstein, Adam Seligman, Einar Thomassen, Gary Waleik and Michael Zank. I also benefited from suggestions and criticisms offered by anonymous reviewers for the *Jewish Quarterly Review, Numen,* and Oxford University Press. My Oxford editor, Cynthia Read, once again was a ready (and patient) source of strong support. Sasha Grossman deftly assisted at each stage. Martha Ramsey copyedited the book with attention not only to the details, but to the general arguments as well. Peter Mavrikis guided the book through production, providing helpful guidance every step of the way.

I gratefully acknowledge that lessons learned in classrooms long ago reverberate here. Alan Segal's spirit hovers all over this work, but especially chapter 3. David Weiss Halivni's influence is palpable throughout, and particularly in chapters 4 and 5. Reaching further back, David Roskies and Zeev W. Mankowitz have left their imprint on chapter 5 too. And although these memories are distant and faded, I do wish to note that I was first introduced to the academic study of Josephus in the classrooms of Shaye J.D. Cohen and Isaiah M. Gafni. I must be forgetting others. But I do remain in eternal debt to the teachers who encouraged and inspired me.

My students at Boston University, Harvard Divinity School, and the Hebrew College contributed a great deal to this project, probably more than they think: nothing encourages reformulating an idea more than a good student's blank stare. My sincere thanks extends to the librarians at these institutions and especially to whomever keeps their electronic services up and running. Although I cannot name (or necessarily even recall) all of the electronic resources I used these past years, I want to acknowledge Google Books and the Internet Archive for making readily available—anywhere, anytime—a great many of the older volumes included in my bibliography. I also want to acknowledge Steve Mason and York University for the Project on Ancient Cultural Engagement (PACE) and Tufts University for the Perseus Project: I used both, six days a week, for a year or more. Maybe I could have written this book without these resources—but it's difficult for me to imagine.

For the last two years, Frances Dora Mansen served as my research assistant, and my thanks to Dorie for her quick, courteous, and accurate help with research tasks early on, and indexing more recently. Fellow members of Temple Israel of Natick were often the first to hear my thoughts on these subjects—I especially thank those hearty souls who came out on cold winter nights over the years to hear some of these presentations and share their reactions. I also gratefully acknowledge Rabbis Dan Liben and Harold Kushner: surely it is no coincidence that I have been paying increasing attention to theology in the years since I first had the good fortune to meet them. All of these friends and colleagues deserve credit for whatever is valuable in this book. The blame for all that is wrong here is mine alone.

Thanks to the Web, a cable modem, and the electronic resources mentioned earlier, I was able to research and write this book largely at home. I am thankful that I have a perfectly functional home office. And I am equally thankful that I live in a noisy—indeed, at times, riotous—household. I wouldn't want it any other way. During the years I worked on this project, my wife Helaine and I were blessed with the births of our older son Ari's two younger brothers, Gabriel and Elijah. Indeed, during my Sabbatical year our littlest was a toddler and mostly at home—sometimes napping but usually not; usually smiling, but sometimes not. As the author of Ecclesiastes might have written if he had enjoyed the company of young children, there's a time for noise. There's also a time for work, and a time for love. Who said it can't all happen at once? I consider myself undeservedly lucky to have been able to do so much of my work on this project with my wife and children so close by. And I therefore dedicate this book to them, in gratitude for the joy and meaning they have brought to my life and, it just so happens, to my work as well.

Contents

Abbreviations

AB	Anchor Bible
AGJU	Arbeiten zur Geschichte des antiken Judentums und des Urchristentums
AJSR	*Association for Jewish Studies Review*
BJP	Brill Josephus Project
BJS	Brown Judaic Studies
CBQ	*Catholic Biblical Quarterly*
CBR	*Currents in Biblical Research*
CRINT	Compendia rerum iudaicarum ad Novum Testamentum
DJD	Discoveries in the Judaean Desert
DSD	*Dead Sea Discoveries*
EJL	Early Judaism and Its Literature
HTR	*Harvard Theological Review*
HUCA	*Hebrew Union College Annual*
JAAR	*Journal of the American Academy of Religion*
JBL	*Journal of Biblical Literature*
JJS	*Journal of Jewish Studies*
JQR	*Jewish Quarterly Review*
JSJ	*Journal for the Study of Judaism in the Persian, Hellenistic and Roman Periods*
JSJSup	Journal for the Study of Judaism Supplement Series
JSPSup	Journal for the Study of the Pseudepigrapha Supplement Series
JTS	*Journal of Theological Studies*
LCL	Loeb Classical Library
PAAJR	*Proceedings of the American Academy for Jewish Research*
RB	*Revue Biblique*
RevQ	*Revue de Qumran*

SJLA	Studies in Judaism in Late Antiquity
SPB	Studia post-biblica
STDJ	Studies in the Texts of the Desert of Judah
TSAJ	Texte und Studien zum antiken Judentum
VT	*Vetus Testamentum*
WUNT	Wissenschaftliche Untersuchungen zum Neuen Testament

A Note on Translations and Editions

TRANSLATIONS OF JOSEPHUS's works typically follow the Loeb Classical Library edition, slightly modified for clarity. Significant divergences from this translation, whether motivated by textual variants or interpretive disagreements, are noted within. I have also consulted all available volumes of the Brill Josephus Project (BJP) edited by Steve Mason, as well as the classic William Whiston translation available (among many other places) on the PACE website, also under the auspices of Steve Mason. For *Antiquities*, I have found Abraham Schalit's Hebrew translation useful; I have also consulted the German edition of *Jewish War*, edited by Otto Michel and Otto Bauernfeind. While I have typically followed the Greek text in the LCL edition, I have also made direct use of Benedictus Niese's text as available on the Perseus and Pace websites, as well as his *Editio Maior*, now (unbelievably) available for download via Google Books and the Internet Archive.

Translations of scripture (Hebrew Bible, New Testament, and Apocrypha) generally follow the New Revised Standard Version (NRSV), modified slightly as necessary. Translations of Talmud follow the Soncino Talmud translation (ed. I. Epstein), but with noticeable modifications. Translations of Qumran literature typically follow Geza Vermes, *The Complete Dead Sea Scrolls*. References to the Dead Sea Scrolls are generally keyed to the text prepared by Martin Abegg, Jr., for *Accordance*, in comparison with the relevant volumes of *Discoveries in the Judaean Desert* (DJD), as well as the *Dead Sea Scroll Study Edition*, edited by Florentino García Martínez and Eibert J. C. Tigchelaar. I have also consulted the recently published first volume of Elisha Qimron's work *The Dead Sea Scrolls: The Hebrew Writings*. Where line numerations differ (e.g., 1QH), I have tried to follow the newest editions. Other translations and editions used are cited in the notes; all are included in the bibliography.

*Josephus and the Theologies
of Ancient Judaism*

I

Theology, Josephus, and Understandings of Ancient Judaism

THE WORD "THEOLOGY" makes some people very nervous. Scholars of religious studies are often wary of theologians, worried—rightly perhaps in some cases, wrongly no doubt in others—lest contemporary religious studies departments and programs be refashioned again after older Christian seminaries (whence, of course, the discipline of religious studies once emerged).[1] One unfortunate side-effect of this can be seen in the failure to develop a neutral space within the academy for a sub-field devoted to the study of religious doctrines. Consider, for instance, the highly developed nature of "ritual studies." There is no comparable field of "doctrine studies." To be sure, certain classic works provide some guidance.[2] But on the whole, religious studies currently lacks a developed discourse devoted to clarifying whatever the interplay may be between social events and religious beliefs. Can theological change be explained as resulting from social changes or political upheaval? What kinds of events can be determined to bring about what types of theological change? Will a given crisis necessarily lead to such change? Despite the significance of these sorts of questions, it seems that many scholars of religion are more likely to be concerned with the potential dangers posed by theology and theologians.[3] One important result for our purposes is the fact that scholars of ancient Judaism—faced with task of tracing developments in Jewish belief between the Maccabean revolt and the destruction of the temple in 70 CE—do so largely, if not entirely, without helpful theoretical or methodological guidance.

Indeed, scholars of ancient Judaism in particular can exhibit a heightened form of anxiety with theology, one that has been understandably hardened by the clearly anti-Semitic descriptions of ancient Judaism by, especially, certain influential central European seminarians. Julius Wellhausen, for instance, praised Christian faith (that is, Protestant faith) and denigrated rabbinic "legalism" and "intellectualism" (in a word, Judaism).[4] To be sure, some important and influential scholars of ancient Judaism, Solomon Schechter and George Foot Moore among them, did attempt to counter these trends with systematic, apologetic theologies of ancient Judaism.[5] But these works have fallen out of fashion. The dominant reaction to Wellhausen among Jewish scholars, rather, has been to focus unabashedly and unapologetically on the study of traditional Jewish legal texts. Within some institutions of higher Jewish learning, Talmudists (like Saul Lieberman) reigned supreme, while theologians (like Abraham Joshua Heschel) struggled for respect.[6] Curiously, this development in some ways aligns with and hearkens back to none other than the first great Jewish intellectual of the modern era, Moses Mendelssohn. For the great Jewish philosopher of Berlin, Judaism is a religion of revealed law. Though few modern Jews, even among academics, uphold Mendelssohn's approach to Judaism in its particulars, we will soon see that a quasi-Mendelssohnian perspective reigns supreme in the study of ancient Judaism: the common scholarly presumption is that Jews of the second temple period—and, by extension, their sectarian disputes—were not all that concerned with theological matters but were just as focused on laws and legal texts as many modern Jews are (or at least are perceived to be). And it is also widely believed—sometimes by the same scholars—that Judaism was, paradoxically, thrust into theological crisis in the wake of the destruction of the temple, from which it emerged only gradually. The common denominator here is that theology was not terribly important in the second temple period. Theological dispute had little to do with sectarianism; and theological discourse was not able to develop sufficient sophistication to withstand the challenge posed by historical catastrophe.

Approaches to ancient Judaism that downplay the significance or sophistication of Jewish theology of the second temple period face one insurmountable problem: developed theologizing is central to the most important single source we have for the study of ancient Judaism: the writings of Flavius Josephus. Taking this fact as the starting point, this book puts forward two interrelated hypotheses with regard to Josephus and ancient Jewish theology. The first hypothesis concerns Josephus's descriptions of the ancient Jewish schools of thought (Pharisees, Sadducees, and Essenes): it will be argued here that these brief, clear and reasonably accurate accounts should play a more central role in the understanding of ancient Jewish sectarian disputes. The second hypothesis concerns Josephus's own theological musings, which pepper all four of his literary works: it will be argued here that this material, too, should figure more prominently in examinations of ancient Judaism in general, and the understanding of Jewish theological responses to the destruction of the temple in particular. Over the course of this book, we will see that the evidence from Josephus should not be overlooked or undervalued when we endeavor to understand ancient Jewish attitudes toward divine providence (chapter 2), life after death (chapter 3), the sources of law (chapter 4), and theodicy, particularly with regard to the destruction of the temple (chapter 5). When compared with other extant evidence, Josephus's theological data proves, on the whole, to be reasonable and confirmable. At times, Josephus's observations seem strikingly sophisticated—even prescient. Therefore, we should not suppose—as is rather common—that these issues were relatively inconsequential, and that Josephus was entirely or largely wrong to present ancient Jewish sectarian disputes as characterized by serious theological differences.

Josephus's Life, Works, and Audiences

But before going any further, a word about Josephus.[7] He was born in approximately 37 CE to a priestly family—he even boasted of his Hasmonean descent, albeit through a maternal ancestor.[8] Reared, we can assume, in wealth and privilege, the young Josephus was exposed to Jewish learning early on, and would later boast of his prodigious learning and unusually sharp memory.[9] Caught in the revolutionary fervor that raged in Galilee and Judea from 66 to 70 CE, Josephus served briefly as a leader of the Jewish rebels in Galilee. Under circumstances that appear suspicious (to say the least), Josephus escaped alive from a suicide pact among doomed rebels, and went over to the Roman side (67 CE). He subsequently witnessed the Roman siege and destruction of Jerusalem from the Roman vantage point. He eventually settled in Rome, where he wrote four works that have survived.[10] His first literary effort, *The Jewish War*, was composed in the 70s.[11] Like all of Josephus's extant works, *War* was composed in Greek, though he speaks of an Aramaic original, now lost (*War* 1.3, 6).[12] Two decades later (c. 93 CE) he completed his magnum opus, *Antiquities*, which is an account of Israelite and Judean history from creation to the first century CE.[13] Sometime later—either in the mid-90s or, less likely, a decade later—he completed *Life*, something of an autobiography, which served as an appendix to *Antiquities*.[14] It is in this late work (*Life* 12) that Josephus tells us he had lived his life as a Pharisee. Josephus's fourth work, *Against Apion,* is an apology, defending Jewish beliefs and practices against Roman detractors; it, too, was likely composed in the mid-90s, though possibly later.[15] If Josephus completed other works before his death (c. 100 CE), they are no longer extant.[16]

Writing in Rome for Greek-readers with money to spare, Josephus's works are certainly addressed, at least in part, to interested Greco-Roman Gentiles who knew little about Judea, Jews, or Judaism.[17] That Josephus also intended or expected a Jewish readership—particularly among wealthy Jews—should not be doubted.[18] Josephus boasts of delivering copies of *War* to both Roman officials (Vespasian and Titus) and to "many" prominent Roman Jews "educated in Greek wisdom," among them Agrippa II (*Apion* 1.50–51; see also *Life* 361–67), Agrippa's brother-in-law Julius Archelaus, and an otherwise unknown, but illustrious, Herod.[19] Considering the controversies Josephus tells us surrounded his works (e.g., *Apion* 1.53), it is not difficult to imagine wealthy, literate Jews wanting to know what the works contained.

But Josephus's fortunes among Jewish readers were soon to change. To be sure, Talmudic rabbis may have had direct or indirect access to some form of Josephus's works, and the medieval Hebrew *Josippon* did circulate widely.[20] But Josephus's works themselves were soon lost to Jewish memory, a phenomenon that may well reflect the fact that their author was suspected of treason even during his lifetime (e.g., *War* 3.439, 5.393; *Life* 425), and remembered for little else by Jews thereafter.[21] As the centuries wore on, it was Christians who took the greatest interest in Josephus, studying his works and preserving whatever manuscript evidence now remains.[22] Indeed, Christian scribes made something of a Christian out of him, doctoring passages in some manuscript traditions, adding passages in others.[23] Josephus's works began to have a direct impact on Jews and Judaism again when, in the nineteenth century, scholars such as Abraham Geiger and Heinrich Graetz published histories of ancient Judaism meant for scholarly and popular audiences alike, making liberal (if selected) use of Josephus's works and views. Josephus's *Jewish War* was published in a Hebrew edition in the 1920s, and a Hebrew edition of *Antiquities* began to appear in the 1940s.[24] In English, however, the relative extent of the Christian popular interest in Josephus is evidenced by the wide circulation of editions of Josephus's works distributed by Christian publishers such as Hendrickson, Kregel, and Thomas Nelson.[25] Tellingly, there is no similar mass-produced edition of Josephus's works addressed to any Jewish market—either Hebrew or English.

Despite these disparities—and whatever Josephus's original intent—this historian's works now find an ecumenical audience, certainly among academics. The discovery of the Dead Sea Scrolls in the late 1940s cemented scholarly and popular interest in the Essenes and their historical background. Yigael Yadin's excavations at Masada in the early 1960s reinforced an already growing interest in *Jewish War* and its account of the fortress's last defenders. Coincidentally, the Loeb Classical Library completed its Josephus project in 1965, with the publication of Louis Feldman's translation and annotation of books 18 to 20 of *Antiquities*. Over the next two decades, works by Feldman, Harold Attridge, Shaye J. D. Cohen, Tessa Rajak, Per Bilde, and Steve Mason set the field of "Josephus studies" on solid footing. Today, dissertations, monographs, conference volumes, research tools (print and electronic) and even commentaries abound; the field is, finally, flourishing.[26]

Josephus as a Historian of Judaism: Sources, Biases, and Veracity

Nothing illustrates the livelihood of a scholarly field better than disagreement. Debates rage—and will continue to for many years—about Josephus's general veracity as a historian, and how scholars should (or should not) make use of his works for the reconstruction of ancient Jewish history.[27] Josephus has been accused of a host of historiographical crimes and misdemeanors, from fabricating documents to suit his ends,[28] to slavishly copying so many sources that he can hardly be considered an author at all.[29] Fueling these disputes is the undoubted fact that contradictions abound within Josephus's own works, particularly when he is speaking about his own participation in the revolt.[30] Closer to our own concerns, many scholars have objected to Josephus's philosophically influenced descriptions of the Pharisees, Sadducees, and Essenes.[31] These are, it is suggested, guided by Josephus's apologetic goals or literary interests, and therefore overlook what *really* mattered to ancient Jews: matters of religious practice, such as the calendar, cultic procedures, and the lineage of the high priest, as we will see. To be sure, we cannot overlook Josephus's apologetic concerns.[32] Nor can we safely ignore his personal biases. As we will soon see, Josephus's biases manifest themselves against the Sadducees in particular, posing a challenge to any understanding of their theological views as he records them.

The situation, however, is not hopeless, at least not for the present project. We can safely leave most general questions about Josephus's historical veracity aside, for we are interested in probing a rather defined set of questions: did Josephus speak accurately when he described ancient Jewish scholastic disputes as theological disagreements? And do his accounts of the contours of these theological disputes ring true? These questions point us to specific observations by Josephus (as we will see in the next section), the accuracy of which we can test in many cases against other extant sources (as we will see in the following chapters). I will argue, throughout this book, in favor of the importance and relative accuracy of the evidence we will consider—but this should not be understood as some apologetic for the veracity of Josephus's historiographic writings in general. I will accept as reliable what can be reasonably verified. The fact that Josephus may have—or even demonstrably—prevaricated about other particular historical figures (e.g., Herod) or events (e.g., suicide at Masada) matters little for our purposes. Even habitual liars sometimes tell the truth. So a prolific historian who exaggerates here, embellishes there, even forges now and then still deserves a hearing. The only way to make progress is to probe selections of data and see what results.

As for Josephan biases, these we will indeed need to track and account for. But the problem is sometimes stated too simply: some accept Josephus's claim (*Life* 12) to have adopted Pharisaic ways and find that Josephus exhibited Pharisaic biases in his dislike of the Sadducees and claims for Pharisaic predominance (at least in his later works).[33] Others, however, doubt the veracity of *Life* 12 precisely by identifying anti-Pharisaic observations in Josephus's oeuvre (e.g., *Ant.* 17.41–45).[34] If both positions can be argued, the question is obviously not so clear-cut. Indeed, Josephus proves difficult to pigeonhole: Of the three groups we will focus on, Josephus seems rather taken with the Essenes. Yet he clearly was not one of their number: he took wives (*Life* 414–15, 426–27), hardly lived a communitarian lifestyle, and survived the war precisely by shunning the martyrdoms that the Essenes (by his account) happily endured (*War* 2.152–53). As noted, Josephus claims for himself a Hasmonean descent (albeit somewhat indirect), yet he does not hesitate to relate to his readers the sordid, murderous deeds of his power-hungry ancestors (see, e.g., *Ant.* 13.372–76 on Alexander Jannaeus's brutal behavior). Josephus's priestly identity may have played a role in his praise for certain priestly figures (such as the moderate Jerusalem leaders Ananus and Jesus, whose noble deaths we will discuss in chapter 3)—but other priests (his Hasmonean ancestors among them) come in for criticism, too. Finally, Josephus's extended criticisms of Herod's homicidal behavior do not prevent him from aligning with the politics of Herod's scion Agrippa II (see *War* 2.345–401).

Although we cannot solve the broader question of Josephan biases as manifested throughout his vast output, it is hoped that this study will contribute something of value to the ongoing discussion. One of the ways scholars try to parse Josephus's bias is precisely by aligning his own views with those of one group or another, or by arguing against such an alignment. Louis Feldman, for instance, argues in favor of Josephus's Pharisaic allegiance by finding echoes of Jewish oral traditions in Josephus's works.[35] Steve Mason, on the other hand, denies Josephus's Pharisaic commitment in part by contrasting Josephus's views with those of the later rabbis.[36] At the same time, Mason points in the direction that we will proceed, by separating Josephus's attitude toward past Pharisaic political behavior (which may well have been critical) from his attitude toward Pharisaic religious beliefs (which, it will be argued here, was rather positive).[37] Indeed, considering what we have observed about Josephus's attitudes about priests, Hasmoneans, Herodians, and Essenes, it seems quite clear that Josephus could praise (or even adopt) a group's religious beliefs or social policies even while criticizing the personal or political behavior of its members or leaders. Josephus's religious beliefs can be discerned, therefore, not by measuring his praises or criticisms of distinct groups' (or their leaders') behavior, but rather by looking at his own theological affirmations. These in turn must be analyzed in light of his descriptions of contemporary religious beliefs as well as whatever external evidence can be brought to bear on Josephus's testimony.

What then of Josephus's sources?[38] There was a time when scholars tried to identify large chunks of non-Josephan material in Josephus's works, and Josephus's descriptions of Pharisees, Sadducees, and Essenes were among those passages believed by some to have been blindly copied from earlier sources—the lost history of Nicolaus of Damascus being a popular choice.[39] A number of developments have taken place in Josephan studies that should give us pause before we attribute this material to someone other than Josephus. Some time ago already, Shaye Cohen systematically compared Josephus's writings with sources that he used that we do still have, such as *Aristeas* and 1 Maccabees. His conclusions are important and unquestionable, for the evidence is now plainly before us: In practically every instance we can evaluate ourselves, Josephus does not slavishly copy his sources, but rather paraphrases and rewrites them so to better suit his literary-historiographic interests and needs.[40] Moving closer to our own interests, Steve Mason thoroughly reviewed Josephus's discussions of the Pharisees (their theological beliefs included) and found, practically without exception, that the material is thoroughly Josephan.[41] His more recent work on Josephus's account of the Essenes reaches a similar conclusion.[42] This is not to say that Josephus did not consult or use sources—indeed he must have done both with great frequency. But if a given passage—say Josephus's account of the Essenes—can be understood in light of Josephus's literary interests, and shown to deploy characteristic Josephan language (an effort made simpler by the availability of electronic texts), then what is gained by hypothesizing that Josephus borrowed from some non-extant hypothetical source? Even when we can determine that Josephus is dependent on earlier material, his habit of paraphrasing and revising the material he co-opts means that hypothetical sources cannot be easily or accurately delineated beneath Josephus's own prose.[43]

Indeed, it has become increasingly clear—primarily through the efforts of Steve Mason—that Josephus's writings must be treated not as a collection of individual nuggets to be mined for whatever particular pieces of material are necessary for the problem at hand, but rather as complete works of literature, the understanding of which requires taking Josephus's literary goals and devices in mind.[44] In this sense, I am highly sympathetic with the recent literary turn in the study of Josephus—a phenomenon that is welcome and, in some ways, long in coming. And therefore, in this book, we will seek to evaluate Josephus's accounts of religious disputes in light of the theological interests reflected throughout his works.

But I do step back from the current literary turn in one key respect. Some current writers—Mason prominent among them—are so taken with Josephus as a creative author that they practically give up on the possibility of discerning historical realities behind his writings.[45] As noted, the broader questions of Josephus's historical reliability will continue, and fuller reevaluations will have to take place elsewhere. For our purposes, this book seeks to demonstrate that we ought not to despair altogether of discerning historical realities behind Josephus's descriptions of ancient Jewish religious arguments. We ought not to let literary methodologies prevent us from reckoning with the possibility that Josephus's own theological statements could represent broader trends in first-century Jewish society. And we ought not to let generally negative evaluations of Josephus's value as a historian get in the way either. When distinctive, significant theological similarities between Josephus's writings and other extant ancient Jewish literature are overlooked or downplayed, then something has gone wrong. I believe—and I hope this work will demonstrate—that Josephus's descriptions of ancient Jewish theological disputes, along with his own related theological observations, constitute a distinct problem set, one that can best be scrutinized when all of Josephus's statements and claims about his own theology and those of other groups he mentions are measured against the treasure trove of ancient Jewish religious and theological literature we have at our disposal. I believe we can and should proceed here embarking on such a broad-based comparison, with due caution. Josephus's Hellenistic terminology must be studied carefully, and his apologetic concerns must not be overlooked. But the effort is not futile, and our confidence is bolstered by the belief that the exercise I propose is worthwhile, if for nothing else than calling into question a number of problematic trends and exaggerated assumptions that currently predominate over the study of ancient Judaism, many of which are, in essence, inversions of what our most informed source, Josephus, tells us.

Josephus on the Schools, God, and the Destruction of the Temple

What kinds of evidence regarding ancient Jewish theology do we find in Josephus? The bulk of the material can be categorized in one of two ways, and we will provide here a brief description of each. The evidence will, of course, be analyzed more closely in each of the following chapters. What follows is a preliminary sketch—a summary description of the evidence, for the purpose of setting a foundation for the arguments that follow.

One sort of evidence that will concern us here is Josephus's descriptions of the ancient Jewish sects or, to remain closer to his terminology, "schools."[46] There are four such passages in Josephus's works that compare or contrast two or more of these groups with regard to matters of belief (though practices, to be sure, come up as well). The longest of these passages, as it happens, is to be found in Josephus's earliest work: *War* 2.119–66. The broader context is Josephus's description of the political upheavals in the years following the death of Herod the Great. The immediate context (2.118) is Josephus's mention of Judas the Galilean, whom Josephus describes as dangerously innovative for his founding of a school of his own, characterized by his refusal to pay taxes to Rome, which in turn is justified by the belief that God alone is king. Josephus then proceeds to describe the Pharisees, Sadducees, and Essenes—the three schools of philosophy that, unlike Judas's group, Josephus deems to be legitimate forms of Jewish thought. His description of the Essenes is the longest (2.119–61), and well known to those familiar with the Dead Sea Scrolls. While it is focused on distinctive Essene practices, theological matters are not overlooked: the Essenes are described as believers in immortality (154–58) and adept practitioners of predictive prophecy (159). This extensive passage is followed by a brief, but dense, comparative description of the Pharisees and Sadducees (2.162–66). Life after death figures here, too, with Pharisees believers in postmortem rewards for the righteous and punishments for the wicked, while Sadducees are described as deniers of both.[47] As for the vexed question of fate and free will, while the Sadducees deny fate's role in human affairs, the Pharisees are described as attributing "all things to fate and to God," even while they, paradoxically, uphold the independent human capacity to choose between good and evil.[48] The passage concludes (166) with a description of the two groups' contrasting social etiquettes: while the Pharisees are praised for their politeness, the Sadducees are denigrated as "boorish" or "uncouth."[49]

Josephus revisits and refines his treatment of these three groups in his subsequent works. A brief treatment of all three groups appears in *Antiquities* 13.171–73. In this passage—which appears in its context seemingly out of the blue, in the midst of Josephus's retelling of the exploits of Jonathan the Hasmonean[50]—Josephus presents a more fully developed treatment of all three groups' views on fate and free will. Once again, Sadducees "do away with fate," ascribing all things to human choice. The Pharisees once again are described as maintaining a position that allows for both fate and free will, although the compromise described in this passage differs somewhat from the compromise described in *War* 2. It is in this passage that Josephus first describes the Essenes as attributing all things to fate, without qualification. A short while later, in *Antiquities* 13.293–300—in the context of describing sociopolitical disputes during the reign of John Hyrcanus—Josephus again contrasts the Pharisees and Sadducees, this time with particular regard to their attitudes toward punishment and law. With regard to punishment, the Pharisees are described as notably lenient, while the Sadducees were stricter (13.294, 20.199). With regard to law, the Pharisees are described as distinctive—and popular (13.288)—because of their adherence to nonscriptural traditions passed down from former generations (13.296–98). The Sadducees reject these traditions, and according to Josephus, are all the less popular for doing so.

Five books later, Josephus presents yet another description of the Pharisees, Sadducees, and Essenes (18.11–22). Once again, the general context is his description of the early first century CE, and the immediate context is the tax revolt led by Judas the Galilean. In this account, Judas is identified more specifically as a Gaulanite, and his deputy in revolt is a Pharisee named Zadok (18.4). Moreover, Judas's philosophy is described— and criticized—more fully (18.4–10, 23–25). Not only did Judas advocate that the Jews ought to recognize only God as king (thereby prohibiting allegiance to foreign rulers), Judas is also described as breaking with Jewish custom by permitting the killing of kinsmen when it should prove necessary (18.5–9, 23).[51] Josephus even goes as far as to describe Judas's ideology as an independent "fourth philosophy" (18.23). Despite this, it remains clear that Josephus views this school with disdain, and questions its legitimate identification as such. In rather close agreement to *War* 2.119, Josephus asserts again in *Antiquities* 18.11 that Jewish thought from ancient times was characterized by *three* (not four) schools: the Pharisees, Sadducees, and Essenes. Once again, the Essene passage is the longest (18.18–22), and the only one of the three to mention distinctive religious practices, such as their withdrawal from the temple rites (18.19) and their communitarianism (18.20). But theological matters pervade all three descriptions, and predominate over the descriptions of Pharisees (18.12–15) and Sadducees (16–17) alike. Once again, the Sadducees deny immortality and fate, while the Essenes affirm both. The Pharisees continue to believe in life after death and to maintain a balance between fate and free will—though the compromise described here is more akin to that of *War* 2.162–63 than *Antiquities* 13.172 (as we will see in chapter 2). Some new points, however, emerge in these passages: the Sadducees are few in numbers but of highest standing (18.17). The Pharisees—who make no concession to luxury (18.12)—are greater in numbers, but even greater in influence (18.15). As in *War* so, too, in *Antiquities*, when the Sadducees are compared to the Pharisees, it is the Pharisees that emerge looking better. But in both books, the highly ascetic—and mostly celibate—Essenes merit highest praise, being compared to the revered Pythagoreans (*Ant.* 15.371).[52]

All three schools are juxtaposed one last time in *Life* 10–12, where Josephus tells us that he spent three years of his early manhood—ending with his nineteenth year—first studying the curricula of the Pharisees,

Sadducees, and Essenes and then living the life of a desert ascetic with a guru named Bannus. At the end of this time, Josephus entered public life, and lived according to Pharisaic ways.[53] It is in this passage that he explicitly compares the Pharisees to the Stoics (*Life* 12), cementing the impression (left unstated, and open to question) that the Sadducees are to be compared to the Epicureans, by virtue of the Epicureans' denial of life after death and divine providence (*Ant.* 10.277–80).[54]

Josephus's works include other sundry observations regarding each of these groups. The legal expertise of the Pharisees is noted in *War* 1.110 (compare 2.162). The Essene penchant for prophecy figures in Josephus's historical narrative in both *War* (1.78–80, 2.111–13) and *Antiquities* (13.311–13, 15.373–79, and 17.346–48). Apparently some Pharisees and Essenes were reluctant to take oaths of allegiance (*Ant.* 15.370–71, 17.41–45). In addition, individual Pharisees, Sadducees, and Essenes figure here and there in Josephus's narratives, as when we are told that leadership roles in the revolt against Rome were held by Simon, son of Gamaliel (*War* 4.159; identified as a Pharisee in *Life* 191) and John the Essene (*War* 2.567, 3.11, 19).[55]

A number of questions must be asked of this data—and indeed, we will do so more systematically in the following chapters. Generally, Josephus's use of philosophic terminology and analogies raises questions concerning the degree to which he refashioned ancient Jewish sectarianism in light of his apologetic concerns.[56] One can also safely wonder—as one always must—whether any given description of a group sufficiently accounts for diversity within the group or change over time.[57] Josephus's self-identification as a Pharisee in *Life* also appears suspicious to some readers, and some have suggested that Josephus only became enamored of the Pharisees in the decades following the revolt, once it became clear to him that the Pharisees were emerging as the predominant power among Jews remaining in the land of Israel.[58] Indeed, a number of differences among the various reports can be identified, and it remains unclear whether they can be explained in light of the development of Josephus's political or religious thought. After all, for all the developments from one writing to the next, there are just as many constants: the Essenes are favored, and the Sadducees are despised—these, too, are questions to be explored. Finally, perhaps the most important question of all is this: on each particular point, can Josephus's claims be confirmed (or refuted) by comparisons with other extant evidence? And what kind of evidence can be admitted for comparison?

With regard to each of these questions, it is important to analyze the data above in light of another set of passages—the portions of Josephus's works where he states his own theological positions. With regard to some of these issues—for example, predictive prophecy, divine providence, and life after death—Josephus's own position is quite clear. As for providence, throughout both *War* and *Antiquities*, Josephus emphasizes his belief in a God who cares for the world and guides human events, such that history comes to align with divine justice (e.g., *Ant.* 1.1–26; *War* 7.453).[59] Book 10 of *Antiquities*—which relates the history of the destruction of the first temple and its aftermath—concludes with a condemnation of the Epicureans and their denial of divine providence, an argument that is rooted in Josephus's affirmation of the truth of Daniel's predictions (*Ant.* 10.267–81). Book 17 similarly concludes with a narrative surrounding successful prophecy, one that Josephus takes as evidence for divine providence as well as life after death (17.339–54). But important issues remain to be considered: for example, what *form* of life after death does Josephus himself affirm? Precisely how does he account for his belief in providence and predictive prophecy: is his belief Pharisaic or more Essene-like? In other cases, the data are even less clear—or at least so it seems on the surface. For instance, it is frequently noted that Josephus's extended paraphrase of the Pentateuch includes no explicit reflections on the relationship between scripture and tradition—a strange omission for a Pharisee.[60] But even with regard to this point, as we will see in chapter 4, a good case can be made that Josephus's own views align rather reasonably with both his own description of the Pharisees as well as with what we learn elsewhere about this group in the first century.

About one particular theological point there can be no question: according to both *War* and *Antiquities*, the destruction of the second temple—just like the destruction of the first—was brought about by God, as a divine punishment for the sins of the Jewish people (e.g., *War* 6.95–110; *Ant.* 20.166; see, on the first temple, 10.131–42).[61] This, in fact, is a fundamental theme of both of these works, and Josephus's attitudes toward providence and predictive prophecy—and even life after death—are, as we will see in chapter 5, all illumined by and, in turn, illuminate Josephus's understanding of the event that stands at the center of his work, and that took place during the middle of his rather eventful life. Above all, Josephus is responding to the destruction of the temple by explaining it, not so much historically as theologically, to both his Greco-Roman and his Jewish readers. Josephus's own deep theological interests are evident throughout all four of his works and help us understand why he wrote about the schools, and what he wrote about them.

Overlooking Josephus: Problematic Trends in Current Scholarship

The full development of the arguments intimated above is to be found in subsequent chapters of this book. In what follows here, we will review instances where the data discussed above are downplayed or overlooked, so as to indicate how the scholarly discussion would change if more attention were paid to Josephus and his writings about ancient Jewish theology.

Sectarianism and Legal Dispute

The clearest indication of the sad fate Josephus's tripartite schema has experienced—especially, it seems, among Jewish scholars—is the regnant assumption that Jewish sectarian disputes are to be understood, first and foremost, as characterized by, and even resulting from, disagreements over points of law and practice.[62] The classic modern articulation of this perspective is Morton Smith's. Dismissing doctrinal issues (such as what Josephus discussed) as "nonessential" and "secondary," Smith provocatively asserted that only legal dispute explains the multiplication of sects among ancient Jews:

> the best known Jewish sects of the late period before 70 A.D. are essentially groups for the observance of particular legal interpretations. Once formed, such a group may glorify its founders in one way or another, may adopt, or at least may tolerate, among its members, all sorts of eschatological speculations and peculiar developments of personal piety, may pick up elements of alien thought, whether from Greek philosophy or from Persian religion, but these things are certainly nonessential to its structure, probably secondary in its development, and possibly, in some instances, no more than peculiarities of individuals among its members. They could be changed or removed, and the sect would go on, as a peculiar community defined and held together by its peculiar legal observances. But touch the Law, and the sect will split, as shown by the fact that the divisions of which we hear before 70 A.D. are, when we can be sure of their nature, the results of disputes over legal questions.

Such are the questions which separate Paul from his opponents, the House of Hillel from the House of Shammai, and the teachers of the Dead Sea sects from their adversaries. The essential contribution, therefore, of the fuller picture of Jewish sectarianism which we have been given by the Qumran finds, is to increase our estimate of the importance of that side of ancient Judaism which conceived of it as the religion of the Law, and to do this by demonstrating the legal origin and nature even of the Jewish sects.[63]

As it happens, Smith's 1961 declaration proved to be practically prophetic, ushering in decades worth of scholarship aligned with this view.

With the discovery of the *Temple Scroll* in 1967—and its full publication a decade later—the centrality of Jewish religious law for the ancient Jewish sects was, it would appear, dramatically demonstrated. Scholars of ancient Judaism began to take a greater interest in the legal documents among the Dead Sea Scrolls—even though many were not yet published.[64] As the contents of 4QMMT (as reconstructed) became known, a number of scholars understood the document as laying out the legal issues that caused the sect to break from the larger Jewish polity (see 4QMMT C 7–9).[65] In the present day, the law-centered approach to Jewish sectarianism has been championed by, among others, Lawrence Schiffman, who also places "halakhic issues at the center of Jewish sectarianism in the Second Temple period."[66] Other prominent proponents of the practice-centered approach to Jewish sectarianism include Aharon Shemesh, Yaakov Sussman, Cana Werman, and at one time—though he has now repudiated this approach—Albert Baumgarten.[67] Perhaps the strongest recent formulation of this view is that of Paul Heger, who treats the approach as the current consensus: "It is a matter of *opinio communis* that issues of belief, whether real or as pretense, lay behind the various disputes among Christians, whereas disputes regarding practical rules, or the appearance thereof, were at the core of disagreements among Jews."[68] Of course, not all scholars would put the matter so sharply. But what matters most for our concerns is this: the law-centered approach requires displacing Josephus's descriptions of ancient Jewish scholastic disputes.

It is not difficult to see that the fate of Josephus's theologically centered schema has been impacted by the relative priorities placed on theology and practice—or, as it were, faith and law—by Jewish and Christian (particularly Protestant) scholars. Generations ago, Jewish religious law was largely discarded as a topic worthy of scholarly study (outside, that is, of Jewish institutions), and the centrality of theology and doctrines was taken for granted (again, Jewish institutions excepted). The inverse characterized Jewish studies, where theology languished and theologians were less regarded than those who worked, say, on the Tosefta.[69] In some important respects, Smith's call for a shift in focus from theology to law— or, in Jewish terms, to halakhah—reflected broader trends in religious studies, evident in the works of Mary Douglas and others, diagnosing long-standing Protestant biases among scholars of religion.[70] To be clear, this sea change is important, justified, and irreversible: no one—let alone an author of two books on purity and sacrifice—should deny the significance of religious law for the understanding of ancient Judaism. But a fundamental thesis of the present book is this: the pendulum of the anti-Protestant counterreaction has swung too far, and it is time to turn again to theology and doctrines for a fuller understanding of the religion of ancient Jews. Indeed, if constructions of ancient Judaism that downplayed law in favor of theology (often discarding rabbinic sources in the process) can now easily be seen as suspiciously aligned with the priorities of Protestant Christianity,[71] then the modern scholarly focus on halakhah (often ignoring Josephus in the process) may well reflect contemporary Jewish priorities as well.[72] Of course, there are important counterexamples, too: even as Joseph Baumgarten welcomed the increased attention to halakhah—that he himself helped pioneer—he long ago warned scholars not to "belittle the significance of religious doctrines" for understanding ancient Jewish movements.[73]

An unlikely ally in the law-centered approach has been the "documentary" approach to the study of rabbinic literature championed by Jacob Neusner, which sets out to study the development of rabbinic Judaism as a sequence of largely self-contained, independent literary compositions.[74] Most of the various controversies surrounding Neusner's method do not concern us here; what matters for our purposes is the fact that Neusner places great significance on the law-centered nature of the Mishnah. Mistaking a literary genre for a complete religious system, Neusner's method isolates the Mishnah from earlier second temple literature, effectively driving a wedge between the early rabbis' religious system and the theologies of the Pharisees, Sadducees, and Essenes, as described by Josephus.[75] In its a priori opposition to the effort of using rabbinic sources for the reconstruction of second temple period religious or social history (let alone to using second temple sources to shed light on rabbinic literature), Neusner's project militates against the kind of work that characterizes the "law-centered" approach to sectarianism; indeed, not one of the scholars who advocate the "law-centered" approach is in any sense Neusnerian. It is precisely for this reason that the alliance of these two approaches is an unlikely one. Even so, Neusner's method aligns with the law-centered approach in three important respects. First, Neusner's historical project is also one that is developed independently of Josephus and his tripartite schema: it is not that the comparisons are drawn and rejected; the very idea of such comparison is rejected at the outset. Indeed—and, second—Neusner's text-by-text approach would suggest, by extension, that Josephus's works need to be studied, too, as literary entities, just as Steve Mason has claimed in his a priori rejection of the use of Josephus for the identification of the Qumran sectarians.[76] Third—and perhaps most important—Neusner's notoriously nasty treatment of scholars who have taken an interest in Jewish theology has done a further disservice.[77] To be clear, Neusner's critiques of G. F. Moore, E. P. Sanders, and E. E. Urbach are not entirely lacking in substance, and it also merits attention that Neusner played an important, positive role in the aforementioned efforts aimed at freeing the study of ancient Judaism from previously prevalent Protestant biases. But there is much more to the works of Moore, Sanders, and Urbach than Neusner allows. Indeed, it is precisely with regard to theological topics that the weaknesses of Neusner's approach become clearly evident: when clear and reasonable theological comparisons between Josephus and later rabbinic literature can be developed—as we will see—why should an unproven and overly strict literary methodology preclude such comparisons or the historical reflections that emerge from them?

The Crisis of 70 CE

If the "law-centered" approach just discussed represents the displacement of Josephus's schools passages, the displacement of Josephus's own theologizing can be seen in scholarly discussions of Jewish responses to destruction of the temple. Seth Schwartz, for instance, asserts that Judaism was theologically "shattered" by the cumulative events of 70 and 135 CE: In an atmosphere of "prevailing gloom," works like 4 Ezra struggled to articulate a meaningful response; but as for the rest, "those whom it failed to satisfy will have reacted with panic, despair, and finally abandonment of Judaism."[78] While Schwartz has stated this hypothesis more boldly than most, the assertion that Judaism in general was stunned into silence by the traumas of the late first and early second century has been articulated by a number of scholars over the years, among them Baruch Bokser, Robert Kirschner, Jacob Neusner, and Robert Goldenberg.[79]

Each of these scholars' approaches to the Jewish response to 70 CE is distinct, but there are some common features: the destruction of the temple brings about a theological crisis marked by an extended and unyielding despair. Recovery—and explanation—takes centuries. We will return to the question of the Jewish response to 70 CE in chapter 5 here. And I have elsewhere argued that at least a number of these writers (Bokser and Neusner prominent among them) have developed their hypotheses with ill-considered analogies to the Holocaust in mind, under the influence of certain strains of post-Holocaust thought that similarly suggest that it took decades before thoughtful responses to the Shoah emerged.[80] For present purposes, it matters here to mention only this: Josephus's *Jewish War* and *Antiquities* have been largely overlooked in these discussions, with problematic results.[81] As intimated above and as we will see, Josephus's theological responses to the destruction of the temple were thoughtful and rather highly developed. And his *War* was written within the decade of the temple's demise. When Josephus's writings are compared with their later rabbinic counterparts (as well as the post-70 CE apocalypses *2 Baruch* and *4 Ezra*) we find more similarities than differences, suggesting that it may not have taken Jews all that long to reach the kinds of conclusions we find in rabbinic literature. Indeed, the comparison will compel us to question whether the extant evidence justifies the claim that the destruction of 70 CE brought about a theological crisis at all. To be sure, the destruction brought about death and destruction. Many lives were lost, and other lives shattered. But Judaism withstood the catastrophe. The *theological* crisis seems most acute only when Josephus's works are set aside, leaving us with a few brooding apocalypses and an otherwise empty void. Looking into that chasm, so created, scholars are then free to conjure an image—perhaps, again, unduly influenced by contemporary concerns—of unyielding despair, mass apostasy, and a shattered Judaism.

Priestly Descent and Sectarian Origins

A third problematic trend in scholarship represents yet another illustration of the displacement or rejection of Josephus's theological scheme: the assumption that the development of Jewish sectarianism is tied closely to—and perhaps even largely explained by—the Maccabean crisis in general, and the break in the Zadokite priestly line in particular.[82] The Zadok of concern here is the one who, according to the biblical account, served as high priest in David and Solomon's time and—working against Eli's descendant Abiathar—supported Solomon against Adonijah in the aftermath of David's death (2 Sam. 8.17; 1 Kings 1.8, 24–48, 2.35).[83] According to the (somewhat inconsistent) genealogies supplied in scriptural texts, this line apparently continued unbroken down into the early second temple period (1 Chron. 6.1–81, 24.31; Neh. 12.1–26). The prophet Ezekiel, in his elaborate vision of the future temple, predicts that the priesthood in general (and therefore, by implication, the high priesthood in particular) will be restricted to sons of Zadok (Ezek. 40.46, 43.19, 44.15–16)—though we have no reason to be certain that this restriction was ever put in place in the second temple period.[84] Indeed, 1 Chronicles 24 suggests the opposite, that non-Zadokite Aaronide priests continued to serve. Presumably (though we cannot know for certain) Zadokite high-priestly dominance over an Aaronide priesthood continued down until the Maccabean crisis, when non-Zadokites assumed the office. A number of scholars then go one step further to suggest that it was precisely this break in the line that brought about sectarian conflicts.

The theory that the Sadducees were named for Solomon's priest and therefore had particular allegiance to his descendants has been prominent in scholarship since the days of Abraham Geiger (1810–1874).[85] This theory was adopted in some influential reference works,[86] and continues to surface in overviews of ancient Judaism.[87] The concern with Zadokite descent has also emerged as an important corollary in the standard formulations of the Essene hypothesis of Qumran origins—the Essene breakaway is often understood as a radical rejection of the non-Zadokite priesthood.[88] Needless to say, centralizing Zadokite descent also plays an important role in recent works tracing the development of "Zadokite" (as opposed to "Enochic") Judaism.[89]

Of course, in one sense, these hypotheses rest on Josephus. To be sure, Josephus does trace the high-priestly lines of descent (*Ant.* 10.152–53, 20.224–51), indicating that the Hasmoneans represented a break in the line that had previously gone unbroken back to Zadok (*Ant.* 12.387, 20.235). And it is Josephus who *implies* that the sectarian disputes came to a head in the wake of the Maccabean revolt, for he first mentions the three schools, as noted, in the midst of his account of early Hasmonean history (13.171–73). But Josephus, of course, describes ancient Jewish sectarian disputes primarily in theological terms, and Josephus does not clearly associate the Sadducees with either the priesthood or the Zadokite line. Nor does Josephus explicitly tie the emergence of sectarian disputes to the time when priestly dynasty was broken. The placement of the notice about the schools and fate and free will in *Antiquities* 13.171–73, in the midst of Josephus's paraphrase of 1 Maccabees 12, relating to the high priesthood of Jonathan the Hasmonean, is rather mysterious, and it is quite questionable whether scholars should take the literary placement—or, possibly, misplacement—of this freestanding passage as historical data about the emergence of these groups.[90] Even if we take this passage as dating the origins of the schools, about fifteen years or more separate the events concerning Jonathan related in *Antiquities* 13.174 from the accession of Alcimus, as described in *Antiquities* 12.387. However, it is unlikely that Josephus in this passage—or in any other—actually means to tell us when these groups emerged. His clearest statement on the subject is *Antiquities* 18.11, to the effect that Jewish philosophy took three forms "from the earliest times."[91] Josephus's most detailed description of the three schools appears in *War* 2—when describing the aftermath of Herod's death. It is difficult to discern what, if any, chronological information can be gleaned from Josephus's placement of these disparate accounts.

More to the point is the fact that Josephus provides no indication that Zadokite descent was a particularly important issue. While Josephus does not obscure the role of Zadok himself, he hardly emphasizes him either. Moreover, Josephus frequently refers to the priests, generally, as "the sons of Aaron" (*Ant.* 10.65)—which non-Zadokites would be, too— and he says nothing about Ezekiel's envisioned restrictions either.[92] Even when describing the deposition of Onias, Josephus describes his successor as "indeed of the stock of Aaron, but not of the family of Onias" (*Ant.* 20.235).[93] If Zadokite descent is not worth mentioning as such, there is little reason to believe the issue was particularly contentious. Indeed, Josephus nowhere suggests that sectarian disputes concerned questions about the legitimacy of the high priesthood. To the contrary, the evidence from Josephus suggests quite the opposite: priestly descent never figures among the sectarian disputes that Josephus mentions. When he discusses conflicts concerning the priesthood, Zadokite descent per se is not a concern (e.g., *War* 4.152–57; *Ant.* 15.40–41; 20.179–81, 213–14); when he explicitly discusses changes in priestly descent, conflict does not usually result (*Ant.* 12.387, 15.22, 20.224–51; note esp. 235–36, 238, 247). To be sure, Josephus does express grave opposition to the appointment, by lot, of Phannis (Phinehas), son of Samuel (*War* 4.152–57), and he suggests that many were bothered by this break in custom (from selection by descent to selection by lot). But once again, it is hardly clear whether or how Zadokite descent figures in this conflict.[94] Even when Josephus relates (Pharisaic) opposition to the legitimacy of the Hasmonean high priest John Hyrcanus, the descent-based argument concerns not the priest's father's status as a (non-) Zadokite but his mother's status as a former captive (*Ant.* 13.292).[95] It would seem, therefore, that Josephus's overall goal in tracing the lines of priestly descent—from Aaron to his own day—is, just as he says, to recall for posterity *all* the legitimate holders of this office (*Ant.* 20.224, 261).

To be sure, it is possible that Josephus has downplayed the significance of this issue, in line perhaps with his own Hasmonean descent (*Life* 1–7). But the problem with this explanation is that Josephus's silence on the issue matches what we find—or, to be more precise, don't find—in other extant sources. As far as the name "Sadducee" is concerned, not a single ancient Jewish source—Josephan or not—associates this term with the Zadokite high priestly line. The rabbinic (and Karaite) sources that do seek to explain the origins of the Sadducees' name all point to some later, nonpriestly figure named Zadok, who purportedly played some role in propagating what were to become characteristic Sadducean views, such as the rejection of life after death.[96] The early Christian "heresiologist" Epiphanius goes one step further than the Jewish sources by suggesting that the Zadok for whom the Sadducees might be named was a priest— but he, too, stops well short of explicitly pointing to the Zadok of David and Solomon's day.[97] Finally, the *Damascus Document* speaks of "Sons of Zadok" (בני צדוק; e.g., 3.20–4.6) as well as an individual historical figure named Zadok (5.5). While it remains entirely unclear who this Zadok was or when he lived, we can be certain this figure lived much later than the time of David and Solomon: David's sins are forgiven, in part, precisely because he lived when the law was not fully revealed (5.5–6).[98]

Indeed, there is good reason to question whether the issue of Zadokite descent was as important to ancient Jews generally (or Sadducees specifically) as scholars assume. Not a single ancient Jewish source—again, Josephan or not—states that disputes over the genealogical descent of the high priesthood played any significant role in fomenting sectarian disputes among second temple period Jews. Geiger's creative theories seemed finally to find firm textual support when the *Community Rule* first appeared, with its references to the leadership of the sons of Zadok

(1QS 5.2, 9; see also 1QSa 1.2, 24; 2.3). Yet subsequent discoveries—including especially the Cave 4 manuscripts of the *Community Rule*, which lack specific mention of Zadokites—have raised serious questions regarding the centrality of Zadokite descent to the Qumran sect, at least with respect to the purported origins of the group in early Maccabean era.[99] It is equally important to ask how, precisely, a presumably celibate sect could give great importance over any length of time to a priestly line of descent.[100] This leads us back to the *Damascus Document*, where the explicit discussion of Zadokites involves a decidedly nonliteral interpretation of Ezekiel 44.15: the reference to sons of Zadok is understood as a metaphor for the "chosen of Israel, called by the name, who will stand at the end of days" (CD 4.3–4).[101] Interestingly, even 1QS speaks repeatedly of the "Sons of Righteousness" (בני צדק; 1QS 3.20, 22; see also 9.14). It remains unclear whether the seemingly literal passages should be read in light of the clearly metaphorical ones.

But even if, at some point, the sectarians assigned leadership positions to the sons of Zadok (in the plural), how can we easily extrapolate from this the notion that the ideal form of leadership in their mind was a *single* Zadokite *high* priest? Indeed, *all* of our sources concerning Zadokites—and there are not all that many—speak of a *group* of Zadokite priests serving in the temple (e.g., Ezek. 40.46, 43.19, 44.15, 48.11; Sir. 51.12i[Heb]), or serving in some capacity at Qumran (e.g., 1QS 5.2, 9; 1QSa 1.2, 24; 2.3; 1QSb 3.22). Over against these sources are a greater number that assert the legitimacy of all the sons of Aaron to serve either at the temple (e.g., Ps. 115.10, 12, 118.3, 135.19; 1 Chron. 23.32–24.6; 2 Chron. 13.10, 26.18, 35.14; Tob. 1.7; Sir. 45.6–25, 50.13, 16; Josephus, *Ant.* 10.65, 20.225–26)[102] or in some capacity for the Qumran community (e.g., 1QS 5.21, 9.7; 1QM 7.10, 17.2; 4QMMT B 16–17, 79; 11QT 34.13).[103] Why is it that we lack even a single second temple period source that explicitly delegitimizes non-Zadokite holders of the high priestly office? Josephus, to be sure, mentions the break in descent—but he makes little of it. Our other sources—even ones that speak of Zadokites—do not appear concerned explicitly with the high priesthood.

It has recently been claimed that the general acceptance by ancient Jews of the Hasmonean line as legitimate could be explained in part by the Hasmoneans being in fact Zadokites.[104] This is an intriguing possibility, and of course it is true that no source—including even the *Habakkuk Pesher*, with its concern for the "wicked priest"—explicitly denies that that this was the case. But no source explicitly affirms that the Maccabees were Zadokites either. There is, therefore, an even more intriguing possibility, one that equally fits the evidence (or lack thereof): the Hasmoneans, and those priests who followed them in the Herodian Period,[105] were not descended from Solomon's priest Zadok, and no one—Sadducees included—cared a great deal about this particular issue. For most Jews, therefore—as for the authors of 1 and 2 Maccabees and of course Josephus—the Zadokites' displacement by the Hasmoneans was likely understood as an outcome well deserved, resulting from the last Zadokites' sinful behavior as described in these three sources.

In sum—and to get back to our main theme—perhaps here, too, we are best off following Josephus's lead: the break in the Zadokite line was noticeable, but not as important as Geiger and his followers have made it out to be.

Despising the Sadducees

We have seen, so far, how three common approaches to ancient Judaism involve overlooking or undervaluing the evidence of Josephus. The law-centered approach to sectarianism undervalues Josephus's theological descriptions of the schools. The assertion that Judaism experienced a great theological crisis in 70 CE undervalues Josephus's own theologizing. The undue emphasis placed by scholars on Zadokite descent undervalues Josephus's historical evidence to the contrary. As we have seen already with regard to the third—and as we will see later with regard to the first two—Josephus's own claims may well match the overall evidence from ancient Judaism better than these currently predominant theories. In this section, we attend to an entirely different problem—an instance where scholars adopt Josephus's view when they ought not. But as we have seen with regard to both law and theology, here, too, the use (or misuse) of Josephus has been unduly colored by contemporary concerns.

Once again, we look back to Abraham Geiger, who set aside in his scholarly and popular works Josephus's tripartite theological scheme, putting in its place a largely binary model, divided along class lines. Placing the literary history of ancient Judaism into these parallel lines, Geiger attributed (for instance) 1 Maccabees and late portions of Proverbs to the Sadducees, and 2 Maccabees to the Pharisees (the Essenes played little role in Geiger's analysis).[106] Going a step or two further, Geiger depicted the Pharisees as democratic and liberal, pitted against the conservative, aristocratic Sadducees.[107] It has long been recognized that Geiger's presentation was colored by his own views of the disputes between advocates and opponents of synagogue reform in nineteenth-century Germany (Geiger himself being a fierce advocate for such reforms). But if Geiger's particular formulation was new and colored by his own experiences, the denigration of the Sadducees in a general sense had a long history, going back to Josephus himself, who was rather disparaging of the Sadducees, viewing them as rude (even "boorish": *War* 2.166), aloof, and ineffectual (*Ant.* 13.298, 18.17).

While much of what Josephus had to say about the sects in general (and the Sadducees in particular) is overlooked or downplayed, the negative view of the Sadducees has had remarkable staying power. Of course, Josephus is not solely responsible for this negativity. It does not help matters that the Sadducees, according to Acts, appear to be at the wrong places at the wrong times (Acts 4.1, 5.17, 23.6–8).[108] Adding insult to injury, the rabbinic sources—at least as traditionally preserved[109]—also display hostility toward the Sadducees (e.g., *Sifre Numbers*, sec. 112; *b. Bava Batra* 115b).[110]

Jewish scholarship, since the days of *Wissenschaft des Judentums*, has endeavored with some success to rehabilitate the reputation of the Pharisees. Yet in many cases, the reevaluation of the Pharisees came at the expense of the Sadducees. If not boorish and rude, they are hardly to be liked; their theology does not stand on principle, reflecting purely their social, aristocratic position. Louis Finkelstein, for instance, spoke blatantly of the "materialistic" and "self-serving" views of the Sadducees, while the Pharisees inherited the mantle of the prophetic tradition.[111] This sort of apology for the Pharisees cleverly co-opts ideals held dear to contemporary Jews and Christians (democracy, liberalism, individualism, prophetic ethics) while transferring to the Sadducees—a Jewish party long gone—attributes not uncommon among anti-Semitic stereotypes of the time (including, especially, materialism and a rigid ritualism).[112] Even when the apology seems left behind, hostility toward the Sadducees can remain: Martin Goodman not long ago associated the Sadducean rejection of immortality with the group's wealth, asserting that Sadducaism "embodies a smug self-congratulation about the status quo that only the rich could accept."[113]

Despite Josephus's anti-Sadducean biases, we will see in the following chapters that his careful description of the group's theological views provides almost all we need for a fair reevaluation of their theology. The irony here is that scholars take from Josephus what they should not (his hostility toward the Sadducees) and leave aside what they ought to accept (his basic understanding of ancient Jewish theological disputes).

As we have seen, many scholars of ancient Judaism have largely side-lined theology in general, or Josephus's discussions of theological concerns in particular. This is not to say that that these topics or texts have been entirely ignored. To be sure, alternate voices are present, and scholarship of ancient Judaism has not entirely abandoned theological subjects. Certain topics—particularly life after death—have received significant attention in the last decade.[114] More comprehensive theological syntheses have also surfaced, despite the shifts in scholarly fashions against such projects.[115] But the place of Josephus's evidence within such works is not always secure. Some studies proceed almost as if Josephus's evidence is rather unimportant or at least secondary.[116] More common is a rather selective use of it. Boccaccini's creative and ambitious rethinkings of ancient Jewish religious history are to be commended for giving theological questions their due.[117] But Boccaccini's entire project—which, in its more mature form, attempts to trace the linear literary histories of "Sapiential," "Enochic," and "Zadokite" forms of Judaism—is, in one sense, an extravagant displacement of Josephus. While Boccaccini would appear to agree with Josephus to the extent that sectarian disputes had theological components to them, Boccaccini proceeds to discount Josephus's identifications of those groups as well as his particular descriptions of the disputes among them. Indeed, while Boccaccini draws freely on Josephus in the effort of illuminating the political and historical background of his literary reconstruction, neither Josephus's own theological observations nor his descriptions of ancient Jewish theology play an important role in Boccaccini's understanding of ancient Jewish theological dispute.

These recent developments and works notwithstanding, it remains true that recent decades have seen, at least in some circles, an increased focus on religious law as the prime focus of ancient Jewish sectarian strife. At the same time, scholars have also undervalued Josephus in the efforts of understanding ancient Jewish theology; and many have virtually ignored him altogether in imagining a post-70 CE Judaism shattered to the core by unprecedented catastrophe. A number of factors may well be at work motivating such approaches and conclusions, but it certainly is suspicious that both the law-centered approach and the catastrophe-crisis dynamic have their analogues in modern Jewish thought, with some writers even explicitly drawing analogies between ancient and modern times.[118] We should also recall the disdain for theology among various scholars of religion generally, as well as the dismissal of the classic works on ancient Jewish theology, particularly by influential groups of Judaica scholars. As for the Sadducees in particular, it is difficult to escape the fact that they have been sacrificed in the effort to rehabilitate the Pharisees. One can also wonder whether the scholarly picture has been muddied by hostility toward (or jealousy of) the ancient moneyed class on the part of modern middle-class academics.

Evaluating the beliefs and practices of ancient Jews should not be dictated by scholarly fashions or contemporary religious concerns. The priorities should be to evaluate the evidence before us, and Josephus's writings deserve pride of place in this evidence. Against Morton Smith and the "law-centered" approach, this book will argue that the division of ancient Judaism into disparate sects was characterized not only by legal disputes, but by theological ones as well.[119] Against Seth Schwartz and others who assume that post-70 CE Judaism was paralyzed into a state of inarticulate shock, this book will argue that Josephus's writings provide our best guide for appreciating the theological vitality of ancient Judaism, before and after 70 CE. Against Gabriele Boccaccini and other scholars who put the issue of Zadokite descent front and center, this book will argue that we would be better off paying attention to the issues Josephus identifies and explains. In short, this work will argue that a fuller understanding of ancient Judaism requires that we reengage Josephus's tripartite account of ancient Jewish theological disputes in a more sophisticated way, by comparing his descriptions of all three groups with relevant comparative evidence, while also taking into account a full evaluation of Josephus's own theological views.

Easier Done Than Said: Josephus's Schools and Comparative Analysis

We can no longer avoid the question we have dodged throughout this introduction: if we want to reevaluate Josephus's descriptions of the Jewish schools of thought, with what should we compare Josephus's accounts? I will argue throughout this work that the positions Josephus ascribes to each of the schools find substantial comparisons in a relatively distinct body of ancient Jewish literature. The theology of Josephus's Essenes will be compared to the sectarian Dead Sea Scrolls, the theology of the Pharisees to later rabbinic literature, and that of the Sadducees to the wisdom tradition, especially as manifest in the Wisdom of Ben Sira. The comparison between Josephus's Essenes and the scrolls is quite commonplace, though by no means uncontroversial. The comparison between rabbinic literature and Josephus's Pharisees was once quite common, but has fallen out of fashion. The comparison between Josephus's Sadducees and the wisdom tradition is the least common of these comparisons, but this may have to do more with a general lack of interest in the Sadducees than anything else.

This chapter is not the place to defend, on substantial grounds, the comparisons to be developed in the body of this book. Over the course of the following chapters, we will construct substantial comparisons between Josephus's Sadducees, Pharisees, and Essenes and, respectively, the wisdom tradition, rabbinic literature, and the sectarian scrolls. The full strength of the comparisons will then emerge, as we shed light on Jewish attitudes toward and debates about fate and free will (chapter 2), life after death (chapter 3), and legal authority (chapter 4). But we need here to clarify and then defend our way of moving forward.

In terms of clarification, one operative word here is "comparison." It is not the purpose of this book to argue for sociological genealogies or historical identifications. Nor are we interested here in refining or altering commonly accepted dates for any of the literature we will be studying, whether in terms of whole compositions or any sources our datable compositions may have used. We are interested, simply, in probing the veracity of Josephus's accounts of ancient Jewish theological dispute by drawing on the clearest and closest meaningful parallels we can find—just as one would do if one were considering the veracity of any given historical source. The strongest arguments I will make will revolve around these claims: that meaningful comparisons can indeed be established, which in turn lends greater credence to Josephus's accounts, as understood in light of the comparisons we have discussed. To be sure, this analysis will in the end provide support to those who wish to defend the Essene hypothesis, the Pharisaic origins of rabbinic Judaism, or wisdom's Sadducean legacy. But the arguments I will make do not require accepting any of these hypotheses (let alone identifications), and I will expend little, if any, effort in this work to defend any particular genealogical or historical connections. Indeed, if "comparison" is one operative term for our approach, "hypothesis" is the other. Perhaps the most important contribution of the so-called Essene hypothesis is that very term. For the purposes of this analysis, all three comparisons being put forward here can and will remain on the hypothetical level. And the relative values of these hypotheses can and should be measured in terms of to what extent they are able to shed light on and, it is hoped, lend credence to Josephus's accounts of ancient Jewish theological disputes.

Even with these caveats, further questions remain. In the rest of this chapter, we will briefly consider some methodological questions and counter certain potential objections to the comparisons we will take up in the bulk of this book.

The Sadducees and Wisdom: An Overlooked Connection

The scholar who seeks a fuller understanding of the ancient Jewish Sadducees faces a number of challenges.[120] Our source material is not extensive, and what we have is purely external: no *verifiably* Sadducean literature exists. Moreover, we can name surprisingly few Sadducees, and we know precious little about the rare figures—like the high priest Ananus—who are explicitly identified as Sadducees in our sources.[121] Unless a truly Sadducean library should turn up, we can never hope to have more sources. Still, I think some progress can be made in understanding better the sources we do have—especially Josephus—and in the process a few matters regarding the ancient Sadducees might be clarified. It is striking that so much of the discussion of the Sadducees is based on speculation concerning their name and priestly affiliation, while comparatively little is spent on exploring the possible scriptural background of Sadducean Judaism. If one were to ask, quite simply, where one might look to explore the origins of a group that is commonly characterized as aristocratic, cosmopolitan, and conservative—all the while believing in freedom of choice, earthly justice, and the finality of death—one obvious candidate presents itself: the wisdom tradition of ancient Israel, as evidenced especially (but not exclusively) in the Wisdom of Ben Sira.

Although the question has not to my knowledge been put quite that way, a number of scholars have suggested in some fashion that there might be some connection between the Sadducees and the wisdom tradition. Long ago, Kaufman Kohler suggested that Ecclesiastes was composed by a Sadducee.[122] More reasonable—and more helpful—is the once commonplace assertion that the Wisdom of Ben Sira articulates a proto-Sadducean theology.[123]

Yet asserting some connection between the wisdom tradition and the later Sadducees is hardly commonplace. Most surveys of the

Sadducees—excepting those mentioned above, among some others, to be sure—say little or nothing about the wisdom tradition, and the same is true for discussions of the wisdom tradition,[124] even those that seek to identify the heirs of wisdom among later second temple period groups or texts, such as apocalyptic literature, the Gnostic sources, or Q.[125]

Of course, perhaps the most obvious divide between the Sadducees and the wisdom tradition is a chronological one. Proverbs, Job, and Ecclesiastes likely had been composed by the Persian or early Hellenistic eras; Ben Sira was likely composed before the Maccabean era.[126] Only Wisdom of Solomon among the clearly identified wisdom documents takes us into the era of the Sadducees, but this document—with its fervent belief in immortality—can hardly be Sadducean, and is likely a product of the Hellenistic Diaspora. Ben Sira, by contrast, circulated in Hebrew in the land of Israel at least until 73 CE, and thus could easily have been revered by and had influence over the Sadducees. Other extant wisdom works, such as Baruch 3.9–4.4, are of unknown date, and could easily stem from the late second temple period. Of course, other sundry wisdom works circulated in late second temple period Judea as well, as evidenced by the Qumran finds.[127] We therefore easily find that the chronological barriers to reconsidering the relationship between the Sadducees and the wisdom tradition break down.

Another wedge can be driven between the Sadducees and the biblical wisdom tradition by recalling the claim that the Sadducees canonized only the Pentateuch.[128] This view is likely mistaken—stemming possibly from the Church Fathers' misunderstanding of Josephus (*Ant.* 18.297).[129] But even if it were correct (as seems unlikely) this hardly militates against reconsidering the connection between the Sadducees and the wisdom tradition, precisely because the greatest similarities are between them and the generally noncanonical Ben Sira. Another motivation for separating the wisdom tradition from the Sadducees is the claim—typically applied to Proverbs, Job, and Ecclesiastes (sans the pious epilogue)—that the wisdom tradition exhibits little concern with either the Mosaic covenant or the priestly cult.[130] But if that is true as far as these books go, the melding of wisdom with priestly and Mosaic concerns is in evidence in various Psalms (e.g., Pss. 1, 34, 37, 73), Tobit 4.3–21, Wisdom of Ben Sira (e.g., 24.1–29), Wisdom of Solomon, and of course the epilogue to Ecclesiastes (12.12–14). Indeed, much of the discussion about the relationship between certain documents (e.g., Pss. 34 and 37) and the wisdom tradition revolves around the question of whether a work that is rooted in the covenant and cult can be considered wisdom at all.[131] Of course, by the time of the Sadducees, the sustained effort aimed at integrating wisdom with Torah was long under way, as evidenced, once again, by the literature just mentioned, along with the appearance of wisdom documents at Qumran (where cult and covenant were surely taken seriously) and the canonization of Proverbs, Job, and Ecclesiastes in the third section of the Jewish Bible, alongside Torah and Prophets. Regardless of how noncultic and noncovenantal wisdom may have been in an earlier era, this cannot preclude the possibility that the synthesis espoused by Ben Sira and others had an influence on later second temple period Jewish groups such as the Sadducees.

A fourth impediment to the linkage between the Sadducees and wisdom is that Josephus makes no such connection. As we will see, subtle connections do emerge from Josephus's description of the Sadducees. As for the lack of explicit discussions of wisdom concerns in Josephus's description of the Sadducees, we should just keep in mind that Josephus does not make much of the wisdom tradition anywhere in his oeuvre. The sage Jesus Ben Sira goes unmentioned, as do the books typically attributed to the wisdom tradition.[132] Even in Josephus's discussion of Solomon (*Ant.* 8.1–211)—which surely does highlight the monarch's legendary wisdom—Josephus does not discuss the books of Proverbs or Ecclesiastes, or make any mention of their purported Solomonic authorship.[133] Indeed, if we had to rely entirely on Josephus, we would have no reason to think that second temple Jewish wisdom literature existed. The fact that he makes no explicit mention of wisdom with regard to Sadducees therefore becomes the kind of absence of evidence that yields nothing but an argument from silence.

A fifth impediment to establishing links between the Sadducees and the wisdom tradition has less to do with our sources, and more to do with ourselves. It seems, simply, that scholarship has not been interested in making such a connection. Perhaps there is insufficient overlap in the interests of those who work in the realms of wisdom literature and ancient Jewish sects. For those under the influence of Gerhard Von Rad, perhaps the hypothesis of the wisdom-apocalyptic connection has absorbed whatever energy there is for exploring echoes of wisdom in late second temple Judaism.[134] For those under the influence of James Crenshaw, perhaps the understanding of the wisdom tradition as a singular, skeptical phenomenon has prevented some from finding its echoes among covenantal Sadducees.[135] Or perhaps scholars are insufficiently interested in the possibility that Ben Sira's synthesis spoke to post-Maccabean second temple period priests and aristocrats. Of course, it is also possible that I am entirely incorrect in taking this connection so seriously. If so, I hope that scholarship can at least learn from this mistake.

The argument can begin with the observation that Ben Sira does not affirm any of the distinctly Pharisaic notions as described by Josephus. There is no beatific immortality of the soul—and certainly no resurrection of the dead (*Ant.* 18.16; compare Sir. 14.11–19, 38.16–23). There is no authoritative body of oral tradition passed down by the generations (*Ant.* 13.297–98; compare Sir. 24.23–33, 38.34–39.11). And there is no effort at fusing fate with free will: human beings are entirely responsible for their behavior and destiny (see chapter 2). These observations in and of themselves cannot simply translate into the assertion that Ben Sira is a Sadducean work. Even if such an assertion were not wildly anachronistic, it would still be methodologically unsound: the absence of Pharisaism is not the definition of Sadducaism.

But there is more to this claim than what the wisdom book lacks. Ben Sira is a cosmopolitan, aristocratic work—characteristics that are common to both the later Sadducees and the earlier wisdom tradition. What is more, Ben Sira at times expresses his disdain for the foolish, sluggish, or unruly in ways that are downright snobbish (e.g., 21.12–22.10, 22.13–15)—could this be, perhaps, the kind of attitude Josephus had in mind when he referred to the Sadducees as boorish (*War* 2.166)? Indeed, with regard to the nature of the Sadducees, Josephus also tells us that it is their nature to dispute with their teachers of wisdom (*Ant.* 18.16)[136]—is Josephus's reference to the Sadducees' teachers' wisdom here a hint that should be followed?

As we proceed in our analysis of Josephus's descriptions of ancient Jewish theological debates, we will seek to establish that the connection between the wisdom tradition and the Sadducees is worth taking seriously. Without much difficulty, we can find within the wisdom tradition—and principally within the book of Ben Sira—precise analogues to practically every perspective that Josephus attributes to the Sadducees. As we proceed with demonstrating this, we will also find the opportunity to go some steps further, venturing to clarify some of Josephus's more ambiguous statements with what we find more clearly articulated in wisdom texts. Certainly, venturing to fill in the gaps left in Josephus's testimony is a perilous business; speculative gap-filling was precisely what was criticized above with regard to the Zadokites. But hereafter, the gap-filling will proceed in a more disciplined fashion. In what follows, we will confine ourselves to working with demonstrable thematic parallels between the wisdom tradition and Josephus's descriptions of the Sadducees. Moreover, we will carefully distinguish between well-established parallels and more inferential ones, remaining cognizant that the Sadducee-wisdom connection is a *hypothesis*, not a fact. Still, having already recognized that Josephus's brief descriptions are in need of a fuller and more sympathetic analysis, it is certainly worth considering whether what we find in Ben Sira can possibly allow us to understand better some of the doctrines ascribed to the Sadducees by Josephus.

Pharisees, Rabbis, and Rabbinic Sources

Just as the Pharisees have received more attention than the Sadducees, the same pertains to Josephus's accounts. Indeed, comparing Josephus's Pharisees with later rabbinic literature has proven tempting to scholars, though there is no current consensus on the extent to which this comparison can be pushed.[137] While older approaches suggest a rather direct linear descent, from Pharisees to rabbis, many current works are more cautious.[138] Still, the comparisons remain. As we have already observed, Josephus's Pharisees struggled to balance fate and free will, believed in life after death, and viewed as authoritative nonscriptural traditions handed down from previous generations. As we will see in the following chapters, each of these positions finds rather precise analogues in later rabbinic traditions. When suggesting a comparison between Josephus's Pharisees and later rabbinic literature, two important questions emerge, one historical and the other methodological. The historical question concerns the validity of the genealogical hypothesis, which is often supported in part by the identification of distinct Pharisees mentioned by Josephus with sages remembered in rabbinic literature. The methodological question concerns the use of rabbinic sources for the understanding of second temple period history.

We can safely shun treating the methodological question here, for two reasons. First, I have argued against the skeptical position in other venues, engaging in the effort of suggesting certain reconstructed Pharisaic views.[139] But more important, this project does not depend on backdating rabbinic documents or individual rabbinic traditions. Indeed, the arguments that follow do not depend on suggesting that any given rabbinic source hearkens back even a generation earlier than whenever the document in question was redacted. Rabbinic sources will be used here primarily for the purposes of illuminating and evaluating Josephus's descriptions of ancient Jewish theologies. Lacking any reliably Pharisaic sources, but granting that Josephus's accounts are verifiably from the first century CE, I propose that we weigh Josephus's accounts against rabbinic sources in order to better evaluate the plausibility of the former. We will not restrict ourselves to rabbinic traditions concerning Pharisees or early tannaitic sages per se. We will, rather, try to find the closest analogues to Josephus's statements wherever they may appear, irrespective of whether the traditions are attributed to figures we can otherwise associate with Pharisees or their heirs. This exercise will, I believe, prove worthwhile, understanding full well that rabbinic sources are later—some significantly later—than Josephus, just as the sectarian Dead Sea Scrolls (which are frequently compared to the Essenes) are significantly earlier than Josephus.

What has been said about the methodological question relates to our approach to the historical question as well. To be sure, many scholars are convinced that rabbinic Judaism emerged out of Pharisaic Judaism, and such approaches will to a certain degree be bolstered by the theological parallels we will consider in the following chapters. For our purposes, however, we need not argue for any particular hypothesis regarding the relation between the earlier Pharisees and the later rabbis. It does not matter whether the rabbinic movement emerged directly out of a Pharisaic ancestor or whether it absorbed elements from various aspects of Jewish society. Even so, we should review and consider some of the reasons why many scholars accept such views, beyond the theological connections that are the subject of this work.

Josephus's repeated assertion that the Pharisees were the leading sect among second temple period Jews (*Ant.* 13.288, 298; 18.15) is certainly an important factor in viewing the eventually predominant rabbis as the successors of the earlier group. Against the veracity of Josephus's claims for Pharisaic dominance is the charge that Josephus himself is participating in Judean politics from afar, advocating (especially in *Antiquities*) the cause of the postdestruction successors of the Pharisees.[140] But as Mason has correctly pointed out, Josephus says less than flattering things about the Pharisees' political behavior practically any time Pharisaic dominance is mentioned or even suggested (*War* 1.110–14; *Ant.* 13.288–98, 400–32, 17.41–45; *Life* 189–98).[141] And depending on how we understand Josephus's reference to the Pharisees as the "first" or "leading" sect (*War*

2.162), Josephus may have made the claim for Pharisaic dominance even in his earliest work.[142] Importantly, the impression of Pharisaic power is also reflected in New Testament sources (e.g., Matt. 23.2–3). So it could well turn out to be the case that Josephus's claims for Pharisaic dominance reflect not his biases or political concerns but the facts as he knew them.[143]

The connection between Josephus's Pharisees and the later rabbis is also suggested by the fact that certain named Pharisees are also remembered as sages in rabbinic sources. The clearest instance is Simon son of Gamaliel, who is identified as a Pharisee in *Life* 191–92, and remembered in rabbinic sources as a sage who lived before the temple's destruction (e.g., *m. Keritot* 1.7). This figure is presumably the son of the man reputed to be Paul's teacher (Acts 22.3). And quite possibly, the rabbinic sage Gamaliel of Yavneh (e.g., *m. Rosh ha-Shanah* 2.8–9) is Simon's son, named as was customary for Simon's father (see *m. Avot* 1.16–18). Other possible overlaps between Josephus's Pharisees and rabbinic sages include the Pharisee Pollion and his disciple Samaias, who were active early in the reign of Herod the Great (*Ant.* 15.3–4, 370; see also 14.172–76).[144] These figures are sometimes associated, respectively, with Abtalion and Shamaiah, the pair of sages who ostensibly flourished in the generation preceding Hillel and Shammai (*m. Avot* 1.10–11, *m. Hagigah* 2.2).[145] As compelling as these connections are, it is important that scholars refrain from going the next step and identifying all early rabbinic sages, such as Hillel and Shammai, as Pharisees. Hillel and Shammai become Pharisees only when we employ a "transitive property" of Pharisaism, whereby the Pharisees-to-rabbis hypothesis becomes the basis of identifying all pre-70 CE rabbinic sages as Pharisees.[146] We do better to keep the Pharisee-rabbi connection as a hypothesis, and to refrain from inferentially identifying individual early rabbinic sages as Pharisees.[147]

A final point should be raised here, concerning the study of rabbinic theology. As noted, this has fallen out of fashion in some circles, with the relatively recent efforts of E. P. Sanders and Ephraim Urbach being grouped together with the earlier efforts of Solomon Schechter and George F. Moore and then criticized for being harmonistic, apologetic, and insufficiently critical.[148] Other important efforts have been criticized less only because they have been ignored more.[149] To be sure, these works have their methodological shortcomings, and scholars have learned, among other things, not to date rabbinic traditions on the basis of the sages named within them. But it seems to me that the criticisms have been taken too far. When it comes to understanding the ways rabbinic texts deal with theological matters—such as those that will be subjects of the coming chapters—there is much that scholars can still learn from careful, critical readings of Urbach and Sanders, and even Schechter, Moore, and Heschel. The rather high level of disrespect accorded to these works in recent times is certainly in part personal, and that can safely be ignored. But we should wonder whether the general acquiescence to these harsh critiques is a reflection of the contemporary tendency among many scholars of second temple and rabbinic Judaism to shunt aside matters of theology while centralizing matters of law. A better approach would be to try to put the study of ancient Jewish and rabbinic theology on a sounder footing. Instead of precluding the possibility of working back from rabbinic sources on literary-methodological grounds, what if we work forward from Josephus, seeing whether Josephus's accounts of ancient Jewish theology anticipate what we find in rabbinic sources? It is hoped that the present effort to reevaluate Josephus's accounts of ancient Jewish theological disputes will aid in this undertaking.

The Essenes and the Qumran Scrolls

Whatever one may say about Josephus's Pharisees and Sadducees, no one could claim that Josephus's Essenes are overlooked or downplayed in current scholarship. Certainly the most robust debate about Josephus among scholars of ancient Judaism concerns the Dead Sea Scrolls and the Essene hypothesis, which asserts that the sectarian scrolls were composed by Essenes of the sort that Josephus describes.[150] Going back virtually to "Day 1" of scholarship on the scrolls—with the publication in 1948 and 1949 of E. L. Sukenik's *Hidden Scrolls*—this hypothesis has had remarkable staying power.[151] It has, of course, also had its critics.[152] Though it may be true that the critics are many, it is equally true that there is little of substance that the critics agree on other than their opposition to the Essene hypothesis. Indeed, many, if not most, of the alternatives to the Essene hypothesis are, literally, *idiosyncratic*: theories articulated by a single major figure, and espoused explicitly by few others.[153] Importantly for our purposes, among the recent critics of the Essene hypothesis is none other than Josephus scholar extraordinaire Steve Mason, who in a series of articles, as well as in a detailed commentary on *War* 2, has argued against the Essene hypothesis and even argued against using Josephus for the purpose of determining who the Dead Sea sectarians were.[154] It is too soon to tell whether this approach will gain support or will be consigned to the assembly of sui generis alternatives. But because Mason's critique focuses on Josephus's description of the Essenes per se—and because Mason's work rightly looms large over all current work on Josephus (including this project)—we do well to briefly consider his arguments here. We can do so briefly for two principle reasons: first, fuller critiques of Mason's approach have already appeared elsewhere,[155] and, second, as this book concerns Josephus's testimony regarding ancient Jewish theology, the fuller questions of Essene history and practice are of less concern here. We will be satisfied to make the following claim: that the theology we find expressed in the sectarian Dead Sea Scrolls—particularly the *Community Rule*, the *Thanksgiving Hymns*, and the *War Scroll*—is remarkably close to that attributed to the Essenes by Josephus.

Before considering a sampling of Mason's specific arguments, it is important to make one further point about the Essene hypothesis. Although Mason downplays the nuances among scholars in his critique of the identification, it is important to recognize differences between what we could call "harder" and "softer" forms of the hypothesis. A classic articulation of the harder form is Frank Cross's oft-cited summary statement:

> The scholar who would "exercise caution" in identifying the sect of Qumran with the Essenes places himself in an astonishing position; he must suggest seriously that two major parties formed communistic religious communities in the same district of the desert of the Dead Sea and lived together in effect for two centuries, holding similar bizarre views, performing similar or rather identical lustrations, ritual meals, and ceremonies. He must suppose that one, carefully described by classical authors, disappeared without leaving building remains or even potsherds behind; the other, systematically ignored by classical authors, left extensive ruins, and indeed a great library. I prefer to be reckless and flatly identify the men of Qumran with their perennial house-guests, the Essenes. At all events, in the remainder of our essay, we shall assume the identification and draw freely upon both classical and Qumran texts.[156]

Two related problems are in evidence in this paragraph, both of which illustrate the "harder" form of the Essene hypothesis. First, Cross moves seamlessly—flatly, in his words—from similarity to identity. Second, he then proceeds to draw freely on both sources. In other words, he will interpret Josephus in light of the scrolls and the scrolls in light of Josephus. A third feature of the harder forms of the Essene hypothesis is also articulated by Cross a few pages later in the same essay:[157] this is the historical reconstruction that assumes a mid-second-century origin of the Essene movement, as a group whose breakaway is rooted in their rejection of the non-Zadokite Hasmonean priesthood.

We have already noted that Josephus's writings do not support the common contentions that sectarianism arose in the mid-second-century BCE or that priestly descent played any particular role in sectarian disputes. We have also noted that the Zadokite connection may be less significant to Qumran than many have assumed. The supposed mid-second-century origins of the Dead Sea sect can be rejected also on literary grounds (insofar as the clearest historical references remembered by the group pertain to the first century BCE)[158] and archaeological grounds (insofar as the relevant occupation layers at Qumran appear datable to the first century BCE).[159] It is important, therefore, to separate all this from the Essene hypothesis, for the identification of the group as comparable to the Essenes does not necessitate any particular view on the question of mid-second-century origins of sectarianism in general or the Essenes in particular. As for the other excesses in this passage (and other similar treatments), many advocates or supporters of the Essene hypothesis are indeed more cautious, carefully speaking of the "Dead Sea sect" or the "Qumran group" (not the "Qumran Essenes") and reaching conclusions to the effect that the group was "a branch of the Essenes."[160] Indeed, these are the characteristics of the "softer" form of the hypothesis: first, origins are to be left aside, as something that lies beyond the capacity of our sources (whether Qumranic or Josephan). Second, the Dead Sea sectarians are not to be flatly identified with Josephus's Essenes, but compared to them. In line with this, sources and terms will be used here with care, such that we will continue to speak of Josephus's (or Philo's, or Pliny's) Essenes as they relate, by means of comparison, to the sectarian literature from Qumran. In short, the hypothesis remains just that: a compelling *hypothesis*. Still, after all these years, the hypothesis remains more convincing to most scholars than any other alternative.[161]

So, to turn now to Mason's criticisms, these take two forms: methodological and substantial. As for the methodological criticisms, some of Mason's points hit their target and should indeed keep scholars from slipping back into the harder forms of the hypothesis. Josephus must be recognized as an author with his own interests and concerns. Even if passages are drawn from sources (such as those concerning the Essenes), the originals have been so thoroughly reworked that attempts to separate earlier sources from Josephan adaptations cannot succeed.[162] Josephus's treatments of the Essenes—indeed, his treatments of all the ancient Jewish groups—must be understood first and foremost in their literary context within Josephus's works. Scholars can now do just that better, thanks in part to Mason's own work. So, for instance, Qumran scholars will have to reckon with the argument that Josephus's account of the Essenes has been shaped in light of Josephus's desire to present the group as Jewish Spartans.[163]

Mason's other methodological remarks are less persuasive, in that they appear to be phrased in such ways as to preclude the Essene hypothesis prima facie. It is quite correct, of course, that "standard historical method requires that the historian gather all contemporary evidence bearing on the phenomenon in question, try to understand it in its own right, and then test hypotheses to find the one that will best explain the evidence."[164] Mason then proceeds to speak of a "strange neglect of standard method in this case"—meaning, of course, the Essene hypothesis. What Mason has overlooked is that for the scholar of religion faced with identifying the group associated with the Qumran finds, the piece of evidence at the center of the question is not Josephus, but the sectarian scrolls (notably 1QS, 1QM, 1QH, etc.). Mason can rightfully wish that scholars had paid more attention to Josephus as an author; but neglect of historical method altogether is a charge too strong to level against, for instance, VanderKam and Flint's *Meaning of the Dead Sea Scrolls*—the tenth chapter of which walks students through each step Mason has outlined, albeit with the scrolls in the center. But Mason himself has not, in fact, followed the method as described. He has, rather, analyzed Josephus in full and considered the scrolls in a rather piecemeal fashion (precisely what he accuses—often correctly—others of doing to Josephus). Moreover, Mason has not considered *all* the alternatives. Indeed, he has hardly considered *any* alternatives to the hard version of the thesis he has rejected, including the all-important (and now probably dominant) softer version of the Essene hypothesis that posits that Josephus's Essenes are something larger (and of course, at least as he describes them, chronologically later) than the Qumran sect. The method Mason follows, it seems, is this: identify as many contradictions as possible, and then consider the case closed. And it's a problematic method. After all, when two sources discuss the same phenomenon—group, person, event, or tradition—aren't there *always* differences—even when the sources stem from similar times and places and are preserved in the same language? (To wit: the Gospels on Jesus; 1 and 2 Maccabees on the martyrs and the revolt; Mishnah/Tosefta parallels, etc.) There isn't a single figure, event, or group from late antiquity that is described consistently among all independent sources. But the Essene hypothesis deniers move shrewdly: *any* contradiction is taken as disproving the case. Attempts at explaining the contradictions are then viewed as being overly accommodating.[165] But what historical question can be answered if we cannot grapple with and attempt to resolve differences among our sources? What historical standard requires such a high level of agreement among disparate sources to permit hypothesizing that they discuss related phenomena? Mason's approach to the Essene question isn't necessarily representative of historical method—it's the preclusion of historical analysis, under the banner of literary purity.

So let us move from method to substance and consider some of the differences identified by Mason. With regard to *War* 2.147 and the Essenes' practice of guarding against certain forms of spitting, Mason duly notes that the scrolls prohibit spitting in public (1QS 7.13–15). But where the Essene behavior as described by Josephus is taken as a sign of their "extraordinary rigor," the Qumranic rule is taken as an indication of the group's "lack of self-control."[166] This instance—which Mason views as representative of the difference between Josephus's Essenes and the group who wrote the *Community Rule*—illustrates the curious way Mason has subjected the two disparate sources to entirely different standards. If we step back and imagine how a self-contained group—one that takes years to join—would maintain discipline and self-control among its members, written rules concerning what is to be controlled comes to mind as a reasonable tool. The appearance of a rule may well indicate that it was, from time to time, broken; but to determine that a group must lack self-control precisely because its rules prohibit spitting is simply astonishing. And it is certainly *not* the kind of conclusion that is based on historical or comparative methodologies. Let us consider one reasonable historical comparison. Anyone who has studied Christian monasticism knows well that (1) monks cultivated the reputation of possessing self-control, and (2) monastic rules prohibit all sorts of sordid deeds. But should we assume, based on inverting their prohibitions (e.g., *The Rule of St. Benedict*, sec. 4), that early Benedictine monks were, in fact, drunkards and gluttons who were fearless of Hell?

A further difference between the two groups—Josephus's Essenes and the Dead Sea sect—concerns their psychology. Mason intriguingly describes the sectarians as a textbook example of William James's "sick souls"—those glass-half-empty types who live, sadly, in a world perceived to be pervaded by evil. Josephus's Essenes, Mason avers, must by contrast be "happy souls," for they appeal to wealthy, aristocratic authors at home in the world.[167] Would that scholars make more use of such theoretical literature for the understanding of ancient Judaism. But the literature must be properly understood first, and Mason has missed some rather important points here. The description of the Dead Sea sectarians as "sick souls" is reasonably sound—assuming, for the moment, that we take the more depressing, introspective *Thanksgiving Hymns* as positive evidence.[168] The other side of the equation, however, is rather problematic since we lack direct (or even indirect) access to the psychology of Josephus's Essenes. But if Josephus's Essenes were as "healthy minded" as Mason suggests, why would they turn away from the world and require a rigorous regimen of initiation? James's sick souls are motivated to be "twice-born."[169] On this particular matter, it is nearly impossible to establish a difference between Josephus's Essenes and the Dead Sea sect: the cultivation of their second births is all but identical.[170] It is not the Josephan Essene but rather Josephus himself who is indeed a "happy soul," in James's parlance: the world is a just place according to Josephus. Whether Josephus's Essenes are best understood in the same light remains, however, a very open question.

The question of Essene sun worship (*War* 2.128; see also 2.148) can serve as our final example. Noting that the *Temple Scroll* prohibits sun worship (11QT 55.15–21), Mason finds here, too, evidence against the Essene hypothesis.[171] Mason is correct insofar as he argues that we ought not to "flatten" Josephus's account into a simple reference to sectarian prayers at dawn (compare, e.g., 1QS 10.10).[172] It does seem inescapable that Josephus views some form of sun-praise as an aspect of Essene prayer practice. But as Mason also notes, Josephus himself tends to personify the sun as a representation of God (*War* 4.382–83, compare, e.g., 2.148). And solar imagery colors Josephus's description of the tabernacle and its worship (*Ant.* 3.100, 115). So it would appear that Josephus views sun worship—or, possibly, adoration of God oriented toward the sun—as an integral aspect of ancient Jewish piety. Of course, evidence of solar worship can also be found in contemporary Greco-Roman literature, as well as in contemporary, local archaeological evidence.[173] But Josephus is not alone among ancient writers in finding such things among Jews. Philo and other writers also described the temple and aspects of its service in cosmic and even solar terms.[174] Solar images also appear later in the traditional Jewish liturgy,[175] and on synagogue floors (e.g., Hammath, Beth Alpha, Sepphoris). Solar imagery associated with God appears in Qumran texts as well (e.g., 1QH[a] 12.6–7, 20.7–14; 1QS 10.1–3). Clearly, for ancient Jews generally, the biblical prohibitions against worshiping the sun (e.g., Deut. 17.2–5, which forms the basis of 11QT 55.15–21) were not understood to have much to do with these solar practices and images. If Jews generally, Josephus's Essenes, and Josephus himself sensed no contradiction here, why should we presume that Josephus's account in *War* 2.128 somehow prevents understanding the sectarian scrolls as Essene-like? Is it really impossible that the sectarian Sons of Light revered the source of all earthly daylight as a "reflection" of the deity?[176] Perhaps there is an inherent contradiction here between Josephus's presentation of the Essenes and our understanding of the Qumran sect and ancient Judaism generally. But I still don't see it.

We can stop here. We need not concern ourselves with all matters concerning the Essene hypothesis, for this is a book about ancient Jewish theologies, not ancient Jewish sectarianism in general. Full-blown defenses of the Essene hypothesis can be found elsewhere. Once again, we can be satisfied with the following claim, which will be demonstrated more fully in the coming chapters: the theology Josephus ascribes to the Essenes is very much like the theology we find among the sectarian Qumran scrolls; at the same time, this theology is very much unlike what is expressed in other known ancient Jewish texts. If that is not enough to put the comparison between Josephus's Essenes and the sectarian Qumran scrolls on solid footing, then what is?

Josephus's Essenes and Philo's Essenes

It is frequently noted that Josephus's descriptions of the Essenes are related in some way to those of Philo. In fact, *Antiquities* 18.18–22 echoes so many aspects of Philo's description in *Every Good Man* 75–91 that scholars frequently entertain the possibility that Josephus drew directly from Philo in this instance.[177] But parallels emerge elsewhere, too, for example with regard to Josephus's description of Essene endurance and suffering (*War* 2.152–53; compare Philo, *Every Good Man*, 89–91) as well as the (clearly hyperbolic) assertion that Essenes live to ripe old ages (*War* 2.151; compare

Philo, *Hypothetica* 11.13). And both writers, alas, describe the Essene attitude toward women in ways that reflect (also) their own misogyny (*War*
2.121; Philo, *Hypothetica* 11.14–17).[78] It is indeed curious that Josephus drew
more from Philo—at least as far Philo's extant works allow us to discern—
in the later *Antiquities* than earlier in *Jewish War*.[79] Even so, similarities
emerge in both works, and we will note these and other comparisons when
relevant in our analysis.[80] But I should explain here why Philo's evidence
will not play a major role in this study. First, as discussed earlier, Cohen
has demonstrated convincingly that Josephus thoroughly reworks any
sources he may have used, a fact that leads us to agree with Mason to the
effect that Josephus's accounts—even if reworked from earlier sources—
are thoroughly his own.[81] Second, all this is particularly true with regard to
the material that is of interest to us—Josephus's accounts of ancient Jewish
theological disputes. Philo says nothing about Pharisaic or Sadducean theology, and he says little of Essene theology. What little he does say—such
as the rather surprising assertion that the Essenes did not attribute to God
responsibility for any evil (*Every Good Man* 84)—seems suspiciously in line
with Philo's own thinking.[82] To his credit, Josephus seems to have been
much more interested in cataloguing Jewish theological debate, and was
clearly willing to record views that disagreed with his own. Added to this,
we should note that Josephus's knowledge of Hebrew and his location in
the land of Israel put him in a better position than Philo to understand all
three groups (regardless of whether we accept Josephus's autobiographical claims to have spent time studying all three curricula). A final point
is methodological. I will argue throughout this work that the best way to
understand Josephus's accounts of ancient Jewish theological disputes
is by considering all such evidence (and not just that with regard to one
group) in light of Josephus's statements about his own theological beliefs.
A fuller understanding of Philo's treatments of the Essenes—which, as we
have pointed out, includes little about theology and even less about theology that is beyond suspicion—would require a similar analysis of larger
amounts of material in light of Philo's own views.[83] This is a task that, alas,
will remain for another scholar to pursue.

Looking Forward

In the following chapters, we will argue that Josephus's descriptions of
ancient Jewish theological disputes are, on the whole, confirmable. With
regard to fate and free will, life after death, and tradition and innovation,

we will find that Josephus's accounts of all three groups—Sadducees, Pharisees, and Essenes—compare reasonably well with, respectively, Ben Sira, rabbinic traditions, and Dead Sea Scrolls. Practically every Josephan statement about theology can be reasonably accounted for. And we will find, I believe, that the results are consistently similar for all three groups. We will also see that the disagreements among Josephus's works with regard to the scholastic debates are largely explainable in light of lessons learned from the comparative evidence.

As we proceed, we will also see that Josephus's own theology is aligned largely with what we can, based on his own writings as well as other sources, associate with the Pharisees (and even early rabbis). Although he is taken with Essene behavior, Josephus's own theology does not accord with what he attributes to the Essenes. Of course, he is hostile to his own simplified (but not entirely false) presentation of Sadducean theology. His own approach affirms divine providence and advocates a partial determinism, supported by his belief in fulfilled prophecy as well as the earthly justice that is manifest in human history. He seeks to find earthly justice where he can, and settles for heavenly postmortem punishments when necessary. But he is not given over completely to the other-worldly immortality he attributes to the Essenes. Josephus's hopes involve bodily hopes, too. And although he cannot be said to advocate the dual revelation (written and oral) that will eventually characterize rabbinic Judaism, a good case can be made for his agreement with the legal ideology of the Pharisees, as he describes them. Of course, we have no way of knowing how Josephus's Pharisees responded to the destruction of the temple. But we will clearly see that Josephus's own response is similar in many respects to what we find in later rabbinic literature.

In the end, we will see that Josephus indeed serves as our best guide to a general understanding of ancient Jewish theological disputes as well as responses to the destruction of the second temple. This in turn has important ramifications for a number of current trends in scholarship, including the tendency to prioritize law over theology in the understanding of sectarian disputes and the common presumption that second temple Judaism was ill equipped theologically to grapple with the disaster of 70 CE.

2

Fate, Free Will, and Ancient Jewish Types of Compatibilism

IN THIS CHAPTER, we turn to the perennial problem of fate and free will, though our focus will be on Jewish efforts of addressing or balancing these two concerns. We do well to begin with this material, for Josephus, too, gives great priority to this issue. When he first introduces the schools in *Antiquities*, he informs us that the three groups can be characterized by differing approaches to "human affairs" (13.171). The Essenes "declare that fate [εἱμαρμένη] is the mistress of all things, and that nothing befalls people unless it be in accordance with her decree" (*Ant.* 13.172). By contrast, the Sadducees "do away with fate, holding that there is no such thing" (13.173). The Pharisees, we are told, hold a middle position, believing that "certain events are the work of fate, but not all; as to other events it depends on ourselves whether they shall take place or not" (13.172). In his earlier, more extended treatment of the three schools in book 2 of *War*, he similarly begins his descriptions of the Pharisees and Sadducees (but not the Essenes) by stating their position on the matter of fate (*War* 2.162, 164). The issue also figures in *Antiquities* 18, being the first theological issue Josephus addresses with regard to both the Pharisees (18.13) and Essenes (18.18; this time the Sadducean position is dropped out).[1]

Additional important data emerge from these passages. For instance, in *War* 2.164–65, Josephus provides a fuller explanation for the Sadducees' denial of fate, informing us that they "remove God beyond, not merely the commission, but the very sight, of evil. They maintain that a person has the free choice of good or evil, and that it rests with each person's will whether to follow the one or the other." The Pharisees, we are told in this passage, "attribute everything to fate and to God; they hold that to act rightly or otherwise rests, indeed, for the most part with men, but that in each action fate cooperates" (*War* 2.163).[2] This Pharisaic *fusion* of fate and free will is also noted in *Antiquities* 18.13:

> Though they postulate that everything is brought about by fate, still they do not deprive the human will of the pursuit of what is in humanity's power, since it was God's good pleasure that there should be a fusion and that the will of humanity with its virtue and vice should be admitted into the council-chamber of fate.[3]

Each of these passages, as we will see, raises important questions and therefore merits further study.

Despite its brevity, *Antiquities* 13.171–73 is particularly interesting. The passage provides a clean typology in which each school is assigned a distinct position regarding the two variables at stake. Moreover, the placement of the passage—as the first mention of the schools in *Antiquities*—suggests that the differences Josephus discusses are important enough, and characteristic enough, that he believed readers could get a handle on these three groups by keeping in mind the differences described in the passage. As we will see, nearly exact parallels seem to present themselves from three distinct realms of ancient literature: rabbinic traditions, the Dead Sea Scrolls, and the Wisdom of Ben Sira.

The passage is also controversial in perhaps just as many respects, and numerous scholars question one or another aspect of it. We have already noted that some scholars have questioned the placement of the passage, for it has no obvious connection to its immediate context.[4] Objecting to the philosophical terminology, some scholars have long questioned whether the passage reflects the interests of ancient Jews in general, some even questioning Josephus's authorship.[5] Moving beyond this particular passage, scholars wonder whether the account here can be squared even with what Josephus says about the schools in the other schools passages.[6] As discussed in the introduction, many scholars believe that the ancient Jewish groups primarily argued about law, not theology.[7] Still others have analyzed ancient Jewish disputes regarding philosophical matters as if Josephus's evidence has little if any importance at all.[8] Of course, some scholars have argued that the passage rings true.[9] In short, practically all the general questions about Josephus and Jewish theology have been or can easily be asked about Josephus's treatment of fate and free will.

Before reconsidering the evidence from Josephus as it relates to ancient Judaism in general, we do well to clarify the philosophical terms that are used, not only in the efforts at translating Josephus's works but also in correlating the views he describes with both ancient philosophical sources and contemporary philosophical and theological treatments. Throughout his descriptions of the three ancient Jewish schools, Josephus speaks of "fate" (εἱμαρμένη), which can be defined broadly as the belief that things are brought about, of necessity, by set causes or impersonal powers.[10] It has long been noted that Josephus's discussion is colored by Hellenistic philosophical concerns, making use of Stoic terminology in particular.[11] It is of course unlikely that ancient Jews who otherwise believed in God granted the existence of a separate or impersonal power—"fate"—governing events. Thus, when speaking of Jewish theologies, one more frequently encounters terms like "determinism," "predeterminism," or "predestination." The first two can be taken, generally, as referring more to the belief that all events, including human behaviors, are inexorably brought about by prior causes.[12] The prefix "pre" is added to the more common philosophic "determinism," particularly in theological contexts, where the writer desires to emphasize that the fixed causation of events follows a previously established divine plan. Predestination is generally understood as a specific form of theistic predeterminism, one that is especially focused on the destinies of individual human beings. Predestination asserts that God has long ago decided that salvation will be extended to some but not to others.[13] Sometimes the term "double predestination" is used for emphasis, to describe the Calvinist belief that just as the righteous are predestined to be saved, so the wicked are predestined to be damned.[14] While the terms can mean rather different things in disparate religious and philosophical contexts, the differences dissipate somewhat in developed theologies of religions such as Judaism, Christianity, and Islam, which put a premium on questions concerning individual salvation and assert the existence of a single omniscient and omnipotent God. Both "predeterminism," and "predestination" assert God's absolute foreknowledge of and control over future events and lead toward the denial of free choice—just as Josephus understands these matters.

Although not with regard to the views of the ancient Jewish schools, Josephus employs other important terms when describing the divine forces that impact human history. In *War* in particular, Josephus describes a number of events—such as Rome's rise—as having been brought about by "fortune" (τύχη; e.g., *War* 3.354).[15] Josephus's use of this term does complicate matters somewhat, but as we will see, we can subsume Josephus's understanding of "fortune" under his more general understandings of divine control over human affairs.

In *Antiquities*, Josephus quite frequently (and perhaps more clearly) uses another word to describe divine control and causation: *pronoia* (πρόνοια), usually translated as "providence." As we will see more fully later in this chapter, Josephus is himself a firm believer in divine providence: God carefully and thoughtfully guides the world, rewarding the righteous and punishing the wicked (e.g., *Ant.* 8.314, 10.278).[16] And Josephus categorically opposes those—like the Epicureans—who deny divine providence (*Ant.* 10.277–78, discussed below). Now while some have questioned the appropriateness of Josephus using the term "fate" (εἱμαρμένη) in discussions of ancient Jewish thought, we can be much more certain that his use of "providence" (πρόνοια) reflects broader ancient Jewish trends, not only theologically, but terminologically. The same term is used to describe God's caring and thoughtful guidance of human affairs in various late second temple period Jewish texts composed in Greek (see, e.g., Wisdom 6.7, 14.3, 17.2; 3 Macc. 4.21, 5.30; 4 Macc. 9.24, 13.19, 17.22; see also Dan. 6.18 [LXX, Old Greek]).[17] The term (and concept) is especially prominent in Philo (e.g., *On Creation* 9, *On the Unchangeableness* 29, and the extant fragments of *On Providence*).[18] And if we jump forward a few centuries, we find the term used, of God, in a number of Jewish dedicatory inscriptions as well.[19]

It has been asserted that Josephus uses the terms "fate" and "providence" interchangeably.[20] Indeed, the terms (and concepts) are identified in classic Stoic philosophy, although distinctions do emerge overtime for some thinkers.[21] To be sure, the terms do overlap for Josephus, especially with regard to predictive prophecy (e.g., *War* 4.622). But I will argue briefly here and more fully later that Josephus's usages of the terms "fate" and "providence" exhibit discernable differences. Josephus consistently speaks of "fate" with regard to the schools' debates because, I will suggest, this term can more clearly express the (debated) belief that *all* events are planned, by God, *in advance* and proceed according to plan in such a way that human freedom to choose is challenged. Josephus's belief in providence, however, does not necessarily involve all-encompassing fixed plans on the part of God. Nor does it pose any particular challenge to human freedom, for it would appear that Josephus believes in freedom of choice, too (*Ant.* 1.14–15, 20–23). Just like the usages of "providence" (πρόνοια) in other Jewish literature noted above, Josephus's belief in providence involves a God who justly and caringly rewards the righteous and punishes the wicked (e.g., *Ant.* 8.314). But this is not necessarily identical to the belief that fate controls all things.

To be sure, Josephus does view some events as fated. While the term "fate" can be employed to describe the views of those who ascribe all things to fate, not everyone who speaks of fate believes that *all* events are fated. Josephus's Pharisees (as described in *Ant.* 13.172) attribute only some events to fate, not all. The relegation of fate to a partial explanation of events is characteristic of various streams of Middle Platonism and Gnosticism, and is also a hallmark of Hellenistic astrology.[22] I will argue that Josephus's own belief in divine providence similarly involves a partial determinism, ascribing some but not all events to fate. Developing this argument will require allowing some distinction between "fate" and "providence"—matters we will attend to more fully later in this chapter.

We must introduce at this point one additional term, although it does not refer to any particular expression used by Josephus or, for that matter, other ancient Jews. Philosophers have coined the term "compatibilism" to refer to the varied efforts—ancient and modern—to maintain that determinism (or fate) and free will are not contradictory but compatible.[23] In particular, the term often refers to the position that holds that a strict determinism can still allow for the possibility that individuals make free and unrestrained decisions, and are therefore responsible for their actions, despite the fact that the decisions and their consequences are all determined in advance. The term has been borrowed and utilized in some recent discussions of biblical (Christian) theology that address the troubled question of divine foreknowledge.[24] Moving closer to our interests, the term also appears occasionally in treatments of medieval or ancient Jewish theology, again with regard to the efforts to balance fate and free will.[25] Yet at the same time, the term "compatibilism"—or the compromise position to which the term ought to refer—has also been applied to other ancient Jewish groups, even the ostensibly deterministic (and possibly Essene) Dead Sea sectarians.[26] Despite these confusions, I believe the term "compatibilism" remains of use to those who wish to better understand the philosophical and theological questions Josephus is addressing. As we try to shed some light on ancient Jewish approaches to fate and free will, we will also offer some helpful clarifications and practical suggestions for the use of the term "compatibilism" in the context of ancient Judaism.

In the first section below, we will take an initial look at Josephus's tripartite theological typology as well as one of his clearer statements about his own view. After that, we will see how confusions have emerged regarding the term "compatibilism" and the varied ancient Jewish approaches to fate and free will. In response to this confusion, a closer survey of the evidence will reveal that Josephus's tripartite schema can be salvaged, once we move past its oversimplifications. Having done this, we will go one step further, observing that at least two distinct modes of compatibilism are spoken of by Josephus and are in evidence in ancient Jewish and rabbinic sources. We will then broaden our analysis in order to consider ways the various modes of ancient Jewish compatibilism described by Josephus differ from their ancient (and even modern) philosophical counterparts. Along the way, but especially toward the end of this chapter, we will clarify various aspects of Josephus's own view, finding that he qualifies as a compatibilist, in line with his controversial claim that he aligned himself with the Pharisees.

In the end, we will find that it is indeed possible to defend the general accuracy and utility of Josephus's typology of the ancient Jewish schools. But doing so requires recognizing both the similarities and the differences between the Hellenistic philosophical and ancient Jewish theological debates. It also requires clarifying the contours and characteristics of the compromise positions that Josephus ascribes to Pharisees, and that were apparently later espoused by a number of rabbinic traditions. Indeed, we will find, ironically, that the term "compatibilism" may prove most useful in the study of ancient Judaism when it is used in a manner somewhat different from the way the term is employed in contemporary philosophy. At the same time, we will find that we need to distinguish between "fate" and "providence"—a move that goes against the current trend in Josephan scholarship, although as we will also see, there is plenty of ancient evidence justifying this maneuver.[27]

Fate, Free Will, and Compatibilism: A Preliminary Sketch

In order to understand better Josephus's use of the term "fate" in the context of ancient Jewish theological disputes, we do well to begin with his descriptions of the school that believes in fate, the Essenes.

Fate among Essenes and the Qumran Sectarians

Josephus's two statements on the Essenes' beliefs regarding fate are brief and rather clear. They believe that "Fate is mistress [κυρίαν] of all things, and that nothing befalls people unless it be in accordance with her decree"

(*Ant.* 13.172). In short, their belief "is wont to leave everything in the hands of God" (*Ant.* 18.18). In the fuller passages from which these observations are excerpted, Josephus makes clear that the Essene doctrine has significant implications for the understanding of human affairs. The unqualified belief in fate poses a challenge for the belief in human freedom. It is precisely for this reason that the Sadducees deny fate (13.173), while the Pharisees struggle to work out some sort of compromise (13.172). But the Essenes seem untroubled by this.

Before the discovery of the Dead Sea Scrolls, we would have had some difficulty identifying among our otherwise extant texts passages that clearly articulate anything even approaching a fully determinist position such as that described by Josephus. To be sure, various non-Qumranic ancient Jewish documents have been understood as deterministic to some degree. These include apocalyptic texts such as Daniel (whose precise predictions imply some predetermination of history) as well as wisdom texts such as Ecclesiastes, with its assertion that there is "a time for every matter under heaven" (3.1).[28] Indeed, the once popular theories drawing strong connections between wisdom and apocalyptic were grounded in no small part precisely by this connection.[29] Again, since all depends on definitions, it is not categorically incorrect to view these texts as deterministic. The problem of doing so, however, is that it makes it more difficult to come to grips with the fate and free will problem, as understood by Josephus and, as we will see, Ben Sira. In order to make sense of the free will problem, we need to recognize that free will can be limited only by stronger understandings of determinism, whereby *all* events are believed to be determined in advance. It is this kind of stronger determinism that precludes alternate outcomes of human choices, raising in turn the question whether divine judgment is deserved (as punishment for choosing evil) or capricious (being the inexorable outcome of actions predetermined by God). Certainly nothing in Ecclesiastes would lead to such a strong determinism.[30] Even careful readings of Daniel suggest that the book holds something other than predeterminism.[31] But we need have no reservations when we turn to the literature from Qumran.

Setting aside the broader question of the Essene hypothesis, we will focus here on the degree to which the theology Josephus attributes to the Essenes finds striking parallels in sectarian literature from Qumran. As is well known, the sectarian *Community Rule* contains what may be the clearest articulation of predestinarian ideas in all ancient Jewish literature:

> From the God of knowledge comes all that is and shall be. Before ever they existed, he established their whole design, (16) and when, as ordained for them, they came into being, it is in accord with his glorious design that they accomplish their task without change. (17) The laws of all things are in his hand, and he provides them with all their needs. He has created man to govern (18) the world, and has appointed for him two spirits in which to walk until the time of his visitation: the spirits (19) of truth and injustice. Those born of truth spring from a mountain of light, but those born of injustice spring from a source of darkness. (20) All the children of righteousness are ruled by the Prince of Light and walk in the ways of light, but (21) all the children of injustice are ruled by the Angel of Darkness and walk in the ways of darkness. (1QS 3.15–21)
>
> But in the mysteries of his understanding, and in his glorious wisdom, God has ordained an end for injustice, and at the time (19) of the visitation he will destroy it forever. Then truth, which has wallowed in the ways of wickedness during the dominion of injustice until (20) the appointed time of judgment, shall arise in the world forever. (1QS 4.18–20)

Similar sentiments are expressed elsewhere in the Qumran corpus, most notably in the *Damascus Document* (e.g., 2.3–10), the *War Scroll* (esp. 1QM 1.1–10), and the *Thanksgiving Hymns* (e.g., 1QH^a 7.25–30, 9.9–22).[32]

Of course, we cannot accurately speak of a simple identity between the theology of Josephus's Essenes and that of the Dead Sea sectarians. As noted, Josephus's discussion of fate is unmistakably colored by the influence of contemporary Greek philosophic concerns (we will return to this issue). Josephus also says nothing about the dualism expressed in 1QS: if his Essenes believed in heavenly powers of darkness, Josephus decided not to tell us this.[33] Yet a remarkable similarity remains: Josephus describes the Essenes as believing in the predetermination of *all* events, apparently to the exclusion of human freedom. The Dead Sea sectarians, it appears, emphasized God's omniscience and his power to such a degree that, as they understood it, all proceeds according to a divine plan, which has been put in place long ago. The wicked play their mysteriously

necessary role, compelled by the powers of darkness, as they were predestined to do by God from the beginning. If this is something other than a
belief in fate, it sure is close.

Free Will among the Sadducees and Ben Sira

The situation is more complicated with regard to Josephus's fate-deniers,
the Sadducees, for no verifiably Sadducean literature has been preserved.
Nevertheless, the Sadducean position on free will finds a strong precedent
in the Wisdom of Ben Sira, a work commonly believed to have been composed in Jerusalem, early in the second century BCE. The book builds on
the wisdom tradition of ancient Israel, but represents a remarkable synthesis of previous biblical traditions and themes. What is important here
can be found in the following passage:

(11)   Say not, "It was God's doing that I fell away";
       for what he hates, he does not do.
(12)   Say not, "It was he who led me astray";
       for he has no need of the sinful.
(13)   Abominable wickedness the Lord hates;
       he does not let it befall those who fear him.
(14)   It was he from the first, when he created humankind,
       who made them subject to their own inclination.[34]
(15)   If you choose, you can keep his commandment
       fidelity is the doing of his will.
(16)   There are poured out before you fire and water;
       to whichever you choose you can stretch forth your hands.
(17)   Before each person are life and death;
       whichever one chooses will be given him.
(18)   For great is the wisdom of the Lord;
       he is mighty in power and sees everything;
(19)   The eyes of God see his handiwork
       and he knows every person's action.
(20)   He has not commanded anyone to be wicked
       nor will he be lenient with liars. (15.11–20)[35]

What we find in this passage is the clear combination of three related,
but separable, ideas: the freedom of choice (esp. vv. 14–17), the denial
that anyone could be destined to do evil (vv. 11–12, 20) and God's absolute

opposition to evil (vv. 13, 20). The combination of ideas is stunningly similar to Josephus's assertion that the Sadducees "do away with fate altogether, and remove God beyond not merely the commission, but the very sight of evil. They maintain that man has the free choice of good and evil" (*War* 2.164–65).

Sirach 15.11–20 is important here for a number of reasons. First, the passage confirms that there were Jews in the second century BCE who articulated a theology that is remarkably in line with what Josephus attributes to the Sadducees at a later period. This in turn lends some additional credence (albeit indirect) to the effort of identifying the beliefs of Josephus's Essenes with other known literature from ancient Judaism, such as the Qumran scrolls. The second important aspect of the passage is its polemical tone ("Do not say ..."). Ben Sira not only confirms that some Jews denied fate in their assertion of free choice but at the same time confirms that these issues were up for debate. Digging just a bit deeper, we find that there are markedly close similarities between Josephus's Essenes and the positions of Ben Sira's opponents: both believed that sinners were destined to sin. The fourth significance of this text is what it reveals about the nature of Ben Sira's dispute with predeterminism: by denying human beings the freedom of choice—and the moral responsibility that comes along with it—Ben Sira believes his opponents implicate God in the commission of evil. Ben Sira and Josephus's Sadducees, however, separate God from evil.[36] By doing so—and by asserting that evil comes about as a result of human choice—God's punishment of the wicked is understood to be both deserved and just. This brings us, at last, to a fifth point: for Ben Sira, the assertion of human freedom is inextricably tied to God's earthly justice. Indeed, it is no accident that the very next chapter of Sirach (16.1–23) contains an elaborate discussion of the punishment of the wicked, along with an assertion of divine justice. Josephus says just as much about the Sadducees: while they deny rewards and punishments after death (*Ant.* 18.16; *War* 2.165), they assert nevertheless (*Ant.* 13.173) that "we ourselves are responsible for our well-being, while we suffer misfortune through our own thoughtlessness" (ἀβουλίαν; see Prov. [LXX] 14.17; Bar. 3.28). All of these striking parallels boil down to two very important general observations. First, everything Josephus says about the Sadducean approach to free will finds an analogue in Ben Sira. Second, Josephus's brief summary of the Sadducean rejection of fate captures the essence of a complicated theological problem that similarly vexed Ben Sira: denying people freedom of choice implicates God in the commission of evil, in turn raising questions about human responsibility and divine justice.

Compatibilism among the Pharisees and the Rabbis

Steve Mason has frequently asserted that Josephus's descriptions of the Pharisaic position on fate display significant differences. Granting that the account in *Antiquities* 13 places the Pharisees squarely in the compromise position, Mason points out that *War* 2.162–63 attributes a strong belief in fate to this group (they "attribute everything to fate and to God"), suggesting that the Pharisees of *War* 2 agree with the Essenes of *Antiquities* 13 and 18.[37] If the issue here were only the belief in fate, the contradiction would be clear; but the problem is that *War* 2 explicitly attributes to the Pharisees a belief in both fate *and* free will—something that cannot be said of the Essenes in any of Josephus's discussions.[38]

Josephus's descriptions of the Pharisaic efforts to balance fate and free will find an analogue, as has long been noted, in assorted statements in rabbinic literature.[39] Perhaps the most frequently cited passage is Mishnah *Avot* 3.16,[40] which is commonly translated, in part, so as to say: "All is foreseen, but freedom of choice is given."[41] So understood, the statement—traditionally and commonly attributed to R. Akiba[42]—embraces the compatibilist paradox and is, therefore, practically philosophic in both form and content.[43] A similar—but not identical—view is attributed to the early Palestinian *amora* R. Hanina bar Hama in a number of passages of the Babylonian Talmud (e.g., *b. Berakhot* 33b), to the effect that "everything is in the hands of heaven, except for the fear of heaven."[44] According to a number of authorities, these statements both characterize the rabbinic position on the whole and exhibit continuity with the Pharisaic position, as described by Josephus.[45]

Josephus's Compatibilism

Josephus revisits the problem of fate and free will one time outside of the schools passages, and it is worth looking at this passage carefully in order to understand better his understanding of the problem's theological implications. After describing Herod's decision to execute his sons Alexander and Aristobulus on charges of sedition, Josephus enquires as to the causes of this domestic tragedy (*Ant.* 16.395–404).[46] He allows three possible avenues of blame. Perhaps the sons themselves are to be held responsible, for their own behavior drove their father to this extreme (16.395; see also 16.66–77). Or perhaps Herod himself is at fault, for his desire to rule knew no bounds—even to the extent of killing family members who stood in his way (16.396).[47] The third possibility Josephus presents is fortune (τύχη), whose power ought not be ignored: "For which reason we are persuaded that human actions are dedicated by her beforehand to the necessity [ἀνάγκη] of taking place by all means [πάντως], and we call her fate [εἱμαρμένη] on the ground that there is nothing that is not brought about by her" (16.397). Having introduced the three possible explanations for the king's killing of his sons, Josephus reviews them, beginning with the last: "Now it will, I think, suffice to weigh against this doctrine [fate] with that according to which we attribute some part of the cause to ourselves and hold ourselves not unaccountable for the differences in our behavior, as has been philosophically discussed before our time in the Law" (16.398).[48] Josephus then proceeds to place the blame elsewhere. The sons are to blame for their malice and disrespect (16.399), but Herod is especially blameworthy: By killing his own flesh and blood (16.400) the king committed an act of immeasurable impiety (16.402). And he did so not on a whim, but after careful consideration (16.403), even when he could have protected his own position by merely imprisoning or exiling his sons (16.401). Subsequently, as Josephus makes clear, God's providence manifests itself—not in Herod's cruelty—but in the excruciatingly painful and humiliating illnesses that assaulted the king in his last days (17.168–71, 192; see also 18.127–28).

This passage is important for a number of reasons. First, Josephus makes clear that there are some people—politely referred to here in the first person plural—who believe in fate to such an extent that all things are brought about by her. Indeed, Josephus goes a step further to explain here that his usage of the term "fate" is related to this particular understanding of it—the belief that *all* events are brought about by fate. This, of course, is the Essene doctrine as explained above, and philosophically educated Greco-Roman readers would recognize the position as characteristic of Stoic determinism. But Josephus then proceeds to challenge this doctrine, pointing out that the belief in an all-encompassing "fate" challenges human freedom to choose, and therefore raises questions concerning human moral responsibility. Human responsibility, Josephus continues, is a fundamental tenet of Jewish philosophy, as expressed in the Law.[49] And responsibility is the problem that drives this whole excursus: can fate— God—be implicated when a tyrant cruelly kills his own sons? No, Josephus assures his readers, fate is not to blame for the death of Herod's sons. The blame, in this instance, rests with the human actors involved, all of whom chose to act poorly and sinfully. As Josephus makes clear elsewhere, all suffer accordingly (17.168–71, 192; see also 18.127–28). So in this passage, Josephus clearly rejects the Essene position, inclining instead toward some kind of balance between free will and fate.[50] As readers of *Jewish War* or *Antiquities*, know, however, Josephus cannot be accused here or elsewhere of suggesting that fate has no place in the determination of human affairs. But fate's power does not extend everywhere either. In other words, when properly understood, this passage presents us with Josephus's affirmation of his own compatibilist position: fate may account for some events, but it does not, without qualification, account for all events.

Confounding Compatibilism

It would be premature, however, to say that the case is closed on the question of whether we can identify the theologies of the rabbis, Ben Sira, and Qumran with, respectively, Josephus's Pharisees, Sadducees, and Essenes. Indeed, once we look beyond the surface similarities outlined above, we need to ask whether Josephus's typology adequately accounts for the levels of nuance we find within the various ancient Jewish sources.

Nuancing Akiba's Position

As noted, there is some dispute concerning the sense of the statement ostensibly attributed to R. Akiba in *m. Avot* 3.16. Despite the frequency with which the Hebrew term *tzafuy* (צפוי) is translated as "foreseen," there are very good reasons to believe that what is meant here is simply that everything is "seen."[51] This would accord with the general force of the sayings attributed to Akiba in this chapter, to the effect that humans are free and God is the overseeing judge (3.14–16). In this respect, the view attributed to Akiba finds a close parallel in *Psalms of Solomon* 9.4:

> Our works (are) in the choosing and power of our souls;
> > to do right and wrong in the works of our hands
> > and in your righteousness, you oversee human beings. [52]

Here, too, we find the assertion of choice coupled with the declaration of God as the overseeing judge. While these statements are indeed parallel, scholars who try to connect *Psalms of Solomon* (esp. 9.4) with the Pharisees, based in part on a comparison with *m. Avot* 3.16,[53] are mistaken: neither statement necessarily affirms determinism at all, so neither statement qualifies as compatibilist. The focus on God as an all-seeing judge is even emphasized in Sirach (16.17): "Do not say, 'I am hidden from the Lord, and who from on high has me in mind?'." As we will see later in this chapter, there are a number of rabbinic traditions that can be viewed as articulating compatibilist perspectives; but the statement traditionally attributed to Akiba in *m. Avot* 3.16 is closer to being libertarian.[54]

Decisions among Essenes and at Qumran

Even for those who associate Josephus's Essenes with the Dead Sea sectarians, it is not uncommon to find the recognition that alongside the deterministic passages quoted above, other passages among the sectarian scrolls appear to step away from such a view. E. P. Sanders noted decades ago that the sectarian literature assumes that the righteous will repent (e.g., 1QS 5.14) and that the wicked follow their own stubborn hearts (e.g., 2.25–26). Such passages, for Sanders, indicate "how far the sectarians were from denying [humanity's] freedom of choice."[55] Indeed, the *Community Rule* itself insists that those who join the community must decide to do so of their own volition (e.g., 1QS 5.8, 10, 22). Eugene Merrill, after surveying references to voluntary repentance in the *Thanksgiving Hymns* in particular, similarly concludes that the sectarians "found it possible to hold for the need for [sic] individual voluntary response to Divine promptings within the framework of a rigid predestinarianism."[56] More recently, Eileen Schuller has pointed out that the predeterminism of the sect did not prevent the group from praying for forgiveness from sin (e.g., 1QHª 19.32–35; see also 8.33–36) and for victory in the final battle against evil (1QM 15.4–5).[57] Yet why would the sons of light have to pray for atonement? And wouldn't their victory already be predetermined? Indeed, Schuller concludes her essay with the suggestion that the Dead Sea sectarians may never have become thoroughly deterministic.[58] As noted, Jean Duhaime moves in a similar direction when he suggests that the Dead Sea sectarians' approach to the issue may have been "compatibilist."[59] Without necessarily making use of this particular term, it has indeed become commonplace to assert that the sectarians reserved some place for free will in their otherwise deterministic system.[60] Some have even settled on the fact that the theology of the Dead Sea sectarians must have been to some extent unsystematic and possibly inconsistent,[61] a conclusion that is really not so far from the view that compares the Dead Sea sectarians with Josephus's Pharisees, since such writers often decline to explain how the sectarians' position is any less systematic or consistent than any other compromise position might be.

Predestination in Ben Sira? Sadducees as Atheists?

Problems also emerge when the beliefs of Josephus's Sadducees are compared with the position espoused in the Wisdom of Ben Sira. The first problem stems from the one clear contrast between them: Ben Sira asserts, along with earlier wisdom traditions, that God sees all, and knows when evil is committed (Sir. 16.17–23; compare Prov. 15.3; Job 34.21–22). Josephus, by contrast, implies that God is removed in some fashion from even seeing evil (War 2.164). Indeed, it is precisely with regard to this curious statement by Josephus that some have asserted that Sadducaism must have amounted to atheism in practice, if not quite in theory: their God was without concern for human morality.[62] So the Sadducees would then indeed be comparable to the despised Epicureans, who deny not only fate but also God's providential care for humanity (see Ant. 10.277–80, discussed below).

Josephus's description as it stands surely poses some challenges: if God were removed from the sight of evil, would he not also be removed from the sight of any good? Would that not then mean (against Ant. 13.173) that there would be no form of even earthly justice? So how to explain this contradiction? Three possibilities present themselves: one is that Josephus (or some source, if he used one) is exaggerating the matter, for polemical or simply rhetorical purposes.[63] Another possibility is that Josephus's comments were influenced by or developed from the biblical idea of God hiding his face from his people, in the event that they choose not to follow God's ways (e.g., Deut. 31.17–18, 32.20; compare Isa. 29.2).[64] Although I find the latter idea tantalizing, I have not been able to find any clear textual linkage between Josephus's description of the Sadducees' beliefs and the biblical notion of God hiding his face. This brings us back to the first possibility that Josephus is exaggerating the Sadducean view in this case.[65] To be sure, there is also a third possibility: that Josephus's Sadducees cannot be identified with the views of Ben Sira.

The second problem for the comparison between Ben Sira and the Sadducees' beliefs comes when we consider the relationship between Sirach 15 (quoted above) and Sirach 33.7–15:

(7) Why is one day more important than another,when the same sun lights up every day of the year?

(8) By the Lord's knowledge they are kept distinct; among them he designates seasons and feasts.

(9) Some he exalts and sanctifies, and others he lists as ordinary days.

(10) So, too, all people are of clay, for from earth humankind was formed;

(11) Yet in the fullness of his understanding the Lord makes people unlike: in different paths he has them walk.

(12) Some he blesses and makes great, some he sanctifies and draws to himself. Others he curses and brings low, and expels them from their place.

(13) Like clay in the hand of a potter, to be molded according to his pleasure, So are people in the hands of their Maker, to be requited according as he judges them.

(14) As evil contrasts with good, and death with life, so are sinners in contrast with the just;

(15) See now all the works of the Most High: they come in pairs, the one the opposite of the other.

At first reading, the passage has a deterministic sound to it (see also 42.24). According to some interpreters, this passage can even be compared to the "Treatise of the Two Spirits" in the *Community Rule*.[66] The appearance, therefore, of an ostensibly deterministic passage such as this within the same work as another emphasizing free choice (15.11–20) leads some interpreters to see Ben Sira as a precursor not of the Sadducean position, but of the Pharisaic or rabbinic one.[67]

Now we have come to the crux of the problem. If we follow one line of thought, then the juxtaposition of the material from Sirach chapters 15 and 33 leads to the conclusion that Ben Sira was a compatibilist, just like Josephus's Pharisees and the even later rabbis. If we follow another line of thought, then we can with some justification compare the theology of the Dead Sea sect with Josephus's Pharisees, too. Did all (or most) of these texts express virtually the same theology?[68] Were all ancient Jews compatibilists?[69] This indeed seems to be the direction in which a number of scholars are moving. But this solution to the seeming contradictions within and among the sources only leads to further problems: if the *Community Rule* is not deterministic, then what might a deterministic ancient Jewish document look like? If the theology of both Sirach and 1QS are to be compared with the compatibilism of the Pharisees and later rabbinic Judaism, then are we not left with an undifferentiated hodgepodge of ancient Jewish compatibilisms? If all ancient Jews were compatibilists of one sort or another, with whom was Ben Sira arguing? And what was Josephus talking about when he stated repeatedly that Jews argued about such matters? If there were disagreements of some sort, does it not behoove us to try to classify them in some manner? I believe we ought not give up on classification. To my mind, the remarkable correlations between Sirach 15 and Josephus's description of the Sadducees suggest, at the very least, that Josephus was onto something.

Confining Compatibilism

So how to make sense of this material? Since we cannot better understand the compatibilist position without understanding the views on either side of it, we will defer for now our consideration of the compromise positions. So the first challenge is to see whether we can identify among ancient Jewish sources distinct approaches taken at either extreme. I think we can.

Clarifying Theological Libertarianism

Let us turn first to the libertarian side, and consider once again the meaning and purpose of Sirach 33. As noted, that chapter—with its discussion of sacred and profane days, as compared to holy and sinful people—has been understood by some interpreters as an assertion of predeterminism or even double predestination.[70] This would then mean that Ben Sira's theology was either compatibilist or contradictory, as Sirach 15 (also quoted above) is rather clear in its assertion of free will.

The resolution of this difficulty can be found when we recognize the difference between predestination and divine election.[71] As we have indicated, predestination is understood here as the belief that all has been determined ahead of time, including especially who will be sinful and who will be righteous. Divine election, by contrast, refers to the idea that a certain group or nation has been singled out from among others for both revelation and responsibility. For Jews, of course, divine election refers to the belief that the covenants established with Abraham and Moses are to be passed down from generation to generation, with the accidents (or providence) of birth deciding who is born into the covenant and who is not. Divine election, however, is not tantamount to predestination; this distinction is at the root of the confusions surrounding Sirach 33.

A careful rereading of Sirach 33 demonstrates that determinism is far from the sage's mind here. The juxtaposition of holy and profane days (vv. 7–9) with holy and cursed people (vv. 10–12) is not meant to suggest that God has determined in advance the actions of individual sinners. The juxtaposition, rather, serves to explain the nature of divine election: just as the Sabbath is holy among days, so the Jewish people are holy among peoples.[72] There is of course a deterministic element to the idea of divine election; people cannot choose to be born as Jews or Gentiles (though through conversion or apostasy, people can presumably change their inherited status). But whatever element of determinism there is in such a notion, this passage hardly articulates ideas that *any* ancient Jews with some remaining fidelity to the covenants of Abraham and Moses would have found surprising or objectionable. Surely, practically all committed Jews—Sadducees and other fate-deniers included—believed that God had chosen Abraham and established a covenant that continued to separate the Jewish people from the other nations. Therefore, nothing we find in Sirach 33 prevents reaching the conclusion that the sage was a firm believer in free will, just as Sirach 15 tells us. If Sirach 33 is predeterministic, then all ancient Jews become predeterminists. Indeed, this description may not be inherently incorrect, as it depends, after all, on how we define the terms. But if we define predeterminism in such a way that it becomes essentially synonymous with divine election, we gain nothing, and we lose the ability to draw a contrast between the book of Genesis (with its belief in divine election) and the *Community Rule* (with its belief in predestination). In order to have analytic value, our definitions must be precise enough to allow for the contrast between divine election (which practically all Jews believed) and predeterminism (which was likely the doctrine of the Dead Sea sect and Josephus's Essenes, but not of Ben Sira).

Still, we have learned something by recognizing that an element of predestination can be found in the notion of divine election. Indeed, this is not the only ancient Jewish idea that contains within itself a small measure of determinism. The notion of prophecy, for instance, assumes an element of divine foreknowledge, at least as far as the predicted events are concerned:

> (3)   The former things I declared long ago
>   they went out from my mouth and I made them known
>   then suddenly I did them and they came to pass.
> (4)   Because I know that you are obstinate
>   and your neck is an iron sinew and your forehead brass,
> (5)   I declared them to you from long ago,
>   before they came to pass I announced them to you. (Isa. 48.3–5)

Indeed, even the most bare-bones Jewish eschatology—the simplest assertion that at the end of days the righteous will be rewarded and the wicked will be vanquished (e.g., Amos 9.9–15)—also assumes a modest degree of predeterminism. But other examples of biblical prophecy foretell the future more precisely, such as the naming of Josiah by the unnamed prophet in 1 Kings 13, and the naming of Cyrus in Isaiah 45 by Isaiah of Jerusalem (for uncritical believers who attribute the entire book to the historical prophet). It should come as no surprise, then, that more recent defenders of biblical determinism have sought to find proof for their doctrine in these and other examples.[73] As we will see, these modern theologians have a partial precedent in Josephus, who pointed to prophetic predictions in defense of his own belief in divine providence (*Ant.* 10.277–80, discussed below). If true prophets can accurately predict the future, then God must indeed have established in advance precisely what will happen.[74]

Regardless of the force this argument holds for believers in predeterminism, it must be emphasized for our purposes that prophecy—like divine election—cannot be considered to be evidence for a general ancient Jewish determinism. Prophecy can be an argument for determinism; it is not evidence of it. We have seen that Ben Sira asserts freedom of choice and denies determinism. Yet he believes not only in divine election but also in the truth of the biblical prophets (Sir. 48.23–25, 49.6, 10). Although we cannot be certain, it is likely that the commonly accepted belief in the conditionality of prophecy is what allows for some balance between human freedom and prophecy's truth (see, e.g., *War* 6.310–11; *Ant.* 8.418, and *b. Yevamot* 49b–50a, all discussed below). Without trying to push the comparison between Ben Sira and the Sadducees too far, it is probably reasonable to suppose that the Sadducees—like practically all ancient Jews, to be sure—believed in prophecy as well as divine election, even as they denied that the moral decisions of individual human beings are determined in advance.

We should go even one step further, to entertain the possibility that Josephus's Sadducees believed in divine providence. To be sure, we are told that the Sadducees reject fate—in the sense that particular human affairs are predestined and must, of necessity, take place irrespective of human decisions. But this in fact leaves room for the Sadducees to believe in *providence*—in the sense that (just as the libertarian Ben Sira would have it) God watches over humanity, rewards the righteous, and punishes the wicked in this world, in line with the decisions each person makes (Sir. 16.1–23; compare *War* 2.165). And note that Josephus never states that the Sadducees deny providence (πρόνοια), though he is aware that the Epicureans would (*Ant.* 10.277–78, discussed below). Josephus also never explicitly states that the Sadducees are like the Epicureans in this particular respect, or in any general sense either. To be sure, the Sadducees, like the Epicureans, deny the afterlife (as we will discuss in the next chapter). And Josephus does indeed say unsavory things about the Sadducees, as we have discussed in the introduction. Moreover, Josephus explicitly identifies the Pharisees with the Stoics (*Life* 12) and the Essenes with the Pythagoreans (*Ant.* 15.371).[75] So isn't it obvious then that the Sadducees are to be compared with the Epicureans?[76]

Josephus, we must admit, left this blank empty, and I for one am not at all certain that we should fill it in.[77] After all, why would Josephus leave this blank empty to begin with? What would prevent Josephus, in Rome, two decades or more after 70 CE, from delivering a damning critique of Sadducean theology if he so intended? But if we do fill in the blank by equating Sadducees with Epicureans, we then trap Josephus in an outright contradiction. In *Against Apion*, in his effort to display Jewish harmony in Judaism's defense, he claims:

> Among us alone will be heard no contradictory statements about God, such as are common among other nations, not only on the lips of ordinary individuals under the impulse of some passing mood, but even boldly propounded by philosophers; some putting

forward crushing arguments against the very existence of God; others depriving him of his providential care [πρόνοια] for humankind. (181) Among us alone will be seen no difference in the conduct of our lives. With us all act alike, all profess the same doctrine about God, one which is in harmony with our Law and affirms that all things are under his eye. (*Apion* 2.180–81)

This is a complicated passage, and surely Josephus exaggerates when he suggests that ancient Jews did not argue about matters of practice or belief. Moreover, I suspect that here—and, indeed, throughout the second half of the second book of *Against Apion*—Josephus is trying to foster or even forge the consensus he boasts about. But is he here suggesting that the Sadducees denied providence and were therefore Jewish heretics of some sort?[78] Since he already claimed that the group exhibited rude behavior, why not spell out their problematic thoughts? In my view, this passage neither contradicts Josephus's earlier testimonies about Jewish scholastic disputes nor condemns Sadducees as heretics who deny providence.[79] We must focus carefully on what is and is not said in this passage. Josephus nowhere denies, for instance, that Jews argued about the afterlife. Nor does he suggest that all Jews agreed about fate or free will—neither issue is even mentioned. Josephus, rather, claims simply that all Jews agree on the existence of a providential God.[80] I would think that any assessment of the Pharisees, Sadducees, and Essenes would have difficulty disagreeing with Josephus on this point, unless one really thinks that the Sadducees were atheists. What is more, the sentiment expressed in this passage is perfectly in line with Josephus's own paraphrase of the Hebrew Bible (let alone Torah), which contains many, many references to providence, but not a single reference to fate (as we will see toward the end of this chapter).

The ancient Jewish debate about determinism—between Sadducees and Essenes, and between Ben Sira and his opponents—concerned questions apart from divine election and prophesied events. And the debate did not concern divine providence in a general sense either. The evidence from Josephus and Ben Sira suggests, rather, that the ancient Jewish theological debate was focused on the narrower question of whether one's individual actions are freely chosen or foreordained, limited by a fixed divine plan. The Jewish libertarians—Sadducees and Ben Sira among them—denied fate, inclining toward free will, lest God be implicated in evil.

Clarifying Theological Predeterminism

When we turn to look again at the sectarian literature from Qumran, we find essentially the inverse of what we found regarding Ben Sira. Scattered references to human decisions can be found in the corpus, but whatever intimations of free will are granted in these texts do not compromise the overall commitment given to predestination. Let us begin with the assertion (e.g., 1QS 5.1) that those who wish to join the community must do so of their own volition. This passage has figured prominently in discussions qualifying the sectarians' determinism.[81] But the issue here is not free will in the theological sense (that human beings are free from divine control). Rather, the issue here seems to be the assertion that joining the community must be voluntary in the sense of being otherwise uncoerced. Regardless of one's view on determinism, there is a difference between intended and unintended behavior, be it accidental or coerced.[82] The difference between murder and manslaughter figures significantly already in the Pentateuch (Num. 35.6–34). The difference between intended and unintended transgression also figures in the rules by which the Qumran community ostensibly governed itself (e.g., 1QS 6.24–7.25). So it is not surprising, and is of little consequence, that the sectarians differentiated between self-chosen and coerced righteous behavior as well. For the Qumran sectarians, one's predestined salvation manifests itself in one's unforced willingness to join the community; no one person can rightly impel another to associate with the elect. That human beings make decisions is a fact. The believer in theistic determinism[83]—if subsequent Christian manifestations are any guide at all—does not deny the reality of human decisions; the predeterminist simply believes that the results of these processes are foreknown and foreordained from above: God knows and establishes what one will choose to do.[84] Some predeterminists actually go further, and allow that human decisions are *freely* made, even though they are nonetheless foreknown and foreordained, for God can know even what one will *freely* choose to do.[85] Therefore, the phenomenon of conversion—to say nothing of other, less dramatic human decisions—poses no threat to a deterministic theology. Strict Calvinists accepted converts in John Calvin's day, just as some Amish groups do in our own. And of course, it is essential to bear in mind that Josephus's Essenes also accepted converts, but only after ensuring their sincerity (*War* 2.137–42). As for other human decisions, Josephus's Essenes distinguish between the weightier decisions that were made by the elders of the group and the more mundane decisions that were left to the discretion of individual members (2.134); but in the end, all was governed by fate.

Repentance is another theme that figures prominently for those who suggest that the sectarians stepped away from a full determinism.[86] But once again, repentance is not an obvious threat to determinism, especially theological determinism. Just as Jewish libertarians had to accept prophecy and divine election as part of their heritage, Jewish determinists had to accept the ever-present biblical calls for repentance as part of their system. Once again, a comparison with Christian determinism proves helpful. Even John Calvin—the Protestant archdeterminist—asserted that sincere repentance is one of the essential aspects of prayer, as properly performed by the elect (*Institutes* 3.20.7). The solution to the problem is simple: if human actions are predetermined, what prevents God from predetermining sincere human repentance? Wouldn't the determinist believe that God controls the mind, too?[87] Strikingly, there is some indication that the Dead Sea sectarians conceived of matters in precisely these terms with regard to this issue. Among the petitionary prayers preserved in the generally predeterministic *Thanksgiving Hymns* is the following assertion: "You set in the mouth of your servant prayers of thanksgiving" (19.36–37; 17.10–11).[88] It would appear that the sectarians—or at least the speaker of these hymns—believed that even seemingly spontaneous words of praise are governed by the all-powerful God who created and controls the capacity for human speech (see 1QH^a 9.25–33).

What we have observed here is really not so surprising. The ancient Jewish disputes regarding fate and free will were limited at their extremes by certain theological tenets that were shared by most Jews: God, prophecy, divine election, repentance, and the legal/moral difference between coerced and willful human behavior. If we allow these issues to cloud the debate, there simply will not be any debate left to clarify. But in this section, as well as earlier in this chapter, we found sufficient cause to identify, so far, two distinct positions within these ancient Jewish disputes. On the one side, we have deterministic Dead Sea sectarians and their compatriots, Josephus's Essenes. On the other side, we have the relatively libertarian Ben Sira and Josephus's Sadducees. It is true, as we have seen, that Ben Sira certainly (and the Sadducees, too, very likely) believed in divine election as well as the predictions of biblical prophecy. It is also true, as we have seen, that the Dead Sea sectarians (and presumably the Essenes as well) differentiated between coerced and voluntary human behavior, and performed acts of penitence in their own religious lives. In all this, these groups remain faithful to the general Judaism of which they were part. But the differences between the groups persist, and for this reason we do well not to elide these differences by viewing them all as "compatibilist," as if they all hovered between some otherwise unattested views that were more extreme.

And what, then, of the middle position? How are Josephus's Pharisees and the later rabbis to be differentiated from these other groups? A simple answer presents itself, one based on the notable similarity between Josephus's testimony and the few rabbinic statements quoted thus far: for the sake of describing ancient Jewish theological debates, we do well to confine "compatibilism" to those ancient Jews who *consciously* and *explicitly* advocated a *compromise* between the seemingly contradictory positions at either side. This is precisely how Josephus describes the Pharisaic position, and it appears to be equally true of the rabbinic traditions that assert, for example, in the words attributed to R. Hanina bar Hama: "all is in the hands of heaven except the fear of heaven" (*b. Berakhot* 33b).

Categorizing Compatibilisms

It is now time to take a closer look at the middle-of-the-road position Josephus attributes to the Pharisees, along with the various rabbinic parallels to this perspective. While there are many discussions of the Pharisaic and rabbinic approaches,[89] there are few that recognize one important fact: in his discussions of the Pharisees, Josephus attributes to them not just one type of compromise between fate and free will, but two.[90] And as we will see, both of the compromise positions attributed to the Pharisees by Josephus find parallels in rabbinic literature. The purpose of this section, however, is not to argue that the parallels between Josephus's Pharisees and the rabbinic sources serve to demonstrate that rabbinic traditions can be a generally reliable guide to Pharisaic thought and practice independent of external confirmation from verifiably second temple period sources. Nor is it our interest here to provide a full account of rabbinic approaches to the theme under discussion. The purpose is, simply, to clarify which particular rabbinic traditions are (or are not) close analogues to Josephus's Pharisees. To the degree to which we do find reasonable parallels between rabbinic sources and Josephus's Pharisees—considering especially the parallels we have already seen between Josephus's typology and other ancient Jewish literature—it may in turn be reasonable to conclude that Josephus could be articulating views that were current in the second temple period.[91]

Jewish Compatibilism, Type 1 (Fusion)

In Josephus's earliest treatment of the schools, he says that the Pharisees "attribute everything to fate and to God; they hold that to act rightly or otherwise rests, indeed, for the most part with men, but that in each action fate cooperates" (*War* 2.163).[92] As noted, one of the more frequently suggested parallels is the statement traditionally attributed to R. Akiba (*m. Avot* 3.16): "all is foreseen, yet free will is granted." I also noted, however, that the statement is problematic in too many respects to be an instructive parallel: as Urbach argues, the passage may well serve to assert, simply, that all is *seen*. And even if the passage does assert a balance between fate and free will, it does so in a most general manner. Josephus, however, does more than attribute a general balance to the Pharisees. He goes further, making three important specifications: First, (1) the framework for the compromise is a strong determinism: everything (πάντα) is determined by fate. For that reason, (2) human free will does not independently rule over anything; rather there are, at most, a great many (τὸ πλεῖστον) actions over which human beings make decisions, but nevertheless, in each of these (εἰς ἕκαστον) fate assists. In other words, fate plays a determining role in everything; choice plays a partial role in only a portion of events. Significantly, (3) these include decisions to do good or evil (τὸ μὲν πράττειν τὰ δίκαια καὶ μὴ; *War* 2.163). So the ideological dispute with the Sadducees (clarified in *War* 2.164) remains: the Pharisaic fusion of fate and free will does indeed implicate God in the human performance of evil.

Strikingly, each of these points is also articulated in Josephus's parallel treatment of the three schools in *Antiquities* 18.13:[93]

> Though they postulate that everything is brought about by fate, still they do not deprive the human will of the pursuit of what is in humanity's power, since it was God's good pleasure that there should be a fusion [κρᾶσις][94] and that the will of humanity with its virtue and vice should be admitted into the council-chamber of fate.

Once again, the starting point is an assertion of divine determinism that applies across the board. Human will has a role, but only with regard to what humans can control, and never fully independently of the fate that pervades everything. But human beings nonetheless have the power to choose good or evil, in some manner that is fused with fate.

Significantly, some rabbinic sources can be identified that agree with this general perspective, to the effect that the human choice to do good or evil takes place under the guidance of divine providence. For instance, commenting on Proverbs 3.34, "At scoffers he scoffs, but to the lowly he shows grace," a tradition attributed to the second-generation Palestinian *amora* Resh Laqish states: "If one comes to defile himself, one is given an opening; if one comes to cleanse himself, one is helped" (*b. Shabbat* 104a; *b. Yoma* 38b).[95] Some interpreters have understood this statement to the effect that God actively helps the righteous but only passively permits wickedness.[96] But the verbs in these passages are parallel in form and meaning (after all, opening a door is a helpful action) and thus ought to be understood as equally active. Even more significant is the general thrust of similar rabbinic statements. Consider the slightly more expanded tradition attributed (in the traditional printed edition) to Rav Huna or R. Eleazar (*b. Makkot* 10b):[97] "From the Torah, Prophets and Writings [it can be proven] that whichever direction a person chooses to go, that person is further directed along that way." The passage goes on to quote Numbers 22.12 and 20, where God is said to have first forbidden and then commanded Balaam to go along with Balak's messengers. The passage then quotes Isaiah 48.17: "I the Lord am your God, instructing you for your benefit, guiding you in the way you will go." For the Writings we are directed, once again, to Proverbs 3.34, quoted above. These traditions, and others like them appearing throughout rabbinic literature,[98] are the closest and most compelling parallels to Josephus's descriptions of the Pharisees in *War* 2 and *Antiquities* 18.[99] In all these traditions, we find a fusion between determinism and free will that in important respects gives pride of place to God's controlling influence over human beings, even at the price of recognizing God's active involvement in the human performance of evil deeds.

Jewish Compatibilism, Type 2 (Partial Determinism)

As noted, it is rarely observed—but true nonetheless—that Josephus's more focused discussion of the three schools' distinct views regarding fate and free will (*Ant.* 13.171–73) presents the Pharisaic position in a way that suggests an entirely different mode of balancing fate and free will (13.172): "As for the Pharisees, they say that certain events but not all [τινὰ καὶ οὐ πάντα] are the work of fate; as to other events, it depends upon ourselves whether they shall take place or not."[100]

In this passage, Josephus states in no uncertain terms that the Pharisees' compromise position is one that limits determinism to certain events—some but not all. For the rest, human beings are allowed to make free and presumably unfettered decisions. Significantly, Josephus here states explicitly that human decisions determine whether or not these nonfated events come about. As the continuation of the passage clarifies, it is the Essenes who see all things as determined by fate, while the Sadducees do away with fate altogether. So the Pharisees do not in fact see all things as determined. Only some events are determined, while those that depend on human decisions are not.

A number of rabbinic passages provide a nearly exact analogue to the view Josephus attributes to the Pharisees in this passage. The famous dictum already cited—"all is in the hands of heaven, except for the fear of heaven" (attributed to R. Hanina bar Hama in *b. Berakhot* 33b)[101]—is one good example. In this statement, just as in *Antiquities* 13, determinism is explicitly limited by whatever events depend on human decisions. The same is true of the fuller, but less frequently quoted, tradition attributed to the third-generation Palestinian *amora* R. Hanina bar Papa:

> The name of the angel who is in charge of conception is "Night," and he takes up a drop and places it in the presence of the Holy One, blessed be He, saying, "Sovereign of the universe, what shall be the fate of this drop? Shall it produce a strong man or a weak man, a wise man or a fool, a rich man or a poor man?" Whereas "wicked man" or "righteous one" he does not mention, in agreement with the view of R. Hanina [bar Hama]. For R. Hanina stated: Everything is in the hands of heaven except the fear of heaven, as it is said (Deut. 10.12): "And now, Israel, what does the Lord your God require of you, but to fear the Lord your God." (*b. Niddah* 16b)[102]

Once again, the significant feature of this tradition is the way determinism is explicitly confined by the allowance given to free will. Some things—even many things—are determined, but the ever-significant variable of human moral decision operates independently of what is determined. The results of these decisions are neither fated nor in the hands of heaven. This is in agreement with *Antiquities* 13.172, but in disagreement with the various rabbinic and Josephan passages quoted in the previous section.[103]

Three further rabbinic traditions address distinct themes related to partial determinism, and will help further illustrate the nature of this particular perspective as articulated in rabbinic literature. The first tradition (attributed to the amoraic sage Resh Laqish) addresses the issue of seemingly accidental deaths:

> R. Simeon b. Laqish opened his discourse with these [two] texts: "And if a man lie not in wait, *but God cause it to come to hand*; then I will appoint for you a place whither he may flee" (Exod. 21.13) and "As it says in the proverb of the ancients: Out of the wicked comes forth wickedness; but my hand shall not be upon you" (1 Sam. 24.13–14). Of whom does the [former] text speak? Of two persons who had slain, one in error and another with intent, there being witnesses in neither case. The Holy One, blessed be He, appoints them both [to meet] at the same inn; he who had slain with intent sits under the step-ladder and he who had slain in error comes down the step-ladder, falls and kills him. Thus, he who had slain with intent is [duly] slain, while he who had slain in error [duly] goes into banishment. (*b. Makkot* 10b)[104]

A number of features of this tradition (and its rabbinic parallels)[105] are significant. Related to matters discussed in the previous section, we find, here, too, confirmation that many rabbinic traditions were willing to countenance God's active guidance of human sinful behavior. But this tradition disagrees with those discussed in the previous section regarding the matter at the heart of our concern. Here, too, we find "type 2" Jewish compatibilism. The first incidents of murder and manslaughter referred to in this text are, we must assume, straightforward instances of human transgression, one willful and the other accidental. It is only the second round of carnage—the unintended killing of the murderer by the manslaughterer—that is orchestrated by God, and this is what is intimated by the problematic biblical phrase (Exod. 21.13) to the effect that God caused this to happen. So once again, we find here a partial determinism: some events are brought about by God, others are purely the result of human decision. It remains only to point out that the general thrust of this particular tradition can be reliably pushed back to the second temple period, independent of Josephus. The tradition quoted above finds an almost exact parallel in the writings of Philo of Alexandria (*Spec. Laws* 3.120–23). Philo, too, based on Exodus 21.13, discusses an incident where a divinely assisted instance of manslaughter serves as providential punishment for previous (and presumably freely chosen) human behaviors.[106]

A further rabbinic tradition, this one focused on the question of human life spans, explicitly espouses a "type 2" compatibilism:

> Concerning "the number of your days I will fulfill" (את מספר ימיך
> אמלא; Exod. 23.26), the tannaim are in disagreement. For it was
> taught: "The number of your days I will fulfill," refers to the years of
> the generations [i.e., the span of life allotted to every human being
> at birth]. If one is worthy one is allowed to complete the full period;
> if unworthy, the number is reduced; so R. Akiba. But the Sages
> said: if one is worthy years are added to one's life; if unworthy, the
> years of life are reduced. They said to R. Akiba: Behold, Scripture
> says [with regard to King Hezekiah], "And I will *add* unto your days
> fifteen years!" (2 Kings 20.6). He replied: The addition was made
> from his own [original allotment]. You may know [that this is so]
> since the prophet stood up and prophesied (1 Kings 13.2): "Behold,
> a son shall be born to the house of David, Josiah by name," while
> Manasseh [Hezekiah's son, Josiah's grandfather] had not yet been
> born![107] And the Rabbis? [How would they respond?]—Is it written
> "from Hezekiah"? It is surely written, "To the house of David" (1
> Kings 13.2); he [Josiah] might be born either from Hezekiah or from
> any other person [of the House of David, but not necessarily from
> Hezekiah]. (b. Yevamot 49b–50a)[108]

The dispute between R. Akiba and the rest of the sages concerns a rather minor matter. It is generally agreed here—perfectly in line with "type 2" compatibilism—that a person's life span is generally predetermined but still changeable as a reward or punishment. What is disagreed is the relatively minor point of whether, as R. Akiba would have it, sinfulness leads to the reduction of years, or, as the sages would have it, virtue leads to the lengthening of years. What is also significant is the particular passage at the focus of the disagreement: the aforementioned nameless prophet's prediction of Josiah's rule in 1 Kings 13. While even Akiba here espouses "type 2" compatibilism in his allowance for the adjusting of predetermined life spans, the rabbis' position goes further by understanding one of the most dramatic biblical illustrations of divine foreknowledge in light of a partial determinism. Yes, the unnamed prophet predicted Josiah's rule by name; but that does not mean that it was predetermined that Josiah would be born as a grandson of Manasseh! Therefore, even the most specific of biblical prophecies becomes conditional or contingent, because the timing and mechanism of its fulfillment are not predetermined. So here, too, we find attributed to various rabbinic sages the view that only some events are predetermined; other events are brought about by human beings as a result of their free and unfettered decisions.

A third set of rabbinic traditions espouse a partial determinism in their discussions of human relationships:

> Rabbah b. Bar Hanah said in the name of R. Yohanan: It is as difficult to pair them [married couples] as was the division of the Red Sea; as it is said, "God sets the solitary in families; He brings out the prisoners into prosperity" (Ps. 68.7). But it is not so; for Rab Judah has said in the name of Rab: Forty days before the creation of a child, a heavenly voice issues forth and proclaims, "the daughter of so-and-so is for so-and-so; the house of so-and-so is for so-and-so; the field of so-and-so is for so-and-so!"—There is no contradiction, the latter dictum referring to a first marriage and the former to a second marriage. (*b. Sotah* 2a)[109]

Once again, partial determinism is assumed in this tradition: the events discussed come about as a result of divine decisions (whether predetermined at birth or providentially guided in relation to people's natures and choices). Regardless, nothing is said that would suggest that *everything* is predetermined. Once again, it is significant that we can identify a parallel tradition among verifiably second temple period sources. The idea that human relationships—at least the ones that work—are predetermined is also clearly articulated in Tobit 6.18, when the angel Raphael reassures the legitimately frightened Tobias with the words "Do not be afraid, for she was set apart for you before the world was made." It is very difficult to make the case that the book of Tobit otherwise articulates a completely deterministic view: the embedded wisdom speech (Tob. 4.5–19) certainly suggests that Tobias and everyone else has free and unfettered decisions to make. But human relationships—at least the important ones—may well be among those select events, like those predicted by prophets, that are predetermined.[110]

It is important not to overemphasize the significance of the differences pointed out here between the two types of compatibilism. After lamenting the fact that few have noticed the difference between the two positions Josephus attributes to the Pharisees, Mason points out that the difference is not major, since all agree that the Pharisees balance fate and free will in some manner.[111] Nevertheless, because so much scholarship concerning fate and free will in ancient Judaism points out the parallels between Josephus's Pharisees and rabbinic literature in a rather indiscriminate manner, surely something can be gained if scholarship were to begin to do so more precisely. This is especially the case when we also consider the various confusions traced above concerning the degree to which we find some elements of freedom or determinism among, respectively, Essenes or Sadducees. Indeed, even Mason has not quite characterized the two views adequately. Mason entertains the possibility that the account in *War* 2 and *Antiquities* 18 (which we termed "type 1") is essentially Stoic in nature, while the account in *Antiquities* 13 is more in line with the Jewish parallels. But as we have seen, both Josephan accounts have Jewish analogues. And as we will see in the next section, *neither* Josephan account of the Pharisaic view is really equivalent to the compatibilism of the Stoics.

The fact that Josephus fails to register the inconsistency could be understood to strengthen the arguments of those, like David Flusser, who claim that Josephus displays insufficient understanding of the philosophical debates.[112] But scholarship should be wary to jump in this direction, if only for the fact that most scholars have equally failed to perceive the very same inconsistency. Moreover, inconsistency and even contradiction may well be expected when it comes to compatibilism. To be sure, a number of important modern philosophers maintain "incompatibilism"—the philosophic position asserting that compatibilism is nonsense.[113] If they are right—or even only partially right—we can hardly blame Josephus for misunderstanding or misrepresenting the paradoxes of compatibilism.

Yet an additional possible explanation for Josephus's twofold presentation of ancient Jewish compatibilism immediately presents itself: perhaps some Pharisaic thinkers—just like the later rabbis as well—explained the tension between determinism and free will in these two different ways. Tempting as it may be to attribute Josephus's inconsistencies to his sources, his biases, or his misunderstandings, it could just as likely be the case that the tensions in Josephus's account reflect tensions in Pharisaic thought (and therefore possibly his own). Indeed, the fact that the two different compromises between fate and free will are clearly in evidence both in Josephus's description of the Pharisees as well as in the various rabbinic traditions we have discussed is itself a further significant parallel between them, this one, so far as I am aware, hitherto unnoticed.

Jewish and Stoic Compatibilisms

It is frequently noted and generally recognized that Josephus's descriptions of the Jewish schools are colored by the use of Hellenistic—and especially Stoic—philosophical terms.[114] A number of studies go further to note and assess the specific parallels between the Pharisaic and Stoic compatibilisms.[115] But a review of the question is called for, not only in light of the observations and distinctions drawn above but also in light of the fact that important developments have taken place in the study of Stoic determinism, such that we can accurately speak of a relatively new consensus concerning the state of Stoic determinism in the first century CE.[116]

The study of Hellenistic philosophy is plagued by a number of problems, the most pressing of which concerns the fact that many key works are lost or only indirectly known from quotations in other sources. Regarding, however, Josephus's description of the three Jewish schools of thought concerning fate and free will, we are relatively fortunate in that we have a number of works preserved that can reasonably be assumed to be possible influences on and models for Josephus's discussion, including the writings of Cicero and Seneca. But it is Cicero's *On Fate* that is arguably the most important text for our concerns. First of all, we can safely assume that Cicero's work was well known and readily available in Rome in Josephus's day. Second, Cicero discusses Stoic determinism in a clear and sympathetic manner. Third, Cicero explicitly describes the determinism of the great Stoic philosopher Chrysippus as a mediating position between strict determinism and absolute libertarianism:

> I indeed see it like this. There were two opinions among the old philosophers; one held by those who judged that all things came about by fate, in such a way that fate imposed the force of necessity. This was the opinion of Democritus, Heraclitus, Empedocles and Aristotle. The other was the opinion of those who thought that there were voluntary movements of minds not involving fate at all. Chrysippus, like a respected arbitrator, seems to have wanted to strike a balance, but in fact inclines rather to those who want the

movements of the mind to be free from necessity. However, by the expressions he uses he slips into difficulties such that he unwillingly supports the necessity of fate. (*On Fate* 39)[117]

Other possible models for Josephus's typology have been presented from time to time.[118] And since we have only fragments of Hellenistic philosophy at our disposal, it may be foolhardy to try to identify the precise source from among our incomplete catalogue. Still the Cicero passage holds appeal at least as a representative sample of the tripartite fate and free will typology in circulation in Rome in Josephus's day.

Cicero's *On Fate* is also helpful for what it can tell us about Chrysippus's compatibilism. This is not the place for a full discussion,[119] but the following selection should prove instructive for our purposes:

> But he [Chrysippus] goes back to his cylinder and cone; these cannot begin to move unless pushed, but, when this has happened, he thinks that for the rest it is by their own nature that the cylinder rolls and the cone moves in a circle.

> "As therefore," he says, "he who pushes a cylinder gives it the beginning of motion, but does not give it the power of rolling; so a sense-impression when it strikes will, it is true, impress and as it were stamp its appearance on the mind, but assenting will be in our power and, in the same way as was said in the case of the cylinder, it is pushed from outside but for the rest moves by its own force and nature." (*On Fate* 42–43)

The cylinder and cone analogy is particularly helpful in explaining the precise nature of Chrysippus's compatibilism.[120] What the Stoic philosopher argues for here is a way of maintaining some semblance of moral responsibility without moving toward partial determinism or indeterminism. What is illustrated in the analogy is the way one's own nature bears partial responsibility for whatever events one is involved with, even though one is impelled to undertake these actions by outside forces. The push is the external stimulus; the spin or the roll of the cone or the cylinder is then determined by the nature of each object, in combination with the external push.

Stoic compatibilism in its Chrysippean form—as described by Cicero and other ancient writers, and as understood by modern writers, including Susanne Bobzien, Dorothea Frede, and Ricardo Salles—is indeed much less attractive to most modern observers than it first appears, for while it allows some place for "what depends on us" (τὸ ἐφ'ἡμῖν; see Cicero, *On Fate*, 43, and Josephus *Ant.* 13.172, 18.13),[121] it does not allow for the possibility that individuals have power to effect alternate outcomes—no more than a cylinder could spin or a cone roll.[122] Free will is given a very small role in this scheme: individuals exercise their will when they assent to what they are driven to do, even though they remain powerless to do anything else. This is illustrated (and dramatized) in an oft-quoted *Hymn to Zeus*, attributed to the early Stoic sage Cleanthes of Assos, and quoted by Epictetus:

> Lead me Zeus and Destiny, wherever you have ordained for me.
> For I shall follow unflinching.
> But if I become bad and am unwilling, I shall follow none the less.
> (*Enchiridion* 53)[123]

Needless to say, the discussion with regard to Stoic philosophy does not end with Cicero's presentation of Chrysippus's view, and readers can follow the subsequent peregrinations in the works of Susanne Bobzien.[124] But we can stop here, for this is where the discussion was in Josephus's day. The Stoics were known for espousing a form of compatibilism. While their compromise position allowed some space to free will in theory, it was hardly a free will "worth wanting," to borrow Daniel Dennett's phrase.[125] If the Chrysippean compromise does not preserve a free will worth wanting, then it also falls short of a compatibilism worth bothering with. Indeed, for this very reason, Cicero was not far off when he remarked that Chrysippus (*On Fate*, 39, quoted above) "slips into such difficulties that against his will he lends support to the necessity of fate." Chrysippus was criticized by other subsequent ancient writers alike for just that reason: his compatibilism is, in the eyes of many ancient and modern observers, simply a rearticulation of determinism.[126]

We can now see very clearly the differences between Stoic compatibilism as understood in Rome in Josephus's day and what was referred to above as "type 2" Jewish compatibilism. The latter is akin to partial determinism, while the former remains a true determinism: whatever space given to free will is not allowed to detract from the given premise that all things are determined by antecedent causes. This is not to say, however, that Stoic compatibilism can be equated with what was referred to above as "type 1 (fusion)" Jewish compatibilism either.[127] That is because

Chrysippus's compatibilism does not countenance the possibility of alternate outcomes, or indeed allow free will any realm beyond what has already been determined. What we termed Jewish compatibilism "type 1" however, in both Josephan and rabbinic formulations, explicitly allows for alternate outcomes. As the rabbinic sources say, for example (b. Makkot 10b), "whichever direction a person chooses to go, they direct that one in that way." Josephus's Pharisees believe that, with regard to what is decided by persons, it depends on them whether they do right things or not (τὸ μὲν πράττειν τὰ δίκαια καὶ μὴ; War 2.163). Indeed, the two-sidedness of Josephus's Pharisees' free will is apparent in all three descriptions of the group (Ant. 13.172: "whether they take place or not"; Ant. 18.13: "virtue and vice").[128]

A second important difference can also be identified between Chrysippus's compatibilism (and especially the cylinder and cone analogy) and the various rabbinic sources: while Stoic compatibilism focuses on human assent to external stimuli (as true determinism would require), the rabbinic sources I have categorized as "type 1" tend to attribute the first move to the human being, with the assistance or opportunity being shaped in response by God. For example (b. Shabbat 104a): "If one comes to defile himself, he is given an opening; if one comes to cleanse himself, he is helped." So even type 1 compatibilism differs from the Chrysippean sort in a rather significant way.

While Susanne Bobzien does not discuss Josephus in any great detail in her masterful, lengthy treatment of Stoic determinism, she mentions him in one footnote in a rather striking way: "The earliest clearly two-sided concept of that which depends on us in the context of the fate debate that I have found so far is Josephus Ant. 13.172" (italics original).[129] Indeed, an important thrust of Bobzien's work—one that influenced what I have written in the previous paragraphs—is that the classic formulations of Stoic compatibilism do not address the questions that characterize what can be termed the "modern" fate versus free will predicament. The modern problem is the difficulty of squaring determinism with a free will that is truly "two-sided," which means that it allows for alternate outcomes. In Bobzien's reconstruction of the discussion, this change comes in the late second century when Stoic philosophy encounters developments in Platonistic and Christian thought, and figures such as Philopator and Alexander of Aphrodisias respond accordingly.[130] There is an important lesson here for scholars of Josephus and Jewish free will debates: while Josephus's discussion is undoubtedly shaped by Hellenistic terminology, it is in a number of important respects quite distinct from contemporary philosophic discussions of the matter, especially when it comes to the accounts of Pharisaic compatibilism as compared to Stoic views. The Pharisaic allowances for alternate outcomes and initial free human action—to say nothing of partial determinism—are not views that can be seen as characteristic of contemporary or earlier instances of Stoic deterministic thought. And there is an important corollary here that Bobzien did not have the opportunity to consider, but which could perhaps contribute to the discussion of the history of Stoic determinism. Instead of viewing Josephus simply as the exception that proves the rule, should we entertain the possibility that Josephus records the earliest—*Pharisaic*—attempt to accommodate Stoic determinism with a two-sided free will? After all, a two-sided free will is not only a Christian or Platonistic idea. It is, as we have seen throughout this chapter, a thoroughly Jewish idea as well (see especially, once again, Sir. 15.11–20, quoted above).

The Essenes as Compatibilists, for the Last Time?

Notwithstanding all that has been said regarding determinism and free will in the sectarian scrolls, it must be admitted here that it is not necessarily incorrect to refer to the Qumranic position as "compatibilist,"[131] or to compare Josephus's Essenes with Stoic determinism.[132] Indeed, in a strict sense, the Qumranic/Essene position approximates Chrysippus's as described by Cicero, and as understood by contemporary scholars of Stoicism. The small room given to free will in either system may well indeed exclude the possibility of alternate outcomes even as moral responsibility is asserted nonetheless.[133] So the limited free will in these systems remains compatible with an absolute determinism.[134] Moreover, note that the Pharisaic and rabbinic position (especially type 2) is not, strictly speaking, compatibilist at all. By attributing some events to fate and others to free will, this position is really a partial determinism. In most philosophic contexts, compatibilism involves, by definition, not a partial determinism but a complete determinism.[135]

So why then not refer to the sectarians as compatibilists? If we have accepted that Josephus likely was influenced by accounts of Chrysippean compatibilism, should we not apply the term to the group that most closely resembles that approach? I think we should not, and for the following reasons. First, Josephus clearly sees the Pharisaic position as the one advocating compromise. If, however, the term "compatibilism" is applied to the Qumran sect by virtue of their adoption of a position akin to Stoic determinism, then the term cannot be meaningfully applied at the same time to Josephus's Pharisees or to the rabbinic sources surveyed above, which more explicitly advocate compromises. If the sectarians are the compatibilists, what term can we use to describe the Pharisaic position? A second problem emerges when we consider the fact that there is no known ancient Jewish group or text that advocated a stronger determinism than what we find at Qumran. If they were the most deterministic of Jews, what value is there in calling them compatibilists? Why refer to the most deterministic of Jews as compatibilists when other groups were explicitly advocating a compromise position while they were not? Doing so would lead directly toward the problem we reached previously—ancient Judaism as a hodgepodge of compatibilisms.

It is also imperative that we not give pride of place to Chrysippus's position when it comes to the larger question of defining and understanding compatibilism as an analytic term. As noted, his compromise position falls short of allowing for alternate outcomes. We could just as well state—in agreement with other ancient writers noted above—that neither Chrysippus nor the Dead Sea sectarians were true compatibilists in that they did not allow room for freedom to do anything more than assent to the predetermined plan. In this respect, the Pharisaic and rabbinic approaches discussed above come closer to a real compatibilism than the positions of the Essenes, the Qumran sectarians, or even Chrysippus, in that Josephus's Pharisees and the later rabbis struggle to maintain some semblance of determinism alongside a real freedom to choose among opposed alternatives and even bring about different outcomes. Finally, it ought to be remembered that Josephus explicitly compared the Pharisees to the Stoics (*Life* 12). As Steve Mason reminds us, Josephus knew much more about both the Pharisees and the Stoics than we do.[136]

It is wiser, therefore, to follow Josephus's lead and view the Hellenistic philosophical debate as *analogous* to, but not precisely identical with, the theological disputes among ancient Jews. We are then free to use the term "determinism" to apply to the most determinist ancient Jews we can identify: the Essenes and their compatriots, the Qumran sectarians. At the other end of the scale, we can meaningfully speak of the (relative) libertarianism of the Sadducees and Ben Sira. We can then meaningfully apply the term "compatibilism" to those ancient Jews who self-consciously articulated a compromise position, including Josephus's Pharisees and the later rabbis. It is true that the range and contours of the philosophical debate are different from those of the theological one, for the ancient

Jewish religious debate is hedged in at the extremes by various generally accepted ideas, such as prophecy, election, and repentance. It is for this very reason that we speak here of "*Jewish* compatibilism," which can then readily be distinguished from, even as it is also compared to, "Stoic" or "Chrysippean" compatibilism.

If we are to draw comparisons between Jewish theological and Hellenistic philosophical approaches, we can do so in only one of two ways. One would be to make the itemized, isolated comparison between, say, Chrysippus and the Qumran sect. But the more useful approach is to follow Josephus's lead, and draw the structural analogy between the two tripartite debates, so that the Essenes, Pharisees, and Sadducees can indeed be instructively compared to (if not identified with) the determinists, compatibilists, and libertarians among the Hellenistic philosophical schools. Because it represents a compromise position, it may be inevitable for compatibilism to be appreciated (or decried) as a paradox. So perhaps it is appropriate that the usage of the term "compatibilism" in the context of ancient Judaism is also paradoxical: the term is most helpful analytically when it is used in a limited fashion, and with a certain degree of philosophical imprecision.

Josephus's Compatibilism: Providence Always, Fate at Times

Now that we have carefully reviewed Josephus's accounts of the Jewish debate on fate and free will in light of ancient Jewish and Hellenistic parallels, it is time to bolster the argument introduced above that Josephus, too, articulates a compatibilist position, perfectly in line with his claim in *Life* to have adopted the ways of the Pharisees.[137]

Toward the very end of *Antiquities* 10, at roughly the halfway point of his magnum opus, Josephus concludes his discussion of the prophet Daniel, emphasizing this seer's uniqueness: while many prophets accurately foretold the future, Daniel alone was able to predict precisely *when* certain future events would happen (*Ant.* 10.267). This remarkable feat leads Josephus to comment further:

> All these things, as God revealed them to him [Daniel], he left behind in his writings, so that those who read them and observe how they have come to pass must wonder at Daniel's having been so honored by God, and learn from these facts how mistaken are the

Epicureans, who exclude providence [πρόνοια] from human life and refuse to believe that God governs its affairs or that the universe is directed by a blessed and immortal being, to the end that the whole of it may endure, but they say that the world runs by its own movement [αὐτομάτως] without a knowing guide or another's care. If it were leaderless in this fashion, it would be shattered through taking a blind course and so end in destruction, just as we see ships go down when they lose their helmsmen or chariots overturn when they have no drivers. It therefore seems to me, in view of the things foretold by Daniel, that they are very far from holding a true opinion who declare that God takes no thought for human affairs. For if it were the case that the world goes on by some automatism, we should not have seen all these things happen in accordance with his prophecy. (*Ant.* 10.277–80)[138]

Once again, it is important to pay careful attention to what Josephus does and does not say in this passage. Josephus is not claiming here that *all* events are planned in advance by God to the extent that *everything* follows a fixed plan. So the implications of Daniel's prophetic powers do not lead inevitably to the position Josephus elsewhere attributes to the Essenes. Indeed, the passage hinges on the rather exceptional nature of Daniel's precise predictions, and suggests that the fulfillment of these particular prophecies at the proper time does not mean that all events follow some fixed, preordered path. The world is not on "autopilot."[139] The world, rather, is constantly guided, in real time, like a well-piloted ship in an open, stormy sea.[140] Josephus makes similar observations elsewhere in *Antiquities*, especially when he comments on God's ability to ensure the equal fulfillment of two seemingly incompatible prophecies (Elijah and Micaiah regarding Ahab: *Ant.* 8.418–19; Jeremiah and Ezekiel concerning Zedekiah: *Ant.* 10.141–42). Yet a single realized prophecy will also do the trick, and the fulfillment of any given prophecy can be a testimony to divine providence and justice, for good (e.g., providential birth of Moses: *Ant.* 2.210–23; Solomon: *Ant.* 8.109) or ill (e.g., brief rule of Zimri: 8.309–14).[141]

We have already noted that some interpreters have had difficulty correlating Josephus's discussions of the schools regarding "fate" with his own observations regarding "providence."[142] Indeed, a rather large number of interpreters believe that Josephus uses the terms interchangeably, perhaps even indiscriminately.[143] As far as *Antiquities* 10.277–80 (quoted above) is concerned, Josephus's appeal to predictive prophecy as evidence for divine providence is somewhat similar to some modern attempts to provide scriptural proofs for predeterminism or predestination.[144] This would suggest that Josephus's position must be rather Essene-like, equating providence with determinism, and thereby curtailing human freedom.[145] To be sure, there is a strong tradition in Western culture of equating providence and predestination (e.g., Calvin, *Institutes*, 1.16.1–9),[146] just as the Stoics identified providence with fate.[147] But these are typically determinist (or predestinarian) moves, which simply preclude compromise positions like those attributed by Josephus to the Pharisees. Ancient thinkers who believed in both fate and human freedom (such as certain Middle Platonists and Gnostics) did distinguish between fate and providence, and typically subordinated fate to providence.[148] So Josephus, unlike the modern predestinarians who see fulfilled prophecy as a proof that *all* events are part of a fixed, predetermined plan, states in the passage above that the bringing about of the few events that are clearly foretold and therefore destined to occur demonstrates not that *all* things are fated but that the world is providentially guided. This passage is not a criticism of the Sadducees (who, we have suggested, denied fate but not providence).[149] Nor is it an endorsement of the Essene view (they viewed *all* events as predetermined by fate). The passage is, rather, just as it says, a criticism of Epicureans, who deny providence. Understanding Josephus's approach requires that we attend carefully to his use of the related, but not identical terms (fate and providence), noticing along the way whether he does (or does not) use the term "all." When we do so, we see that we can summarize his own belief in this way: Providence always, fate at times.

We have by now quoted and discussed some of the key passages regarding Josephus's belief in divine providence (in addition to *Ant.* 10.277–80, see *Apion* 2.180–81, discussed earlier in this chapter). Beyond these, references to "providence" (πρόνοια) liberally pepper both *Antiquities* and *War*.[150] Without using the word, the concept also dominates the introduction to *Antiquities*:

> Speaking generally, the main lesson to be learned from this history by any who care to peruse it is that people who conform to the will of God, and do not venture to transgress laws that have been excellently laid down, prosper in all things beyond belief, and for their reward are offered, by God, felicity; while, in proportion as they depart from the strict observance of these laws, things (otherwise)

practicable become impracticable, and whatever imaginary good thing they strive to do ends in irretrievable disasters. (15) At the outset, then, I entreat those who will read these volumes to fix their thoughts on God.

(20) ... God, as the universal Father and Lord who beholds all things, grants to such as follow him a life of bliss, but involves in dire calamities those who step outside the path of virtue. (*Ant.* 1.14–15, 20)[151]

Three general themes emerge here: divine guidance, personal responsibility, and divine justice. Of course, these themes appear in various guises throughout *Antiquities*, and the correlation between providence and earthly punishment for the wicked is emphasized at various points (e.g., *Ant.* 8.314, 17.170, 17.354, 18.127, 19.16; *War* 1.82, 1.593, 7.451–53).[152] So far, these beliefs reflect general ancient Jewish ones (see *Apion* 2.180), and the sentiments are not incommensurate with other usages of "providence" in second temple Jewish literature (some of which were cited at the beginning of this chapter). Indeed, when Josephus claims, in *Ant.* 16.398 (quoted earlier in this chapter), that the human responsibility has been discussed "philosophically" in the Law, this is likely what the passage refers to: Josephus's general sense that biblical history proves that God is watching, and will punish the wicked. Indeed, even Sadducees would have believed in this sort of providence and justice. Like theirs, Josephus's belief in providence is matched by his belief in human freedom to choose, underscored by his hopes that his readers will choose to do good (*Ant.* 1.14–15, 20–23, 4.180–83, 8.125–29). But Josephus, for one, is no Sadducee: a dollop of fate will be thrown into this mix, too.

If the earthly enactment of divine justice is one major manifestation of divine providence, the fulfillment of prophecy is the other.[153] As we have seen, Josephus is taken with the power of predictive prophecy, viewing its fulfillment as a clear demonstration of God's power and providence. How different this is from a belief that all events are fated can be better appreciated when we observe that Josephus is also taken by prophecy's nonpredictive function, as a call for repentance. Commenting in the doubly predicted, duly deserved death of Ahab, Josephus notes that "nothing is more beneficial than prophecy and the foreknowledge [πρόγνωσις] that it gives, for in this way God enables us to know what to guard against" (*Ant.* 8.419). Prophecy is said to serve a similar function—as a warning, not simply a prediction—in a number of other instances. Sometimes, the prophetic warnings are heeded, repentance occurs, and judgment is averted (e.g., Jehoahaz's repentance: *Ant.* 9.175–76; Manasseh's repentance: 10.36–46). Other times, the warnings are disregarded and punishment ensues (e.g., Joash and the murder of the prophet Zechariah: *Ant.* 9.167–68).

Josephus believes that the same dynamic played out in his own lifetime. Like the prophets of old before him, Josephus claims he called on the people of Jerusalem to repent of their sins, in order to prevent the coming disaster (*War* 5.415–19).[154] Josephus even claims that other prophetic warnings preceded his own, giving the people of Jerusalem the fair chance to repent and avert the disaster (e.g., *War* 2.650, 6.288–309). These omens and portents were misunderstood or simply ignored by the sinful, unwise populace (6.301–15).[155] Nonetheless, the omens, dreams, and prophetic predictions ought to have been clear enough. Just as God had empowered the Babylonians and then Persians in biblical times (5.389–93; compare *Ant.* 10.89, 106, 112–13, 272–77), it ought now be clear to all that "fortune" (τύχη)—the unmerited gift of political hegemony—had passed to the Romans (*War* 3.354, 4.622, 5.367).[156] Keeping in line with these paradigms and precedents, sinful people refuse to submit, rebelling against the designated power, be it Babylon or Rome. Still, even ignored prophecies teach something: "Reflecting on these things one will find that God has a care for people, and by all kinds of premonitory signs shows his people the way of salvation, while they owe their destruction to folly and calamities of their own choosing" (6.310–11). The conditionality of prophecy means, for Josephus, that not all events are fated to take place. Empires may indeed rise and fall in line with Fortune. But Jewish temples fall as divine punishments—and these come about as a result of people disregarding divine guidance and prophetic warnings, choosing instead to be sinful.

If prophetic events are providential, but not necessarily fated, what events *are* fated for Josephus? The undeniable inevitability of death has greatly influenced Josephus's use of the term "fate" in both *War* and *Antiquities*. In *Antiquities*, "fate" appears only six times; three of these occur in the context of describing ancient Jewish theological disputes (13.172, 173; 18.13), and a fourth occurs when Josephus reflects on his own view of the fate versus free will debate, in light of Herod's shockingly unnatural execution of his sons (16.397). The other two instances both appear in indirect speech, when dying heroes—Mattathias and Agrippa I—reflect on their coming deaths, neither of which occur as executions of divine judgment (Mattathias: 12.297; Agrippa I: 19.347). A more telling passage concerns the story of the death of Ahab, where the doubly fulfilled prophecy brings down Ahab by "necessity" (τὸ χρεών; *Ant.* 8.409, 412, 419). Although the term is frequently translated as "fate,"[157] Attridge argues persuasively for seeing here something quite distinct from a general notion of "fate" (εἱμαρμένη), with "necessity" (τὸ χρεών) referring in general to the inevitability of death,[158] and in this instance to Ahab's deserved and decreed demise.[159] Even so, the use of the term "necessity" and the dynamic of judgment in this passage sheds light on the way Josephus correlates providence, prophecy, and judgment, in such a way that, at times, approaches a notion of fate. But despite the overlaps between fate, providence, fortune, and necessity, we can parse Josephus's compatibilist position this way: he views as fated only those events deemed absolutely necessary by God's providence—and these events are often the ones that are predicted by prophets. Stoic determinists, as we have observed, may well equate fate, providence, and necessity. But for compatibilists, the terms just overlap: fated events are those deemed necessary by providence, from the time of divine determination until the plan's earthly fruition.

The term "fate" appears more frequently in *War*.[160] Three of the twelve instances involve the scholastic debate on free will (2.162, 163, 164), and, as in *Antiquities*, a number of other instances relate in some way to the inevitability of any given individual's death (*War* 1.662, 4.297, 6.84; see also 1.79), at times in indirect speech (1.628; see also 1.79, and 4.257).[161] Of course, one important fated event—one also clearly predicted by prophets and omens—is the rise of Vespasian (3.321–22, 399–404; 4.622).[162] But there is above all, in *War*, a single, major, fated event: the destruction of the temple. On the one hand, Josephus is adamant—as we have seen— that the people of Jerusalem were duly warned by portents and prophecies and given due opportunities to repent and avert the disaster. On the other hand, a turning point is reached about halfway through the work, in the events leading up to the murders of the high priests Jesus and Ananus. (Their moderate speeches and the events leading to their murders occupy much of book 4.) Jesus' speech itself raises the possibility that the city is fated for destruction (4.257). Josephus then sees the guiding hand of fate (4.297) in Ananus's skipping his routine inspection of his sentries (some of whom then fell asleep) while a thunderstorm provided cover for the Zealots to allow the Idumeans to enter the city, defeat Ananus's faction, and then murder Ananus and Jesus (4.288–317). In other words, the evil killers are aided providentially, by a string of unlikely circumstances. Yet these murders, Josephus makes clear, constitute the true turning point

(4.318): "the capture of the city began with the death of Ananus." In other words, we could very well borrow a term from the study of Hellenistic philosophy and say that the fall of Jerusalem was *conditionally fated*—the inexorable result of the people's free choice to sin.[163]

Ambiguities remain: Josephus suggests that the death of Ananus came about *after* a divine decision was reached: "because God had, for its pollutions, condemned the city to destruction and desired to purge the sanctuary by fire" (*War* 4.318). Yet Josephus will depict himself as calling for repentance even later (5.415–19).[164] Still, at some point, the process put in motion around the death of Ananus becomes irrevocable.[165] There is no escape from decreed judgment (6.314: τὸ χρεών). By book 6, the city and people are condemned to their fate (6.108, 428), and divine justice manifests itself in the destruction of the temple on the same fated day that saw the destruction of the first temple centuries before (6.250, 267).

Taken together, Josephus's account of the destruction of the temple in *Jewish War* displays three key elements of his compatibilism. First, we have one undoubtedly fated event—the destruction of the temple— although it's not clear, even with hindsight, precisely when the temple's destruction became inevitable. Second, the final fate of the city was determined not from the beginning of time, but much later, as a conditional result of the people's sinful behavior. Third, we also have acts of injustice—the murders of Jesus and Ananus—in which Josephus sees the arm of divine fate guiding the hands of human killers. Josephus's God is not in this instance, like the Sadducean deity, removed from the very sight of evil. He is, to the contrary, deeply implicated in these crimes, opening doors (*War* 4.298–300; compare *b. Shabbat* 104a; *b. Yoma* 38b) in order to allow the wicked to do their bidding, for which they will be duly and justly punished.[166] This is compatibilism as Josephus understands it: fate and free will cooperate, under the guidance of providence.

To complete the picture we are drawing of Josephus's compatibilism, it is now necessary to illustrate examples of events Josephus believes are neither fated nor even caused by divine providence. There are at least three categories of such events. The first are, simply, accidents. Bad weather, military setbacks, human errors, and perhaps many other minor details just happen, without God's specific intentionality (*War* 1.374–77, 4.40; *Ant.* 15.144, 299).[167] To be sure, sometimes the weather can be providential (18.284–85). Josephus even claims that when the temple was being rebuilt in the days of Herod, as a manifestation of divine power and approval, it rained only at night (*Ant.* 15.425).[168] But other times rain is just rain; life brings twists, turns, advances, and reversals (*War* 2.113).

Related in some way is another category of events, though this category is more ambiguous. According to Josephus, the fortunes of princes and empires naturally rise and fall, sometimes suddenly, not always in direct relation with virtue (e.g., *War* 2.184, 360, 373, 390; *Ant.* 17.191–92, 18.129, 19.16).[169] To be sure, Josephus believes that no empire can rule without God's permission (*War* 2.390; see also 2.140). But God's providence is seen most of all in the final outcome, and not necessarily in every step along the way (e.g., *Ant.* 2.236, 19.16; compare Sir. 11.4–6, 27–28).[170]

Certainly the most important category of unfated events includes the acts of evil that occur without God's participation, being purely the result of human wickedness. Examples abound, especially in *Antiquities*, but also in *War*. In his biblical paraphrase, earthly injustices enacted by wicked humans include the murders of Abel (*Ant.* 1.53), Naboth (8.355–61), and Zechariah son of Jehoiada (9.168–70), as well as the unfair imprisonment of Jeremiah (10.115).[171] Postbiblical examples include the murders of the high priest Johanan (11.297–301, a patricide), the prophet Onias (14.22–28), Herod's wife Mariamme (15.232–46; see also 16.185, 17.180–81),[172] John the Baptist (18.116–19), the high priest Jonathan (20.160–66) and James, the brother of Jesus (20.197–203).[173] We have also already mentioned Herod's killing of his own sons (*Ant.* 16.395–404; though in this case, the sons were hardly innocent). We should also add the innocents slaughtered in the temple by Archelaus (*War* 2.12–13, 30; but see *Ant.* 17.213–18). The references to righteous Jews who heroically withstood tortures in the context of religious persecutions would also, I think, qualify as examples of innocent people unjustly persecuted by the wicked (*War* 1.34, 2.152–53; *Apion* 1.42–43, 2.232–35). As we will see in the next chapter, some of these events play an extremely important role in Josephus's theological approach to history. But here it is sufficient to note that these events are an important illustration of Josephus's compatibilism. These events do not occur because God wills them to happen; they occur, rather, because the way of the wicked is to "carry out plans as if no divine power exists" (*Ant.* 17.130).[174] Divine providence is seen later, when the wicked suffer for their crimes. There are times, to be sure, when God cooperates with wicked people in order to bring about divine justice (e.g., Nob in the time of Saul; Jerusalem in the time of Josephus). In these rarer cases, for the ultimate purpose of bringing about earthly justice, we can say that fate and free will cooperate in such a way that God is implicated in evil (see *War* 2.162–65), as the wicked are aided in their sordid plans. But most events, for Josephus, are brought about either by God or by people. In other words, Josephus's compatibilism is not a full fusion of fate with free will, but a partial determinism, one well characterized by the catchphrase "Providence always, fate at times."

Conclusion

Over the course of this chapter, we have seen that Josephus's tripartite description of ancient Jewish debates on fate and free will is corroborated in a great many respects by the range and diversity of positions articulated in ancient Jewish literature. This is especially true with regard to the Qumran scrolls, the Wisdom of Ben Sira, and rabbinic literature, where we find, respectively, very close analogues to the Essenes' determinism and the Sadducees' libertarianism, and also the two types of compatibilism Josephus attributes to the Pharisees. The assorted evidence regarding ancient Jewish disagreements concerning fate and free will proves, therefore, to be reasonably compatible. What is more, Josephus's brief descriptions also hit the nail on the head with regard to the issues at stake for ancient Jews. We can confirm (from Ben Sira) that some Jews were driven to the libertarian view in order to deny that God is complicit in human decisions to commit evil. We can confirm (from rabbinic sources, Josephus's own writings, and the Dead Sea Scrolls) that other Jews moved toward the compatibilist or even determinist positions in relation to their beliefs in divine power and predictive prophecy. Josephus's descriptions, therefore, are not only descriptively accurate; they are also analytically insightful.

We have also seen that Josephus's own approach to the matter appears decidedly compatibilist. To be sure, Josephus does see the workings of fate impacting on human affairs (especially in *Jewish War*). Certain events—especially the specific future occurrences predicted by prophets—are indeed destined to occur. And Josephus views the fulfillment of some prophecies as proof par excellence of the wide power of divine providence. But unlike Calvinist predestinarians or Stoic determinists, Josephus distinguishes between fate and providence: while all events are seen and guided by providence, only some are fated. Fate must make room for freedom of choice, since human responsibility—but not an all-encompassing fate—is an irrefutable doctrine of the Jewish Torah, as Josephus understands it. Josephus's own discussions of fate are informed by his discussions of the scholastic debates, and vice versa. He uses the term "fate" when he is accounting for specific, predicted events or trying to explain ancient Jewish debates about fate and free will. So he does not incline toward an Essene determinist view, as is sometimes asserted. Nor does he contradict himself when he asserts (in *Apion*) that Jews agree on divine providence even while he explains (in *War* and *Antiquities*) that Jewish schools of thought differ on the question of fate and free will. Josephus is a consistent compatibilist. His discussions of the concepts are guided not by a Stoic determinism (that equates fate with providence) or even a Chrysippean compromise (that attributes all things to fate, with a slight nod toward free will). Josephus's own approach is akin to the one he attributes to the Pharisees in *Antiquities* 13, a position we also find among various Middle Platonists and Gnostics: a partial determinism that attributes all things to providence, but only some to fate, in order to allow for a truly two-sided free will.

To be sure, Josephus's accounts of the Jewish debates remain somewhat exaggerated (at each extreme). They are also, quite likely, simplified: there may well have been Sadducees, Pharisees, or Essenes whose views differed from those Josephus describes—though in his defense, the confirmations far outweigh any contraindications. Josephus's accounts also fall short in the respect that he does not explain the ways the Hellenistic philosophic and Jewish theological debates differed. He also does not fully reckon with the difference between the two distinct compromise positions attributed to the Pharisees in his works. Finally, it ought to be noted once again that Josephus hides neither his affection for the deterministic Essenes nor his disdain for the libertarian Sadducees. So there is room to criticize Josephus for certain shortfalls both as a historian and as a philosopher.

But the criticism is, I think, frequently overdone on this matter. Instead of criticizing Josephus's tripartite typology as an example of apologetic fancy, biased historiography, or substandard philosophy, it might be better for modern historians of ancient Judaism to embrace Josephus's tripartite typology as an example of good pedagogy, which can as a matter of course require both simplification and the use of clear, but imprecise, analogies. On the basis of this standard, Josephus's typology can be praised highly. If he fell short of explaining all his terms and reckoning with all the philosophic complexities, we just need to remind ourselves that most modern efforts to reckon with these debates have stopped short of fully explaining the theological and philosophical issues at stake. It's not Josephus's fault that we are less informed than he expected. Evaluating the accounts of the Jewish scholastic disputes in light of Josephus's own context and purposes, we must conclude that Josephus has clearly, efficiently, sympathetically, and memorably schematized important debates among ancient Jews and translated them into terms (to say nothing of the language) understood by his first-century readers. And he has done so with reasonable accuracy as well.

3

Afterlives and Noble Deaths

WE TURN IN this chapter to a consideration of Josephus's testimony regarding ancient Jewish views on the afterlife.[1] As in the previous chapter, our primary task is to evaluate Josephus's descriptions of the three Jewish schools in light of relevant comparative evidence. And here, too, we are also interested in determining where Josephus's own position on the matter can best be placed on the map his evidence helps us draw. But the task in this case is a bit more complicated. As we will see, in order to best locate Josephus's views among the options he describes, we will need to consider his attitude toward the noble deaths of warriors and martyrs in general and, in particular, the Sicarii's seemingly heroic suicidal deaths at Masada (*War* 7.252–406).[2] Josephus intriguingly tells us that Eleazar ben Yair was able to motivate his followers to take their own lives, in part, by speaking eloquently of the promises of immortality (7.341–57). If Josephus intends for us to view these deaths as truly noble, presumably that would mean that he wants readers to adopt the views toward the afterlife expressed so eloquently in Eleazar's second speech. But are we to sympathize with the Sicarri? Is Eleazar articulating Josephus's beliefs? In order to answer these questions, we will endeavor, toward the end of this chapter, to carefully parse Josephus's views on noble deaths—suicidal and not—and to correlate these with his views on the afterlife. By doing so, we hope to shed some light on the Masada episode in particular, but also on ancient Jewish views of suicide, martyrdom, and mortality more generally.

Before Afterlife

Before turning to Josephus's accounts of the schools, some preliminaries are in order. As in the previous chapter, it is necessary first to offer a few terminological clarifications. Once our terms are clarified, we will then be in a better position to comment briefly on some matters that concern other recent scholarly treatments of the afterlife: when did the Jewish beliefs in immortality and resurrection emerge and develop? And can we discern among our sources any reasons why these doctrines emerged?

Immortality and Resurrection: Two Options or More?

For the most part, scholarly discussions of the afterlife in ancient Judaism are careful to distinguish between two general forms of afterlife beliefs: the immortality of the soul and the resurrection of the dead. In this respect, the scholarly discussions of today rightly follow the ancient material at our disposal, in which, as we will see, one can frequently isolate one or another of these ideas. But there is an important difference between the ancient and modern discussions: there are no treatments in ancient Jewish sources of the "afterlife" per se—discussions typically concern one or another of the subconcepts (e.g., Acts on resurrection, Philo on immortality) or, more rarely, both (e.g., Hippolytus—see the appendix). This is because the general, neutral catchall terms we have the benefit of using today—"afterlife," "life after death"—are not in evidence in the ancient literature. Most ancient discussions of the concept are couched exclusively in the specific terms that best express the belief espoused by the source in question. When a source tells us that a given group denies resurrection, that may or may not mean that the group denies all forms of afterlife. Even when we are told that a group denies immortality of the soul, other afterlife notions may have been believed nonetheless.

The immortality of the soul—of which Josephus, for instance, speaks often—posits that on death, the soul separates from the dead body, and lives an eternal disembodied existence, perhaps in the heavens, among angels or stars. This belief is often characterized by both duality and immediacy. The desired afterlife commences right when death detaches the immortal soul from the deceased body. The resurrection of the dead—of which the New Testament and rabbinic literature speak more frequently—posits that at some point after death, an individual's life is restored back to a living body. This belief is characterized by both delay and an eventual nonduality. Resurrection will not take place immediately on death, and what happens in the interim is not always so clear. But the eventual result is nondualistic, in that soul and body—if separable—are (re)united in the resurrected body. Therefore, the two notions—immortality and resurrection—are not mutually contradictory. Indeed, they can be rather compatible, especially during the delay that precedes resurrection: we know that some ancient Jews believed that immediately after death the soul lives an unembodied existence, but that later the soul will be returned to a resurrected body (e.g., 4 Ezra 7.32–37, 75–103). But the beliefs clearly do not always go hand in hand, and a number of ancient Jewish texts are rather emphatic in focusing on one notion or the other.

We can illustrate the difference between the two doctrines by comparing the martyrological narratives that appear in 2 and 4 Maccabees. The belief in bodily resurrection is articulated quite clearly in 2 Maccabees—possibly for the first time in an ancient Jewish text. When the second son prepares to die, he articulates his confidence that the "King of the Universe will raise us up to an everlasting renewal of life" (7.9). When the third soon-to-be-martyred son stretches forth his hands, he confidently asserts "I got these from Heaven, and because of his laws I disdain them, and from him I hope to get them back again" (7.11; see also 14.46). As the seventh son nears his death, his mother comforts him:

> I do not know how you came into being in my womb. It was not I who gave you life and breath, nor I who set in order the elements within each of you. Therefore the Creator of the world, who shaped the beginning of humankind and devised the origin of all things, will in his mercy give life and breath back to you again, since you now forget yourselves for the sake of his laws. (7.22–23)

As Daniel R. Schwartz points out, the allusion to creation here is an important aspect of the book's belief in bodily resurrection: just as God created physical matter—from nothing (7.28)—so God can easily restore bodily existence to the righteous dead.[3]

That some Jews rejected these notions in favor of a disembodied immortality of the soul can be seen in the reworking of 2 Maccabees 6.1–7.42 found in 4 Maccabees.[4] With perfect consistency, every allusion to bodily resurrection is elided, and the newer text speaks exclusively and clearly of the immortality of the soul: after death, the righteous dead live a heavenly afterlife with God and the patriarchs. The book imagines the brothers comforting themselves before their deaths:

> Let us not fear him who thinks he is killing us, for great is the struggle of the soul and the danger of eternal torment lying before

those who transgress the commandment of God. Therefore let us put on the full armor of self-control, which is divine reason. For if we so die, Abraham and Isaac and Jacob will welcome us, and all the fathers will praise us. (4 Macc. 13.14–17)

Similar assertions appear throughout the work (7.19–20, 16.25, 17.5).

The views of other texts and authors are also rather clear: Philo (e.g., *On the Birth of Abel*, 5–20; *Life of Moses*, 2.288–91) and Wisdom of Solomon (e.g., 3.1–9) articulate beliefs in the immortality of the soul; early rabbinic literature speaks of resurrection of the dead (e.g., *m. Sanhedrin* 10.1).[5] But between 2 and 4 Maccabees are various shades of gray, and this is to say nothing of the darker hues in the background of these texts—the murkier presages of resurrection or "intimations of immortality" that are in evidence in earlier ancient Jewish texts, and even the Hebrew Bible itself.[6]

The first term we should introduce is *resuscitation*. This term accurately describes an important foreshadowing of resurrection—the various instances in the Hebrew Bible and later literature when a person is miraculously brought back from the brink of death.[7] In the case of a resuscitation, the person brought back to life isn't actually dead—just mostly dead. Moreover—and more to the point of introducing this distinction—the person whose health and vigor are miraculously restored will still, eventually, die a normal death. The classic instances of this are found in the Elijah/Elisha cycle of narratives embedded within the Deuteronomistic History (1 Kings 17.17–24; 2 Kings 4.18–37, 2 Kings 13.20–21). Related to resuscitation is *revivification*: the transformation of a fully deceased—and even decomposed—body back into a living amalgam of flesh and breath. This is what is described (albeit as a metaphor) in Ezekiel 37.1–14. The common denominator of these passages is their affirmation that God, as the author of life, has power to reverse death and restore life. But these texts do not necessarily affirm any belief in the afterlife per se. Those restored to life have been given a second chance at a finite earthly life. When people speak today of resurrection of the dead, however, they are interested in an afterlife hope: resurrection to an eternal life—but that is absent from these biblical texts.

Even in the absence of evidence for a belief in bodily resurrection, there are indications that Israelites did believe in some form of immortality, albeit not a *beatific* one. A beatific afterlife can take various forms—immortality of the soul and bodily resurrection among them—but what they share is the general sense that the afterlife is something to anticipate, not dread (at least insofar as the virtuous are concerned). We can quickly appreciate the significance of this distinction by reviewing the biblical story of the medium at Endor who, at Saul's desperate request, calls up the deceased prophet Samuel (1 Sam. 28.1–25). This story figures prominently in practically any discussion of afterlife in ancient Israel (and as we will note, the story interested Josephus too). Rightly so, for the story is in many ways the clearest indication we have that the prohibitions of necromancy found in the Hebrew Bible (e.g., Exod. 22.17, Deut. 19.10, 1 Sam. 28.3, 2 Kings 23.24) were rooted in a firm belief that the dead could indeed be brought back—at least temporarily—to consciousness in order to communicate with the living.[8] Moreover, the story may well provide the clearest indication we have of where Israelites believed the deceased were: underneath the earth (1 Sam. 28.14–15), in Sheol (Gen. 37.35; Num. 16.30–33). And Samuel's prediction of Saul's death is a telling one: "Tomorrow you and your sons will be with me" (1 Sam. 28.19). Most scholars take this narrative as the unambiguous confirmation of what appears to be hinted at all over the Hebrew Bible. The underworld is, in George Mendenhall's phrase, the "democracy of death," where the wicked and righteous shades equally endure a dark and dreary postmortem existence, cut off from the living and God alike.[9] As stated in Psalms, "The dead cannot praise God." (117.17). Wishing for death, Job imagines a place where the kings persist among the poor, the prisoners among their captors, the wicked among their victims (Job 3.1–19). Death comes to all, and no one can escape Sheol's clutches (e.g., Ps. 89.49, Eccles. 9.10).[10] Sheol, then, is the dark, dreary place where the shades of the righteous Samuel and the wicked Saul persist together, for eternity.

Considering such traditions, we could say that Israelites did believe in immortality all along, expecting an afterlife in Sheol. But to put the matter this way obscures more than it clarifies. The biblical democracy of death is a world away from the second temple Jewish beliefs in immortality or resurrection. In the previous chapter, we noted Daniel Dennett's derision of Stoic compatibilism as failing to provide a free will "worth wanting." We could justifiably utilize the same criterion to distinguish second temple notions of afterlife from the intimations we find in the Hebrew Bible. What separates them is the fact that one is desirable—*beatific*—while the other is not. In the Hebrew Bible, Sheol is not something to look forward to: Job's desire for death is illustrative of his utter despair. For in Sheol there is neither justice nor divine company. But according to a number of the second temple beliefs that will concern us in this chapter, the afterlife becomes something to be desired, awaited with great hope. It is where the righteous dead come closer to God, receiving the rewards denied them in the physical world while they were alive. For some ancient Jews, as we will see, hopes in an afterlife better than any earthly existence motivated warriors, martyrs, and other suicides to willingly—even happily—surrender their lives prematurely.

Jon D. Levenson has recently reevalutated the common understanding of the Israelite underworld, by asking an intriguing question: were Abraham, Moses, and Job really consigned to Sheol?[11] Levenson does not deny that some texts speak of Sheol as the universal, inescapable destination for the deceased.[12] But he finds another view in evidence as well, one that suggests that different postmortem fates await righteous persons who live out their lives and die fulfilled and contented. Levenson points out that some texts speak of Sheol as a dreary place *for the wicked* (e.g., Job 18.5–21); others speak of Sheol with regard to the fear of premature deaths (e.g., Ps. 18.6) or brokenhearted ones (e.g., Gen. 37.35). Still other texts famously allow select persons, beloved of God, mysteriously to escape death altogether (e.g., Enoch: Gen. 5.21–24; Elijah: 2 Kings 2.1–12).[13] Levenson suggests, therefore, that an alternate view began to emerge, considering Sheol to be the sad abode of those who lived an unfulfilled life. The righteous dead—who lived out their years and left behind sufficient progeny to carry on their name and memory—live on in this world, through the legacies they passed to their descendants. "In sum, the biblical Sheol is the prolongation of the unfulfilled life. There is no equivalent prolongation of the fulfilled life precisely because it is fulfilled."[14]

If Levenson is right, then common understandings of the biblical "democracy of death" are mistaken, or at least overstated in their belief that ancient Israelites unanimously believed that Sheol was the universal destination for the deceased. Since we are interested in a later period, we need not resolve this dispute here. But we can draw two important lessons from the questions Levenson has asked. First, he is no doubt correct that we should be open to the possibility that the Hebrew Bible expresses or intimates a multiplicity of views, not all of which are necessarily extensions of pre- or nonmonotheistic thought. Second, he has asked a question that clearly resonates: the fate of the patriarchs plays a curiously prominent role in second temple literature concerning the afterlife. 4 Maccabees speaks of immortality as "living with God," *like Abraham, Isaac, and Jacob* (4 Macc. 7.19, 13.17, 16.25). In the New Testament, Jesus is said to have proven the doctrine to doubting Sadducees by arguing that since the living

God is the God of Abraham, Isaac, and Jacob, therefore the patriarchs live on in eternity (Mark 12.26//Matt. 22.32//Luke 20.37–38). And Josephus, in his retelling of Genesis 22, imagines Abraham comforting his soon-to-be-sacrificed son Isaac, to the effect that the divine command means that God wants Isaac to be with him (*Ant.* 1.229–31). The thought that God's chosen were destined to be eternally confined in Sheol—even though this is precisely what some biblical texts clearly state—was so counterintuitive to many ancient Jews that the opposite assumption became a powerful argument in favor of the existence of some sort of beatific afterlife. And ancient Jews who were inclined to do so could point to the mysterious, postmortem ascensions of Elijah, Enoch—and even, possibly, Moses—as examples.[15] Yet if the later material confirms that some Jews believed the patriarchs were with God, other later literature—such as Ben Sira and Josephus's descriptions of the Sadducees—confirms that at least some Jews continued to deny the existence of a beatific afterlife, even for the truly righteous.

Afterlife in Ancient Judaism: When and Why?

The question we must now briefly consider is this: when and why did these shifts in Israelite/Jewish intuition take place? One possible explanation is acculturation—that the Jews in the Hellenistic period adopted ideas common to their cultural context. But immortality is neither a uniquely Hellenistic view nor a particularly novel one in the Hellenistic Near East (to wit, Gilgamesh). And *resurrection* is not paralleled in Hellenistic thought at all. Moreover, according to Josephus, the Sadducees (who had the support of the wealthy, who were, presumably, the most acculturated of the Jews) continued to deny both doctrines, as we will see. Clearly acculturation, while perhaps part of the answer, is not a solution.[16] The material evidence testifies to diversities and developments in practice—note the contrast between Herodian period ossuaries and the cemetery at Qumran. But broader cultural practices were similarly diverse and developing in this period, and there's no clear way to associate particular Jewish burial practices with developments in afterlife beliefs.[17]

   Other writers have suggested that the break with biblical theology was brought about by some sort of crisis. Based on the coincidence that early references to immortality (Dan. 12.1–3) and resurrection (2 Macc. 7.9, 14, etc.) are embedded in accounts of the Maccabean conflicts, one commonly expressed view has it that the persecutions of righteous Jews under the reign of Antiochus IV constituted a calamity significant enough to warrant a dramatic change in Jewish theology.[18] A number of arguments can be raised against this view, however.[19] The first is the fact that we can now reliably date various ancient Jewish textual references to a beatific afterlife—particularly 1 *Enoch* 22.1–14—to the third century BCE.[20] The second is the fact that 1 Maccabees and Josephus suggest to us that many ancient Jews—even those who believed in the afterlife—saw no particular association between these events and the doctrines espoused by Daniel and 2 Maccabees. While tragic, the sufferings of the mid-second century were not seen by all as unprecedented. And other Jews—Sadducees prominent among them—persisted in their denials, long after the events in question. We will review some ancient Jewish understandings of martyrdom in particular later in this chapter. Subsequently, we will go one step further (in chapter 5 and the conclusion) to suggest that there is very little reason to associate any particular theological changes with any known historical crises.

Levenson has suggested a powerful theological argument, briefly stated in the subtitle of his book: "The Ultimate Victory of the God of Life." Rejecting the views that Jewish beliefs in immortality emerged out of specific crises or as an accommodation to external cultural pressures, Levenson sees resurrection as the natural, logical, and even necessary consequence of the belief in a singular, all-powerful God:

> What has happened to the biblical Sheol…is that the affirmation of faith in the omnipotent and rescuing God of Israel…has collided with the brute fact of death.…Something had to give. What gave was not the faith in the limitless power of the Rock of Israel and their redeemer. What gave was death.…In the case of Resurrection, the last word once again lies not with death—undeniably grievous though it is—but with life. Given the reality and potency ascribed to death throughout the Hebrew Bible, what overcomes it is nothing short of the most astonishing miracle, the Divine Warrior's eschatological victory.[21]

This theological argument is important, especially for its striking independence from the more common, more problematic, explanations rooted in culture or crisis. Moreover, Levenson's argument represents a paradigm shift, moving the argument from external historical or sociological causes to internal ideas. Theology here is not the object but the subject.

As we will see, Josephus's accounts of the ancient Jewish schools can shed light on these questions in important ways. On the one hand, Josephus supports those, like Levenson, who refuse to associate the emergence of afterlife beliefs among Jews with the martyrdoms of the second century BCE. Like Levenson, Josephus, too, suggests that ancient Jewish debates about the afterlife are long-standing and there is no tipping point that can be associated with any particular historical crisis. Moreover, there can be no question that afterlife is associated, by those who believe in it, with God's unlimited power as well as the destiny of biblical heroes. Yet Josephus also helps us understand that even if the debates on the afterlife are to be dissociated from any particular historical crisis, they ought not be dissociated altogether from theodicy. Josephus's accounts of the schools' approaches to the afterlife are carefully constructed so as to illustrate that ancient Jewish debates on these matters involved serious and sincere disagreements about the nature and location of divine justice and the extent of divine or human responsibility for evil. Josephus's discussions also suggest that afterlife expectations impact personal decisions to do good or evil—especially when the risks are high.

Josephus on the Schools and the Afterlife

There can be little doubt that Josephus was a firm believer in some form of afterlife, and that the topic interested him a great deal.[22] Descriptions of the afterlife beliefs of all three schools are included in both *War* 2 and *Antiquities* 18. Beyond that, the afterlife is a central theme of *War* in particular, with various leadership figures depicted as affirming a belief in the afterlife in the context of encouraging their followers to risk death (e.g., the two teachers: 1.648–50), surrender (e.g., Josephus himself: 3.361–82), fight to the death (e.g., Titus: 6.46–49), or commit suicide (e.g., Eleazar at Masada: 7.320–88). Although somewhat less prominent in *Antiquities*, affirmations of afterlife appear at key points in the book, both as Abraham comforts his son Isaac on the altar (1.229–31) and when Josephus himself concludes book 17 with the argument that the downfall of Archelaus constitutes proof of divine providence and the immortality of the soul (17.354).[23] Afterlife beliefs are also included in Josephus's general description (and defense) of Judaism in *Against Apion* (2.218). Although the traditions have been well studied, certain questions linger. One question concerns the relative accuracy of Josephus's accounts of the theological disputes, and in the sections that follow, we will review Josephus's schools passages, with an eye toward demonstrating, once again, that his accounts are reasonably confirmable. A second lingering question concerns the causal correlations between the afterlife beliefs Josephus describes and the life-and-death decisions first-century ancient Jews faced. That question will concern us later in this chapter.

The Sadducees and Their This-Worldly Mortality

The descriptions of the Sadducean afterlife beliefs in *War* 2 and *Antiquities* 18 are not identical, but they are largely commensurate. In *War* 2.165, Josephus tells us that "as for the persistence of the soul after death, penalties in the underworld, and rewards, they will have none of them." In *Antiquities* 18.16 we are informed, simply, that "the Sadducees hold that the soul perishes along with the body."[24]

As is well known, this account is largely paralleled in the New Testament, although the Sadducean denial is there phrased with regard to rejecting resurrection. In Acts, we are told that the Sadducees deny resurrection, angels, and spirit, while the Pharisees acknowledge them all (Acts. 23.8).[25] And in all three of the Synoptic Gospels (Matt. 22.23–33// Mark 12.18–27//Luke 20.27–40), the Sadducees are depicted as renouncing resurrection. Indeed, all three texts—despite their differences—give us a picture of a dispute about resurrection that for both sides is rooted in scripture. The Sadducees ask a shrewd question, one characteristic of some later rabbinic sources in being both practically unlikely but legally troubling.[26] What if a woman married a series of seven brothers, one after the other, in fulfillment of the biblical institution of levirate marriage (Deut. 25.5–6): when the deceased are resurrected, whose husband will she be?[27] Jesus' response to the Sadducees is also telling in a number of ways. After accusing them of denying scripture and divine power (Matt. 22.29//Mark 12.24), Jesus first suggests that the resurrected will remain unmarried, like the angels in heaven (Matt. 22.30//Mark 12.25//Luke 20.35–36). Then he develops an intriguing argument rooted in an analogical exegesis of scripture. Referring to the Lord as the living God, and quoting Exodus 3.6 ("the God of Abraham, God of Isaac, God of Jacob"), Jesus asserts that God is not God of the dead, but of the living (Matt. 22.31–32// Mark 12.26–27//Luke 20.37–38). In sum, if the living God (see Jer. 10.10) is identified by his relation to the patriarchs, then they, too, must still be alive.[28] Perhaps few nonbelievers would be brought in by this argument, but it's not bad as far as scriptural proofs for resurrection go.[29]

This fascinating passage is important in a number of respects. First, the Sadducean opposition to resurrection as described here is rooted, at least in part, in their refusal to accept what they perceived to be the doctrine's ultimate bodily implications. Quite possibly, Jesus' scriptural argument suggests another motivation for the Sadducean view: the doctrine's oft-acknowledged lack of clear scriptural justification. Either way, there are important disconnects between the Sadducean question and Jesus' reply. Jesus explains that resurrected bodies are unlike normal living ones, in that the former will be celibate, angel-like—and perhaps (although we cannot be certain) nonphysical altogether.[30] And the scriptural argument seems better suited for defending not resurrection, but immortality— after all, has Abraham's resurrection taken place? Abraham's postmortem eternity proves not resurrection, but immortality. Moreover, according to Acts 23.8—though not according to Josephus—the Sadducees denied that angels existed. So Jesus' reply is additionally strange in appealing to an angelic analogy to illustrate the nature of resurrected bodies to Sadducees.[31] It has recently been argued that this passage stands a good chance of reflecting an authentic event in Jesus' life.[32] But there is one aspect of these passages that surely is not historical—the implication that Sadducees found these arguments at all persuasive, or even to the point of the question asked. Even so, we can, quite reasonably, draw on this passage in order to confirm what Josephus implies—that the Sadducees would deny any form of beatific postmortem life or justice, whether it be immortality of the soul or resurrection of the dead. Moreover, we find in this passage confirmation that ancient Jewish understandings of resurrection were likely confused and muddled—what would be the nature of the resurrected body? This is a question to which we will have reason to return again later.

The Sadducean denial of resurrection is also attested in rabbinic sources, albeit rather late ones. According to *Avot de-Rabbi Natan* A 5, B 10 (ed. Schechter 13b), the Sadducees were founded by two students of Antigonus of Socho, named Zadok and Boethus. Unlike the Pharisees— who, according to their own tradition, shunned material wealth in this world, hoping for reward in the next—these Sadducees "used gold and silver vessels every day of their lives," dramatically illustrating their contrary belief that rewards in the next world were not to be expected.

Our best guide to fleshing out—and at the same time confirming— Josephus's brief description of the Sadducees may well, again, be the wisdom tradition, and especially the Wisdom of Ben Sira. Ben Sira articulates a number of reflections on death. Death awaits all (14.17, 17.30, 38.22, 41.1–4), is final (10.10–11, 38.21, 41.4), and is not particularly worth looking forward to (7.17, 10.11, 14.11–19). On a few occasions, Ben Sira speaks of bodily decomposition as the punishment for sinners (7.17, 10.11, 21.9). But presumably, Ben Sira is not suggesting that the wicked suffer after death in a particularly distinct way; the point seems to be, rather, that the sinners will slip to their deaths early (21.9), or after some well-deserved earthly suffering (11.25–28). Everyone's end is in Sheol, where there will be no pleasure (14.16), no praise for God (17.27–28), and no argument (41.4; compare Eccles. 9.10). The only ways around mortality are to be survived by progeny (Sir. 30.4–5, 40.19, 44.12–13) and to be remembered for righteousness by subsequent generations (41.11–13, 44.14–15). Yet Ben Sira hardly denies afterlife in all its forms. The nonbeatific, nondualistic afterlife that characterizes those few biblical passages that do speak of Sheol (Job 7.9–10, 17.13–16; Eccles. 9.10) is precisely what Ben Sira affirms (esp. 14.12–19 and 41.1–4, both extant largely in Hebrew).

With good reason, we can surmise that the Sadducees—with their reverence for scripture and their conservative theology—would have held similar views, including a belief in Sheol.[33] In order to be fully understood, the Sadducean denial of immortality needs to be translated into a number of distinct affirmative statements. First, the Sadducees affirm—precisely as Josephus puts it—that the soul and body *perish together* (*Ant.* 18.16). This is not an absolute denial of all forms of immortality; what they deny (*War* 2.165) is that the soul could persist after death apart from the body. The Sadducees affirm—in line with the general biblical record—that human life consists of an inseparable amalgam of what others (including Josephus) refer to separately as body and soul.[34] For the Sadducees, death is a final, single, unitary experience: body and soul (which Sadducees would not separate) together descend to Hades (i.e., Sheol).[35]

Josephus also tells us that the Sadducees deny that either rewards or punishments await the deceased in Hades (*War* 2.165). Once again, it is important to pay careful attention to precisely what is and is not denied. The Sadducees' rejection of rewards and punishments in the underworld does not need to mean and most likely does not mean that they rejected belief in an underworld altogether. The Sadducees' approach to death is unitary in this second way, too. They would likely affirm that Sheol is the "democracy of death," where the wicked and righteous reside together, for eternity, in a shady afterlife—precisely what we find in Ben Sira (38.21–23) and indeed in much of the wisdom tradition (e.g., Job 17.13–16; Eccles.

9.10–11).[36] If some Jews did limit Sheol, understanding it as the destination only for those who deaths brought premature conclusion to an unfulfilled life, the Sadducees were, most likely, not among them.

Having considered two important parallels between Josephus's Sadducees and the wisdom tradition—that both affirm the finality of death and that the same destiny awaits the righteous and wicked alike—I turn now to the corollary of this second notion: the belief in earthly justice. Josephus intimates as much when he tells us (*Ant.* 13.173) that the Sadducees believe "we ourselves are responsible for our well-being, while we suffer misfortune through our own thoughtlessness" (ἀβουλίαν; compare Prov. [LXX] 14.17; Bar. 3.28). Apparently, Josephus is telling us that the Sadducees believe that the righteous and wicked are punished in this world, and in this world alone. This of course is a perspective that is commonly expressed in the wisdom tradition (e.g., Prov. 10.27–31; Sir. 16.1–23, 39.28–31, 40.12–17).

Josephus does not give us any further indication of how precisely this earthly justice was meted out. Because of the Sadducees' aristocratic status, it is commonly inferred (as noted in chapter 1) that they would have viewed their wealth as a sign of divine approval. There is, to be sure, some confirmation of this in the wisdom tradition: Wealth is one of the ways the righteous wise could be rewarded in this world (e.g., Prov. 11.18, 24–26; 13.4; Job 1.1–10, 42.10–17; Sir. 29.1–13, 31.8–11), and we can reasonably surmise that some wealthy Sadducees viewed their wealth as a gift bestowed by God (compare Eccles. 5.18). But even a cursory reading of the wisdom tradition should caution against the assumption that all Sadducees—or other ancient Jews for that matter—would have viewed current wealth as an assured or irrevocable reward for righteousness. One thread running throughout the wisdom tradition is the recognition that the current state of affairs by no means reflects God's final judgment: fortunes can change suddenly and rapidly (e.g., Prov. 13.11; Eccles. 4.14, 5.12–13, 9.12; Sir. 11.4–6, 27–28, 18.25–28, 22.23–26). Moreover, to whatever degree wealth is one way God may choose to bestow blessings on the righteous, there are certainly many other methods as well, including illness (Sir. 38.9–15, see also 30.14–17), natural disasters (39.28–31), mental anguish (40.1–10), and a premature (21.10) or painful (11.27–28) death. Because God views discipline as a value, there are also times when the righteous are tested with suffering such as disease or poverty (Prov. 3.12; Job 1.13–2.10; Sir. 2.1, 4.17, 44.20). Precisely because of the complexities involved, the wisdom texts across the board deny that humans can know at any given time their status in God's eyes (Prov. 20.9; Eccles. 3.11; Sir. 5.4–8, 7.5).

The claim that the Sadducees viewed their wealth as a positive sign of God's favor is—like the Zadokite hypothesis—an unjustified inference. In this case, the juxtaposition of Josephus's Sadducees with the wisdom tradition reminds us that even a rich person can be made miserable by illness, anguish, or other sufferings, and life brings constant surprises. Surely the Sadducees knew this, just as Ben Sira and Job did. There is, therefore, no basis for asserting that the Sadducees would as a matter of course see their wealth as a God-given reward for unquestionable merit.

Having established this point, we can now counter one common explanation for why the Sadducees resisted the afterlife trend that was gaining momentum all around them in the ancient world. It is frequently asserted that the Sadducean denial of the afterlife is reflection of their satisfaction with their socioeconomic status.[37] Not to put too fine a point on it, the Sadducees ostensibly denied the afterlife because they didn't need it. Living in wealth and power, their lives were heaven on earth already. We need only remind ourselves here of the persistence of anti-Sadducean slurs among modern scholars to take pause. Does this argument really make any sense at all? Does wealth bring happiness? Is heaven really the wish of only the poor? It may be true, as one of my two wise grandmothers used to say, that there are few problems made worse by having more money. Surely wealth has its advantages (see Eccles. 9.7–9). But money is no guarantor of happiness, any more than it assures physical health, marital bliss, or multiple progeny. Nor can money protect one from natural disasters, foreign attack, or thieves (see Job 1.10–19). As the rich but dour Ecclesiastes understood well, wealth cannot bring happiness, just a modicum of comfort. But surely the afterlife could bring more.

So how do we explain, then, the Sadducean rejection of belief in a beatific afterlife? The difficulty ancients and moderns have in finding scriptural support for the doctrine could well be one reason, though some caution is in order. Scriptural support for immortality does appear clearly in Daniel (12.1–3) and arguably elsewhere (at least as Jesus, the Pharisees, and the later rabbis would claim). Indeed, medieval Jewish scripturalists—the Karaites—agreed with rabbinic Jews insofar as the scriptural authority for resurrection of the dead was concerned.[38] Quite possibly, the Sadducees remained unpersuaded by these texts and interpretations—but we would still have to ask why they rejected traditions or arguments accepted by others. Simple, principled conservatism may therefore be a safer explanation. But the best explanation is the combination of these, along with the recognition that it's not sufficient to say, negatively, that the Sadducees *deny* the afterlife because of their *inability* to prove it from scripture or their *refusal* to accept postbiblical developments. Rather, understanding the Sadducean position requires that we recognize the strong support in biblical and postbiblical texts—such as Proverbs and Ben Sira—for their "this-worldly," even rationalist focus.[39] They believed—like many sincere Jewish and Israelite sages before them—that divine justice rewarded the righteous and punished the wicked in this world. If justice was not worked out over one's lifetime, it would manifest itself—for good or ill—in one's descendants. The only immortality one should wish for is to be remembered for good, by plenty of progeny. And when things go wrong—when, say, the righteous suffer at the hands of the wicked—the blame for this falls back not on God but on the wicked themselves. As demonstrated in the previous chapter, the Sadducees find it theologically intolerable to view God as having a hand in evil. Only the wicked are evil's authors, exercising their God-given free will. And in *War* 2.164–65, Josephus juxtaposes the Sadducees' affirmation of free will with their denial of life after death. In just a few tightly packed lines, Josephus has given us enough to understand that Sadducean theology was built on scripture and buttressed by commitment to these intellectually consistent, this-worldly ideals.

The Pharisees: Immortality, Resurrection, or Both?

Josephus's descriptions of Pharisaic afterlife beliefs are somewhat more elaborate than his accounts of Sadducean views, though the additional data does not in this case bring additional clarity.[40] In *War* 2.163, the Pharisees maintain "that every soul is imperishable, but the soul of the good alone passes into another body, while the souls of the wicked suffer eternal punishment." In *Antiquities* 18.14, the Pharisees maintain that "souls have the power to survive death and that there are rewards and punishments under the earth for those who have led lives of virtue and vice: eternal imprisonment is the lot of evil souls, while the good souls receive an easy passage to a new life." In both accounts, these statements immediately follow the brief descriptions of Pharisaic compatibilism discussed in the previous chapter.

At first pass, these descriptions seem somewhat distant from our external knowledge of ancient Jewish beliefs. Just as is the case regarding descriptions of what the Sadducees deny, both the New Testament and rabbinic sources are wont to speak of various Jewish groups (Pharisees, early

Christians, rabbis) as believing in resurrection of the dead, not immortality of the soul. The Pharisees are unmentioned in the Sadducee/Jesus dispute concerning resurrection in the gospel traditions discussed above, but Acts 23.8 explicitly attributes resurrection to the Pharisees. Rabbinic sources—again, rather late ones—also confirm that the Pharisees maintained afterlife beliefs (see esp. *Avot de-Rabbi Natan* A 5, cited above). It is also surely relevant, as is equally well known, that the early rabbinic sages maintained a clear faith in the resurrection of the dead, as expressed in the Mishnah (*m. Sanhedrin* 10.1) and as emphasized in early Jewish liturgy as well (e.g., the second blessing of the Eighteen Benedictions).[41]

As we have seen in the previous chapter, on this matter, too, Josephus's descriptions of the Pharisaic (and, as we will soon see, especially Essene) beliefs are clearly couched in Hellenistic/philosophical terms. Indeed, it is with regard to Josephus's descriptions of afterlife beliefs that C. D. Elledge helpfully spoke of Josephus's "apologetic translation."[42] But the question we face is whether behind this translation we can discern anything of historical value. The answer to this conundrum depends on our own understandings—and translations—of Josephus's curious descriptions of Pharisaic beliefs: what does it mean for the souls of the righteous to "pass into another body" (*War* 2.163: μεταβαίνειν δὲ εἰς ἕτερον σῶμα) or to gain "easy passage to a new life" (*Ant.* 18.14: ῥᾳστώνην τοῦ ἀναβιοῦν)?

H. St. J. Thackeray, in his notes to the Loeb translation of *War*, takes the phrase he translates as "passes into another body" as articulating a belief in "reincarnation."[43] In the notes to his Loeb translation of the final books of *Antiquities*, Feldman argues that Josephus's use of the term ἀναβιόω (18.14; compare, e.g., 2 Macc. 7.9) indicates that he understood the Pharisees as believing in *resurrection*, just as rabbinic literature and the New Testament also testify.[44] Steering a course between these two, Elledge argues that Josephus speaks of "transmigration"—a phenomenon quite distinct from, in his view, the resurrection ostensibly espoused by the Pharisees.[45]

In order to elucidate this debate—and, especially, the Josephan passages at the heart of it—we need to clarify the terms being bandied about. As commonly understood, believers in *reincarnation* maintain that the (immortal) soul of the deceased is reborn into another body.[46] But even after this rebirth, the immortal soul has not found an eternal bodily existence. The new body is destined to die, too. The ultimate goal—for Plato (e.g., *Phaedo* 81d–82c), as in Hindu mythology—is to break free of this cycle altogether. Short of that, on its own, reincarnation into new physical, mortal bodies is not really an afterlife belief at all, and certainly not what Josephus has in mind regarding the Pharisees in *War* 2.163, where the reward for immortal souls is clearly to pass into some *immortal* body, in parallel contrast to the eternal punishment suffered by the wicked.

It is precisely for this reason that a number of scholars reject the term *reincarnation*, referring to the belief Josephus attributes to the Pharisees as, instead, *metempsychosis* or *transmigration*.[47] If we consult standard English dictionaries and thesauruses, we find that all three terms are technically synonymous, or at least overlapping in meaning. But the fact that the terms "transmigration" and "metempsychosis" are used less frequently in popular discourse—and perhaps more precisely by some religious studies scholars—allows historians of ancient Judaism to describe Josephus as attributing to the Pharisees something in between reincarnation and resurrection. The argument goes like this: on the one hand the righteous souls in question pass indeed into new, truly immortal, bodies (unlike standard reincarnation). On the other hand, these "different" or "new" bodies are something quite other than the original bodies once possessed by the deceased (unlike standard resurrection).

To be sure, some ancient Jewish texts imply that resurrected bodies would be identical with, or at least very similar to, those bodies the souls lost on death. As one of the Maccabean martyrs maintains, looking at his hands, "I hope to get these back again" (2 Macc. 7.11: ταῦτα πάλιν ἐλπίζω κομίσασθαι; see also 14.46). In his discussion of this matter, Elledge frequently cites a liturgical fragment (possibly, but not certainly, tannaitic) preserved in the Babylonian Talmud (*b. Berakhot* 60b), thanking God who "returns souls to deceased bodies" (המחזיר נשמות לפגרים מתים).[48] These texts appear to envision the soul's *return* to the *same* body, while Josephus speaks of a passage into *another* body. Elledge therefore concludes that the Maccabean and rabbinic sources articulate a belief in resurrection, while Josephus attributes to the Pharisees a belief in transmigration or metempsychosis.[49]

The problem with this argument is that it denies subtlety to ancient Jewish belief in bodily resurrection. While it is likely true that those who believed in resurrection imagined that their renewed bodies would be recognizably theirs (2 *Bar.* 50.1–4), it is equally true that a number of the fuller reflections on the nature of resurrected bodies also imagine that the new bodies would be in many ways different from the old ones (2 *Bar.* 51.1–5). After all, how could a human body be identifiably human and also immortal? We should recall here Jesus' answer to the Sadducees in the gospel passages discussed earlier, to the effect that resurrected bodies would be angelic and celibate (Mark 12.25).

It may also be instructive to recall Paul's description of resurrected bodies:

> (40) There are both heavenly bodies and earthly bodies, but the glory of the heavenly is one thing, and that of the earthly another. (41) There is one glory of the sun, another glory of the moon, and another glory of the stars; indeed, star differs from star in glory. (42) So it is with the resurrection:
>
> What is sown is perishable, what is raised is imperishable. (43) It is sown in dishonor, it is raised in glory. It is sown in weakness, it is raised in power. (44) It is sown a physical body [σῶμα ψυχικόν it is raised a spiritual body [σῶμα πνευματικόν If there is a physical body, there is also a spiritual body.
>
>   (1 Cor. 15.40–44)[50]

It is not insignificant that Paul's clear distinction between mortal and resurrected bodies also finds parallels in later rabbinic literature. One partial parallel also draws on the image of a planted seed in order to illustrate the difference between buried and resurrected bodies (*b. Sanhedrin* 90b).[51] But more important—and likely more illustrative of the rabbinic tradition than the liturgical fragment cited previously—is the following tradition attributed to the early Amoraic sage Rab:

> A favorite saying of Rab was: [The future world is not like this world.] In the future world there is no eating nor drinking nor propagation nor business nor jealousy nor hatred nor competition, but the righteous sit with their crowns on their heads feasting on the brightness of the divine presence, as it says, "And they beheld God, and did eat and drink" (Exod. 24.11). (*b. Berakhot* 17a)

Other traditions in the Talmud wonder in different ways about the nature of the resurrected body, affirming that even if the deceased was lame or blind, the resurrected body would be healed (*b. Sanhedrin* 91b).

Although it may at first seem reasonable to take 2 Maccabees 7 as the paradigm for Jewish understandings of bodily resurrection, it may in fact turn out to be the case that the classic Maccabean martyrdom narrative is rather extreme and possibly unique its emphasis on the similarity between mortal and resurrected bodies. Indeed, if we take as our standard a more reliable first-century defense of resurrection—such as that attributed to Jesus in the Synoptic Gospels—we then can find this perspective echoed in Paul, as well as later rabbinic sources. Having done so, we can turn back to Josephus and quite easily understand Josephus's description of Pharisaic doctrines as phrased in such a way as to preempt the kind of materialistic counterargument offered by the Sadducees in the Synoptic Gospels, and perhaps by Paul's opponents at Corinth as well. In sum, taken all together, Josephus, the New Testament, and rabbinic sources provide evidence that many Jews believed that resurrection was in some ways something more—but in other ways something less—than getting one's old body back. And for good reason: after all, decomposed skeletons will hardly do. By any understanding—celibate or not, angelic or not—resurrected bodies would, as a matter of course, have to be reconstituted, revitalized, re-formed, and reclothed so as to rise again and persist for eternity.[52] There can be little doubt that Josephus's descriptions of the Pharisees are cryptic; but one possible explanation for this ambiguity is, in fact, accuracy: it appears that the precise nature of resurrected bodies was something of a conundrum among ancient Jewish believers in bodily resurrection.

It will be helpful now to examine two other passages where Josephus speaks about afterlife beliefs. In suggesting that *War* 2.163 intends to speak of reincarnation, Thackeray compares the passage to *War* 3.374 and *Apion* 2.218.[53] In the first of these passages (to which we will return) Josephus depicts himself as appealing to a similar belief when trying to convince his fellow defenders not to commit suicide: the souls of the righteous dead, Josephus states, "are allotted the most holy place in heaven, whence, in the revolution of the ages [ἐκ περιτροπῆς αἰώνων] they return to find in sanctified bodies a new habitation [ἁγνοῖς πάλιν ἀντενοικίζονται σώμασιν]." In *Apion* 2.218, Josephus claims to describe the ancient Jewish view in general terms: "to those who observe the laws...God has granted a renewed existence [γενέσθαι τε πάλιν] and the gift of a better life [βίον ἀμείνω] in the revolution of the ages [ἐκ περιτροπῆς]." Now in neither passage is Josephus claiming to present the Pharisaic view, although the case for aligning Josephus's own beliefs with views he ascribes to the Pharisees continues to grow. But regardless, two important aspects of these passages may shed further light on what we have said heretofore regarding Josephus's description of the Pharisaic view. First, both of these passages—in agreement with Josephus's accounts of Pharisaic views—are rather emphatic in going beyond mere immortality. The Jews of whom, or for whom, Josephus speaks in these passages expect more than immortality: there will be a bodily renewal (*War* 3.374) or a better life (*Ap.* 2.218). What is more, in both these passages Josephus indicates that he believes that the ultimate renewal does not take place immediately on death (when immortality would be effected) but after the "revolution of the ages"—presumably the end-time. The delayed implementation of this second stage of the afterlife is a second way these two passages explicitly reach beyond the more straightforward beliefs in immortality of the soul, coming much closer to the two-stage process involved in resurrection of the dead. Yet, as we will see in the next section, Josephus's descriptions of the Essenes' beliefs are consistently different from what we have seen so far.

The Essenes and Their Other-Worldly Immortality

Josephus's description of Essene afterlife views in *Antiquities* couldn't be clearer or more to the point (18.18): "They regard the soul as immortal."[54] The earlier description in *War* could not differ more, at least in form. Quite unlike the description of any other doctrine in relation to any other group, Josephus elaborates freely on the Essene affirmation of immortality (2.154–58).[55] To be sure, Josephus's entire account of the Essenes is distinctively detailed when compared to the descriptions of the Pharisees and Sadducees. Josephus can summarize the Pharisaic or Sadducean view on afterlife with a few well-crafted (if cryptic) lines—just as he could describe all three schools' views on fate with extreme economy of words. But his report on the Essene afterlife beliefs is remarkably rhapsodic, relating the postmortem ascent of the soul, and comparing Essene beliefs explicitly to Greek ideas. Like Plato (*Phaedo* 80d–81d, 82d–83d, etc.),[56] Josephus's Essenes view the soul as imprisoned in the body (*War* 2.154), and death for them comes as a release (2.155). Josephus even mentions specific mythological figures—Sisyphus, Tantalus, Ixion, and Tityus—whose punishments in Hades are similar to the eternal woes the Essenes expect the wicked will face (2.156).

Scholars are particularly suspicious of this account, and not without cause. After all, allusions to Greek myths and Platonic dualism would seem to be out of place in any description of first-century Judean society, even if we grant that all schools of thought and layers of society were thoroughly Hellenized.[57] Some of those who adhere to the Essene hypothesis are particularly troubled by Josephus's description, believing it much more likely that the theologically conservative, Hebrew-writing Dead Sea sectarians would have maintained a belief in bodily resurrection, like contemporary Pharisees and early Christians as well as later rabbis.[58] Those willing to engage in source-critical analyses of Josephus's writings can then point to Hippolytus of Rome, whose *Refutation against All Heresies* contains an account of the Essenes, doubtless related to Josephus's treatment in *Jewish War*, that attributes to them not only the belief in immortality, but also the belief in bodily resurrection (see the appendix).[59]

But the skepticism can be overdone. We ought not to dismiss Josephus's account as an apologetic fancy invented for the occasion or an inaccurate confusion freely copied from a misinformed source. We ought, rather, to read this account allowing for the fact that Josephus is—explicitly—*comparing* Essene and Greek ideas. The question, therefore, is not whether Qumran sectarians or any other Jews would have spoken this way. The question is whether there were ancient Jews who, like the Platonic Greeks Josephus has in mind, viewed the physical world with sufficient disdain so as to look forward to a fully unembodied future existence.

Scholars who nevertheless reject the value of Josephus's report have struggled mightily to center bodily resurrection within Essene/Qumranic thought. There are two ways to go about this. One is to defend the historical accuracy of Hippolytus's resurrection-laden account of the Essenes. The other is to isolate scrolls passages that articulate some notion of resurrection. As I argue in the appendix, it is most unlikely that Hippolytus's *Refutation* is anything other than a free modification of material drawn from Josephus. As for the Dead Sea Scrolls, references to bodily resurrection are few and far between.

It is generally granted that only a few scrolls explicitly speak of bodily resurrection. The most commonly cited texts include *Pseudo-Ezekiel* (4Q385–88, 391) and the *Messianic Apocalypse* (4Q521).[60] Both of these texts are fragmentary. Although unknown outside Qumran, neither document exhibits distinctively sectarian ideas, terminology, or orthography.[61] *Pseudo-Ezekiel* appears to be an expansive rewriting of Ezekiel. As such, the reworking of the dry bones vision of Ezekiel 37 in 4Q385 (fragment 2) contains, as a matter of course, a vision of bones coming back to life. Some see here evidence that *Pseudo-Ezekiel* presents the biblical prophetic vision as a prediction of an eschatological bodily resurrection.[62] But while such a reading is plausible, it is not inevitable: explicit mention of a bodily resurrection to eternal life for all the righteous is at most implied in our extant fragments. The *Messianic Apocalypse* is even less well preserved, extant only in a single copy. But the reference to a future eschatological resurrection of the dead (ומתים יחיה) is perhaps incontestable (4Q521 fragment 2, 2.12). For some scholars, this is the smoking gun, the key piece of evidence around which a fuller argument for sectarian belief in resurrection can be constructed.[63]

Elledge, though, is more cautious, concluding that the evidence merely shows that "the Community was quite capable of adopting belief in the resurrection."[64] Facing the relative weight of the evidence, Geza Vermes's ironic conclusion regarding 4Q521 remains apt: "if this poem is an Essene composition and not a psalm dating to the late biblical period, it can be said that one out of many hundreds of Qumran manuscripts definitely testifies to the sect's belief in bodily resurrection."[65] As Collins concludes: "it would be unwise to treat [4Q521] as the key to the eschatology of the sect in the matter of resurrection."[66] And as Mladen Popović points out in a recent survey, even if we determine that these documents do speak of resurrection, we still do not know what *kind* of bodies—corporeal or angelic, recognizable or transformed—the texts imagine the resurrected would receive.[67]

Over against these texts, we find other passages, more frequently preserved and arguably more central to the sectarian outlook, that seem focused on a heavenly, angelic immortality, distant from sinful society, and divorced from any earthly reembodiment. We can begin with 1QH[a] 11.20–23:[68]

> (20) I thank you, O Lord, for you have redeemed by soul from the pit and from the hell of Abaddon (21) you have raised me up to everlasting height.
> I walk on limitless level ground and I know there is hope for him (22) whom you have shaped from dust for the everlasting Council.
> You have cleansed a perverse spirit of great sin,
> that it may stand with the (23) host of the Holy Ones,
> And that it may enter into community
> with the congregation of the Sons of Heaven.

Similar expectations and sentiments—some detailing also the fate of the wicked—are expressed elsewhere in the Hymns in particular (1QH[a] 7.27–34, 12.21–23, 14.14–22, 19.13–17).[69] Because these sentiments are echoed in other Qumran sectarian documents (1QS 4.6–8, 11.5–9; 1QSb 4.24–26; CD A 3.20), a number of scholars maintain that the Qumran sectarians, like Josephus's Essenes, believed in immortality, but not resurrection.[70]

What is particularly important for our purposes, first, is the fact that the texts express hopes that are on some level meaningfully comparable to Greek ideas as Josephus describes them. Equally important is the continuation of the hymn just quoted:

> And yet I, a creature (25) of clay, what am I?
> Kneaded with water, what is my worth and my might?
> (1QHª 11.24–25)

This sentiment, too, appears elsewhere in the *Thanksgiving Hymns*, frequently developed more strongly with language of defilement used to describe the human condition (1QHª 4.29–37, 9.23–25, 12.30–32, 20.27–39).[71] But the passage quoted here is significant for our purposes, for the speaker's hope for eternal life among the angels is juxtaposed with—and presumably, directly related to—his disdain for the human condition of which he spoke a few lines previously. The hope for an unembodied afterlife may well go hand in hand, at Qumran, with the contempt for corporeal existence.

Clearly, the scrolls on the whole—and particularly the identifiably sectarian scrolls—are, to say the least, notably reticent about bodily resurrection. Considering the sect's concerns with defilement and desire, it is not hard to imagine why. Possibly, they believed in some form of bodily resurrection and developed some way of imagining possessing physical bodies entirely transformed so as to be utterly unlike the sources of pollution they possessed during their lifetimes. But if the sect imagined this, they did not express it. Their expressed hopes, on the other hand, are not so far off from the disembodied, other-worldly afterlife Josephus describes. And to the degree that the sectarians viewed the body negatively and hoped for their souls' release and angelic ascent, their views may even be worthy of the Hellenized comparisons Josephus draws.

Just as in the previous chapter, we have seen once again that Josephus's descriptions of ancient Jewish theological disputes are, on the whole, confirmable. On the most general level, his assertion that ancient Jewish groups had long-standing disputes about life after death appears to be quite accurate. Without equating Pharisees with later rabbis, Essenes with Dead Sea sectarians, or Sadducees with earlier wisdom sages, we find, at the very least, that Josephus's evidence withstands comparative scrutiny reasonably well. Virtually every statement he makes about the Pharisees, Sadducees, and Essenes finds close analogues in comparable evidence. Some scholars seem reluctant to believe that any Hebrew-speaking Jews might have believed in an incorporeal, other-worldly immortality, holding that such a belief could only reflect diasporic, more Hellenized milieus. But there is simply no reason, a fortiori, to reject Josephus's suggestion that there were Jews in the land of Israel who believed in an incorporeal immortality. Josephus's claims regarding the Essenes withstand comparison to the Qumran material, and indeed Josephus's juxtaposition of an incorporeal afterlife with negative attitudes toward the body seems strikingly apt in light of that evidence. Some scholars have overlooked the careful distinctions Josephus draws between immortality and reembodiment, eliding the differences Josephus draws between the afterlife beliefs of the Pharisees and Essenes. But Josephus's careful—if still somewhat cryptic—recognition that some Jews expected an eventual return to renewed bodies finds confirmation among rabbinic and early Christian sources. Some scholars have taken 2 Maccabees 7 as the gold standard of Jewish resurrection belief, eliding beliefs in other forms of reembodiment with reincarnation, metempsychosis, or transmigration. But the evidence from the New Testament (as well as later rabbinic literature) suggests that Josephus was not alone in his understanding that believers in resurrection understood resurrected bodies to be distinct from those that humans possess in the present world. If the Essene afterlife is incorporeal and other-worldly—and if the Sadducean denial of immortality is decidedly this-worldly—then the Pharisaic belief, as Josephus describes it, is somewhere in between, right where Josephus suggests the Pharisees' theology belongs in general. So we find, once again, that we have in Josephus a rather reliable guide to ancient Jewish theological disputes. As we will find in the next section, Josephus also allows us to understand better other disputes among Jews—related to the afterlife—concerning martyrdom and suicide.

Afterlife, Martyrdom, and Suicide

There are three important ways Josephus's description of Essene afterlife beliefs differ from his accounts of the Pharisaic beliefs, two of which were discussed in the previous section. The first is that the accounts concerning the Essenes are absolutely bereft of any hints of bodily resurrection:

Josephus's Essenes believe in the immortality of the soul, but not any form of reembodiment. Related to this is the fact that the Essenes are depicted as adopting rather negative attitudes toward their mortal bodies. Viewing the body as a prison, the Essenes see death as liberation. The third difference between Josephus's Pharisees and Essenes—the one we have not yet discussed—concerns their attitude toward martyrdom.

According to Josephus's account in *War* 2, the Essenes were fearless (2.151):

> Even so, the war with the Romans tried their souls through and through by every variety of test. Racked and twisted, burnt and broken, and made to pass through every instrument of torture, in order to induce them to blaspheme their lawgiver or to eat some forbidden thing, they refused to yield to either demand, nor ever once did they cringe to their persecutors or shed a tear. Smiling in their agonies and mildly deriding their tormentors, they cheerfully resigned their souls, as if[72] they would receive them back again. (2.152–53)[73]

The account is strange, if for no other reason than the fact that Josephus does not elsewhere indicate that the Romans forced Jews to commit blasphemy or eat forbidden foods.[74] But this is precisely what we hear of in 2 Maccabees and, especially, 4 Maccabees. Indeed, as Steve Mason has pointed out, this passage is rife with allusions to 4 Maccabees in particular, where we also find depictions of submission to cruel tortures,[75] as well as a motivating belief in immortality (7.19–20, 13.17, 16.25, 17.5). Indeed, the transition from the passage quoted above to the discussion of Essene immortality discussed in the previous section makes the causal connection quite clear: for Josephus, it would appear that martyrdom is motivated or encouraged by the belief in an unembodied immortality. Perhaps he thought that the fear of death and bodily harm can be more easily overcome when one believes that the future life will be unembodied.[76]

We can find striking confirmation that Josephus is trying to establish a connection between risking death (even suicidal behavior) and believing in unembodied afterlife, especially in *Jewish War*. Indeed, the earliest reference to immortality in *War* appears when Josephus relates the efforts of some hotheaded youths to remove the golden eagle Herod placed on the temple gate (1.648–55).[77] The insurgents were, Josephus relates, inspired by two "sophists"—popular experts in the nation's laws[78]—who persuaded their disciples to take this action,

> telling them that, even if the action proved hazardous, it was a noble deed to die for the law of one's country; for the souls of those who come to such an end attained immortality and an eternally abiding sense of felicity; it was only the ignoble, uninitiated in their philosophy, who clung in their ignorance to life and preferred death on a sick-bed to that of a hero. (1.650)[79]

So persuaded—and believing that Herod was dying—the disciples took action, daringly (and acrobatically) hacking at the eagle with hatchets. Not surprisingly, they were quickly arrested and brought before Herod. The king wonders at their at joy when facing death; they respond affirming their confidence that greater happiness will follow their deaths (1.653). Aroused by anger, Herod gets up from his sickbed (1.654; see also 1.651) to ensure that the rebels receive the deaths they seek. The popularity of the teachers now evaporates, and the people—fearing Herod's wrath—agree that the rebels and teachers should die for their crimes. Herod burns them alive. The eagle was removed, but Josephus's narrative can leave the reader wondering: was courting—indeed, achieving—death the best way to go about it? We will return to this narrative and the question it raises when we consider issues relating to martyrdom later in this chapter.

At the other end of Josephus's *Jewish War*—in the famous narrative of Masada in Book 7[80]—the expressions of belief in an unembodied afterlife are once again depicted as motivativating suicidal behavior.[81] When Flavius Silva's siege of Masada has progressed to the extent that Roman victory appears inevitable, the rebel leader Eleazar is depicted as delivering two extensive speeches to his followers, encouraging them to take their own lives. The first of these (7.323–36) makes arguments more or less closely related to the principles that readers of *War* would have already associated with the radical rebels. Since they refused to accept Roman rule before (7.323–24, see also 2.117–18, 7.254–58), why should they let themselves fall to the Romans now? Moreover, since the only benefit the Romans could derive from the victory would be to enslave the survivors (7.326–27, 335–36, 387), why not deny the Romans the reward they wish?[82] The second speech, however, includes Josephus's longest oration on life after death (341–88). Josephus imagines Eleazar drawing explicit comparisons with foreign (this time Indian) ideas, all the while clearly alluding to well-known passages from various Greek philosophical and dramatic classics.[83] What matters for our concerns is that we find here a striking development of the themes already presented in Josephus's description of the Essenes. The freedom-loving rebel leader is depicted as describing the soul as imprisoned in the body, such that death comes as a liberation (7.344–48; compare 2.154–55). "Life, not death, is humanity's misfortune" (7.344), Eleazar states, balancing the life-hating sentiments of Ecclesiastes (2.17, 3.16–4.3) with the other-worldly hopes of Plato (e.g. *Phaedo* 80d–81d).[84] So once again, the hope for incorporeal immortality combines with disdain for the body and earthly life to yield suicidal behavior. But curiously, while the Essene hope for a beatific immortality is balanced by a fear of postmortem retribution (*War* 2.156–57), Eleazar's description of immortality curiously—and conspicuously—lacks any concern with punishments for wicked souls.[85]

In between these two speeches there is one more, an oration ostensibly delivered by Josephus himself at Jotapata as part of his unsuccessful bid to persuade his fellow defenders to surrender to Rome rather than commit mass suicide (3.355–91).[86] Josephus offers a number of arguments against suicide in general, and against doing so in the present situation in particular. Granting that it is honorable to die for liberty when necessary, why (3.365–68) should one do so when the Romans have offered an escape? And why perish for a freedom that has already been lost? As for the more general arguments, Josephus points out that suicide is an impiety toward God, and contrary to nature—just as no animals commit suicide, no humans should (3.370–71). Respecting life as a gift from God, one should depart from life only in accordance with divine laws (3.371–74). On a natural or lawful death, one can hope for three rewards: eternal renown, security for progeny, and a better life after death (3.374). But punishments await those who sinfully take their own lives: agony after death for the sinful deceased, as well as suffering here on earth for the suicide's progeny (3.375).

Regarding their appeals to immortality, there are clear similarities between Josephus's and Eleazar's speeches, including, once again, allusions to Greek literature. Similarity, however, should not surprise— Josephus, of course, penned *all* of the speeches in *War*, in keeping with Greco-Roman historiographic fashions. But the conundrum here is how one speech appeals to life after death to persuade suicide, while the other does so in order to argue against it. A number of scholars, taking the overall perspectives toward the noble death and afterlife in these two speeches as generally similar, focus on the variable of "necessity"—in Josephus's speech, suicide at Jotapata was not necessary (3.365), while in Eleazar's, suicide at Masada has become so (7.358–60, 370).[87] But this is at best a partial argument: if the situation at Masada has now become hopeless, the rebels only have themselves to blame for this, as Josephus himself emphasizes (7.262), and as Josephus depicts Eleazar as admitting (7.332). So we do well to look for other variables, too, and indeed, there are a number of important differences between the afterlife sentiments Josephus depicts himself as expressing and those he later depicts Eleazar as articulating. First, Josephus does not view the soul as imprisoned in the body. To the contrary, body and soul are "fond companions" (3.362: τὰ φίλτατα). The soul is a "portion of the deity" (θεοῦ μοῖρα) that is "housed" (ἐνοικίζεται)—not imprisoned—in the body (3.372; see also 374). Therefore—and this is the second difference—the decision to end life ought remain in God's hands (3.371). Suicide is not heroic but cowardly (3.365–68); and taking one's own life or that of close kin is sinful (3.362, 369, 379–80). Third, unlike Eleazar—but in agreement with the Essenes—Josephus depicts himself as concerned with both rewards for the righteous and punishments for the wicked after death (374–75). Eleazar's affirmation of a beatific immortality, by contrast, in unbalanced by any fear of postmortem punishments. Finally, Josephus's views as expressed here are decidedly more materialistic than those of the Essenes or Eleazar. Wicked souls will be punished in the hereafter, but sufferings may visit their progeny here on earth as well (3.375). As for the future life of the righteous, Josephus expresses a hope not just in immortality, but in an eventual reembodiment (3.374), the same sort of resurrection belief he ascribes to the Pharisees earlier (2.163). Moreover, Josephus's more body-oriented perspective can also be seen toward the end of the speech, when he brings up the concern with burial (377–78).

These observations suggest that we ought to consider these matters further. How do we account for these differences between Eleazar's afterlife hopes and Josephus's? Can Eleazar's suicidal behavior be correlated with his afterlife hopes in some way? How deep is the causal connection Josephus sees between the Essenes' willingness to undergo martyrdom and their hope for incorporeal immortality? Is it the case that Josephus intends to associate martyrdom and suicide with an incorporeal immortality, as opposed to the reembodiment others hoped for? And what, then, are Josephus's own views of immortality and martyrdom? What does he want his readers to learn and do?

Maccabees, Martyrs, and Murders

The evidence we have just reviewed is complicated, and a number of questions need to be addressed in order to bring greater clarity to the understanding of these matters. Some scholars associate Josephus's apparent praise for Essene endurance with an admiration and amazement for the suicides at Masada (7.388, 406), with the result that Josephus emerges as a spokesman for the "noble death" with praise for the "martyrs" of Masada.[88] In my view, recent treatments have not paid due attention to key variables that differentiate the assorted accounts of noble death in Josephus's works, and as a result some of the messages of *Jewish War* (admittedly subtle ones) have been missed. One problem concerns definitions—categories such as noble death and martyrdom have expanded too far, so as to jumble together phenomena that need to be differentiated. A related problem concerns the ways these definitions are constructed. Studies of noble death and martyrdom often focus on the structural components of the subnarratives, such as the trial or death scene—surely an essential step—without as much regard for the equally important place these disparate subnarratives take within the broader works (e.g., 2 Maccabees or *Jewish War*).[89] As a result of these two tendencies, studies have not yet noticed the degree to which *Jewish War* hinges not around quasi-sacrificial martyrdoms, but around their inversion: sacrilegious murders.

In order to bring some sense to the disparate forms of noble death and their multifarious motivations and aftermaths, we need to take a step back and present a preliminary typology of three types of noble deaths that appear in ancient Jewish literature more broadly: "Maccabees," "martyrs," and "murders."[90] All three of these models are at least echoed in Josephus's works, though only two of them (the first and the third) are developed fully. The third is developed more fully in Josephus than anywhere else; and, as we will see, it is the antithesis, or inversion, of the mode that seems to move Josephus the least ("martyrs").

Maccabees

In a nutshell, I intend with this term to refer to the nonmartyrological death stories of Maccabean heroes, especially as told in 1 Maccabees. While 1 Maccabees remains the paradigmatic expression, the model is also echoed in *Antiquities*, and not just in the cases where Josephus paraphrases his Maccabean source. Key elements of this mode of noble death narrative include (1) a decision by the heroes to risk or accept premature violent death at the hands of foreign enemies, (2) in order to live by the law or defeat an enemy, (3) comforted by the knowledge that their deaths will be noble. However, (4) the lesson drawn is typically a negative one. While the nobility of the death remains revered, the message to the reader is not to imitate the deceased, but rather to be more moderate regarding the law (less sinful or less extreme) and more careful regarding one's military exploits.

In 1 Maccabees, the first and paradigmatic example of this kind of noble death concerns those who refused to fight on the Sabbath (1 Macc. 2.29–41). The heroes in this story choose to die assured of their innocence rather than fight, lest they profane the Sabbath day (2.34–37). The enemy easily dispenses of them, such that thousands of men, women, and livestock are killed (2.38). But their nobility and heroism impel Mattathias and his friends—the real heroes—to make a startling decision. Rather than die like that, they declare (2.41): "Let us fight against anyone who comes to attack us on the Sabbath day; let us not all die as our kindred died in their hiding places."[91]

A number of other stories in 1 Maccabees are in more or less the same vein, including the deaths of Eleazar Avaran (6.40–47) and Judas (1 Macc. 9.1–22). In each of these cases, although the death in question is revered as noble, the praise is qualified, and balanced with a critical evaluation of the hero. In the case of Judas's death, the narrator makes it clear— through the advice given by Judas's subordinates (9.9)—that escape is possible, leading perhaps to other victories. Judas, however, chooses death with glory (9.10). Though his wish is fulfilled—and he is indeed praised for his heroism (9.20–22)—it is his brother Jonathan who lives to achieve the full victory (9.73). In the case of Eleazar, too, the criticism is oblique, but discernable nonetheless. His desire is to save his people and seek an everlasting name (6.44). Although some of the enemy fighters are killed, the result of Eleazar's decision is his death, his army's flight, and his enemy's victory (45–47). Far from achieving glory and an everlasting name, his narrative merits all of four verses. In short, this mode of noble death is ultimately an unfortunate and avoidable one. The heroes should be revered, but their deaths should not be emulated or imitated.

Josephus's narratives also contain examples of this model. Of course, his own accounts of the Maccabean era closely follow 1 Maccabees,[92] so Josephus, too, presents the noble, but still somewhat mistaken, deaths of the strict Sabbath keepers (*Ant.* 12.272–74) as well as the heroic but unsuccessful battles led by Eleazar Avaran (*War* 1.42–44; *Ant.* 12.373–74), and Judas (*War* 1.45–47; *Ant.* 12.420–34). Other examples of the warrior death model include Josephus's elaborations of deaths of Samson (*Ant.* 5.317) and Saul (6.344–50, 370–72).[93] It is clear that these premature violent deaths are in one sense noble: these figures fight to the end, making the most of their final moments, taking some of the enemy down with them (Samson: 5.317; Saul: 6.344–45; Judas: *War* 1.47, *Ant.* 12.430). Josephus, characteristically for a general, has praise for those who died heroic deaths on battlefields. Yet in the cases of Samson and Saul, Josephus also makes clear that the premature violent deaths bring conclusions to lives led poorly, characterized by passions and violence (*Ant.* 5.301–2, 317; 6.262–68, 378). Certainly, these figures do not present role models to be followed, whether in life or death. Even in the parallels to 1 Maccabees, Josephus allows the reader to discern, beneath the valor, that the deceased could have decided things differently. With regard to *War's* account of Eleazar Avaran's death in particular, Josephus is even more emphatic than 1 Maccabees that martial derring-do is simply another way of courting death (*War* 1.44).[94] The takeaway for the reader in all these cases is to lead a different life—characterized by greater virtue or better decisions—and to hope for a longer one. It may be good to die a death of valor. But it's better to live and experience the victory.

Martyrs

Martyrdom is quite different from the noble deaths described earlier. Although the term "martyrdom" rarely appears in Jewish sources, I suggest that we retain the term here—as has become scholarly custom—to refer to the self-chosen premature violent (but nonbattlefield) deaths of the heroes whose reverence for God and divine law is placed far above their love of life.[95] The Jewish martyrdom narratives from the second temple period (principally 2 and 4 Maccabees) exhibit distinct features that allow us to differentiate the deaths of the martyrs described here from those of the warriors described earlier and the murders to be described later.[96]

For our purposes, the key elements of martyrdom include (1) a decision by a righteous person to risk or accept premature violent death at the hands of foreign power (typically off the battlefield), (2) in order to die nobly rather than break the law, (3) comforted by a hope for a better future life, (4) with the result that God's mercy is swayed by the innocence of the martyrs, so that the enemies of the Jewish people are defeated. After the martyrdoms, oppression ends, and victory soon results, not so much from the might or valor of warriors, but from God's mercy, as swayed by the martyrs.[97] In both 2 and 4 Maccabees, Eleazar, the mother, and her seven sons die the martyr's death, refusing to worship idols or eat forbidden foods. In both texts, as we have seen, the martyrs comfort themselves with hopes for a better life (resurrection in 2 Macc.; immortality in 4 Macc.).[98] And in both texts, it is the deaths of the martyrs that sways God's mercy, and brings about the subsequent victories (2 Macc. 6.12–17, 7.32–38, 8.1–4; 4 Macc. 1.11, 6.28–29, 9.24, 12.17, 17.19–24, 18.4). Indeed, in 4 Maccabees in particular, the martyrs' deaths serve quasi-sacrificial functions, expiating for the people's sins (1.11, 6.29, 17.21–22).[99] An interesting additional example in 2 Maccabees involves the suicidal death of Razis (14.37–46). In this case, the setting is a battlefield, not a religious persecution—though the text implies that Razis has already risked his life in earlier persecutions (14.38). Facing overwhelming forces, Razis chooses suicide over surrender, by falling on his own sword (14.39–42). This hero, however, did not succeed in killing himself immediately. He then threw himself off of a wall, finally tearing out his own entrails (14.43–46). Unlike the deaths of Eleazar or Judas as described in 1 Maccabees—but quite like the deaths of the martyrs described in 2 Maccabees 6 and 7—the death of Razis is followed by a dramatic Jewish victory, and the death of the enemy, Nicanor, who had instigated Razis's arrest (2 Macc. 17.1–36).[100] In short, martyrs are models in both their lives and their deaths. Their lives are ones of virtue, and their apparently unjust earthly deaths bring better afterlives to themselves but also—and perhaps more important—better earthly fortunes to the Jewish people.

As noted, Josephus's accounts of the Maccabean era follow 1 Maccabees, and his account of the Antiochene persecution is no exception. While 1 Maccabees is aware of the persecution and the steadfastness of the many suffering righteous Jews (1 Macc. 1.54–64), it is the zealous heroism of Mattathias, his sons, and their followers that turns the tide (2.1–28). Similarly, in *Jewish War* and *Antiquities*, the persecution is remembered, briefly, as an anonymous tragedy (*War* 1.34–35; *Ant.* 12.253–56). The victims are not promised an afterlife, and their deaths are not said to achieve anything in this world either. The agonies of those persecuted in the days of Antiochus only impact history insofar as their sufferings encourage the Maccabees to rebel (*War* 1.35).

Indeed, no single narrative anywhere in *War* or *Antiquities* shares all of the criteria for a full-blown martyrdom as described earlier, whether relating to the Maccabean era, the war against Rome, or any other period of Jewish history. Even Josephus's description of religiously oriented persecution of Jews in Antioch lacks all the key characteristics of full-blown martyrdom (*War* 7.50–53): there are no named righteous victims to remember fondly, no accounts of heroic endurance, no appeals to immortality, and no earthly good comes out of the sufferings. But Josephus seems aware of the kinds of martyrdoms described in 2 and 4 Maccabees, as demonstrated not only by the brief acknowledgments of the Antiochene persecutions but also by his description of Essene martyrdom (*War* 2.152–53). Like the Maccabean martyrs, the Essenes are depicted by Josephus as choosing to die rather than eat forbidden foods. Presumably, off the battlefield—and offering no physical resistance in this context—the Essenes heroically withstand cruel tortures. Indeed, going a step further than 2 or 4 Maccabees, the Essenes even suffer happily (*War* 2.153; compare 3.321; *Apion* 1.42).[101] And just as with the martyrdoms of 2 and 4 Maccabees, the Essenes are remembered as comforting themselves with hopes for a better afterlife. Moreover, as we have already pointed out, Josephus's description of Essene martyrdom unmistakably echoes 4 Maccabees in its particular descriptions of tortures and endurance.[102] But there is one essential difference between the ways these stories are developed in 2 and 4 Maccabees and the way they are echoed by Josephus. There is no transformative earthly aftermath to the Essenes' deaths. The Essenes die nobly, to be sure. And perhaps they even achieve some postmortem reward for their righteousness. But their deaths do not achieve anything on earth, other than, perhaps, making a point.[103] Their postmortem fame is at best anonymous, and reserved by Josephus to a mere few lines. God's mercy was not swayed, and subsequent Jewish victories did not come about.

Perhaps the clearest example of a somewhat successful martyrdom in Josephus's works concerns the aforementioned tale of the two teachers, their disciples, and Herod's eagle (*War* 1.648–55; see also *Ant.* 17.146–63). Risking death—and encouraged by an expectation of an ensured, unembodied immortality—the teachers' disciples succeed in removing the eagle from Herod's temple. But the subsequent deaths of the teachers and their students leaves one wondering whether the achievement was worth the cost.[104] An interesting contrast is provided by two subsequent stories: Pilate bringing standards to Jerusalem (*War* 2.169–74; see also *Ant.* 18.55–59) and Caligula's plan to have his own statue installed in the temple (*War* 2.184–203; see also *Ant.* 18.257–309).[105] In both cases, masses gather to declare their willingness to risk death. But the Roman overlords in these two cases are unwilling to engage in such mass slaughter, and back down. In these two cases, the goal is achieved in the end without bloodshed. Could the teachers have achieved the removal of the eagle in a similar way? Since Herod was on his deathbed, would it have been more prudent to wait until after his death to seek the eagle's removal?

In *Against Apion*, Josephus boasts of a Jewish willingness to submit to death in order to demonstrate fidelity to the law (1.42–43, 2.232–35). The martyrs he has in mind in this instance are motivated by a hope not just in immortality, but in eventual reembodiment as well (2.218, compare *War* 3.374). Moreover, in this passage Josephus clearly differentiates between willing[106] submission to torture and martyrdom by small numbers of righteous Jews, when matters of Jewish law are at stake, and the easier deaths—including suicides?—of many on battlefields (*Ap.* 2.232–35). In this passage—surely Josephus's highest praise of martyrdom—we find that he praises the martyrs' endurance, highlighting the impact their heroism has on the Jews' enemies. But even here, we do not find what is characteristic of the ancient Jewish martyrologies we do have: the belief that martyrdom sways God and changes the course of human history for the betterment of the Jewish people.

It is worth recalling at this juncture, for the sake of comparison, the well-known rabbinic ambivalence toward martyrdom.[107] On the one hand, certain rabbinic heroes—Rabbi Akiba prominent among them— are remembered for having risked death in order to teach Torah, suffering until death as a result (e.g., Akiba: *b. Berakhot* 61b; Hananya ben Teradyon: *b. Avodah Zarah* 8a).[108] The martyrdom stories at the heart of 2 and 4 Maccabees are also echoed in rabbinic literature, though the setting is transferred from the Seleucid to the Roman era (*b. Gittin* 57b; *Lamentations Rabbah* 1.16).[109] And we even find instances of children choosing suicide (by drowning) to avoid being sexually abused by the Romans, with the traditions assuring doubters that even the drowned will be resurrected (*b. Gittin* 57b; *Lamentations Rabbah* 1.16).[110] On the other hand, the few rabbinic martyrs find their counterweight in Yohanan ben Zakkai—who, like Josephus, shunned martyrdom in favor of survival.[111] Indeed, rabbinic literature limits the legitimate causes for martyrdom to three grave sins (idolatry, sexual sins, and murder). In all other instances—including notably, the food laws[112]—rabbinic law requires Jews to figure out some way to live by the laws (see Lev. 18.5) as opposed to dying for them (*b. Sanhedrin* 74a).[113] At the same time, the tannaitic promise of resurrection for all Israel (*m. Sanhedrin* 10.1) undercuts the force of the afterlife guarantees assumed in some martyr traditions and echoed by the hopes expressed by certain would-be martyrs in the works of Josephus (e.g., *War* 1.650, 653). Finally, it is imperative to appreciate the significance of the fact that the rabbis date these martyr-doms—including the stories of the mother and her seven sons—to the post-70 CE, Roman era. For the rabbis, as for Josephus before them, mar-tyrdom is not a prelude to victory, as in 2 or 4 Maccabees. Martyrdom, rather, is the aftermath of defeat, and a divinely ordained defeat at that (as we will see in chapter 5).

Murders in the Sanctuary

If full-blown, transformative martyrdom is largely absent from Josephus's works, there is another form of transformative noble death that plays, roughly, the same role in *Jewish War* that the martyrdoms play in 2 and 4 Maccabees. But these events differ from martyrdoms in a number of important respects. Martyrdoms are quasi-sacrificial deaths, after which the innocence and purity of the victim sways God's mercy. These deaths are sacrilegious killings, after which the guilt of the murderers kindles God's wrath. Although some formal similarities with martyrdoms could also be identified, these murders differ significantly from the martyrdoms discussed in the previous section. The pattern looks something like this: the heroes in question (1) make a decision to risk or accept premature violent death at the hands of fellow Jews (2) in order to publicly condemn wickedness among the Jewish people, (3) but then suffer sacrilegious deaths at the hands of the wicked Jews, (4) with the result that God's anger is inflamed and the Jewish people suffer national catastrophe.

Alone among the three forms of noble death in the present typology, this one has a clear scriptural precedent in the brief story of the murder of the prophet Zechariah (son of the priest Jehoiada; 2 Chron. 24.17–24).[114] Late in the reign of King Joash of Judah, the king has led the people astray, abandoning the house of God, and worshiping sacred poles and idols (24.17–18). The prophet Zechariah bravely confronts the people, con-demning them for their transgression (24.20). Far from listening to the prophet, the people stone him to death—at the command of the king—in the court of the temple (24.21). As he lies dying, the prophet calls for his revenge (24.22). Indeed, in short order a small contingent of Aramean soldiers arrives, and God delivers Judah's more numerous army into their hands, so as to execute judgment on Joash (24.23–24). The king is subse-quently murdered for his crimes (including the killing of the prophet) and is not even buried in the royal tomb (24.25).

It appears that this brief biblical story had a profound effect on Josephus. Of course, he retells the story (*Ant.* 9.166–72), and he includes in his paraphrase each of the key elements we have identified: a brave prophet is killed by the people, in the temple, bringing about God's wrath and a national catastrophe. But the powerful influence this kind of tale has on Josephus can be seen by subsequent examples in *Antiquities*, as well as (especially) *Jewish War*.

The very first postbiblical episode Josephus relates fits this pattern very closely, though not quite perfectly (*Ant.* 11.297–301).[115] Immediately on concluding his paraphrase of the book of Esther, Josephus seeks to explain why the Persian king Artaxerxes II[116] succeeded in defiling the sanctuary. Although there is no prophetic confrontation in this story, there is a murder in the sanctuary—a priestly fratricide, no less (298–99). This sacrilege provokes God, with the result that the people are defeated and the temple is defiled by the Persians (300). The pattern recurs with the murder of the rainmaker Onias (*Ant.* 14.22–28).[117] Once again, a prophetic figure is murdered by his own people, this time for refusing to place a curse on Aristobulus and his forces (22–24). Sure enough, the people suffer mightily for the sin of killing a prophet (25–28). Somewhat similar is Josephus's treatment of the murder of John the Baptist (18.116–19)—the execution of a virtuous figure is followed by the defeat of a Jewish army.[118] The pattern clearly appears once again, and this time at a particularly key moment. In *Antiquities* 20.160–66, Josephus relates the conspiracy to kill the priest Jonathan, during the reign of Felix. Although Jonathan was no prophet, he is described as admonishing Felix to improve his administration; and "incessant rebukes are annoying to those who choose to do wrong" (162). So Felix arranges for Jonathan's murder at the hands of the Sicarii (164). Although it is not explicit that the priest was killed at the temple, that may be implied since the killers' cover was their intent to worship God. Regardless, Josephus is quick to point out that the Sicarii carried out other murders in the temple (165). And divine judgment is the result:

> This is the reason why, in my opinion, even God himself, for loathing of their impiety, turned away from our city and, because he deemed the temple to be no longer a clean dwelling place for him, brought the Romans upon us and purification by fire upon the city, while he inflicted slavery upon us together with our wives and children; for he wished to chasten us by these calamities. (*Ant.* 20.166)

In *Antiquities*, the scriptural story of the sacrilegious murder of Zechariah serves as a model for explaining subsequent traumas, including, in *Antiquities* 20.166, the destruction of the second temple.[119]

If this pattern peppers *Antiquities*, it plays an even more central role in *Jewish War*. The most elaborate examples appear about halfway through—at what Steve Mason identifies as the central, turning point of the narrative[120]—when two former high priests, Ananus and Jesus, are depicted as bravely delivering speeches encouraging the people to turn against the Zealots and abandon their rebellion.[121] Condemning the people for their internecine strife and for committing bloodshed in the temple (4.162–92, 238–69), both of these figures are, in turn, killed along with their followers; the temple is left defiled by blood, and the priests' corpses are left unburied, to be devoured by beasts (4.312–16, 324).[122] As Josephus's encomium on their deaths makes clear, these figures were heroes whose sacrilegious murders swayed God to abandon the Jews and deliver the temple to the Romans (318–25).[123] Yet the sinful bloodbath continues, with the Zealots next turning on the virtuous (and wealthy) Zechariah, son of Baris: he, too, is killed in the temple, after attesting to his innocence (334–44).

To my knowledge, the fullest development of this scripturally inspired pattern is to be found in the works of Josephus. But we can find examples and echoes elsewhere, including rabbinic sources.[124] A particularly striking instance appears in Acts, which elaborates on the story of Stephen's execution (often called a martyrdom; 6.8–7.60).[125] True to the form as we have described it, Stephen prophetically condemns his compatriots for sinfulness (6.8–10), leading to a conspiracy against him (6.11–15). Using his trial as an opportunity to maintain his innocence, Stephen delivers one last oration (7.2–53). Dragged from the city, Stephen meets his death by stoning. On the one hand the fact that the killing is completed outside the city deviates from the model. On the other, it is rather clear that the memory of Zechariah's murder hovers over the incident. Zechariah is, it appears, mentioned earlier in Luke 11.50–51 (//Matt. 23.35), and Stephen himself speaks of the killing of prophets (Acts 7.52). Quite clearly, the murder of Zechariah lurks in the background of Acts 6–7.[126] But even more important for our purposes is the similar role this murder plays in Acts compared to the murders of the priests in *War*: in Acts, too, the lynching of Stephen is a pivotal moment, heralding God's rejection of the temple, and introducing a young man named Saul (7.58), whose conversion and teaching will occupy much of the rest of Acts.

It is important to admit that we could, if we wish, call all these deaths martyrdoms. And since all depends on how we define our terms, it would not necessarily be incorrect to do so. But the distinction we have drawn here allows us to appreciate the way these particular murder narratives constitute virtual inversions of the paradigmatic martyrdom stories as related in 2 and 4 Maccabees. In 2 and (especially) 4 Maccabees, the noble, quasi-sacrificial deaths of the innocent martyrs at the hands of foreign enemies secure God's mercy, eventually leading to Jewish victories. In the instances we have seen in this section, shameful, sacrilegious murders of prophets and priests are committed by the Jewish people. This in turn conjures God's wrath, bringing about Jewish military defeat and the destruction of the temple.

Suicide, Masada, and Murder-Suicide

We can now turn back to the Masada narrative. The articulate, emotional speeches, the appeal to immortality, and the defenders' rugged determination to deny Rome the spoils of victory lead some to view this account as a martyrdom.[127] But the typology we have laid out suggests otherwise. The Masada narrative lacks the key element of the fully worked out martyrdoms of 2 and 4 Maccabees: God's anger is not assuaged, and salvation—whether in heaven or on earth—is not forthcoming.[128] To the contrary, Masada seals the Jewish defeat. The greater differences between the Masada narrative and martyrdoms concern, however, not the aftermath but the preliminaries. The defenders of Masada were the sinful Sicarii—the first to put into deadly action the dangerously mistaken beliefs attributed to Judas the Galilean (*War* 2.117–18):[129] they refused to accept any political authority other than God, and they were willing to kill their own kin in order to further their political program (2.254–57, 7.254–62) or simply to secure supplies (e.g., the Passover massacre at Ein Gedi: 4.398–405).[130] As we have noted, Josephus has Eleazar recognize his faction's sins (e.g., 7.329), and Josephus himself minces no words condemning their murderous behavior (7.259–62). So it is unwise even to compare the deaths at Masada to the suicidal death of Razis in 2 Maccabees 14.[131] Razis's suicide brings an unjust end to a life led by virtue, but at least a Jewish victory will quickly ensue. The suicides (and murders) at Masada bring a just end to lives lived sinfully (7.271–74), and nothing but Jewish defeats are in store for the Sicarii or anyone else who continues to fight (7.437–42).

The contrasts just noted between the stories of Razis in 2 Maccabees and Masada in *Jewish War* highlight the vast range of sentiments that are expressed in second temple period stories of suicide and voluntary death. On occasion, the suicidal death of a military leader on the battlefield is seen as paradigmatic of military valor. This is clearly the case in the tale of Razis in 2 Maccabees and in Josephus's treatment of the deaths of Samson and Saul. But even here, there's a key difference: Josephus's evaluations of Samson and Saul follow both scripture and Josephus's general proclivity in depicting these characters as demonstrating both heroic and sinful qualities.[132] Even as he praises Samson's heroic death, Josephus notes his shortcomings (*Ant.* 5.317). Similarly, Josephus does not hide Saul's murderous deeds, elaborating on his guilt for the massacre at Nob (*Ant.* 6.242–70, esp. 262–68, recasting and expanding 1 Sam. 21.1–22.1; see also *Ant.* 6.378).[133] In other cases, Josephus follows scriptural precedents, describing semisuicidal deaths on the battlefield as a clear sign of divine punishment (e.g., Abimelech: *Ant.* 5.251–53, following Judg. 9.50–57; Zimri: *Ant.* 8.309–11, following 1 Kings 16.18–19; see also *Ant.* 8.314–15).[134]

Most of Josephus's other accounts of suicidal death—and there are a great many of these stories—fall clearly into one of two other categories. In a number of cases, suicidal deaths are one of many tragic or pathetic events involved in Josephus's descriptions of military defeats. When fighters realize their situation is hopeless and death is certain, Josephus frequently relates that the soon-to-be-vanquished throw themselves off precipices, into rivers, or onto raging fires (curiously, suicides by sword are relatively rare in these cases).[135] Not dissimilar are the narratives of priests who choose to die as their temples burn.[136] The frequency with which such suicide notices appear suggests that the motif has become a stock one for Josephus, likely inspired by Greco-Roman models.[137] Indeed, a number of the accounts are rather formulaic: the reasons preventing escape or surrender are presented, the decision is made, and the deed is described in gory detail.[138] Even so, the historical possibility that despondent Jews resorted to suicide in such situations cannot be excluded. Perhaps Jewish rebels were in fact encouraged by the same Hellenistic influences that have permeated the literary accounts.[139] Either way, these stories fit into Josephus's general message: the rebellion against Rome was a tragic mistake, with deadly consequences; but when all military hope is lost, there can be a modicum of valor in suicide. Typically, however, the suicides that Josephus explicitly respects take place only *after* fighting to the end (see *Ant.* 5.317, 6.344–50). This important element is lacking in Josephus's account of Masada.[140]

But there are a few instances where Josephus makes abundantly clear that things can go too far—and not only in his speech at Jotapata. One such story appears when he describes Herod's campaign against the cave-dwelling brigands (λῃστάς) of Arbel (*War* 1.304–13; *Ant.* 14.415–30). These robbers were, we are told, guilty of "evils no less than war" (*War* 1.304). Herod attacked the brigands in their high cliff caves by lowering troops with ropes (1.310–11). Although Herod offered to take prisoners, most fought to the death (311). But when a mother wished to save her seven children, the patriarch of the family refused, slaughtering each one by the sword, finally casting the corpses from the heights. Herod, we are told, looked on with dread, begging the man to stop. Finally, the murderous father threw himself off the cliff, on the dead bodies of his murdered family. Surely it is notable that even Herod—the brutal despot who will himself later murder adult members of his own family—is depicted as being horrified by the father's slaughter of his wife and children. This brief narrative—the first mass murder-suicide recorded in *War*—is an important clue for how we are to read the Masada episode. Self-slaughter by fighters after losing a battle is one thing; killing your own family members is quite another matter, one that makes even a murderous despot quaver.

Josephus tells of another mass murder-suicide, this one at the beginning of the great war (2.469–76). Once again, the person at the center of it—Simon, son of Saul, of Scythopolis—has excelled in internecine warfare (2.470). As a fitting punishment to his killing of fellow Jews (471)—but also as a sad result of trusting his non-Jewish neighbors (476)—Simon finds himself trapped with his wife, children, and parents. In a fit of rage, he kills them all and then himself (473–76). Thackeray, for one, labeled the episode as a tale of "heroic death."[141] But the judgment dispensed by Josephus—and ostensibly articulated by Simon himself (472–74)—suggests otherwise.

I will grant that Simon's tale—and the Masada episode, too—resembles in a few resepects the heroically suicidal death of Saul, especially as related in *Antiquities*: a murderous man is able to muster the strength to die with perhaps a modicum of dignity, accepting his deserved death while refusing to yield to Israel's enemies to the last (see esp. 6.344–50). Moreover, Josephus does not intend readers to live lives modeled on Saul's (6.262–68, 378). But Saul's death is something different: he was able to show his best at his last moments, fighting honorably to the last without directly killing any of his own kin (344–46). Can we say the same for Simon of Scythopolis or the defenders of Masada?

Some interpreters have suggested that deaths at Masada are in some way redemptive—as if the "defenders" atoned for their sins by their suicidal deaths.[142] But even if the death of a criminal can atone for grievous sins (so, e.g., *m. Sanhedrin* 9.5, *m. Yoma* 8.8), how does killing of innocent women and children figure into this picture? Not only should we stop speaking of "martyrs" at Masada; we should stop speaking of "suicides" at Masada, and insist on speaking, more accurately, of "murder-suicides."[143] While heroic suicide of warriors on a losing battlefield is a stock element of Josephus's stories, mass murder-suicides, including the slaughter of women and children, are rarer, and not something he sympathized with in any particular way.

At Masada, the take-away message is a negative one. Perhaps the *Romans* will be amazed and impressed, drawn in by these figures' philosophizing, and less troubled by the deaths of women and children (see Tacitus, *Histories* 5.5.3).[144] But if so, then Josephus's Masada narrative is rife with irony—double meanings that would be read differently by Jews and Romans.[145] For every praise, there is also a condemnation; the suicides' philosophizing is offset by their madness (7.389). For his Jewish readers, if not for his Greco-Roman readers as well, the message is not to emulate these figures, whether in life or death. The story is a cautionary tale, whose messages are not difficult to discern: refusal to accept the sovereignty of Rome is suicide; the killing of one's own is a crime that will not go unpunished.[146]

Whatever nobility the rebels manage to eke out of their suicidal last moments, their deaths are simply reflections of their guilt. As they were the first to rise up in revolt by adopting the practice of killing their own kin, so at the end they suffer the just punishment for their misdeeds (7.259–62, 271–74).[147] These crimes include not only the murders they enact themselves (2.254–57), but also the sacrilegious murders of Ananus and Jesus—for the perpetration of these killings involves enacting lessons the Sicarii themselves have taught the nation (7.262, 329). Josephus has also not forgotten here the Passover massacre at Ein Gedi (4.398–405), and Jewish readers would certainly not miss the powerful irony that the murder-suicides occurred on the fifteenth of Xanthicus—Passover (7.401, compare 5.98–99, *Ant.* 2.308). Living to witness the destruction of their sacred shrine, they are doomed to kill themselves, murdering their wives and children, in madness (*War* 7.389–97), desecrating once again the holy day they besmirched years before. Even their final wish—that *all* the defenders would die this way (7.398)—is thwarted by some sagacious women who hide with some children, and survive, presumably to tell the tale (7.399, 404).

What, then, of Eleazar's eloquent description of an incorporeal immortality? Here, too, Josephus's message is consistent. He wants his careful Jewish readers to understand that Eleazar's life-negating, other-worldly afterlife—unbalanced with a fear of postmortem retribution—is a dangerous component of his fratricidal refusal to submit to Rome. Those who view life as misfortune (7.343; compare 358), pinning their hopes on a seemingly ensured other-worldly incorporeal afterlife, will be all too quick to risk leaving this world, forcing others, including women and children, to quit this world prematurely as well. Josephus made different decisions for himself, choosing to submit to Rome in the hope of living (3.380, 391). It may be no accident that his doing so coincided with his Pharisaic views about what happens after death.

For Josephus, the moderate, priestly victims of sacrilegious murder merit eulogies of the highest praise. Jews willing to fight heroically until death are also worthy of honor, though Josephus make no effort to hide these figures' strategic miscalculations or previous shortcomings. Josephus appears to be even more equivocal regarding martyrdom. The willingness of the Essenes in particular to submit to and endure tortures certainly impresses Josephus, and he expects it to impact his readers as well. And certainly he expects that there are situations when Jews should submit to death rather than betray their laws or freedom. But there is no full-blown martyrdom in Josephus's works: there is simply no case where a virtuous Jewish person submits to death at the hands of foreign oppressors that in turn leads to a positive outcome for the Jewish people. In Josephus—quite unlike 2 and 4 Maccabees—God is not swayed to compassion by the worldly, sacrificial suffering of righteous heroes. It is the inversion of this pattern that is operative in Josephus: the sacrilegious murder of worthy priests and prophets conjures God's wrath, bringing on doom for the Jewish people. If 2 and 4 Maccabees can be called Jewish "martyrologies," we can perhaps capture the similarities and differences by referring to *Jewish War* as a "murderology."

The murder-suicides of Masada do not quite fit any of these patterns, but seem to be a hybrid of two other motifs. In general, mass suicide is a stock element of a decisive defeat, and so it makes sense for the fall of the last rebel fortress to include suicide as well. Murder-suicide, though, is a special case for Josephus. There is nothing noble about the murder-suicides; they are, rather, the ignoble ends of lives unjustly lived, with the additional suffering of innocent (or less guilty) women and children thrown in. The murderer-suicides lose their lives and their progeny all at once, thus ensuring one of the punishments promised to all who choose suicide—the visitation of the crime on the future generation (*War* 3.375). Those who do so will surely be denied the eventual reembodiment they don't deserve or even seem to expect (see 3.374). They will likely even be denied the incorporeal immortality they do hope for, suffering instead the postmortem punishments they don't even acknowledge.

In each of these ways, Josephus's views align most closely with the Pharisees, as he has described them. Josephus believes that immortality will be followed, eventually, by a reembodiment. Josephus is consistently more worldly than the Essenes but more other-worldly than the Sadducees. We would know, even from *Jewish War*, that Josephus chose not to live the Essene way (he was no ascetic communitarian, for instance). We also know from *War* that Josephus chose not to die the Essene way when he was given the chance. By the time we read *Life*, we learn explicitly of his deciding against the Essene way in favor of the Pharisaic (8–12), and of his taking of wives (414–15, 426–27). Mysteriously, scholars persist in emphasizing Josephus's sympathies with the Essenes and underestimating the degree to which his own beliefs match those of the Pharisees as he describes them.

Conclusion

As in the previous chapter, once again Josephus proves to be a reasonable—and underutilized—guide to understanding ancient Jewish theological disputes. A careful reading of Josephus's descriptions, when measured against the extant evidence, suggests that he accurately describes positions we can find articulated among other Jewish sources. The this-worldly, rationalist position he attributes to the Sadducees finds parallels, once again, in the wisdom literature (particularly Ben Sira), where we also find the rejection of beatific afterlife combined with a belief in earthly justice. The other-worldly hopes for an incorporeal afterlife that Josephus attributes to Essenes (and various suicidal rebels) find confirmatory echoes in 4 Maccabees and, to some extent, among the Qumran finds as well. Josephus's Pharisees once again take up the middle position, balancing other-worldly afterlife hopes with decidedly this-worldly concern for future reembodiment. And Josephus's descriptions find confirmation on these matters among rabbinic sources and the New Testament, especially with regard to the complexity of Pharisaic hopes regarding reembodiment. Unlike the simpler hopes apparently expressed earlier in 2 Maccabees, most first-century believers in resurrection seem to have understood that any future bodies they might be blessed to receive would have to be new enough to be worth wanting. To be sure, the reality was likely even more complex than Josephus's brief, pedagogic, descriptions allow. And we cannot really know for certain whether Josephus is accurately describing the general theological motivations of martyrs and suicides, but the correlations he identifies seem reasonable. Once again, the rough guide Josephus provides finds much more verification than disconfirmation.

Earlier in this chapter, we raised the historical questions concerning immortality, and noted that some have pointed to cultural shifts or historical crises to explain the rise of afterlife beliefs among ancient Jews in the second temple period. The evidence from Josephus pertains to these questions, I believe, in two ways. First, Josephus's account does not provide any evidence in favor of theological changes resulting from theological crises. Indeed, in the material we have seen this chapter, Josephus emphasizes long-standing debates on life after death. If any particular event or catastrophe helped bring about a sea change in ancient Jewish afterlife beliefs, Josephus seems to know nothing about either a sea change or a causal crisis. Indeed, as we will see in chapter 5, Josephus's works attest that various Jewish theologies can withstand the destruction of the temple, too. While this of course does not disprove the possibility that a crisis brought about such a change in belief regarding life after death, Josephus's evidence should at least be weighed against such theories, instead of being ignored or overlooked.

The second significance of Josephus's works with regard to the history of afterlife beliefs is the curious fact that while Josephus seems unaware of, or uninterested in, social causes of the doctrine, he seems acutely aware of, and quite interested in, the opposite phenomenon: the social impact of distinct afterlife beliefs. Most generally, Josephus's discussions suggest that warriors, sages, and other religious stalwarts can be motivated to risk death, submit to martyrdom, or even commit suicide when comforted by a belief in the afterlife, especially an other-worldly one. So perhaps instead of seeing afterlife beliefs as a theological response to certain kinds of social events, Josephus suggests we should reverse the equation, recognizing that some theological beliefs may help bring about certain kinds of personal decisions and social events. Josephus's own position seems influenced by such concerns, for his own theological moderation emerges in his subtle critique of incorporeal afterlife beliefs. Recognizing the symbolic value of heroic martyrdom, Josephus remains alarmed by murderous and suicidal behavior. Afterlife beliefs may well be comforting, but they are also potentially dangerous. As Eleazar's speech demonstrates, one who pins too much on the promises of after-worldly bliss may lose his moral compass and bring about undue suffering for himself and his family, not just in this world, but in the next one as well. For Josephus, therefore, the hope for immortality ought to be balanced with the concern for future reembodiment; the hope for an other-worldly existence should be balanced with a fear of eternal punishment. And here, then, is the great irony. As Josephus makes clear, afterlife beliefs are an integral component to Pharisaic and Essene theodicies (and of course his own). But when taken to the extreme, these hopes can bring about greater suffering in this world. In other words, the problem of theodicy can be exacerbated by some of its solutions.

4

Torah, Tradition, and Innovation

IN THIS CHAPTER, we consider Josephus's descriptions of Jewish scholastic disputes and disagreements regarding scripture and "traditions," especially insofar as these relate to legal authority. Our goals will be, once again, twofold. First, I will seek to draw a revised typology of ancient Jewish views on these subjects, by correlating a careful rereading of Josephus's accounts with a cautious effort to compare Josephus's evidence with other extant ancient sources. Second, we seek to clarify Josephus's own position on these matters; I will argue, once again, that Josephus's view aligns with that of the Pharisees, *as he describes them.*

The nature of the material to be covered in this chapter differs in some respects from what we have seen previously. In chapters 2 and 3, we have seen Josephus delineating tripartite disputes, differentiating rather clearly between the approaches of the Pharisees, Sadducees and Essenes. With regard to topics of this chapter, however, Josephus describes a binary dispute between the Sadducees and the Pharisees, and it proves more difficult to discern where the Essenes stand on these matters. This fact will make our first goal that much more complicated. Our second goal—delineating Josephus's own view—is made more challenging by both the mass of legal material he presents and his reluctance to clarify his own position. Josephus, of course, presents substantial summaries of Jewish religious practices both in *Antiquities* (esp. 3.102–87, 224–86; 4.196–308) and *Against Apion* (esp. 2.151–219). And following scriptural and Greco-Roman precedents, Josephus assures his readers that he will neither add nor subtract to his authoritative source (*Ant.* 1.17, 4.196).[1] Yet he neither slavishly follows the biblical text as we have it nor clearly links these legal excursuses with the scholastic debates regarding scripture, tradition, and authority.

Indeed, Josephus's legal excursuses appear rather haphazard—at least by whatever standards we can establish.[2] In one classic discussion, Louis

Feldman presents thirty-six cases where Josephus's legal position diverges from the plain sense of scripture. In eighteen of these, Josephus's view agrees with rabbinic halakhah, but in the others Feldman suggests that Josephus's view articulates an "earlier or alternate version of the Oral Torah."[3] In his own review of the question, Mason, too, notes various agreements and disagreements between Josephus's legal excurses on the one hand and rabbinic sources, Philo, and Josephus's own accounts of sectarian behavior on the other. For instance, Mason notes that in *War* 2.161, Josephus indicates that the marrying Essenes consider it forbidden to have intercourse with their pregnant wives; in *Apion* 2.199, Josephus suggests that this rule is to be followed by all Jews.[4] We are left, it seems, without any "single explanatory logic" for Josephus's legal views.[5] More recently, Eyal Regev and David Nakman reviewed a different data set and identified seven cases where Josephus's own legal position agrees with views attributed to Pharisees in rabbinic sources, three cases where his legal position agrees with views attributed to Sadducees (again, in rabbinic sources), and six cases where his view agrees with positions that can be discerned in other halakhic traditions, including the *Temple Scroll*, 4QMMT, and *Jubilees*.[6] Their conclusion—that Josephus's legal material reflects a "halakhic eclecticism"—seems ineluctable.[7]

Unfortunately, Josephus does not elsewhere in his works seek to clarify his own position. As we have seen, Josephus rather clearly espouses his own beliefs in providence and life after death, often at key points in his narratives. But this is not the case with regard to the matter at hand. Moreover, Josephus's aforementioned tendency to use technical vocabulary in confusing ways is also apparent in his unfettered deployment of terms such as "laws" (οἱ νόμοι, τὰ νόμιμα) and "customs" (τὰ ἔθη, τὰ πάτρια) in seemingly interchangeable ways, in assorted combinations, in singular and plural forms, sometimes speaking of Pharisees and other times speaking of Jews in general (e.g., *War* 1.648: "the laws/customs," τὰ πάτρια; *War* 1.649: "ancestral laws," οἱ πάτριοι νόμοι; *War* 1.654: "the law," ὁ νόμος).[8] One particularly interesting example occurs when Josephus, with apparent accuracy, notes the Jewish acceptance of polygamy—but this is described as an "ancient custom" (*War* 1.477, *Ant.* 17.14), despite the clear scriptural precedents noted by Josephus himself (e.g., Jacob: *Ant.* 1.298–306). Therefore, classifying Josephus's view based on either his legal positions or his statements about Jewish law has proven something of a challenge. Still, as noted, some scholars do accept as reasonable Josephus's late-life assertion of Pharisaic allegiance (*Life* 12).[9] Against this current, Mason has argued that Josephus's agreement with nonrabbinic legal traditions, as well as his incorporation of nonbiblical legal traditions into his biblical paraphrase—without any clear or consistent terminological distinction—speak against his claimed Pharisaic allegiance.[10] But as we will see, there is a third source of information that has not been sufficiently exploited in the effort of discerning Josephus's own view: when we attend to Josephus's historical narratives regarding specific legal developments (e.g., warfare on the Sabbath during the Maccabean period) and disputes (e.g., Herod's violations of Jewish customs) we will find good reason to associate Josephus's own position with the approach he ascribes to the Pharisees.

Discerning Josephus's view on the matters of scripture, tradition, and legal authority is significant for reasons beyond the understanding of Josephus. As I intimated in chapter 1, there is a "law-centered" approach to ancient Jewish sectarianism, some of whose proponents seek to trace the interrelated histories of Jewish sectarianism and halakhic development.[11] As we will see, these efforts can be illumined—and challenged—by a fuller understanding of Josephus's approach to these issues. First-century Jewish legal theory is also of interest to scholars of the New Testament, some of whom seek to discern the historical Jesus' approach to the legal matters that come under dispute in the New Testament.[12] I hope that this review of Josephus's position can inform these efforts as well.[13]

The Pharisee-Sadducee Debate on Scripture and Tradition

The Evidence from Josephus

Josephus's most detailed treatment of the debate between the Sadducees and Pharisees regarding legal matters is found apart from the three schools passages that have been the starting points for our discussions heretofore. In *Antiquities* 13.230–300, Josephus describes the eventful reign of the Hasmonean high priest John Hyrcanus I (r. 134–104 BCE).[14] Elaborating on the much briefer treatment this ruler is given in *War* (1.54–69), Josephus describes in some detail a conflict that ensued at a dinner party, when a Pharisee named Eleazar adjures Hyrcanus to give up his high priestly duties and serve only as the ruler (*Ant.* 13.289–91). When asked why, Eleazar claims that Hyrcanus is unfit for service in the temple, alleging that his mother was a captive during the time of Antiochus

Epiphanes (13.292). Josephus quickly adds that the allegation was false—
but the lines of conflict are drawn nonetheless. Hyrcanus then receives
advice from a Sadducee named Jonathan, who urges the king to ask the
Pharisees what Eleazar's punishment ought to be for his slander (13.293).
Hyrcanus figures that he will thereby determine for certain whether the
Pharisees truly side with Eleazar or not. Indeed, Jonathan's advice is cun-
ning, for the Sadducee knows that the Pharisees are lenient in punishment,
and will therefore not recommend the death penalty for slander (13.294).
Although we don't learn what happened to Eleazar, it was likely worse
than the "stripes and chains" the Pharisees recommend. Convinced by
their leniency that the Pharisees endorse Eleazar's allegation, Hyrcanus is
persuaded by Jonathan to switch his allegiance to the Sadducees (13.295).
In the process, Hyrcanus abrogates the Pharisaic regulations, at the same
time lowering his reputation among the people (13.296).

Josephus's account bears a striking resemblance to a story preserved
in the Babylonian Talmud (b. Qiddushin 66a). The rabbinic tradition in
question is curiously distinctive, in part for its style: the Hebrew gram-
mar of the passage is more biblical than rabbinic. There are, to be sure,
important differences between the tradition preserved in rabbinic sources
and the version as told by Josephus. For one thing, the rabbinic tradition
situates the conflict during the reign of one of Hyrcanus's successors,
King Alexander Jannaeus (r. 103–76 BCE). For another, the Sadducees
go unmentioned in the Talmudic tale: we have Pharisees opposing the
Hasmonean house, but no Sadducees are involved one way or another.
Still, the parallels are so striking that virtually all concerned—even Steve
Mason—admit that in this particular case, Josephus has more or less
incorporated a traditional Jewish story, one that has also found its way
into the rabbinic tradition.[15]

But what matters more for our concern is the explanatory aside that
follows this story in Josephus's retelling of it, for it is here that Josephus
spells out for his readers the nature of the sociolegal dispute between the
Pharisees and the Sadducees:

> For the present, I wish merely to explain that the Pharisees had
> passed on [παρέδοσαν] to the people certain regulations [νόμιμά]
> handed down by former generations [ἐκ πατέρων διαδοχῆς] and not
> recorded in the Laws of Moses, for which reason they are rejected by
> the Sadducean group, who hold that only those regulations should
> be considered valid which were written down [in scripture],[16] and

that those which had been handed down by former generations need not be observed. (298) And concerning these matters the two parties came to have controversies and serious differences, the Sadducees having the confidence of the wealthy alone but no following among the populace, while the Pharisees have the support of the masses. But of these two schools and of the Essenes a detailed account has been given in the second book of my *Judaica*. (*Ant.* 13.297–98)

The information Josephus provides here is not paralleled in the Talmudic account, and the passage is best understood as Josephus's editorial addition to the story he has just transmitted.[17] Yet, readers who follow this cross-reference back to *War* 2 will find that the issues discussed in this passage are not included in Josephus's earlier, lengthier treatment of the schools—though, as we will discuss later, Josephus does refer to the Pharisees as the more accurate interpreters of the law (*War* 2.162). This has led Mason to suggest that the information Josephus provides in *Antiquities* 13.297–98 reflects contextual needs more than Josephus's own interests in the groups. Left to his own devices (and interests), Josephus chooses to focus on other issues.[18]

The disparity between the kinds of information presented in *Jewish War* 2 and *Antiquities* 13 may well indeed reflect Josephan priorities to a certain extent. But Josephus bridges the gap between these accounts in his final treatment of the schools in *Antiquities* 18, where, along with the theological data discussed in his previous chapters, he draws contrasts on matters of legal significance. The Sadducees, we are told, "own no observance of any sort apart from the laws" (18.16). And although the causal connections are not fully spelled out, Josephus also emphasizes once again that the Sadducees are unpopular and, therefore, largely ineffective (18.17). Josephus's statement regarding the Pharisees is not entirely clear: "They follow the guidance of that which their teaching [λόγος] has deemed good and handed down, attaching the chief importance to the observance of those things which it has seen fit to dictate" (18.12).[19] Although translations and understandings vary somewhat, the passage certainly suggests, once again, that the group follows distinctive practices dictated by their own teaching, which has been handed down. The very next point Josephus raises emphasizes their respect for their elders. Of course, we have already noted and problematized Josephus's biased assertions that the Sadducees were rude and boorish (*War* 2.166; see also *Ant.* 18.16), and we cannot evaluate the praise here for the Pharisees without bearing this in mind. But the juxtaposition of this generalization with the preceding notice regarding distinctive Pharisaic traditions may ring true: it stands to reason, of course, that elders would play an important role for a group that prides itself on transmission of traditions from earlier generations.[20] Be that as it may, as the passage continues, we are told again of the popularity and influence of the Pharisees—but this time Josephus informs us that the public sacred rites are performed according to their views (18.15).

There is an additional passage that speaks of the Pharisees' distinctive legal traditions. In *Antiquities* 17.41–45, expanding on *War*'s rather brief reference to Pharisaic opposition to Herod (*War* 1.571), Josephus describes the Pharisees' role in a conspiracy against Herod instigated by the wife of the king's brother, Pheroras.[21] On mentioning the Pharisees, Josephus informs his readers that they were "a group of Jews priding itself on its adherence to ancestral custom and claiming to observe the laws of which the Deity approves" (17.41). These men—there were more than six thousand of them—refused to take an oath of allegiance to the king, and were therefore fined (17.42). Apparently, the Pharisees in general were not exempt from this oath (unlike the Essenes, the Pharisaic sage Pollion, and Pollion's disciple Samaias; see 15.368–71). When Pheroras's wife paid the Pharisees' fine (see also *War* 1.571), the Pharisees used their prophetic skills to foretell Herod's downfall, leading Herod in turn to put some Pharisees to death (*Ant.* 17.44).

This passage has received less attention than those discussed above, in part because the passage's apparent hostility to Pharisaic pride and contrivance convinced many that it must have originally been penned not by Josephus himself, but by one of his literary predecessors (typically, Nicolaus of Damascus).[22] Mason, however, has convincingly argued that the passage exhibits Josephan language and content, even with regard to the negative evaluation of the Pharisees' behavior.[23] What matters for our concerns is that the passage speaks, once again, of distinctively Pharisaic ancestral traditions. In this case, however, the opposing view is left unarticulated.

Pharisaic Traditions, in Josephus and Beyond

And what can we say about the nature of these traditions? Josephus makes it clear that the regulations he has in mind could be set aside or reinstated by a political authority: Just as Hyrcanus is said to have repudiated

Pharisaic traditions (*Ant.* 13.296), his successor, Queen Alexandra, is said to have restored them (13.408).[24] That Pharisaic traditions concerned public practices is also evident from Josephus's claim that the sacred rites were performed in accordance with their rulings (18.15). Josephus also emphasizes, as we have seen, that the Pharisaic traditions were popular (13.298, 18.17). Precisely how the Pharisaic (and Essene) refusal to take the oath of allegiance to Herod fits in here is unclear (15.368–71): perhaps they opposed all such oaths, or perhaps they opposed taking such an oath in allegiance to Herod in particular.[25] The clearest general example Josephus provides of a lenient Pharisaic tradition concerning public matters that would likely prove popular is the Pharisees' approach to punishment, which apparently limited the use of capital punishment, at least when compared to the harsher Sadducean position (13.293–94, 20.199).

Beyond this, we could only hazard guesses, wondering *perhaps* whether the Pharisees espoused nonscriptural leniencies articulated by later rabbis, such as the *eruv* (the Sabbath boundary, easing certain restrictions and rejected by the Sadducees according to *m. Eruvin* 6.2) or the *tevul yom* (the daytime immersion, easing certain ritual purity restrictions, again rejected by the Sadducees according to *m. Parah* 3.7). A great deal of circumstantial evidence from Qumran suggests that the Pharisees were in fact proponents of a lenient position on the *tevul yom*, over against the stringent position attributed to the Sadducees in rabbinic literature and articulated emphatically, even polemically, in Qumran documents (11QT 45.9, 50.4, 15 and 4QMMT B15, 72).[26] The Sadducean opposition to establishing an *eruv* finds an apparent parallel in the *Damascus Document* (11.7–9), though in this case reconstructing the Pharisaic leniency requires greater degrees of speculation or sufficient confidence in the historical value of rabbinic literature to permit attributing the rabbinic *eruv* to Pharisaic authorities.[27] Ultimately, however, there's really no way to be sure what legal traditions Josephus may have had in mind, beyond the few matters, such as punishments, that he explicitly mentions.

Still, there is value in measuring Josephus's evidence against what we find reported about the Pharisees, the Sadducees, and their legal disputes in rabbinic literature and the New Testament. Significantly, the Greek texts of the New Testament allow us to confirm that other late first-century writers also believed the Pharisees to be in possession of distinctive, nonscriptural "traditions" that were "passed down" (Matthew 15.1–20// Mark 7.1–23)—notions expressed in terms strikingly similar to those Josephus uses in passages such as *Antiquities* 13.297–98, 17.41, and 18.12.[28]

Moreover, the New Testament specifies some of the traditions, allowing us to expand the repertoire of Pharisaic rulings to include matters such as hand-washing and vows.[29]

The rabbinic evidence, however, confuses the matter somewhat. Many scholars have rushed to associate the Pharisaic nonscriptural traditions with rabbinic "Oral Torah."[30] But as Mason, Steven Fraade, and others have correctly pointed out, there are important differences here.[31] First, while Josephus and the New Testament do, as we have seen, indicate that the Pharisees preserved, transmitted, and considered authoritative, certain nonscriptural legal traditions, it is not necessarily the case that these traditions remained in exclusively oral form. Josephus's observations in *Antiquities* 13.297–98 and elsewhere indicate the nonscriptural origin of these traditions, not their inherently oral form.[32] Moreover, while Josephus and the New Testament describe these traditions as going back many generations, both stop well short of the later rabbinic claim that Oral Torah comes from Sinai, just like the Written Torah (e.g., *b. Shabbat* 31b). As a result, it is therefore not clear that the Pharisees gave ancestral traditions equal weight to scripture, as later rabbinic teachings imply.[33] So while Josephus's Pharisees may well illuminate the background of rabbinic claims concerning their "Oral Torah," it is important to differentiate the two. Rabbis will come to believe that their purely oral traditions— which, for a time, it was forbidden to write down[34]—are of equal authority and antiquity with the text of the Pentateuch. We could even say, to borrow an apt Christian term, that the full-blown rabbinic doctrine held the Oral Torah to be "coeternal" with the written one. Josephus knows nothing of the "coeternity" of the oral traditions with the Mosaic Torah, and there's no reason to think that he should have, or that *any* first-century Jews believed that nonscriptural legal traditions—even if valid and authoritative—were of equal status with the Mosaic Torah. To be sure, *Antiquities* 17.41 suggests that the Pharisees believed their traditions to be divinely ordained—but not necessarily divinely given. All we can say of Josephus's Pharisees is that they were willing to ascribe authority to nonscriptural legal traditions. In other words, while they would justify some laws by rooting them in scripture, they would justify others by appeal to tradition.

We ought, by now, also be able to understand better the difference between Pharisaic traditions and rabbinic legal exegesis (midrash halakhah). Josephus frequently speaks of the Pharisees as expert, or precise, *exegetes* of laws (e.g., *War* 2.162; see also 1.110).[35] Indeed, it is often averred that the Pharisaic traditions involved efforts in proto-midrashic legal exegesis.[36] It is, of course, quite possible that rabbinic midrash builds on earlier models of legal exegesis.[37] But the attribution of legal exegesis to Pharisees per se can be problematized from two ends. From the rabbinic side of the equation, it is imperative to distinguish between the ideology of "Oral Torah"—which asserts the coeternity and complete authority of autonomous, nonscriptural halakhic traditions—and the practice of midrash halakhah, which involves the effort of deriving (or justifying) legal positions in relation to passages from the Pentateuch. Indeed, the two phenomena operate to a certain degree in tension: laws that are derived exegetically need not be justified by appeal to nonscriptural tradition—exegesis provides its own justification. And if nonscriptural traditions have their own independent validity, what need is there to justify them by tying them to scriptural verses?[38] Moreover, the belief in an independent Oral Torah asserts a duality of revelation—Two Torahs—that need not be assumed by those engaged in legal exegesis of the singular Written Torah.[39] So the fact that Josephus attributes traditions to the Pharisees ought not be taken, by itself, as suggestive of the Pharisees' exegetical activity. Indeed, this conceptual tension separating legal exegesis from traditional authority lends further support to recent understandings of Josephus's accounts of the Pharisees. Paul Mandel, in particular, has demonstrated convincingly that Josephus's references to Pharisees as "exegetes" (e.g., *War* 2.162) means something quite different from scriptural midrash, and more likely refers to the Pharisaic expertise in remembering, transmitting, and explaining their legal traditions that were neither recorded in scripture nor explicitly derived from scripture by means of what we now refer to as exegesis.[40]

The parallels between Josephus's Pharisees and the later rabbis ought not be entirely dismissed, however. Although we cannot demonstrate—and therefore should not assert—that Josephus's Pharisees either engaged in midrash halakhah or were early transmitters of "Oral Torah," the fact remains that there are striking phenomenological, if not terminological, correspondences between Josephus's Pharisees and the general nature of our earliest rabbinic text, the Mishnah. This document, to be sure, does contain laws that are derived exegetically (e.g., *m. Berakhot* 1.3), as well as laws whose general scriptural justification may have been assumed (e.g., *m. Berakhot* 1.1: that the *shema* must be recited at night, based presumably on Deut. 6.7). And on rare occasions, distinct traditions are identified as "a halakhah of Moses from Sinai" (e.g., *m. Pe'ah* 2.6).[41] But the bulk of the traditions preserved in the Mishnah are transmitted anonymously, while many others are attributed to specific named authorities, most of whom lived in the first or second centuries CE. The Mishnah's presentation of this material is not characterized by any consistent effort at deriving law exegetically or justifying rulings by appeal to tradition. Although the vaguest of transmission histories is provided (*m. Avot* 1.1–2.1), this passage is remarkable both for its lack of clarity regarding the nature of the (singular) "Torah" that is transmitted and for the fact that the sayings this tractate seems to be concerned with transmitting are all *aggadic* (nonlegal) in nature. Tractate *Avot* hardly serves as an effective "apologetic" for the Mishnah.[42] The nature of the Mishnah is better described in *m. Hagigah* 1.8: some laws have much scriptural support, others have less; and some are "like mountains hanging by a hair," with the scantest of support from scripture, and some laws hover in the air, having no scriptural support whatsoever. There may well be something important here to bear in mind. Instead of trying to understand Josephus's Pharisees in light of the more full-blown efforts at justifying law that are characteristic of post-Mishnaic rabbinic literature, we may do better to try and understand the Pharisees in light of the inchoate and, to a degree, less consistent efforts at categorizing and justifying nonscriptural laws that are in evidence in the Mishnah. So, for what it is worth, perhaps we can say this much: the Mishnah confirms the possibility that the Pharisees were known for preserving and transmitting traditions apart from scripture in the two senses we have noted: their traditions are not necessarily found in scripture, and they are not necessarily justified exegetically either. Nonscriptural rulings are justified by the belief in the authority of such traditions.[43] So once again, the various lines converge, confirming that the Pharisees were known for giving weight—unequal weight, but weight nonetheless—to nonscriptural laws that they viewed as venerable traditions.

One final piece of evidence lends support to the argument we are making that Josephus understood that nonscriptural traditions passed down from one generation to the next were neither exegetical nor necessarily all that ancient. When summarizing Herod's temple renovation project, Josephus relates:

> And it is said that during the time when the temple was being built no rain fell during the day, but only at night, so that there was no interruption of the work. And this story, which our ancestors have handed down to us [καὶ τοῦτον τὸν λόγον οἱ πατέρες ἡμῖν παρέδωκαν], is

not all that incredible if, that is, one considers the other manifestations of power given by God. (*Ant.* 15.425)

The story Josephus here describes as having been passed down by his
ancestors is paralleled in a tannaitic tradition that makes strikingly similar claims: during the construction of Herod's temple, it rained only at
night, as a sign of divine favor (*b. Ta'anit* 23a; *Sifra be-Huqotai* Perek 1, on
Lev. 26.4 [ed. Weiss 110b]; *Leviticus Rabbah* 35.10). This instance also allows
us to confirm that Josephus does not believe Pharisaic ancestral traditions
to be as old as scriptural ones. After all, this particular tradition can go
back no further than the time of Herod. Though potentially quite important, this passage is not, however, the smoking gun that confirms beyond
any doubt Josephus's Pharisaic allegiance. Nor does the passage solidify
the identification of Josephus's Pharisaic tradition with the later rabbinic
one. Although Josephus uses here the terminology he uses elsewhere to
describe Pharisaic traditions, all that we have said about Josephus's terminological inconsistency weakens any argument based on terminology
alone. Moreover, the tradition in question is nonlegal in nature—*aggadic*,
in rabbinic terms—and Josephus's statements about distinctive Pharisaic
traditions focus on their legal nature. Still, we are perhaps safe in saying
that these parallel accounts of providential weather stand where the various lines we have already traced above appear to converge—with Josephus,
like the Pharisees, giving weight to extrascriptural traditions.

Sadducean Scripturalism in Josephus and Beyond

And what can we say about the Sadducees? In *Antiquities* 13.297, the
Pharisaic adherence to nonscriptural traditions is countered by the
Sadducean acceptance of only those laws that are written down (νόμιμα τὰ
γεγραμμένα). As many commentators—and even translators (see above)—
have pointed out, the sense of this contrast concerns not the procedure
of transmission (orality verses textuality) but the Sadducean rejection of
the Pharisaic appeal to nonscriptural tradition as a source of authority.
If the Pharisaic traditions were not necessarily oral, then the Sadducean
rulings were not necessarily in written *form*: the issue at stake is whether
the rulings were perceived to be scriptural or traditional.[44] The notice
in *Antiquities* 18.16 is briefer and even less clear, to the effect that the
Sadducees restrict their observances to "the laws." Clearly, the Sadducees
deny validity to the nonscriptural traditions accepted and transmitted by

the Pharisees, and give scripture greater weight in the process. But how precisely did their scripturalism operate? Were the Sadducees literalists? Did they derive laws by means of exegesis? Did they perhaps appeal to, or even contrive, revised scriptures like the *Temple Scroll*? As we will see, each of these suggestions has been articulated (or assumed), but some approaches are more problematic than others.

The problems we face in this case include those that also prevent fuller understandings of other Sadducean views, as we have discussed already. Here, too, what Josephus tells us about the Sadducees is largely stated negatively: it is clear that they reject the Pharisaic traditions, but Josephus does not tell us how the Sadducees defend their own views. Unfortunately, the New Testament does not provide much information that is of help in this respect either. Of course, Acts confirms the general opposition of Pharisees and Sadducees (23.6–8), but the Sadducean view that would oppose giving authority to Pharisaic traditions is not explicated. It is worthwhile to remember (as discussed in the previous chapter) that the gospel traditions recall—or imagine—Sadducees opposing the doctrine of resurrection on scriptural grounds (Matt. 22.23–33//Mark 12.18–27// Luke 20.27–40). But the exegetical methods evident here, even if genuinely Sadducean, cannot be reliably generalized, on their own, to explain Sadducean legal theory vis-à-vis the Pharisees.

A further problem that resurfaces with regard to Sadducean legal theory is the hostility toward the Sadducees that persists, curiously, among modern scholars. One manifestation of this hostility is the presentation of Sadducees as conservative literalists. Of course, literalism need not be presented in a hostile fashion, but surely it is notable that Sadducean conservative literalism typically is. Jacob Lauterbach spoke of the Sadducean approach as "simple and literal"—they were "blind slaves to the letter of the law."[45] Salo Baron spoke of the literalist Sadducees as insisting on "rigid application of Jewish law...having lost contact with the living currents of their faith."[46] These treatments—and others as well[47]— are not analyses of Sadducean literalism but partisan criticisms of it, in the service of some more flexible, modern-oriented variety of rabbinic Judaism.

If the problem were only negativity, such approaches could (perhaps) be reformulated. But the problems go deeper than that. If the Sadducees believed they were literalists of some sort, what exactly did they insist on taking literally? The Torah?[48] The Jewish Bible? The Sadducees flourished at a time when neither the general contours of the Jewish canon nor its particular textual formulations were settled.[49] I have argued at length that Ben Sira articulates views Josephus attributed to the Sadducees—but we cannot know the status this book held in their eyes. And it is often observed, as we have already noted, that various Dead Sea Scrolls—including the *Temple Scroll*—articulate legal positions attributed to Sadducees in rabbinic literature. Yet no document can be convincingly characterized as articulating exclusively Sadducean views. We will consider below the approaches that treat the *Temple Scroll* and other Qumranic texts as articulations of Sadducean law. But we must point out here that the phenomenon of "rewritten" scripture seems ubiquitous in the second temple period. Indeed, although it's not always described as such, a good case can be made that Ben Sira's book is, at least in part, a rewritten Proverbs, with a summarized Deuteronomistic History (Sir. 44–49) thrown in for good measure. How can we be sure that that the Sadducees didn't revere these or other parabiblical documents? Even if, therefore, the Sadducees claimed to be literalists, we simply have no idea which documents they were trying to read literally.

Moreover, we cannot know how literal their readings were. Literalism is more a slogan than a system.[50] Contemporary authorities—religious, political, and judicial—can argue at length about literal understandings of the Bible or the U.S. Constitution. In the modern case, at least we can ascertain which texts are, ostensibly, being read literally. But even then, we cannot necessarily eliminate the possibility that one group would claim as a literal reading an understanding that to others would seem to be interpretive. Whenever interpretive questions arise, the "literal" understanding of the passage in question is disputed. So even if the Sadducees *claimed* to be literalists, that doesn't mean that their views would be restricted to what other contemporaries or later authorities would consider a "literal" reading of the texts at hand.

But there is an even better reason to doubt that the Sadducees even claimed to be literalists: Josephus, our main source about the Sadducean view, doesn't clearly say so.[51] And rabbinic sources, as Urbach noted, may well suggest quite the opposite, that the Sadducees engaged in exegetical activity.[52] It is for all these reasons problematic and even precarious to describe Sadducean legal theory as literalist. All we can say, so far, is that the Sadducees were characterized by their rejection of the Pharisees' nonscriptural traditions, in favor of their own scripturally justified law.

The Qumran Legal Tradition: Sectarian
or Sadducean?

An important alternative to the view that considers Sadducees to be literal-ists has emerged, in particular among those maintaining the "law-centered" approach to ancient Jewish sectarianism. A trend among many of these scholars—Aharon Shemesh currently prominent among them—is to take a binary approach to the history of halakhah, whereby the generally accepted hypothesis viewing the rabbis as heirs of the Pharisees is balanced by the supposition that Qumranic/sectarian legal documents represent the priestly legal tradition of the Sadducees.[53] This view finds its basic support in the fact that, as we have already had occasion to note, various laws attrib-uted to the Sadducees in rabbinic sources (e.g., *tevul yom*) are articulated or echoed in legal texts from Qumran. At the same time the approach itself is more conservative than innovative, in that it is something of a throwback to the pioneering work of Abraham Geiger.[54] Geiger, as we have also noted already, attributed most ancient Jewish literature to either Sadducean or Pharisaic streams, and largely sidelined the Essenes.[55] Moreover, reject-ing the validity of Josephus's testimony, Geiger denied that the Sadducees were either literalists or rejecters of all nonscriptural tradition. Following rabbinic literature, Geiger believed that the Sadducees had legal traditions of their own.[56] Yet Geiger didn't have what his contemporary heirs possess: nonrabbinic halakhic material that is verifiably datable to the late second temple period, the very time when the Sadducees flourished.

It is important to note that these scholars are not necessarily identify-ing the Qumran sect as Sadducean. It is possible to claim that the Qumran sect inherited and developed a Sadducean halakhic system, even as the group became quite distinct from the urban and perhaps more Hellenized first-century Sadducees known to Josephus and the New Testament.[57] But as far as the history of halakhah is concerned, the identification of Qumranic law as Sadducean leads to a binary approach, imagining that ancient Judaism was characterized by two overarching legal systems: the Pharisaic/rabbinic and the Sadducean/Qumranic.[58] And some practitio-ners of this approach exhibit a sincere desire to counter ancient and mod-ern hostility toward Sadducees, depicting their system as principled and complex. Upending older attitudes and, in this sense, inverting Geiger's approach, Shemesh speaks of Sadducean/Qumranic textualism as inno-vative—even a "reform" (albeit a stringent one)—going against the status quo of Pharisaic traditionalism.[59] In response (according to this approach) the rabbis will eventually enact an innovative exegetical revolution of their own, by embracing powerful hermeneutic tools allowing them to read the Pentateuch in radically nonliteral ways.[60]

Though I sympathize with the effort to rehabilitate the Sadducean view, approaches that trace the history of Jewish law and legal exegesis in this dual, evolutionary fashion are extremely problematic, both for their duality and for their evolutionary nature. First, as Albert Baumgarten has pointed out, legal agreement is weak evidence for positing the historical identity of religious groups (or, by extension, the identity of halakhic systems).[61] In many of these cases—as, for instance, in the case of the *tevul yom*—there are more known groups than there are legal options: it could be that various groups rejected the purity of the *tevul yom*, without necessarily doing so for the same reason or agreeing on everything else. What is more, with regard to the Sadducean material in particular, the identifiable agreements between various Qumranic laws and legal positions attributed to Sadducees in rabbinic literature are balanced by identifiable disagreements between the same two data sets.[62] One could resort to diachronic variables to account for such differences, positing that the single Sadducean tradition would have evolved over time.[63] But this rather weak argument actually highlights the problematic foundation on which binary approaches rest: it stands to reason that Sadducean law evolved, just as it stands to reason that all of the groups we can identify from Josephus, the New Testament, and rabbinic literature evolved over time. Once we grant this, identifying a late second temple period text discovered at Qumran as Sadducean on the basis of partial agreements with a data set drawn from third-century-CE and later rabbinic material becomes all the more problematic. Finally, it remains to point out, once again, that these "law-centered" approaches sideline Josephus not just by placing law over theology but also by ignoring the fact that Josephus makes it abundantly clear that Essenes and Sadducees disagreed on matters of practice, not just theology. Why should scholars identify only two legal traditions when Josephus would suggest to us that there were (at least) three? And why should scholars imagine textual "revolutions" and exegetical "chain reactions" that left no impact on our various historical/narrative sources? For all these reasons, it is precarious to try and reconstruct the early history of Sadducean legal practice (or theory) based on Qumranic legal documents.

Even if the Qumranic documents will not tell us very much about Sadducees per se, we can still glean information about second temple legal practice and dispute that will help us contextualize Josephus's evidence.

First, a good deal of the sectarian literature suggests that the group's distinctive practices were justified neither by appeal to tradition (like the Pharisees) nor by direct appeal to scripture (as we might expect of Sadducees). Rather, it appears that the sect believed its distinctive practices were things "hidden" (נסתרות) from the rest of Israel, being things "revealed" (נגלות) to them, presumably (at least at first) by the "Teacher of Righteousness" (CD 3.12–16).[64] Qumran texts also speak of an "Interpreter of the Torah" (דורש התורה) who was, to be sure, very likely understood to be an exegete of some sort (CD 6.7–11, 7.18–21; see also 1QS 8.11–16).[65] Indeed, the terms "hidden" and "revealed"—taken from an infamously cryptic verse, Deuteronomy 29.28—demonstrate the significance of exegetical activity for sectarian self-understanding.[66] Yet it appears that the sect believed the Teacher of Righteousness and the Interpreter of the Torah were particularly gifted—even prophetically gifted—such that their disclosures of hidden laws and teachings take on the status of new, esoteric, legal revelation.[67] The Teacher and Interpreter may not have been alone in this; various passages suggest that the sect viewed the prophets in general as revealers of law (1QS 1.3, 8.16).[68] Whether derived by exegesis or not, the authority of new revelation at Qumran depends not on exegetical credibility, but on the authority of its prophetic teachers. Indeed, the extant Qumranic texts are largely, but not entirely, bereft of explicit legal exegesis; this, too, suggests that the authority of their laws rests primarily on esoteric revelation, not scholastic interpretation.[69] Although the largest legal document from Qumran—the *Temple Scroll*—is often characterized as an exegetical work, the fact remains that it presents itself as the content of the older Sinai revelation, not as the product of inspired (let alone scholastic) exegesis.[70] By contrast, later rabbinic approaches explicitly bestowed power on tradition and scholastic exegesis, and earlier Pharisaic approaches explicitly bestowed power on tradition (the role of exegesis being less clear in this case). Both did so, it would seem, over and perhaps against sectarian appeals to prophetic (or even quasi-prophetic) revelation.[71] The neoprophetic revelation of legislation (be it new or hidden previously) therefore emerges as a third means (beyond scholastic exegesis and ancestral tradition) for supplementing scriptural law in the second temple period.

Josephus and the History of Jewish Law

The material reviewed in the previous section has been well studied, though some important questions remain, particularly with regard to the understanding of Josephus's own attitude toward the relative authority of scripture, custom, and tradition. In what follows, we will pursue a slightly different line of argument, trying to discern as well as possible Josephus's personal approach to the matter of legal development. Who, according to Josephus, is empowered to introduce changes into Jewish religious practice? What is the status of new rulings with regard to law or custom? What kinds of innovations does Josephus oppose, and why?

Defensive Fighting on the Sabbath and Legal Development

By all accounts, one major halakhic issue that Jews faced in the second temple period was whether or not, or the degree to which, biblical Sabbath restrictions prohibited warfare on the seventh day of the week.[72] Josephus's writings discuss the issue in greater detail than any other ancient source, presenting about as much information as can be gleaned from the rest of our pre-Josephan sources combined, if not more. It is worth reviewing the matter here, not so much to determine historically what may have been decided by whom and when—or what, precisely, Josephus's halakhah was[73]—but rather to discern the various ways Josephus and other sources justify or explain any perceived change in practice or policy. So in what follows, we turn back to review some biblical precedents as well as pre-Josephan second temple treatments of the matter. As we will see, the sources in general suggest a variety of approaches and justifications. This will then allow us to see more clearly that Josephus's treatment of the issue, even when more detailed, is selective in rather interesting ways.

Perhaps surprisingly, the conflict between Sabbath and warfare remains unrecognized or at least unaddressed in the Hebrew Bible. The few passages that prohibit certain activities on the Sabbath (e.g., Exod. 20.8–11, 31.12–17, 34.21) or allude to such prohibitions (e.g., Jer. 17.19–27, Amos 8.5) say nothing one way or another about warfare. Other texts, like the book of Deuteronomy, articulate concerns with the Sabbath, leaving the restrictions unspecified (e.g., 5.12–15). Yet according to the Deuteronomistic book of Joshua, the siege of Jericho took place for seven days, without stop (Josh. 6.3–4). So at least one of those days was a Sabbath. Quite possibly, in accord with traditional Jewish understandings, the Sabbath was the seventh day, on which the walls came tumbling down.[74] According to 2 Kings 11.4–20 (see also 2 Chron. 23.1–21), the bloody, armed insurrection against Queen Athaliah led by the priest Jehoiada with the boy-prince Joash took place on a day when the incoming and outgoing priestly courses overlapped—presumably also a Sabbath (2 Kings 11.5, 7, 9//2 Chron. 23.4, 8).[75] As for defensive action, we are told that when Nehemiah supervised the building of Jerusalem's walls, guards were posted day and night (Neh. 4.10–17) for fifty-two days (6.15).[76] Indeed, it is highly unlikely that Israelites could have successfully defended themselves, even for short periods of time, against Canaanites, Philistines, Edomites or any of their unfriendly neighbors—to say nothing of Egypt, Assyria, or Babylonia—had they avoided military conflict on the Sabbath. And when, in the Persian period, Jews served in Persian forces at Elephantine and elsewhere, they, too, presumably addressed the matter in a practical way, though our extant sources do not let us know whether a conflict was sensed or how the matter was decided.[77]

We must admit that one possible explanation for what we have seen so far could be that the Sabbath was neither widely nor strictly observed. But what matters more for our purposes is the fact that documents that do express concern for Sabbath observance (whether that observance transpired or not) exhibit no worries about warfare. In this light, it is notable that biblical law mandates that the daily sacrifices would be offered on the Sabbath, with additional burnt offerings called for as well (Num. 28.1–10). The various overlaps between cultic and military activity—especially when it comes to "Holy War"[78]—suggests that any military conflict believed to be divinely ordained would justifiably take place on the Sabbath, just as cultic activity does. Indeed, rabbinic literature moves decidedly in this direction, permitting even maintaining a siege on the Sabbath, in the context of offensive, elective war—though the siege must begin at least three days prior to the Sabbath.[79]

The late second temple period sources, however, differ from the explicit permissive posture of the later rabbis as well as the apparent nonchalance of the biblical traditions. Indeed, the extant evidence suggests that many Jews were inclined, by the late second temple period, to draw different implications from the biblical evidence. Some, dissatisfied with the biblical record, sought to clarify it. In this spirit, the expanded Sabbath law attributed back to Moses in *Jubilees* 50.1–13 includes an explicit prohibition of engaging in warfare on the Sabbath, mandating capital punishment for violators (50.12–13).[80]

The explicit prohibition of *Jubilees* 50.12–13 likely reflects the fact that this issue came to a point of crisis during the Maccabean period.[81] Both 1 and 2 Maccabees record tales of pious Jews who died, refusing even to defend themselves when attacked on the Sabbath (1 Macc. 2.29–38; 2 Macc. 5.25–26, 6.11; see also 8.25–26).[82] But over and even against such idealistic pieties, both 1 and 2 Maccabees endorse more practical approaches. 1 Maccabees is rather explicit about the policy change, depicting Mattathias and his cohorts quickly reaching agreement that defensive fighting is justified on the Sabbath (2.39–41). Their reasoning, as depicted in the brief account of 1 Maccabees, is based neither on scripture nor tradition, but simply good sense and the desire to survive: "Let us fight against anyone who comes to attack us on the Sabbath day; let us not all die as our kindred died in their hiding places" (2.41). 2 Maccabees, however, leaves the matter unsettled until late in the career of Mattathias's son Judas. When Nicanor's army plans to attack the Judean forces in Samaria on the Sabbath, the Jews who are pressed into his army beg for mercy, appealing to their divinely given command to follow the seventh day (15.1–2). Nicanor, however, is depicted as asserting his own sovereignty on earth, commanding the Jews to fight on the Sabbath (15.3–5). Judas then encourages his own soldiers by quoting "from the law and the prophets" and reminding them of their many victories (15.9). Judas also describes a vision he had seen of the pious priest Onias praying for the Jews and their city and of the prophet Jeremiah stretching out his hand to give Judas a sword with which Judas is to strike down his enemies (15.12–16). Assured that Judas's prophetic and priestly vision provides divine sanction to defend themselves, their city, and the temple against Nicanor's Sabbath attack, the Jewish forces press on with the fight, indeed, even taking an aggressive posture (15.17–50). Yet the divinely ordained decision described in 2 Maccabees leaves the general questions unanswered: can the Jews defend themselves on the Sabbath in any case, or just when Jerusalem is in danger? Or perhaps Judas's dream applies only in the case at hand? Indeed, some readers of 2 Maccabees have argued that the work opposes the legal position endorsed in 1 Maccabees.[83]

Turning to Josephus, the first thing we should note is that his biblical paraphrase provides neither a hint of any problem nor any intimation of potential solutions. Arguments from silence are, of course, precarious: but had Josephus felt it was important to provide a scriptural basis or precedent for the issue—one way or another—he certainly could have worked something in. As we have seen, Josephus imagines that Abraham reassured his bound son Isaac by describing the immortality of the soul (*Ant.* 1.230–31). In so doing, Josephus plants a scriptural seed of sorts that will eventually provide a root for the later Pharisaic doctrine of immortality.

But Josephus's treatment of Sabbath laws in his biblical paraphrase does not appear in any way to be shaped so as to support or point toward the directions the law will take in the Maccabean period. Indeed, Josephus hardly elaborates on the Sabbath at all in his paraphrase of the Pentateuch (Exod. 20.8–11 is briefly summarized in *Ant.* 3.91). In *Antiquities* 5.20–30, Josephus follows Joshua in describing a seven-day siege—even intimating that the siege began on the Passover holiday (compare Josh. 5.10–11). But Joshua's fighting on the Sabbath or even the festival is neither recognized as a problem nor identified as a precedent for later decisions.[84]

Yet Josephus tells us quite clearly that second temple period Jews eventually perceived conflicts between observing the Sabbath and militarily defending themselves. Ptolemy I Soter was apparently the first to have exploited this when he took Jerusalem essentially unopposed (c. 301 BCE; *Ant.* 12.4–6). To be sure, Josephus's account suggests that a variety of issues were at stake: the Jews were fooled into thinking Ptolemy only wished to worship in Jerusalem and therefore admitted him into the city when they were unprepared to defend themselves (12.4–5).[85] Yet Josephus then ostensibly quotes a passage attributed to Agatharchides of Cnidus (12.6) that describes the Jewish refusal to take up arms on the Sabbath in unambiguous terms, and he does nothing to counter this impression.[86] Whatever the historical reality, Josephus is clearly persuaded by Agatharchides—and, as we are about to see, by 1 Maccabees—that some Jews were in fact opposed to fighting, even defensively, in the pre-Maccabean era.

As noted, Josephus's account of the Maccabean era is based closely on 1 Maccabees, while it is not clear that he made any use of 2 Maccabees.[87] This pattern holds true here, too. *Antiquities* 12.272–77 largely follows 1 Maccabees 2.29–41, with a few notable differences. First, Josephus suggests that some of the pietists escaped and survived (12.275). Second, Josephus glosses over 1 Maccabees 2.40, which suggests that Mattathias's cohorts deduced that refusal to fight would mean death for all. Instead, Josephus tells us that the survivors were instructed to fight on the Sabbath directly by Mattathias (12.276). Then Josephus concludes with one further editorial clarification: "to this day we continue the practice of fighting even on the Sabbath, whenever it becomes necessary" (12.277).

According to Josephus, a century after Mattathias's decree regarding defensive warfare, Pompey (along with the Hasmonean Hyrcanus II) was able to exploit Jewish sabbatical scruples in a rather shrewd way.[88] Knowing that the Jews would defend themselves only if directly attacked, the

Roman general instructed his men to build the siege works on a Sabbath, but without actually engaging the Jewish forces in combat. Pompey's soldiers were therefore able to set the stage for the subsequent attack without any risk (*War* 1.145–47; *Ant.* 14.61–63; see also *War* 2.390–94). Josephus's description of the state of affairs in *War* is brief and to the point: "on the Sabbath the Jews fight only in self-defense" (1.146). The description in *Antiquities* is fuller, and instructive: reminding readers of the Jews' "custom" (πάτριον) to rest on the Sabbath day, Josephus explains: "the Law [ὁ νόμος] permits us to defend ourselves against those who begin a battle and strike us, but it does not allow us to fight against an enemy that does anything else" (14.63). This passage is remarkable for a number of reasons. First, it is one of the clearer statements we have concerning what was considered permitted and forbidden—at least, according to Josephus—in the post-Maccabean period. But it is also remarkable for the way Josephus has used the terms "custom" and "Law."[89] He describes as a "custom" the general Jewish observance of the Sabbath, despite its scriptural origin; he describes as "the Law" the rule permitting defensive fighting only, despite the fact that neither Josephus nor Josephus's Mattathias offers any scriptural support for the decision to this effect that, Josephus also maintains, was reached only in the early Maccabean period. The usages here certainly confirm that Josephus is not really concerned with determining which practices stemmed from scripture and which stemmed from later customs: the category of "Law," apparently, is a fluid one.[90]

Josephus's other references to fighting on the Sabbath are notable, and not entirely irrelevant to the matter at hand. In *War*, Josephus notes that the rebels made a point of setting out on murderous rampages and other offensive actions on Sabbaths or other holidays (e.g., 2.449–56, 517–18; 4.398–405; 5.100–105).[91] In *Antiquities*, Josephus presents documentary evidence to the effect that various communities of Jews received exemptions from military service in deference to Jewish customs regarding food or Sabbath (e.g., 14.226–27, 233, 234, 237).[92] Josephus's account of the two Babylonian brothers also notes their initial reluctance to defend themselves on the Sabbath (*Ant.* 18.322–24)—even though they lived long after the Maccabean decree. Although seemingly contradictory at first glance, there are identifiable common denominators to Josephus's treatment of this issue. Apparently, Josephus understands the Maccabean ruling to apply to Jews legitimately defending Jewish interests, such as Jewish territory or institutions. The ruling does not necessarily permit or excuse Sabbath warfare by Jewish mercenaries, conscripts, or adventurers living abroad, or by otherwise sinful rebels at home. Be this as it may, the entire issue is worthy of further study, especially in light of the developments in the study of both Josephus and ancient Jewish law.

And what have we learned from Josephus's understanding of this matter as it relates to the themes of this chapter? First, Josephus's treatment of the issue provides us with a perfectly clear example of the way *he believed* a legal question could be addressed. There was a traditional way of observing the Sabbath in the pre-Maccabean period. The stringent practice became unworkable, so the law was changed by a legitimate political authority, and the people accepted the new ruling. To be sure, Josephus does not at any point equate the new ruling with the Pharisaic ancestral tradition per se. Indeed, the legal dispute appears to have been settled in his mind before Pharisees or Sadducees walked the streets of Jerusalem.[93] But what originates as an innovative decision approved by consensus becomes, simply, "the Law" (*Ant.* 14.63). Moreover, it is significant that the issue is settled in a decidedly non-Sadducean fashion: no precedents from scripture are cited in favor of the Maccabean approach, despite their being readily available. No scriptural exegesis is offered either.[94] It is also notable that Josephus is not interested in settling the matter in the way of 2 Maccabees (if indeed this book renders a decision at all). Neither in this instance—nor, as we will soon see in any other—is Josephus at all interested in settling a legal matter by dreams, omens, or any other prophetic mechanism.

Other Innovations: Tithes and Festivals

The material reviewed above constitutes, to my knowledge, the fullest test case we have for discerning Josephus's own views regarding legitimate legal development in the second temple era. But there are other instances when Josephus records explicit instances of legal developments of which he approves. One such example concerns Nehemiah.[95] Providing information not found in scripture or other extant sources concerning this figure, Josephus describes Nehemiah's policies for increasing Jerusalem's population. After encouraging priests and Levites to move into houses he built in Jerusalem at his own expense, Nehemiah then instituted a change in the practice of tithing: thenceforth, the people were to bring their tithes to Jerusalem to support the priests and Levites now living there (*Ant.* 11.181–83; Neh. 10.32–39). We are not given a lot of details, but the general sense of Nehemiah's policy, as Josephus describes it, diverges not only from what is recorded in the Pentateuch (Lev. 27.30; Num. 18.25–32; Deut. 14.22–26)

but also, more important, from Josephus's own summary of Mosaic tithing law (*Ant.* 4.205).[96] Josephus clearly understands Nehemiah's policy as
both innovative and considered—and as just one example of this figure's
praiseworthy leadership (11.183). What is important for our purposes is
that, once again, a rightful leader is praised for making necessary changes
to the law, and no scriptural or prophetic justification is provided. Rather,
the legitimacy of Nehemiah's innovations is demonstrated by their acceptance by the people and their successful implementation.

A number of other examples of legal innovation in Josephus's narratives concern the declaration of new holidays.[97] Following one clear scriptural example, Josephus tells approvingly of the decree creating the new
festival of Purim (*Ant.* 11.291–96). Curiously, Josephus gives the credit
for this matter entirely to Mordecai, while the biblical book bearing her
name gives credit for the institution of the holiday also to Queen Esther
(Esth. 9.20–32). Following 1 Maccabees, Josephus describes, and accepts
as duly legitimate, the establishment of the Festival of Lights (Hanukkah;
Ant. 12.323–26; 1 Macc. 4.52–59; 2 Macc. 10.1–8), as well as Nicanor Day
(*Ant.* 12.412; 1 Macc. 7.48–49; 2 Macc. 15.36).[98] Josephus's slight editorial
changes to 1 Maccabees 4.59 are particularly interesting, in light of what
we have observed already: where the earlier document speaks of a *decision*
by Judas, his brothers, and the council, Josephus puts the matter more
boldly, asserting that celebrating the new holiday was established as a law
(*Ant.* 12.324: ὡς νόμον θεῖναι; see also 12.412) and accepted as such by the
people (12.325). Of course, we have no reason to believe that Josephus's
acceptance of these new holidays is in any way distinctively Pharisaic.
Sadducees and most others likely observed these festivals as well, though
the Dead Sea sectarians likely did not.[99] But it surely does matter that
Josephus, once again, exhibits no interest in any effort to provide scriptural precedent for these innovations. Nor are they justified by any appeal
to prophetic authority. Yet the innovations become law. Legitimate leadership is justified in making such decisions, as is evidenced by the continued acceptance of these practices by the people (11.296, 12.325, 412).

A Striking Absence: Legislative Prophets

Further instances are worth mentioning in light of the above examples,
not for what Josephus does say but for what he deletes from his sources.
Just before describing the establishment of the new festival of rededi-
cation, 1 Maccabees notes that Judas and his men were uncertain what

to do with the stones from the defiled altar they had just torn down (1 Macc. 4.45). In the end, they decided to store the desecrated stones on the temple hill "until a prophet should come and tell them what to do with them" (4.46).

It is frequently noted that Josephus's decision to elide this passage is connected to the fact that he believes prophecy to continue in his own day.[100] Indeed, Josephus also glosses over 1 Maccabees' other explicit reference to the cessation of prophecy (1 Macc. 9.27; *Ant.* 13.5). And as we will see in the next chapter, Josephus seems to have believed that the experiences of his own life testify to the ongoing nature of prophecy.[101] Be that as it may, it is imperative for present purposes to point out, once again, that for Josephus, prophecy serves a largely predictive purpose.[102] Indeed, Josephus completely eliminates from his accounts of prophecy—whether from biblical times or his own day—any legislative function whatsoever. Only Moses, the greatest of all prophets, merits being a legislator (4.327–31; Deut. 34.10). Josephus devotes time to narratives concerning Isaiah (*Ant.* 10.34–35), Jeremiah and Ezekiel (10.74–142), and he characteristically focuses on their predictions. He says nothing of these (or other) prophets' ethical admonitions, to say nothing of Ezekiel's extensive legislative material. Indeed, as we observed in the introduction, Josephus appears to know nothing of the concerns for Zadokite descent voiced by this prophet (Ezek. 40.46, 43.19, 44.15–16). And perhaps now we can understand the reason: For Josephus, the biblical prophets predict and warn; they do not lay down law.[103] Josephus's source for the early second temple period—1 Esdras—imagines Ezra speaking of the prohibition of intermarriage as a commandment given by the prophets (8.80; Ezra 9.10–11). But Josephus's Ezra makes no such appeal (*Ant.* 11.140–53).[104] In Josephus's narratives concerning the later second temple period, prophets appear with reasonable frequency, but again in a purely predictive (or cautionary) role (e.g., *War* 6.283–87; *Ant.* 15.373–79).[105] In Josephus's world, not once does a post-Mosaic prophet address, let alone solve, a legal matter.[106] So Josephus's elision of 1 Maccabees 4.46 is characteristically Josephan in two distinct ways, one much less frequently noted than the other. First, as commonly recognized, prophecy has not ceased. But second, not since Moses has prophecy served as a legitimate way of addressing legal questions or justifying legal change. When individual prophet-like figures do arise to change the law, Josephus will reject their novel teachings soundly.

This phenomenon may well illumine Josephus's account of the Essenes, especially when compared to the sectarian Dead Sea Scrolls. As noted, various scrolls suggest that some of the sect's distinctive practices were revealed by a quasi-prophetic Teacher of Righteousness (e.g., CD 3.12–16). Other passages suggest that the sect bestowed legal significance on prophetic literature (e.g., 1QS 1.3, 8.16). These of course are among the important aspects of Qumran self-understanding that find no parallels in Josephus's description of the Essenes. Yet Josephus does spend a good deal of time relating Essenes to prophecy in general (e.g., *War* 2.159) or speaking of individual Essene prophets (e.g. Menaham: *Ant.* 15.373–79).[107] The phenomenon we have just noted—Josephus's adamant refusal to recognize, let alone legitimize, post-Mosaic prophetic legislation—may well explain this discrepancy. Of course, we cannot *prove* that Josephus was aware of sectarian (or Essene) beliefs in a neoprophetic legal revelation. Nor can we *prove* that Josephus's Essenes were closely related to the Dead Sea sect. But we can say this: The scrolls prove that some ancient Jews believed in post-Mosaic, quasi-prophetic legislative revelation. Our review of Josephus's overall approach to the matter demonstrates that he was categorically opposed to this phenomenon—so much so that he rewrote scriptural and historical sources so as to avoid even mentioning that some Jews believed such a thing.

A Prophesied Transgression? The Curious Temple of Onias

In the wake of the crises leading up to the Maccabean revolt, the deposed high priest Onias established himself in Egypt, and even received permission to construct a Jewish temple at Leontopolis.[108] Josephus discusses the temple in both *War* and *Antiquities*. Indeed, the temple serves as a frame-story for the former work. The temple's construction is mentioned quite early on (1.33), and its destruction comes toward the very end (7.433–36). In *Antiquities*, Josephus's fuller treatment appears in its proper sequence (*Ant.* 13.62–73). As always with Josephus, there are some discrepancies between the two accounts. In *War*, we are told that the temple resembled a tower (7.427); in *Antiquities*, Onias's temple resembled Jerusalem's in appearance, though it was "smaller and poorer" (13.72). In *War*, we are told straight out that Onias's motives were off: he wished not to serve God but to rival the Jerusalem temple he had left behind (7.430–31). In *Antiquities*, Josephus is more oblique, telling us that Onias sought eternal fame (13.63), just what Menahem the Essene predicted for Herod (13.376). But there is one important detail that both accounts share: Onias the priest is said to have justified his actions by appeal to a prophecy of Isaiah that was understood to mean that a Jewish temple would be constructed in Egypt (*War* 7.432, *Ant.* 13.64, 68, 71; Isa. 19.19).

In light of what we have observed above regarding Josephus's struggle to separate prophets from law, the report regarding Onias's justification for his behavior is quite intriguing. But of course, this is not an instance of a prophet directly addressing a legal question. It's an instance (alleged, of course) of a priest appealing to an ancient, scriptural prophecy, in order to support a practice that others are, quite obviously, questioning (*Ant.* 13.70–71). Indeed, Josephus himself criticizes Onias outright in *War* and obliquely in *Antiquities*. And as we will have occasion to note again, Josephus believes in the unquestioned, singular authenticity of the Jerusalem temple (*Ant.* 4.200–201; *Apion* 2.193). Moreover, Isaiah's prophecy was not enough to prevent the Alexandrian governors Lupus and Paulinus from shutting down and despoiling this temple, just a few years after the destruction of Jerusalem (*War* 7.433–36). This case, therefore, hardly challenges Josephus's opposition to prophetically answered legal questions. If anything, the narrative provides not evidence for the sectarian approach but a caution against the Sadducean one. Scripturalism has its unforeseen dangers that Shakespeare put best: "Even the devil can cite Scripture for his purpose" (Antonio in *Merchant of Venice,* 1.3.98). Josephus's warning, however, is subtler.[109] Even resorting to interpreting scriptural prophecies as means of prediction—no doubt the prime function of the prophetic texts, according to Josephus—is similarly precarious: ambiguous oracles can be misunderstood, and apparent contradictions among the prophecies can foster further misunderstanding (e.g., *War* 6.310–15; *Ant.* 8.401–20, 10.103–42).[110] How, then, could legal questions be settled by such documents?

The Limits of Legitimate Legal Evolution

We have seen that Josephus recognizes and approves of certain legal developments. If a situation arises that requires a change in law or custom, legitimate, nonprophetic authorities who prudently implement new policies are praised for their leadership, and the new directives in time become indistinguishable from other facets of the Jewish legal tradition. But looking at the changes Josephus approves of is only one side of this coin. In a number of instances, he explicitly rejects innovations introduced to traditional Jewish practices, and it is instructive to review these cases as well, with an eye toward understanding Josephus's legal theory better.

Rejected Innovations: Rebels

Perhaps the clearest and best known Josephan condemnation of legal innovation involves his discussion and critique of the so-called fourth philosophy, in *Antiquities* 18.4–10, 23–25 (here expanding on the much briefer report in *War* 2.118). Scholarship has long been skeptical of Josephus's categorization here, and for good reason: it certainly seems that isolating this group serves his apologetic purpose, supporting the suspicious claim that most Jews were not rebellious by nature or ideology.[111] And in light of the concerns and approach of this work, it merits pointing out that we lack external confirmatory evidence regarding the full independence of this "fourth philosophy" from the other groups, while the independent existence of Pharisees, Sadducees, and Essenes can be confirmed by multiple external accounts. Some scholars, however, have been more sanguine regarding Josephus's reports of the fourth philosophy, accepting the possibility that a distinctive rebellious ideology emerged in this period.[112] Our interest here is not in probing the veracity of Josephus's claim that the fourth philosophy was sociologically, or even just ideologically, distinct from its Pharisaic, Sadducean, and Essenic siblings. The question we will consider is whether Josephus's largely unverifiable report on this group helps us understand better his attitude toward law, tradition, and innovation.

When it comes to describing the thought and practice of this group, Josephus attributes to them two distinct beliefs, each of which translates into certain types of rebellious behavior. Their first characteristic belief is their "passion for liberty," guided by the belief that "God alone is their leader and master" (*Ant.* 18.23, see also 18.4–5). Their second characteristic belief is their belittling of death, to the extent that they submit to martyrdom without fear, and worry even less over killing their kin. Indeed, we are told that they consider it permissible to kill other Jews in the pursuit of their own passion for freedom and independence (18.23, see also 18.5). As we have seen, Josephus claims, in *War*, that these ideologies were put into distinctively violent practice by the Sicarii (e.g., 7.323, 410), who at the end suffer accordingly for their many sins.

A number of points require emphasis for our purposes. First, it is clear that Josephus opposes the fourth philosophy's characteristic ideologies as well as the dangerous practices they engender. Indeed, following his first mention of the group in *Antiquities*—and preceding his extended discussion of the Pharisees, Sadducees, and Essenes—he takes a moment to draw a general lesson about the dangers of legal innovation. Arguing that the rebellious philosophy introduced by this group led eventually to the destruction of the temple (18.8), Josephus draws a lesson regarding the dangers of illegitimate changes[113] to ancestral customs (τῶν πατρίων)— suggesting that such can indeed be a nation's undoing (18.9). Of course, it is clear from all we have seen that Josephus does not oppose all inno- vation. And it is equally clear from what follows that he does not oppose all disagreement or diversity within the Jewish polity. This "fourth" phi- losophy is indeed illegitimate, even while the Pharisees, Sadducees, and Essenes exhibit differences in thought and practice that find a rightful place within the Jewish polity. Moreover, Josephus's opposition to the fourth philosophy is much more "Pharisaic" than "Sadducean," at least by Josephus's own understanding of these groups. The fourth philos- ophy has broken not with scripture, but with traditional customs. And although we cannot be certain of the matter, it stands to reason that any historical fourth philosopher would have appealed to scripture for justi- fication, citing passages such as Judges 8.22 and 1 Samuel 12.12, which oppose monarchy on theological grounds. Josephus, of course, does not allow for any such understanding of the group—both of these passages being elided in Josephus's own biblical paraphrase (*Ant.* 5.232, 6.91). To be sure, Josephus's God (as well as Moses and Samuel) prefer aristocracy over monarchy—but monarchy is endorsed as a legitimate possibility in *Antiquities* 4.223–24 (compare Deut. 17.14–20).[114] Bereft of scriptural or political legitimacy as far as Josephus is concerned, the fourth philosophy is, simply, the dangerous, self-serving sophistry of its founder, Judas the Galilean (18.3–4, 9–10; *War* 2.118).

In *Jewish War* 2.409–18, Josephus describes another instance of politi- cally dangerous legal innovation, when the priest Eleazar son of Ananias persuaded temple officials to refuse the offerings from—and, apparently, for—foreigners. Once again, neither the accuracy of Josephus's account nor the history of Jewish practice on this matter is our present concern.[115] What does matter, however, is how Josephus describes the innovation in question, and the arguments that he suggests were offered to coun- ter it. Noting that sacrifices had been offered for Rome since the time of Augustus (2.409, see also 2.197), Josephus depicts the chief priests oppos- ing this change in custom (ἔθος); the rebels however, relied on Eleazar's authority (2.410). As the circle of controversy widens, leading citizens and Pharisees enter the fray, warning the people of the dangers of Eleazar's proposition, and reminding them of the established customs of accepting gifts from foreign rulers and welcoming offerings from all (2.411–13, 417). Josephus continues, emphasizing the opponents' condemnation of this "strange innovation" (414), arguing also that abandoning the sacrifice for Rome would be tantamount to revolt (415–16). Once again, just as in his description of Judas's fourth philosophy, Josephus describes a dangerous innovation as violating customary practice, and he does so without recognizing the role that scriptural justifications could play either way. Innovation is measured not against scripture but against tradition; danger is not inherent in innovation per se but in certain kinds of politically sensitive breaks with national customs.[116]

Rejected Innovations: Royals

If rebellious innovations represent the dangers of "bottom-up" breaks with the national customs, Josephus's narratives regarding Herod I in particular illustrate Josephus's views regarding problems inherent in "top-down" breaks with law and custom.[117] To be sure, Josephus views Herod's innovative reconstruction and expansion of the Jerusalem temple as praiseworthy, even divinely sanctioned (*Ant.* 15.425).[118] But in a number of instances, Josephus explicitly criticizes Herod for breaking specific Jewish laws, customs, or traditions (e.g., *Ant.* 15.365; further instances cited and discussed below).[119] This is apart, of course, from Josephus's criticisms of Herod's flamboyantly murderous behavior (which, on the whole, Josephus has no need to describe as violating Jewish law or tradition—that much is patently obvious).[120] Setting aside once again questions of historical veracity—as well as, in this case, any evaluation of Herod himself[121]—it is worth reviewing this material in order to assess whether Josephus's critiques of Herod's illicit behavior shed further light on Josephus's approach to law, custom, and tradition.

One of Herod's first formal breaks with Jewish law occurred early in his reign, when the king deposed one living high priest in favor of another, something Josephus tells us was against the law (παράνομα; *Ant.* 15.40). Herod was urged to do this by his wife, Mariamme, who desired see her brother Aristobulus occupy the position, thereby bringing the priesthood back into Hasmonean hands (15.31–38). But doing so meant taking the position away from Ananel, the Babylonian priest Herod had installed in the position only a short while earlier (15.22).[122] To be clear, what bothers Josephus about Herod's handling of this matter—and what strikes him as violating Jewish legal norms—is not so much a question of descent (whether Babylonian or Hasmonean, to say nothing of Zadokite) as the fact that the high priesthood was apparently understood to be a life term. Now Herod, Josephus points out, was not the first to break this practice, but the third (15.41): Herod was preceded by Antiochus Epiphanes (who deposed Jason; see *Ant.* 12.238, 2 Macc. 4.23–29) and Aristobulus II (who deposed his brother Hyrcanus II; see *Ant.* 14.6–7, 41–42).[123] Characteristically, Josephus does not explain the origin of this thrice-broken tradition. Nor does his scriptural paraphrase contain any ruling that would mandate life terms for high priests.[124] In fact, if anything, Josephus's paraphrase provides scriptural support for Herod's behavior: following 1 Kings 2.26–27, Josephus relates that King Solomon deposed and banished the high priest Abiathar in favor of Zadok (*Ant.* 8.10–11). Nevertheless, Josephus still holds Herod to account for breaking with the traditional practice in this regard.

A more serious category of transgressions concerns Herod's introduction of foreign practices into Jewish areas, in violation of Jewish "national customs" (*Ant.* 15.267: τῶν πατρίων ἐθῶν).[125] Included among the problematic practices introduced by Herod are periodic athletic games, as well as the construction of a theater in Jerusalem and amphitheater nearby (15.268).[126] The buildings themselves caused controversy, we are told, because the trophy-laden décor itself (15.272) was considered a violation of Jewish custom (276: πάτριον). But the games themselves also violated Jewish mores, particularly the gladiatorial games of deadly combat (274–75). Josephus clearly tells his readers that such impieties were considered gross violations of Jewish customs—but, curiously, he does not in this case accuse Herod of breaking "the Law"—even though such a case could easily constructed, and perhaps was constructed by at least some of the Jews who opposed Herod's behavior.

Josephus also relates condemnation of Herod for his construction of Roman temples (*Ant.* 15.328–30).[127] We are told that Herod constructed such temples in Sebaste (*War* 1.403; *Ant.* 15.298), Caesarea (*War* 1.414; *Ant.* 15.339), and Paneion/Banias (*War* 1.404; *Ant.* 15.363–64), as well as other locales (*War* 1.407, 416; 422–28).[128] Here, too, Herod seems to stop just one step short of outright idolatrous behavior, for Josephus grants that Herod built such structures only in non-Jewish territory, for use by his non-Jewish subjects (*Ant.* 15.329). Yet Josephus states quite clearly (*Ant.* 15.328) that Herod's behavior violated Jewish "customs" (τῶν ἐθῶν) and "laws" (τῶν νομίμων).[129] Still, Josephus makes no effort to provide scriptural explanations or justifications—satisfied, apparently, that Herod's breaking with established custom is bad enough.

Herod's most controversial act in the arena of idolatry was no doubt his installation of a golden eagle above the gate of the newly renovated Jerusalem temple (*War* 1.648–50; *Ant.* 17.149–63).[130] We have had occasion to mention this episode before, for Josephus relates that two experts in Jewish law fomented fierce opposition to the eagle, inspiring their students to tear down the eagle with promises of eternal fame (*War* 1.650; *Ant.* 17.152–54) and even immortality (*War* 1.650). Josephus's description of this conflict in *War* largely fits the patterns we have traced above, where even a violation that could be presented as a clear abrogation of scripture (or "the Law") is decried, with characteristic ambiguity, as abrogating "customary laws" (1.649: τοὺς πατρίους νόμους).[131] In *Antiquities* 17.151, however, Josephus comes closer than we have seen in any case heretofore to accusing Herod of violating a Mosaic statute. In Josephus's own explanation, Moses remains unmentioned, and no biblical law is quoted; but Josephus does explain that "the Law" (ὁ νόμος) prohibits setting up images in the temple (17.151; see *War* 1.650, and compare also *Ant.* 3.91). In the trial scene depicted a few lines later, Josephus goes even further, albeit indirectly, depicting two legal experts, Judas and Matthias, as pitting Herod's decrees against Moses's God-given laws (17.159). While the plurals here would suggest that more is at stake than just the golden eagle, the contrast between Herod's illegitimate decrees and the divine Mosaic laws is, finally, clearly drawn—albeit only in the most general sense.[132]

Josephus notes many more Herodian impieties, such as the pillaging of David's tomb (*Ant.* 16.179–83). Josephus also speaks generally of Herod's impiety (e.g., 16.1, 17.168). Indeed, many further examples of Herod's violations of Jewish law and practice can be adduced, especially when readers measure Herod against standards other than Josephus's clearly stated ones.[133] And this, of course, is to say nothing of the king's murderous behavior, which Josephus believes incurred divine wrath, manifest in Herod's painful illnesses (e.g., *Ant.* 15.241, 17.168–71). But reviewing Josephus's narratives on these matters won't illumine the question we are considering here: the legal grounds that undergird Josephus's criticism of Herod's policies. There is, however, one last incident we must discuss, perhaps the most remarkable incident of Herod's law-breaking for our purposes, for in only this instance does Josephus clearly indicate how a legal innovation offered by Herod violates a particular law of Moses.

In *Ant.* 16.1–5, Josephus relates that Herod introduced a policy by which thieves caught breaking into houses would be sold into slavery to foreign masters.[134] So by Herod's new law, Jewish criminals suffered both slavery to Gentile masters and exile. This, of course, is well beyond what scripture mandates, as Josephus makes clear. Paraphrasing Exodus 21.37–22.2, Josephus explains that the Law mandates that such criminals either pay a fourfold fine or serve as slaves to fellow Jews for up to six years (compare *Ant.* 4.272–73).[135] Herod's policy, indeed, violates the biblical statute in a number of ways: the punishment is harsher, and when forced into service to Gentiles, the punished criminals would no longer be able to live in the manner of Jews (*Ant.* 16.2).

But what really matters for our purposes is that in this instance, we learn that Josephus is perfectly capable of explaining, both briefly and clearly, how a given royal decree violates not only "customs" in a general sense, but the Mosaic Law in a very specific sense. If Josephus had been, say, a Sadducee—by his own understanding of the group's concerns—he likely would have described *every* Herodian violation of Jewish law this way. Yet even in this case, when a clearly identifiable pentateuchal law of Moses is violated, Josephus introduces the discussion by describing Herod's flouting of the "national customs" (τῶν πατρίων ἐθῶν).

Josephus on Laws, Customs, and Traditions

How do we explain Josephus's failure to carefully distinguish between scriptural laws and nonscriptural traditions? Is this simply a reflection of his adoption of a Greco-Roman concept?[136] Does this put the lie to his repeated promise not to add or subtract from the scriptural record? If what is characteristic about the Pharisees is their adherence to nonscriptural traditions, doesn't it stand to reason that they would distinguish one category of laws from the other?

Well, it may stand to *our* reason that they would do so, but that doesn't mean that it stood to *their* reason to do so. Indeed, even full-blown rabbinic-Talmudic Judaism lacks any systematic effort at differentiating scriptural laws from oral traditions, so there may be little value in contrasting Jewish and Greco-Roman usages in this score. There are categorical distinctions that are bandied about, to be sure. We have already mentioned that a (rather small) number of *halakhot* are identified as nonscriptural traditions going back to Moses at Sinai. And the rabbis do, when it serves their purposes, distinguish between laws that are *de-Oraita* (from the Torah) and *de-Rabbanan* (from the rabbis). But this distinction does not at all cohere with the categories that interest Josephus. The category *de-Oraita* includes many laws derived exegetically; the category *de-Rabbanan* includes the rulings that are understood to be later, postbiblical expansions or additions to the legal tradition (therefore having less force).[137] A nonscriptural "halakhah of Moses from Sinai" would not be considered *de-Rabbanan*.[138] And it's difficult to predict from any abstract generalizations (let alone any precise definitions) how these categories might be used. To be sure, the rabbis view the command to build a booth on the festival of tabernacles to be a biblical ordinance, in contrast with the construction of an *eruv*, which is recognized as rabbinic (*b. Sukkah* 2a). But less predictably, the twice-daily recitation of the *shema*—understood already in the Mishnah as derived from Deuteronomy 6.7—is deemed a rabbinic ordinance, not a biblical one (*b. Berakhot* 21a; but compare *m. Berakhot* 1.1–3).

Another illustration of rabbinic Judaism's relative disinterest in clearly or consistently distinguishing biblical from nonbiblical rules can be drawn from traditional Jewish practice. The Jewish tradition recognizes the fact that the festival of Hanukkah is a postbiblical development, established by the Jewish community of that time and place (*b. Shabbat* 21b).[139] Yet when the Hanukkah candles are lit, a standard formula is recited, blessing God "for commanding us to kindle the Hanukkah lights." If we are looking for a comparative model to confirm the academic suspicion that Pharisees would, as a matter of course, have clearly distinguished biblical laws from their nonbiblical traditions (or even postbiblical interpretations), Talmudic Judaism, as manifest in rabbinic literature or traditional Jewish practice, does not fit the bill.

If we turn back to Josephus's description of the Pharisees, we can observe that Josephus never claims that the Pharisees neatly categorize their observances as either "scripture" or "tradition." He simply says that they accept the validity of both types, and emerge, nevertheless, as the "more precise" interpreters of the law of his age (*War* 1.110, 2.162). So we cannot argue against Josephus's Pharisaic allegiance by pointing to his scriptural adaptations and terminological confusions.[140] Neither his Pharisees nor the later rabbis were necessarily any clearer on these matters. And why should they have been? If one passionately believes that nonbiblical traditions are as legitimate as biblical laws, what difference does it make whether any given practice is in one category or another? Such a categorization might have mattered to a Sadducee, who would likely reject the customs for which scriptural justification was deemed lacking. But the rabbinic evidence—especially, *m. Hagigah* 1.8—suggests that those who accepted such traditions found no need to separate them out.

Clearly, Josephus is not a Sadducee, by his terms, and he's certainly not an Essene either (even a marrying one). We learn from the sectarian scrolls that many of that group's distinctive legal rulings were attributed to an inspired Teacher of Righteousness. Although Josephus does not address this issue head on, Josephus's paraphrasing of prophetic books and 1 Maccabees suggests that he was adamantly opposed to the idea that legitimate legal change could be introduced by a prophetic figure. From all that we have seen in this chapter, it seems that Josephus's own legal priorities align reasonably well with those of the Pharisees *as he describes them*. This is a significant conclusion, and it is one entirely independent of the more fraught question of whether Josephus's legal material coheres with Pharisaic halakhah, to whatever degree this can even be determined. Indeed, efforts aimed at identifying the scholastic milieu of Josephus's various positions on points of Jewish law have proved inconclusive at best.[141] But we can evaluate Josephus's legal theory in light of what he himself says about the Pharisee-Sadducee debates on these issues. Just like the Pharisees he describes, Josephus bestows great authority on traditions and even newly declared laws, without very much concern for scriptural justifications or precedents. He is fully capable of manipulating scripture to support certain ideals (e.g., resurrection) or to forward his apologetic purpose. But he demonstrates no interest in either bringing scripture in line with his later legal interests or justifying his legal interests by pointing back to scriptural passages or precedents. Nothing could be more Pharisaic than this: his indifference to precise categorization illustrates the fact that he has internalized the equal authority of both scripture and tradition.[142]

Diversity and Consensus

As we have seen, Josephus speaks against rebellious legal innovations as well as royal decrees that violate ancestral customs or scriptural laws. This is not to say, however, that he is intolerant of all innovations or diversities in ancient Jewish customary practice. As for innovations, we have already noted that he is not categorically opposed: he speaks approvingly of a variety of changes to the ancestral laws, provided they were introduced by legitimate leaders, with the consent of the Jewish populace. It remains to note here that Josephus is also accepting of at least some differences in custom and practice, as is evident in his generally laudatory treatments of the Essenes and John the Baptist. But how does Josephus square this accommodation with his general opposition to changes in Jewish law? His first strategy is to deny the innovative nature of such diversity, and his second strategy is to downplay the legal significance of any such diversity. Both strategies are evident in his treatments of the Essenes and John the Baptist.

Stringency and Innovation: Essenes and John the Baptist

Josephus asserts clearly that the Essene school was one of three, all stemming "from ancient times" (*Ant.* 18.11). The general tone of his two descriptions of Essene practice is quite positive, and he even asserts outright that the Essenes are, in almost all respects, of the highest character (*Ant.* 18.19). Josephus does, to be sure, make it clear that this group's practices differ from the rest with regard to matters such as celibacy, shared goods, oaths, and worship. And he does offer one explicit point of criticism, when he notes that the Essenes worship by themselves, apart from the temple (*Ant.* 18.19).[143] But in other cases, Essene discipline presumably involves accepting additional obligations above and beyond the general observances accepted by all, without necessarily rejecting general practices. In some instances, we are led to believe that distinctive Essene practices—such as the prayers they offer toward the rising sun (*War* 2.128)—were performed in accordance with their own, presumably longstanding, customs (πατρίους).[144] In other words, Essene practices do not need to be understood as legal innovations per se—and Josephus, importantly, does not describe them as such. It is true that one *could* criticize the Essenes for breaking with wider Jewish traditions by adopting their own stringencies. But not everyone would necessarily be receptive to such a criticism. Today, there are Jews who are vegetarians, vegans, or even teetotalers, going well beyond the mandates of ancestral laws concerning diet or customs concerning sobriety. Yet these practices are not generally perceived by contemporary Jews as outright breaks with traditional practices. Josephus's attitude toward the Essenes seems to have been similarly accepting. Indeed, as we have also noted, Josephus singles out the Essenes for their devotion to the Law, maintained, if need be, until death (*War* 2.152–53).

There is one particular matter where, quite possibly, Josephus goes out of his way to avoid lending credence to a critique of Essene legal innovation. Among their most notable practices was their celibacy, something noted by not only Josephus (*War* 2.120–21; *Ant.* 18.21) but also Philo (*Hypothetica* 11.14–17) and even Pliny (*Nat. Hist.* 5.73).[145] In one respect, this is a rather striking practice, one that would appear to fly in the face of the plain sense of the twice-repeated divine command given first to humans created on the sixth day and later again to Noah: "be fruitful and multiply" (Gen. 1.28, 9.1). Now I suspect that Josephus's Essenes would have had an answer to any scripturally based challenges to their practice, as he implies: if their celibacy was in fact motivated by the fear that women cannot be trusted in matters of sexual behavior (*War* 2.121), then they could justify their celibacy by appeal to the biblical command not to commit adultery (e.g., Exod. 20.14 [MT: 20.13]). But Josephus has, intriguingly, made the matter much simpler. Readers of *Antiquities* would never suspect that there was a legal innovation or, quite possibly, a scriptural violation involved in the acceptance of celibacy. Josephus's rewritten Torah does not include paraphrases of either Gen. 1.28 or 9.1.[146] There's no way to know for certain why Josephus chose to gloss over these commands, but one effect of his editorial decision is clear enough: the celibate Essenes he describes cannot be accused of violating the scriptures he has rewritten.

Josephus's description of John the Baptist is similarly shaped in such a way as to avoid giving the impression that John's preaching or practices were either novel or of any legal consequence (*Ant.* 18.116–19). Obviously, we cannot weigh in here on the fraught questions concerning the historical value of this account over against those of the New Testament (John's life: Matt. 3.1–17//Mark 1.2–11//Luke 3.1–22, and also John 1.19–35; John's death: Matt. 13.3–12//Mark 6.17–29//Luke 3.19–20).[147] Nor can we fully consider here the nature of John's baptism.[148] But we must observe here that Josephus evaluates John quite positively: he was a "good man," who encouraged piety (18.117).[149] His unjust death resembles in some respects the prophet-killings discussed in the previous chapter. To be sure, John makes no predictions and is executed in Machaerus (not Jerusalem). Moreover, Josephus grants that Herod Antipas was fearful of potentially seditious crowds gathering around John (18.118). But the killing of John is viewed as unjust nonetheless, and Herod's subsequent defeat is understood as divine punishment (18.116, 119).

What matters most for our purposes is one particularly distinctive aspect of Josephus's account: his emphatic insistence that John's baptism was not, in truth, a new ritual of atonement in and of itself but a symbolic, bodily counterpart to a prior change in behavior: "they should not employ it to gain pardon for whatever sins they committed, but as a consecration of the body, implying that the soul was already thoroughly purified by right behavior" (18.117). This, of course, is very different from the Gospels' more straightforward description of John's call to practice "baptism of repentance for the forgiveness of sins" (Mark 1.4: βάπτισμα μετανοίας εἰς ἄφεσιν ἁμαρτιῶν; compare Matt. 3.6; Luke 3.3, 6)—a phenomenon that was apparently rather controversial (see John 3.25). In an earlier treatment of this matter, I have argued that the Gospels are likely closer to the truth on this matter than Josephus.[150] Without reviewing the entire matter here, I would suggest that the present analysis may well suggest a motive for Josephus's special pleading on John's behalf: Josephus is at pains to stress that John's baptism was neither a legal innovation nor a radical break in ancestral custom; it served merely to encourage piety. Josephus's description of John is somewhat similar to his description of the Essenes, and entirely unlike his account of Judas the Galilean. In contrast to Judas's dangerous innovations, John's preaching and practices were—Josephus avows—symbolic, legally inconsequential, perhaps even quaint, and certainly harmless.

Josephus, the Pharisees, Consensus, and Stasis

Josephus repeatedly claims, as we noted, that the Pharisees are more popular than the Sadducees (*Ant.* 13.288, 298; 18.15, 17).[151] Josephus also indicates that the popularity of the Pharisees rests, at least in part, on their willingness to bestow authority on ancestral traditions, over the opposition of the Sadducees (*Ant.* 13.298; see also 18.15, 17). While some have questioned the historicity of these assertions, there is good reason to consider them carefully, for one can find echoes of Pharisaic power in the New Testament and, perhaps, reflections of Pharisaic popularity in the eventual predominance of rabbinic Judaism.[152] Given these possibilities, it stands to reason that the people might have been more willing to support a group that would have bestowed authenticity on customary practices. There is, however, no way to be certain of this, and we will therefore set aside the historical problems here. What we do need to probe now is whether Josephus's understanding of the dynamics of law and custom in determining Jewish religious practice relates in any way to his association of popularity with the Pharisees, as well as his claim to have lived a Pharisaic life.

A striking irony on these matters emerges when reading Josephus's oeuvre. As we have seen, his works provide a good deal of information regarding disputes among disparate ancient Jewish schools of thought. At the same time, he frequently boasts of Jewish unity with regard to both practice and belief. His emphasis on unity and consensus is particularly strong in his last work, *Against Apion* (2.179–83). Here we find him celebrating Jewish harmony of practice and belief. Jews act alike, and all agree on the matter of divine providence (2.179–81). Jews lack innovators, adhering in unison to the ancestral customs (2.182–83). Has something happened between *Antiquities* and *Apion* such that the one-time describer and defender of diversity has now become an advocate of consensus?

While there are differences between *Antiquities* and *Apion* in this regard, there are also important similarities. In both *Antiquities* and *Apion*, Josephus repeats what may well have been an ancient Jewish slogan of sorts: that the uniqueness of the Jerusalem temple represents the singular God and befits the united people of Israel (*Ant.* 4.200–201; *Apion* 2.193, see also 2.179).[153] In both instances, this assertion serves as a proud point of departure, introducing the summaries of Mosaic law that follow. This suggests that we ought not read *Apion* against *Antiquities* on this score, for the same assertion serves the same purposes in each work.[154] Even as we again grant that Josephus is engaged in apologetic exaggeration—especially in *Apion*, his *apology*—we must allow that Josephus is not necessarily engaging in pure fancy when parading aspects of Jewish unity; nor is he clearly contradicting himself.[155] Indeed, the overall unity of the Jewish people is a motif of both *Antiquities* and *Apion*, with *Antiquities* emphasizing historical continuity under divine providence (esp. *Ant.* 1.1–26) and *Apion* emphasizing general unity of practice and belief (esp. *Apion* 2.179–87).[156] Yet the unity of the Jewish people is also a motif in *Antiquities*, articulated symbolically by the singularity of the temple (4.200–201) and illustrated practically by the rite of pilgrimage (4.203–4, see also 17.155, 20.105).[157] The scholastic diversity that, in truth, is a rather minor theme of *Antiquities*, does not undercut Josephus's overarching emphasis on Jewish historical continuity and political unity.[158] Moreover, whatever threat scholastic diversity poses to Josephus's impression of Jewish unity is, in part, countered by his repeated assertion of Pharisaic predominance and popularity. The other groups, we are told, are of great interest but much less influence.

There are further common denominators among *Antiquities* and *Apion*—and even *War*—that deserve mention here. We have reviewed many instances where Josephus opposed changes in custom or law introduced by wayward teachers, rebels, or royals. The various details we have reviewed find their most general expression in *Apion*, where Josephus takes pride that the Jewish people lacks "innovators" (2.182–83). Unlike other nations, who alter their ancestral customs at will (2.182), the Jews steadfastly oppose whatever their ancient law prohibits (2.183).[159] To be sure, to some scholars this sounds as if Josephus has taken on a new-found opposition to all legal change or diversity.[160] But it is important as always to tend carefully to what Josephus does and does not say. In at least some respects, as with regard to divine providence (2.180), the assertions of unity in *Apion* are carefully phrased so as not to preclude the legitimate scholastic differences operating within the consensus. In *Apion* 2.180, Josephus asserts that all Jews accept divine *providence*; as argued in chapter 2, this does not preclude the legitimacy of the Sadducean denial of *fate*.[161] With regard to law, even in *Apion*, Josephus allows that legal and judicial decisions will be made carefully by human judges (2.187). What he opposes in *Apion* 2.182–83 is lending legitimacy to those who would consciously, proudly, and *individually* innovate in ways that go against the law and customs of the people. So understood, this is not a new interest of his at all. Indeed, he expresses the very same concern, in very similar terms, when he earlier opposes the dangerous innovations of Judas the Galilean (*Ant.* 18.9).[162]

There is no reason to presume, therefore, that Josephus has changed his mind (in *Apion*) about the rare, and relatively minor, legal innovations he describes and accepts as legitimate in *Antiquities*. He has not decided late in life that the Maccabean alteration to Sabbath law was misguided. Nor is he necessarily now opposed to the quaint, rigorous practices added to the law by Essene or other pietists. He does not understand these harmless stringencies as changes to the Law at all. And the legal changes he supports are those that were proposed by legitimate leaders and quickly accepted by the people as a whole. In other words, he accepts decisions approved by *consensus*; such changes cannot, of course, threaten the unity of the Jewish people or the integrity of their constitution. The changes or reforms he would oppose in *Apion* are those that would change the very nature of the law and threaten the legal consensus. Josephus is here asserting what he would have asserted all along: that pious Jews would sooner lay down their lives than give up the Law's commands, such as the Sabbath, circumcision, or food laws (*Apion* 1.42–43; see *War* 1.34–35 and *Ant.* 12.253–56, on the Antiochene persecutions; and *War* 2.152–53, on Essene martyrdoms).

For Josephus, the real threats to consensus are twofold: individual innovation and civil strife. And again, a common denominator among

Josephus's works can be discerned on these matters. Both *Antiquities* and *Apion* are ill disposed toward individual innovation (*Ant.* 18.9, *Apion* 2.182). And his celebration in *Apion* of peaceful unity is the flip side of his concern in *Antiquities* with the most dangerous innovation of all, Judas the Galilean's willingness to permit the killing of other Jews in the pursuit of his political program (*Ant.* 18.7–8, 23). And of course, both books in this respect reflect concerns with the breakdown of consensus that preoccupied Josephus decades earlier, when writing *Jewish War* (e.g., 1.10, 12; 5.257).[163] Indeed, it may not be mistaken to see his apologetic embrace of Jewish unity and harmony in *Apion* as the mirror image of *War*'s Masada story.[164] For Josephus, the Masada story's mass murder-suicide constitutes the self-inflicted, just punishment of those Jews who pioneered the kin-killing stasis that typified the rebellion against Rome. The conclusion of *Apion*, by contrast, celebrates the unity and harmony of the Jewish people, providing the ideal counterweight to the aberration that, Josephus hopes, ended with Masada.

Hovering between these black-and-white depictions of ideal unity and suicidal stasis—but moving decidedly closer to the former—are the popular Pharisees. If stasis is suicide, then consensus—both theological and halakhic—is the only real hope. And where there is moderate diversity, popularity surely is the next best thing to an unquestioned consensus. We can, I think, go one step further: even if popularity is one step short of consensus, the interest in consensus is by no means contradicted by the inclination toward popularity, when necessary. To the contrary, Josephus's remarks about Pharisaic popularity, the ideal of Jewish unity, and his endorsement of legal changes put forward by legitimate leaders and adopted by consensus are all cut from the same cloth.[165] Perceptions of legitimacy and popularity are equally essential in establishing and maintaining a consensus.

There are, to be sure, undeniable shifts in emphasis between *Antiquities* and *Apion* in particular.[166] Of course, *Antiquities* is a historical work that cannot deny the changes—or mistakes—of the past. *Apion* is not only an apologetic essay but possibly a forward-looking one as well. But the common denominators among Josephus's compositions are measurably larger than the shifts in emphasis. These works were penned by the same author, and he did not make some dramatic about-face on the matters we are discussing here. His literary efforts all stand against internecine strife, and favor consensus. When we examine his response to the destruction of the temple in the next chapter, it will be helpful to consider whether

Josephus's emphasis on consensus—evident in all his works, though above all in *Apion*—plays a part in that response.

Conclusion

We have seen, once again, that Josephus's thumbnail sketch of ancient Jewish scholastic disputes proves reasonably confirmable. The Pharisees did, as is widely recognized, adhere to nonscriptural ancestral traditions. We have no reason to believe that they considered these traditions to be of equal antiquity with scripture. Nor does the evidence support the claim that the Pharisees consistently defended these traditions on exegetical grounds. The Sadducees, by contrast, adhered to a more scripturalist view, in that they rejected nonscriptural ancestral traditions. They were not, however, literalists. There was no fixed scripture, and there was no opposition to interpreting scripture when needed. It is even possible that Sadducees engaged in rewriting scripture, but this evidence is tenuous, based as it is on the appearance of Sadducean laws in the *Temple Scroll* and the reworkings of biblical narratives and proverbs found in the Wisdom of Ben Sira, a work whose theology prefigures later Sadducean thought.

Unfortunately, Josephus does not explain precisely how the Essenes fit into this picture, but a few points can be noted. First, he gives us no reason to believe that the Essenes agreed with either the Sadducees or the Pharisees, whether on specific matters of Jewish law or with regard to the method by which their distinctive practices were derived. Curiously, the scrolls suggest that the Qumran sect's distinctive practices were revealed by an inspired Teacher of Righteousness. However, this evidence from Qumran meets up with a decidedly suspicious silence: Josephus's description of the Essenes says nothing about a neoprophetic teacher of laws, and this will remain an important difference that prevents simply equating one data set with the other. But as we have seen, Josephus appears to categorically reject the legitimacy of *any* post-Mosaic prophetic-style legal teaching. Even the biblical prophets were never involved in legal innovation in Josephus's retelling. And the prophets of his own time served in purely predictive or cautionary capacities. Therefore, if Josephus had been aware of an Essene or sectarian belief in a quasi-prophetic legislative revelation, he likely would not have mentioned it. We must admit that the correlation in this matter is weaker than, say, that shared by Josephus's Pharisees and the ideology of the Mishnah. But even so, there is a tantalizing correspondence among Josephus's silence on the derivation of Essene law, his interest in Essene prophecy, and his consistent refusal to grant any prophets but Moses the power to legislate.

Once again, we have found that Josephus's own views align reasonably well with those of the Pharisees, as he describes them. Josephus himself bestows legitimacy on both written laws and ancestral customs. Indeed, he often describes them interchangeably, even allowing that "the Law" can come to include newly adopted practices or changes, provided they have been proposed by legitimate authorities and approved by consensus. His concerns with both scripture and tradition can also be discerned in the ways he opposes innovative policies that he rejects, such as Herod's decrees and the innovations of what Josephus himself identifies as the "fourth philosophy." Scripture matters to Josephus, but so do nonscriptural customs, and violators of either stand to be criticized. As we have seen, consensus matters to Josephus as well. Legitimate changes to law are all approved by consensus, while the most dangerous innovations are those that foster civil strife. Although Josephus does not explicitly attribute to the Pharisees an interest in consensus per se, his repeated assertions of Pharisaic popularity, whether historically valid or not, serve the same purpose: popularity is what consensus is made of.

Along the way here, some important things are to be learned about ancient Jewish law and legal dispute as well. Some have pointed to Josephus's terminological inconsistency to argue against his Pharisaism, arguing that a good Pharisee would have been more careful to distinguish between scriptural laws and ancestral traditions. But we have suggested good reasons to think that Pharisees—like Josephus and the later rabbis—probably would not have struggled to categorize all laws as either scriptural or traditional. Those who accept practices that can be justified in multiple ways are not the ones who need to carefully distinguish the categories.

Other scholars have largely overlooked Josephus's evidence in the efforts to support binary approaches to the understanding of ancient Jewish halakhah, pitting a Sadducean-sectarian approach against the Pharisaic-rabbinic one. Various lessons from this chapter caution against such simplifications of the matter. Even if Sadducees and sectarians agreed on (some) important matters of law, there is no evidence—whether from Josephus or anywhere else—that the Sadducees accepted what appears to the characteristic justification for distinctive sectarian practices: the quasi-prophetic revelation of what had been hidden to all, and remains hidden from the rest of (nonsectarian) Israel. Josephus's testimony about the Essenes certainly would suggest that there were at least three—and not just two—approaches to ancient Jewish legal matters. His testimony about the Pharisees (and his own views, too) would suggest that the Pharisees did not justify their positions by exegetical means, but rather by defending the validity of nonscriptural traditions. If we knew more about the Sadducees, perhaps we would be able to determine whether Urbach was right when he surmised that they—and not the Pharisees—were the pioneers of legal midrash. Still, the general impression we get from Josephus about both of these groups lends further validity to Urbach's claims. But even if not, the evidence from Josephus should caution us against understanding the history of Jewish law in binary terms, whether with regard to the number of distinct groups or to the methods of deriving law—from scripture, custom, or prophecy.

Josephus's studied disinclination to even mention the possibility of post-Mosaic prophetic legislation is an overlooked piece of this puzzle. Although we can only surmise, this may well explain why he doesn't describe the Essene legal theory in comparison to Sadducees and Pharisees. Surely his reticence to allow neoprophetic figures to weigh in on matters of law would have put him in opposition to the Dead Sea sectarians and their ilk. At the same time, his attitude on the matter prefigures a number of rabbinic traditions, some of which will object to laws derived from prophetic texts (e.g., *b. Hagigah* 10b) while others reject the possibility that neoprophetic revelations could solve legal questions (e.g., *b. Bava Metzi'a* 59b). But as we will see in the next chapter, this intriguing phenomenon is just one of a number of important ways Josephus prefigures later rabbinic thought.

5

Josephus and Judaism after 70 CE

IN THIS CHAPTER we consider Josephus's works as responses to the destruction of the second temple. Although we will draw evidence from all of Josephus's literary creations, we will focus as much as possible on *Jewish War*, for that work alone constitutes his *explicit* response to the destruction of the temple. But we will look beyond *Jewish War* when relevant. Doing so will prove particularly informative when we consider *Antiquities*'s account of the aftermath of the destruction of the *first* temple. We will also consider material of interest in relation to what both *Antiquities* and *Against Apion* have to say about Judaism in Josephus's own day.

Up to this point, we have been gathering support for the contention that Josephus's theological and even legal views align reasonably well with the Pharisees, as he describes them—perfectly in line with his claim to this effect in *Life* 12. Unfortunately, Josephus does not describe the Pharisaic response to the destruction per se, so the same kind of support for this aspect of our argument is not available. Still, we will see that Josephus's response points in the general direction that the later rabbis will later follow. To be sure, this phenomenon in and of itself would not constitute much of an argument in favor of describing Josephus's theology as Pharisaic. Nevertheless, the case we have been constructing to that effect does find confirmatory support in the general similarities with later rabbinic theology that we will consider in this chapter.

It is, of course, widely accepted that the destruction of Jerusalem and its sacred shrine in 70 CE was a cataclysmic event in the history of the Jewish people. Indeed, it remains quite common, despite some objections, for scholars of ancient Judaism and teachers of religion to view 70 CE as a turning point for the purposes of periodization, marking the time when the second temple period comes to an end and the rabbinic period begins.[1] The purpose of this chapter is neither to downplay the significance of the events of 70 CE nor to argue for rethinking the standard periodizations of Jewish history. But there are three problematic trends in current scholarship that this chapter does seek to counter. The first is a general tendency to assume that Judaism in general was not able—theologically or religiously—to respond adequately to the catastrophic events of the era. According to some authorities, Judaism was shocked into silence by the temple's demise, only producing thoughtful responses generations later. In the meantime, the Jewish experience was characterized by despair and apostasy. A second, and related, problematic tendency is to overlook or downplay the significance of Josephus's evidence regarding the Jewish response to the destruction of the temple. A third problematic tendency, related equally to the previous two, is to assume that certain groups in particular—such as the Sadducees or Essenes—were unable to withstand the catastrophe, and disappeared *for that reason*. The purpose of this chapter is to show how different things look when we do give Josephus's works the credit they deserve. Josephus's *Jewish War* and *Antiquities* may well constitute the most thorough and thoughtful early Jewish response to the fall of Jerusalem that we have. Moreover, his works provide the benchmark by which we can evaluate both the novelty of the later rabbinic response and the alleged inadequacy of predestruction Judaism to weather the storm of 70 CE. We will of course devote the bulk of our efforts in this chapter to a fuller understanding of Josephus. But because so much scholarship on 70 CE seems unduly influenced by contemporary concerns, we must spend a few paragraphs explaining and countering these trends.

Shattering the Myth of a Silent Crisis

In his justly praised and self-consciously controversial rethinking of rabbinic history, Seth Schwartz asserts that Judaism was "shattered" by the cumulative events of 70 and 135 CE, and that rabbinic Judaism emerged as we know it only centuries later.[2] Judaism's near disappearance, Schwartz avers, is to be explained as resulting, in part, from the theological challenge presented by the destruction, one that remained unmet:

> Probably everywhere, though, the failure of the revolts had led to disaffection with and attrition from Judaism. 4 Ezra ... gives an idea of the gloom prevailing among some of the literate elites and subelites

of Jewish Palestine after 70. What point is there, the author argues, in trying to observe an unobservable covenant when God rewards our efforts by destroying us.... But [4 Ezra] cannot have satisfied everyone, and those whom it failed to satisfy will have reacted with panic, despair, and finally abandonment of Judaism.[3]

In characterizing the period as one of gloom and apostasy, Schwartz is hardly alone. Robert Goldenberg also claims that "many must have reacted to the catastrophe with despair and total abandonment of Judaism."[4] Adiel Schremer has recently discerned within various rabbinic traditions echoes of "a theological and existential crisis with which many Jews of the time were confronted, namely, the possibility that Rome's victory meant the obliteration of God Himself."[5]

In some respects, these recent studies echo the now classic (and frequently cited) studies of Baruch Bokser, describing the rabbinic response to 70 CE as one that emerged in stages, over the course of the tannaitic and amoraic periods.[6] At first, Judaism was completely traumatized by the events of 70 CE. Jews remained enamored of the temple (as witnessed by Mishnah *Seder Qodashim*) but they also embraced the newer phenomenon of statutory prayer. Eventually, according to Bokser, rabbinic Jews had sufficiently reacted to the loss of 70 CE by boldly claiming that the newer institution of statutory prayer had "superseded" the cultic institutions of the past: prayer *is* greater than sacrifice, as stated in the tradition attributed to R. Eleazar ben Pedat in *Bavli Berakhot* (32b).[7] In some of these articles, Bokser goes even one step further, bolstering his argument by appealing to a historical analogy. In 1983, echoing a voice commonly heard in post-Holocaust thought of that time, Bokser asserted that survivors of the Holocaust and Hiroshima were "able openly to talk about these events only after a considerable number of years and they still find it difficult to evaluate the full implications."[8] So the ostensibly delayed rabbinic response to the events of 70 CE can be understood by comparison with reactions to the more recent destruction of European Jewry.[9]

Bokser was neither the first nor the last scholar to draw a comparison between these two events. In relatively recent publications, partial analogies between 70 and 1945 have been drawn, for instance, by Martin Goodman, Jonathan Price, and Lawrence H. Schiffman (among others).[10] Also drawing modern analogies, Birger Pearson locates the (Jewish) origins of Gnosticism within circles that lost faith in response to ancient catastrophes.[11] Lurking behind Bokser's views in particular may well be the views of his teacher, Jacob Neusner, who linked the events in a number of publications, including some produced during the time Bokser was studying with him at Brown University.[12] Neusner has also disclosed, in an autobiographical essay, that his personal grappling with the Holocaust shaped his life in general and his academic work on ancient Judaism in particular.[13] Of course, it bears remembering that both Jacob Neusner and Baruch Bokser—along with practically two full generations of Jewish academics—studied with Shoah survivors and refugees at the Jewish Theological Seminary and other institutions. For these and perhaps other reasons as well, explicit comparisons between the Jewish responses to 70 CE and 1945 are not uncommon.

At the root of these comparisons is a common trope in post-Holocaust thought, one associated with well-known figures such as Richard Rubenstein, Emil Fackenheim, and Irving Greenberg, all of whom asserted that the response to the Holocaust was muted or delayed until the 1960s.[14] Although these writers disagreed among themselves, they agreed that traditional theologies were inadequate to the challenge posed by Auschwitz; and they agreed that it took a generation before this consensus could be reached. This perspective has become almost a doctrine in certain circles, and it has been "canonized" in some anthologies of post-Holocaust thought.[15] In some cases, post-Holocaust writers themselves, somewhat paradoxically, looked back to 70 CE as a model or partial precedent for the contemporary catastrophe as well as Jewish reactions to it.[16] Bokser and others followed and reinforced this trend in their own works on the earlier catastrophe.

I have dealt with this issue more fully—and still, no doubt, inadequately—elsewhere.[17] For present purposes, we need only mention the following. First, the very notion of comparing the two events may well be entirely misguided. Whether considering the absolute numbers of victims, or the relative number of victims versus survivors, the contemporary catastrophe surely exceeds all that happened in 70 CE.[18] Indeed, a common trope in contemporary Jewish thought on the Holocaust asserts that the event is historically unique—a reasoned assertion that can and has been questioned.[19] But certainly a narrower claim still stands: the Holocaust is commonly believed by modern Jews to be an unprecedented catastrophe *in the Jewish experience.*[20] And what matters most of all for our concern is this: no one thought the same about 70 CE. Indeed, no one even asked whether 70 CE was unprecedented. As we will see, the Jewish responses to 70 CE are all predicated on the comforting assertion that the destruction of the *second* temple in 70 CE is, by contrast, a precedented event, the response to which can be guided by the scriptural accounts concerning aftermath of the destruction of the first temple in 586 BCE.

We must also point out here that the specific hypotheses being projected onto the past—the notions of shocked silence and delayed response to catastrophe—have been proven false. As both David Roskies and Hasia Diner have demonstrated, the belief that the Jewish response to the Holocaust—be it literary, theological, or even liturgical—was delayed is, simply stated, a myth: A vast literary output occurred both during and immediately after the war.[21] And this is to say nothing of the rather practical—but no less meaningful—responses, such as aiding the survivors,[22] or supporting the building and defense of the nascent state of Israel.

One final point must be mentioned: the notion of delayed response is decidedly biased, favoring the liberal, philosophical approaches of the 1960s over all others. It did not take any time at all for those that were so inclined to interpret the destruction of European Jewry within the traditional, covenantal theodicies. Indeed, various writers did so both during and immediately after the war (blaming primarily, in turn, Zionists, assimilationists, or even anti-Zionists).[23] It similarly took very little time to reach for the equally traditional noncovenantal theodicies, whereby (for example) during the Holocaust, God hid his face (see Deut. 31.17–18).[24] As already noted, it also took no time at all for a great many survivors and refugees to respond to the Shoah pragmatically, by helping create and defend the State of Israel. The assertion, therefore, that there was a delay in responding to the Holocaust is predicated on denying the power of the traditional theodicies (whether covenantal or not)[25] and prioritizing the value of intellectual philosophizing over various important, and meaningful, practical responses.

It may be true that the traditional theodicies are ineffective in the post-Holocaust age. But it is fair to point out that these theodicies were just as ineffective (for atheists and religious liberals at least) before 1945 as well. The Lisbon earthquake of 1755 brought many of the same questions to the fore long ago.[26] It was in 1791 that Immanuel Kant published his essay questioning all philosophical theodicies.[27] Indeed, for sensitive religious liberals, the death of a single child can shatter the traditional, covenantal theodicies, and did so before 1945 as well.[28] Yet as we have already observed, for many Orthodox or "Ultra-Orthodox" theologians, the traditional theodicies—even the covenantal ones—continue to work just as well as they always did.[29]

Much more can and has been said on the myth of Jewish shocked silence and delayed response to the modern catastrophe. For present purposes, it suffices to emphasize that the reading back of this falsehood onto ancient Judaism—whether explicitly or implicitly—is a practice that simply has to stop.

To be sure, some scholars have bucked these trends. Among recent studies, Moshe Beer's survey of the Jewish responses to 70 CE (including Josephus's) grants the anguish of the apocalyptic texts, but sees less of a theological crisis in evidence in rabbinic literature.[30] Jonathan Price also sees precedents of the later rabbinic response in the early Josephan one.[31] And Martin Goodman has observed that for most Jews, Judaism "was not shattered."[32] Shaye Cohen pointedly questioned whether the evidence for the analogy discussed above is in the sources or in scholars' minds, and reminds us that before 1945, scholars often claimed that the events of 70 CE did not result in a theological crisis.[33] Indeed, in an essay published during the *First* World War, R. Travers Herford's description of Pharisaic Judaism is essentially the inverse of Seth Schwartz's. Granting that the destruction was a source of great grief, Herford asserts nonetheless that the destruction "was not a fatal blow" and that the Pharisees "were not thrown into confusion as if there were an end to their Religion."[34] Herford's essay is problematic in its own right—particularly in its then common assumptions regarding the historical value of the late rabbinic legends concerning Yohanan ben Zakkai. But the essay remains instructive, if only as a reminder of how different 70 CE seemed almost a century ago, at least to those scholars willing to give the Pharisees and early rabbis the benefit of the doubt.

When we leave the modern analogy out of the picture, the myth of shocked silence after 70 CE should shatter under its own weight. When we examine the evidence for early Jewish literary responses to 70 CE, what do we find? It is well known that very little Jewish literature produced in the immediate aftermath of the destruction has been preserved. From the four decades following Titus's victory (70–110 CE), we have some apocalyptic literature (4 Ezra and 2 Baruch)—and we have the works of Josephus. The vast majority of the Jewish *Pseudepigrapha* are of uncertain date, so perhaps another apocalypse or testament, too, was composed during this time frame.[35] Of course, our sources tell us about other writings that we no longer have—the history by Justus of Tiberias, for instance (Josephus, *Life* 336–67).[36] And a great deal of Christian literature was produced, at least some of which was composed by people who still considered themselves Jews. The Christian responses to the destruction of the temple are not uninteresting; nor is it always possible to discern whether a given text from this period is exclusively Jewish or Christian—the boundaries remain permeable.[37] Still, the demonstrably Christian responses to the destruction (even if Jewish-Christian) are not directly relevant to my argument here because scholarship rarely claims that the destruction of the temple posed a theological crisis for Christians. Nor do scholars who argue that the Jews experienced a theological crisis point to Christian (or Jewish-Christian) sources as evidence for this claim.[38]

Regardless of what we decide to include, the fact remains that the literature responding in some way to the destruction of the temple and known to have been produced in the four decades following 70 CE is not as vast as, say, what the rabbis later produced, or what the Dead Sea sectarians ostensibly composed or copied centuries earlier. However, we must also point out that the extant literature datable to the four decades following the destruction is, arguably, vaster than the extant Jewish literature datable to the four decades preceding the destruction. What literature was produced by Jews from 30 to 70 CE? Late Philo, the letters of Paul, early portions of the Gospels, and perhaps other assorted documents, such as, possibly, Wisdom of Solomon or even *Megillat Ta'anit*.[39] We can, I think, dispense with statistics: the numbers (whatever they are precisely) do not seem to support the conclusion that Jewish literary production declined precipitously after 70 CE.

Of course, we cannot assume that the surviving literature is a reliable indication of rates of literary production. Perhaps a great deal of literature composed both before and after 70 CE has been lost forever. Indeed, we could just as well conclude—from the general lack of literature from various periods preceding the destruction—that Jews were shocked into silence by the Roman conquest of Judea in 63 BCE, by Herod's reign of terror, or even by Jesus' crucifixion. And the point being offered here remains valid nonetheless: the evidence we do have—however little it may be—does not support the claim that Jewish literary production experienced a marked decline after 70 CE.[40]

Josephus, the Rabbis, and the Theological Response to 70 CE

A curious fact alluded to earlier characterizes much of this discourse on 70 CE, even as it renders the results all the more problematic: Josephus's

Jewish War has been largely overlooked in these discussions. Of course, it is much easier to imagine Judaism's theological silence in the face of catastrophe when the later rabbinic response is compared to the meager— and to some, depressing—responses of *2 Baruch* and *4 Ezra*. According to Neusner, the apocalyptic authors of *4 Ezra* and *2 Baruch* raise and address head on the important questions of the day concerning suffering and atonement, while the rabbinic Mishnah remarkably passes over these issues with "utter silence."[41] According to Robert Kirschner, the apocalyptic visionaries conceive of God as transcendent, mysterious, and vindictive; the rabbis of the aggadic midrashim, according to Kirschner, imagine an immanent God who identifies with his people and suffers along with them.[42]

For some reason, comparisons between the rabbinic response and Josephus's are more difficult to come by.[43] Perhaps this is because the anonymously authored apocalypses express their messages in a canonical genre, and presumably represent a distinct group of religious Jews. The known and individual author of *Jewish War*, by contrast, expressed himself in a "secular" genre, and may well only represent his own views. It may also be that Josephus is more likely to be studied by historians, while apocalyptic and rabbinic literature is more likely to be studied by historians of religion; and our topic may more likely be studied by the latter than the former. Socioreligious factors may also be at play, for it is true that post-Holocaust thought has had little, if any, discernable impact on the study of Josephus.[44] Be that as it may, there are nonetheless a striking number of similarities between the later rabbinic responses to the destruction and Josephus's, especially as articulated in *Jewish War*. A careful consideration of these comparisons is instructive, for it allows us to see the extent to which the answers eventually reached by the rabbis were already reached long before by Josephus, within a decade or two of the temple's demise. The comparison also allows us to appreciate the degree to which Josephus's response points in the directions that much of Judaism will later follow.[45] Indeed, the comparison will compel us to question whether the extant evidence justifies the claim that the destruction of 70 CE brought about a theological crisis at all.

Theodicy and Covenant

Although *Jewish War* is, primarily, a work of history, we have seen throughout this book that Josephus's account is liberally peppered with theological observations.[46] It remains to argue here that these theological observations cohere in such a way that we can meaningfully speak of the work as offering a thorough, theological explanation for the destruction of the temple. Simply put, Jerusalem fell for its sins (*War* 6.95–102; *Ant.* 20.166). This is not meant to deny that Josephus also sees other historical forces at work in bringing about the revolt. He presents a reasoned, nontheological survey of the causes of the revolt, describing (especially in *War*, books 1–3) the gradual breakdown of trust between the Roman procurators and their Jewish subjects.[47] From the very opening lines of *Jewish War* (1.10–12), Josephus clearly lays the blame with the "Jewish tyrants," who caused violent civil strife and brought ruin on the temple. As the narrative progresses, we learn that civil strife for Josephus is not a historical cause of the Jewish defeat, but a moral one. It is not that the strife allowed the Romans to win—that victory was inevitable. The strife, rather, renders the Roman victory just (5.257). Indeed civil strife and bloody tyranny are just two of the many sins Josephus attributes to the contemporary Jewish populace (5.401–15, 429–45, 565–66; 6.200–213). So despite all the practical explanations he offers along the way, the extensive Jewish defeat and the destruction of the temple were, ultimately, brought about by God as punishment of the sinful Jewish polity.[48]

Josephus's discussions of Jewish transgression are focused particularly on two sorts of sin: bloodshed, and profanation of sancta. Josephus records the slaughter of many whom he considered innocent: the named figures include the priests Ananus and Jesus (4.314–25), and the upright Zacharias, son of Baris (4.334–44).[49] Various unnamed innocents were also killed, including, for example, the slaughtered population of Ein Gedi (4.402–3), random worshipers at the temple (5.15–18), and the infant consumed by Mary of Bethezuba (6.200–13). As for the profanation of sancta, Josephus points out that the rebels often violated the Sabbath or festivals (2.456; 4.102–3, 402; 5.100–105). In a large number of instances, a single act will do double duty for Josephus, as when early on in the revolt, civil strife led to bloodshed in and around the temple (2.424, 443–46) or later when the Sicarii murdered the population of Ein Gedi on Passover (4.402–3). The defilement of the temple by bloodshed committed in or near it is an important leitmotif of *Jewish War* (4.150–51, 201, 215; 5.15–18, 100–105; 6.95–110). For Josephus, this bloodshed—especially the murders of priests in the sanctuary (4.314–25)—plays a particular role in bringing about the divine punishment that concludes the rebellion (see also *Ant.* 20.165–66).

Josephus's theodicy—like many biblical and second temple theodicies—proceeds along two planes, one personal and the other communal.

On the personal level, Josephus duly reports that many sinful people—especially sinful leaders—eventually get their just deserts (e.g., Aristobulus: 1.84; Herod: 1.656; John of Gischala and Simon bar Giora: 6.433–34; the Sicarii and other rebels: 7.259–74). He even concludes book 7 of *Jewish War* by describing the painful illness of one of his enemies, and asserting that "God in his providence inflicts punishment on the wicked" (7.453). But Josephus's personal theodicy does not assume a timely earthly reward or punishment for all. Indeed, sometimes punishment is delayed, so as to come at a fitting time later (4.104). Other times, as we have already observed, Josephus notes that innocent people suffer at the hands of the wicked. Since Josephus—like the Pharisees (2.163), the Essenes (2.154–58), and even Titus (6.46–49)—believes in life after death (3.372), justice can be worked out on the personal level in the next world.

On the communal or national level, Josephus clearly believes that God holds the people accountable for their sins, and that the political fortunes of the nation depend largely on the behavior of the people toward each other and God. Such, indeed, is the message of Josephus's own lengthy speech in book 5 (esp. 376–419), ostensibly delivered to the people of Jerusalem. The same sentiment serves as Josephus's overriding understanding of what befell his people in his day (e.g., 1.10, 12; 5.391–93, 442–45). What remains to be noted is that the communal theodicy of *Jewish War* is, in the author's mind, closely tied to the sins the people committed; in particular, the bloodshed in and near the temple—including, above all, the murders of Jesus and Ananus (4.288–317)—tips the scale (318).[50] The pollution of the temple by bloodshed (4.150, 201, 388; 5.15–18, 100–105; 6.95–110, 126) and other transgressions (4.242; 5.402) leads to God's abandonment of his sanctuary and people (4.323; 5.19–20, 411–12; 6.300), and the inevitability of Roman victory (3.354; 5.367–68; 6.110; see also *Ant.* 20.165–66).

The Jews are not the only people whose fate is governed by God, according to Josephus. Various passages in *Jewish War* assert that God—whether by fortune (τύχη), providence (πρόνοια), or fate (εἱμαρμένη)—is on the Romans' side (e.g., 3.354, 4.622, 5.367).[51] With regard to God's support for the Roman Empire in general, Agrippa is early on given the opportunity to point out that no empire could rule so vast a kingdom without God's permission (2.390), and Josephus himself says much the same thing in his speeches (5.367–68).[52] Not only is the Roman Empire's dominion ordained by God, the particular victory at hand is brought about by God as well, as asserted by Titus (3.484, 494; 6.41), unnamed Roman generals (4.366, 370), and Josephus himself (3.293; 6.110). One further aspect of Roman rule and victory is also ordained by God, and that is the rise of Vespasian and Titus to imperial power (3.6, 401, 404; 5.2).[53]

In understanding the events of his day, Josephus is clearly guided by his strong belief—rooted in Jewish scriptures—in a God who exercises control over major political events in the world at large while at the same time maintaining a special relationship with the people of Israel, whose fortunes rise and fall as a function of their virtues and vices. In other words—as we have seen in chapter 2—Josephus believes in both divine providence and election. Although the term "covenant" hardly plays a prominent role in Josephus's works,[54] it is clear nonetheless that a covenantal concept pertains.[55] As far as Josephus is concerned, this special relationship between God and Israel is not ruptured by the events of 70 CE. Although the temple is gone, God has not been defeated, for he brought these events about. Moreover, earthly divine justice remains in evidence.

That much of what is outlined above finds parallel expressions in rabbinic literature will come as no surprise to those who have familiarity with these sources.[56] The assertion that the temple's demise came about because of God's anger over transgressions by the Jewish people is commonplace in rabbinic literature and traditional Jewish liturgies. The destruction is sometimes blamed, vaguely, on transgression in general (e.g., *b. Berakhot* 3a) and other times connected to various sins (see. e.g., the catalogues of sins listed in *Mekhilta ba-Hodesh* 1 [ed. Horovitz/Rabin 203–4] and *b. Shabbat* 119b). In a few instances, the sins discussed by the rabbis as causing the temple's destruction resemble or recall those focused on by Josephus. As for civil strife, a well-known tradition preserved in the Tosefta and the two Talmuds (*t. Menahot* 13.22; *y. Yoma* 1.1, 38c; *b. Yoma* 9a–b) asserts that the second temple was destroyed on account of senseless hatred (the Tosefta and Palestinian Talmud also mention greed). The fuller rabbinic accounts of the destruction of Jerusalem more specifically recall civil strife–induced famine, and various horrors resulting from it (see esp. *b. Gittin* 55b–56b).[57] We also find rabbinic traditions that link the destruction of the temple to bloodshed and defilement (*b. Shabbat* 33a; *Sifre Num.* sec. 161 [ed. Horovitz 222]).[58] More to the point, a rabbinic tale preserved in the Tosefta (*t. Yoma* 1.12, *t. Shevuot* 1.4) and later texts (e.g., *y. Yoma* 2.2, 39d; *b. Yoma* 23a–b) speak of priestly manslaughter in the second temple.[59] Presumably, the fight is over the opportunity to perform priestly duties, but the result is bloodshed in the temple, which is followed in turn by demonstrably bad judgment by all involved: the concern was more with ritual defilement (from the corpse) than it was for the murder in their midst. As for other sins, both Josephus and the rabbis speak rather specifically of corruption and greed among late second temple period priests (e.g., *Ant.* 20.181, 205–7; compare *t. Menahot* 13.21; *b. Pesahim* 57a). Some have even suggested that in the case of this particular parallel, there may be some reason to suspect that the rabbis had access to Josephus (in some version) or a source he used.[60] Finally, the rabbis also agree that the Roman victory, the destruction of the temple, and even the rise to power by Vespasian are events orchestrated by God, in order to bring about the covenantally deserved punishment of the Jewish people (*b. Gittin* 55b–56b; *b. Avodah Zarah* 18a).[61]

Perhaps we should not make too much of these comparisons, for there are, to be sure, differences as well. Josephus, for instance, is particularly (but not exclusively) focused on the defilement of the temple by bloodshed, while the rabbis are less focused on this particular issue,[62] and willing to blame the destruction (at least for homiletic purposes) on all sorts of sins (*b. Shabbat* 119b). Surely other differences between Josephus and the rabbis can also be identified. Of course, the bulk of the rabbinic sources surveyed here are from later strata, and some are Babylonian in provenance. So the rabbinic sources will no doubt have taken their own social and geographic context as well as later developments (such as the rise of Christianity) into account. Yet the common denominators here are important ones. The Jewish defeat was a punishment by God for transgressions—including bloodshed committed in or near the temple. The temple was destroyed by a Roman empire whose victory was orchestrated by God, and by a Roman emperor whose rise was predicted by a Jewish sage. Surely there were other views on these matters as well, but the evidence from Josephus allows us to demonstrate conclusively that these core aspects of the rabbinic approach—which are largely scripturally based—were already in place, at least in some circles, within a decade of the temple's demise.

Lament and Precedent

Let us turn back to Josephus and Josephus's belief that God has destined his people and temple to destruction for their sinful engagement in civil strife and temple profanation. It is fair to point out that there seems little comfort in this interpretation of the revolt. Indeed, Josephus more than once records his own sadness at the defeat, in addition to noting the

lamentation of the other Jewish people experiencing it.[63] It has been suggested that *Jewish War* is a largely tragic book, written when the author
"felt that Judaism without the Temple could not survive."[64] Generalizing
further, one can perhaps understand why scholars might speak of pervading gloom after 70 CE, and imagine widespread disaffection, apostasy, and
even the shattering of Judaism itself.[65] But such conclusions overlook one
key fact, readily apparent to any reader of either *Jewish War* or the Hebrew
Bible: this has all happened once before. What Josephus describes—in all
its gory detail—is, after all, the destruction of the *second* temple.

The precedented nature of the destruction of the temple is emphasized
by Josephus a number of times in *Jewish War*.[66] Most simply—and, from
a literary point of view, most emphatically—Josephus concludes book 6 of
Jewish War on precisely this note: "Thus was Jerusalem taken... Captured
on five previous occasions, it was now for the second time devastated"
(6.435). Books 5 and 6 in particular are liberally peppered with references
to the previous destruction, and comparisons between the past and the
present. Josephus indeed claims that he repeatedly reminded Jerusalem's
residents of the first destruction—and the reasons for it—on the eve of
what would turn out to be the second (5.391–93, 411–12; 6.103). Josephus
also takes note of the calendrical coincidence that highlights the connection: the destruction of the second temple took place on the very same
"fated" day (the tenth of Av)[67] that Nebuchadnezzar burned the first temple (6.250, 267–68).

Because the destruction followed a pattern, it was also predictable—or
so it seemed, after the fact, to Josephus. He believes that a number of signs
indicated, even before the destruction, that great tragedy would befall the
people *again*. Above all else, the extensive sin that Josephus describes
could have made everyone aware that, by God's power, the Jews would be
punished one way or another. Having described John of Gischala's sinful plunder of the temple—the latest of many transgressions—Josephus
emotes:

> Nor can I here refrain from uttering what my emotion bids me say.
> I believe that, had the Romans delayed to punish these reprobates,
> either the earth would have opened and swallowed up the city, or
> it would have been swept away by a flood or have tasted anew the
> thunderbolts of the land of Sodom. For it produced a generation far
> more godless than the victims of those visitations, seeing that these
> men's frenzy involved the whole people in their ruin. (*War* 5.566)

Josephus is so convinced of the people's sinfulness, at least after the fact, that he believes the temple would have been destroyed inevitably, even without Rome.

But the logic of covenantal theodicy is not the only sign Josephus speaks of. The historian claims that publicly visible or audible omens of various sorts should have served as sufficient reminders that the temple is not inherently invulnerable to destruction (*War* 2.650; 6.288–300).[68] Still, as Josephus reminds us (2.650; 6.287) the problem with omens is that they can be too easily misinterpreted. Josephus also recalls the efforts of seers who ostensibly foresaw the doom, such as Jesus, son of Ananias, who publicly lamented for Jerusalem starting four years before the war. He continued to do so—lamenting that destruction will come *again* to Jerusalem—until he was struck dead by a Roman *ballista* (6.300–309). But then again, the problem with "true" seers is they can be too easily foiled by "false" ones (6.286–87), just as in biblical times (e.g., Deut. 13.1–6; Ezek. 13.1–23). A further mode of warning available to Jews before the destruction involved the interpretation of scriptures and other writings. Josephus speaks of these sorts of predictions too (6.109–10, 250, 310–15). Indeed, Josephus's *Antiquities* later asserts that the Roman defeat of the Jews was predicted by Jeremiah (10.79) and Daniel (10.276).[69] But as we have already noted, Josephus grants that the problem of alternative interpretation of scripture remains (e.g., *War* 6.310–15).[70] Curiously, the memory of such public warnings has also been preserved in the independent records of Tacitus (*Histories* 5.13),[71] the New Testament (esp. Mark 13.1–2, 14),[72] as well as rabbinic literature (*y. Yoma* 1.4, 39a; *b. Yoma* 39b; *b. Pesahim* 57a; *b. Gittin* 56a). Whether anyone actually accurately predicted this event cannot be known; the fact that it was widely believed (after the fact) to have been predicted (before the fact) tells us something of the way various groups—Jews no doubt included—were able to incorporate the event within their religious paradigms.

A number of times in his narrative, Josephus presents himself as an agent of prediction, experiencing dreams and portents (*War* 3.351–52; 405–8) or interpreting the prophecies of the past (4.385–88; 5.375–419). He indeed seems to have imagined himself as a latter-day Jeremiah—predicting defeat, counseling surrender, and even comparing the abuse hurled in his direction to the sufferings of the biblical prophet (5.391–93; compare, e.g., Jer. 20.1–8 and *Ant.* 10.114–15).[73] This comparison, however, ought not be pushed too far, for the figure (and book) of Daniel also figure prominently in Josephus.[74] Unlike Jeremiah, Daniel, the wise dream interpreter, was, after all, taken into the court of Nebuchadnezzar (*Ant.* 10.186–89). And Josephus similarly took up residence in a foreign capital in the wake of the temple's demise.[75] Moreover, as we noted previously, Josephus states that he believed that Daniel predicted the rise of Rome (*Ant.* 10.276), prefiguring, perhaps, Josephus's own predictions regarding Roman rulers. To be sure, Josephus's prophetic self-description may be self-serving, and may also be drawn largely after the fact—what Josephus *really* thought and said before the destruction is not knowable. But whether we accept Josephus's self-portrait as historically accurate is beside the point. Even if he came to see himself this way on arriving in Rome, the phenomenon still illustrates his ability to quickly embrace— even embody—biblical precedents.

Moreover, with regard to each of the categories of prediction discussed above—the logic of covenantal theodicy, public omens, and the predictions of prophets past and present—Josephus never claims for himself exclusive access to any one. So even if we entirely dismiss Josephus's self-portrait, we are still left with his various accounts of omens and predictions with which he was not personally involved, to say nothing of the omens and predictions recorded in Roman, Christian, and rabbinic sources. With or without the insight of prophecy, the coming doom may have been clear to many, and Josephus implies as much when he describes—quite reasonably—the dejection of moderate Jews and the efforts of many, both early on and closer to the end, to flee to the Roman side (e.g., *War* 2.455, 556, 649; 4.128). After all, a Jewish victory would have required a miracle. Short of that, a Roman victory was to be expected. So the destruction of the temple may not have been as shocking as some assume. Certainly for Josephus, the catastrophe did not shatter his faith. To the contrary, the destruction affirms that God guides the universe with both providence and justice, just as in biblical times.

Once again, parallels between Josephus and later rabbinic literature are easily found. The earliest of rabbinic documents—the Mishnah— preserves a tradition that speaks of mourning for the temple's loss, and does so in a way that emphasizes the connections between the destruction of the second temple and earlier events: one is to fast and mourn on the seventeenth of Tammuz and the ninth of Av as a result of both destructions, as well as other events relating to biblical and postbiblical history (*m. Ta'anit* 4.6–7; see also *t. Ta'anit* 3.9–13; *b. Ta'anit* 29a). Although the point is often missed or underappreciated, even the classic Yohanan ben Zakkai legend ties back to the aftermath of the destruction

of the first temple: the sage's proof that acts of loving-kindness will suffice for atonement comes, importantly, from the behavior of the postex-
ilic prophet Daniel, driving home the point that the post-70 CE reliance
on loving-kindness as a means of atonement is therefore not only scripturally justified, but follows historical precedent (*Avot de-Rabbi Natan* A
4 [ed. Schechter 11a]). Indeed, the precedented nature of the second temple's destruction is specifically emphasized in the great many rabbinic
sources that speak of both destructions or compare one to the other (e.g.,
t. Menahot 13.22; *y. Yoma* 1.1, 38c; *b. Yoma* 9a–b). So thoroughly are the two
events tied together that often it is difficult to decide whether a rabbinic
tradition speaking generally of the destruction of the temple or Jerusalem
intends to speak of 586 BCE, 70 CE, or both (see, e.g., *b. Shabbat* 3a).[76]
The rabbis also juxtapose 586 BCE and 70 CE to other catastrophes earlier and later, including the shattering of the tablets by Moses and the
fall of Betar (*m. Ta'anit* 4.6–7). Yet they differentiate between the two
temples (*b. Yoma* 18a, 21b; *b. Menahot* 27b) and between their destructions
as well, suggesting that these catastrophes came about as a result of different sorts of sins (e.g., *t. Menahot* 13.22; *y. Yoma* 1.1, 38c; *b. Yoma* 9a–b).
The rabbis also recognize that while 586 BCE was followed by exile, 70
CE was not.[77]

The rabbis also, like Josephus before them, believed the catastrophe of
70 CE was predictable, and indeed was predicted before the fact. Rabbinic
traditions regarding omens of destruction have been mentioned already
(e.g., *b. Yoma* 39b; *b. Pesahim* 57a; *b. Gittin* 56a). Other rabbinic traditions
speak (like Josephus) of the withdrawal of the Shekhinah from a sin-laden
sanctuary prior to its destruction (*Avot de-Rabbi Natan* A 34 [ed. Schechter
51b]; *b. Rosh ha-Shanah* 31b).[78] Just as Josephus presents himself as properly understanding these signs, so rabbinic literature describes Yohanan
ben Zakkai as the correct reader of such omens (*b. Yoma* 39a; *y. Yoma* 1.4,
39a, 6.3, 43c–d). Indeed, just as Josephus likely saw himself as Jeremiah,
scholars sometimes compare Yohanan ben Zakkai to Jeremiah as well.[79]
And just like Josephus before them, the rabbis believed the Romans to be
Daniel's fourth kingdom (e.g., *b. Avodah Zarah* 2b; *Leviticus Rabbah* 13.5, on
Lev. 11.2–7 [ed. Margulies 1:281–95]; compare *Ant.* 10.276).[80] Various other
biblical passages are understood by the rabbis (after the fact, of course) to
be predictions of the temple's destruction (e.g., *Sifra be-Huqotai, perek* 5.2
[ed. Weiss 111b]; *Sifre Deut.* sec. 328 [ed. Finkelstein 378–79]; *Lamentations
Rabbah* 1.5 [ed. Buber 32b–33a]); and they believe these meanings to have
been known already to biblical figures (e.g., Joseph: *Genesis Rabbah* 93.12,

to Gen. 45.14 [ed. Theodor/Albeck 3:1170]; Adam and various prophets: *Leviticus Rabbah* 13.5, on Lev. 11.2 [ed. Margulies 1:281–95]).

Once again, many of these rabbinic traditions are from the later, amoraic strata of the rabbinic period. Moreover, we could easily isolate many minor differences among the varied rabbinic sources and between them and the earlier Josephus. But it is the basic common denominators between Josephus and the later rabbis that matter most, as they constitute the core interpretation and understanding of the destruction. For both Josephus and the later rabbis, the regrettable loss of the temple is to be mourned, but it is at the same time easily explainable, for the answers are all there in the Hebrew Bible. The destruction of 70 CE was a precedented event, and a predictable one.

Memory, Hope, and Atonement

Three further aspects of Josephus's approach to the temple are, to my mind, insufficiently appreciated when evaluating the various Jewish responses to the destruction of 70 CE. Neusner famously argued decades ago that an important aspect of the rabbinic response to the destruction was to assert in the face of catastrophe that nothing had changed, and it is for this very reason that the Mishnah devotes a good portion of its content to describing how the temple ought to look (esp. tractate *Middot*) and how the cultic rites ought to be performed there (esp., but not exclusively, tractates *Tamid* and *Zevahim* and the portions of *Seder Mo'ed* devoted to sacrificial offerings).[81] Cohen correctly challenged one important aspect of this view when he argued, against Neusner, that the Mishnah's general silence regarding the destruction raises serious questions as to whether the Mishnah is addressing a theological crisis caused by the destruction.[82] It remains here to point out, once again, that the novelty and distinct nature of the rabbinic sources are both challenged by comparison with Josephus's writings. If continuity—along with, perhaps, hope—is what is asserted by remembering the temple's structure and practice, then the rabbis' efforts in evidence in the Mishnah can be seen as a continuation of Josephus's lengthy passages describing the temple and priesthood (esp. *War* 5.184–237) and sacrificial practice (esp. *Ant.* 3.224–57), passages in which Josephus at times speaks as if the temple were still standing (see also *Apion* 2.193–98).[83] And long before the rabbis devoted as much as a third of the Mishnah to remembering and detailing sacrificial practice, Josephus, too, emphasized the centrality and singularity of the Jerusalem temple (*Ant.* 4.199–203; *Apion* 2.193). But the parallels do not stop here: just as Josephus recalls the temple's particular splendor (*War* 6.260), so do the rabbis (*b. Bava Batra* 4a). Yet both also record that this splendor was bestowed on the place largely by the sinfully cruel king, Herod I (*War* 1.401–2; *b. Bava Batra* 3b–4a). Commenting on this paradox, the Talmudic tradition asserts, very practically: "if it were not for the monarchy, the temple would never have been built" (*b. Bava Batra* 4a) Although we cannot be certain of this, it is likely that Josephus would have said much the same. So Josephus as well as the later rabbis fostered memory of the temple in its splendor, but did so in a way that stopped short of a moral whitewash. The temple of old was built by rather sinful human hands, but it was glorious all the same.[84]

It is commonly asserted that Josephus's works are particularly reticent when it comes to eschatology or other hopes for Jewish restoration.[85] But there are indications—especially in *Antiquities*, but even in *Jewish War*— that Josephus expected an eventual reversal of the situation he witnessed. This is at least implied in all the evidence collected and reviewed already regarding the precedented and predicted nature of the destruction. Since the destruction had happened once before (esp. *War* 6.250, 267–68, 435–38; see also *Ant.* 10.135–42), then, following the same script, a reversal too would be expected (*Ant.* 11.1–7). Moreover, if the destruction was predicted—for example, by understanding Daniel's fourth kingdom as the Romans (*Ant.* 10.210, 276–77; see also *War* 6.109–10, 250)—then the ultimate triumph of the Jews (*Ant.* 4.125–30) as well as the Romans' eventual demise is just as clearly predicted.[86] After all, once Josephus clearly indicates that Daniel predicted Rome's rise and Jerusalem's fall (*Ant.* 10.276), any Jewish reader of Josephus would know what the next step has to be. Daniel's various prophecies never end with the victory of a foreign king: it's always the God of Israel who gets the last laugh. Josephus, more vaguely—perhaps now with his non-Jewish readers in mind—follows his final mention of Daniel with some vaguer, but not contradictory, statements on divine providence (10.277–80; discussed in chapter 2).

We are back in the dark with regard to the nature of the temple Josephus (presumably) wished to see restored. But the impression cast by his works suggests that there is an important contrast with apocalyptic expectations, even as there is a comparison with early rabbinic literature. Along the lines of Ezekiel, the *Temple Scroll*, the *New Jerusalem* texts, and especially (for our purposes) 4 Ezra 10.25–27, 44–54, it appears that a good number of ancient Jews expected that a future temple would be quite different from, and much greater than, the temple of old.[87] While some late rab-binic and medieval traditions speak of a jewel-encrusted future temple,[88] the dominant trend is to imagine a future without even implying any defi-ciency or critique of what was lost. The rabbis could have put forth visions of the future that in some fashion implied an overturning of the past by imagining a temple of vastly greater size, operating by different rules, run by different personnel. But they do not do this. The Mishnaic discussions of temple practice are practical, realistic, and *conservative*.[89] Indeed, if we were to characterize the rabbinic hopes on the basis of the memories of the temple preserved in extant tannaitic sources, we would conclude that the rabbis wanted the temple back *pretty much just the way it was*.[90] And the same, it seems, holds for Josephus. In *Antiquities*, he has little to say about Ezekiel (*Ant.* 10.74–141) and nothing to say about the prophet's temple vision. Just like the later Mishnaic rabbis, Josephus betrays no hints that the next temple would look any different from the last one.

Because the memory of the structure of the second temple played an important role for both Josephus and the rabbis, one can wonder whether Josephus or early rabbinic sages held out hopes for the rebuilding of the temple without at the same time overturning the world order, just as happened after 586 BCE. As Martin Goodman points out, rebuilding a destroyed temple would have been more the norm than the exception in the Roman world.[91] It is also rather certain that some Jews held more violent expectations, as articulated in extant apocalyptic works, and evidenced by subsequent Jewish revolts.[92] While there are aspects of Josephus's works that can be compared with apocalyptic literature—such as his treatments of Daniel's prophecies[93]—there is one key difference: Josephus's immedi-ate hopes were likely focused on working within the Roman system, not against it. We will never know precisely what the sages of Josephus's day thought about this matter. While the degree of rabbinic involvement in the second Jewish revolt against Rome remains unclear,[94] the rabbinic movement's survival through the second war against Rome suggests that at least a number of key figures were not involved. While the apocalyptic strain is not to be entirely disconnected from the rabbinic one,[95] the bulk of our earliest rabbinic evidence (namely, the Mishnah) suggests that the rabbis' memories and hopes were more like those of Josephus than those of the apocalyptic seers.

One final matter must be addressed. It is frequently claimed that the destruction of the temple created a crisis precisely because the people were then left without means of atonement.[96] It is true that rabbinic sources raise this very question—most famously in a tradition recording R. Joshua asking it of Rabban Yohanan ben Zakkai (*Avot de-Rabbi Natan* A 4, B 8 [ed. Schechter 11a–b]).[97] But a number of points must be considered with regard to the significance of these traditions. First, these sources have no difficulty finding an answer: in the absence of the temple, various forms of piety (prayer, study, acts of loving-kindness) can suffice—just as they did in the days of Daniel, after the destruction of the first temple. It is also important to note that these sources, taken as a whole, do not uniformly suggest that atonement per se is the issue. While one well-known tradition referred to above does raise the problem of atonement without the temple, other equally poignant traditions mourn the temple without direct reference to this concern (e.g., *b. Makkot* 24a–b). Indeed, the Jewish daily liturgy appears to have incorporated prayers of atonement early on.[98] And unlike the traditional *musaf* prayers recited on Sabbaths and holidays—which ask God to accept prayer in lieu of sacrifice—the atonement blessings of the daily *amidah* do not include any apology regarding the matter of doing so without sacrifice.[99]

We also find different approaches to the matter of atonement as it relates to the temple's demise, including the assertion that the punishments entailed in the destruction itself released Israel from further obligations regarding, at least, the sins committed up until that point.[100] Finally, we must note that the traditions asking and answering the question of how to atone in the absence of the temple do not stem from the earliest strata of the rabbinic tradition.[101] It is true that the question of non-sacrificial atonement is answered clearly only in later rabbinic traditions such as *Avot de-Rabbi Natan*. However, it is equally important to bear in mind that, at least as far as our extant evidence is concerned, the question remains unasked until these later texts as well.

The last point is crucial: if we are to believe that the destruction of the temple posed an existential or theological crisis because of the elimination of the means of atonement, it would be wise to find sources from the earliest decades following the destruction that assert this point. To my knowledge, there aren't any. When the destruction is described in apocalyptic literature, various questions are raised, but the problem of atonement is not among them (see, e.g., 4 Ezra 3.1–4.52, 2 *Bar.* 10.1–19). The apocalypses are full of gloom, to be sure, but there is a glimmer of hope in them as well, and the possibility for reconciling with God remains (e.g., 4 Ezra 8.19–36; 2 *Bar.* 48.2–24).[102] Similarly, when reacting to the violation of the temple by Antiochus IV, both 1 and 2 Maccabees express various emotions and raise sundry questions, but neither seems particularly concerned with the problem of atoning for sin without the temple (see, e.g., 1 Macc. 1.62–2.14; 2 Macc. 6.12–17). Daniel 9.4–19 is even more explicit: the temple has been ravaged, so Daniel *prays* for repentance. Presumably, Daniel's request was granted.

More important for our concerns, Josephus betrays no evidence of a crisis regarding atonement in his reaction to the events he witnessed. In one of the few passages in *Jewish War* explicitly addressing this theme, Josephus portrays himself calling on the people to repent of their sins to avert the coming doom (5.415–19). While this call precedes the temple's destruction, it follows the defilement of the temple by bloodshed and other transgressions, as well as the abandonment of the sanctuary by God (5.19–20, 411–12; 6.300). Moreover, there is nothing in the speech to imply that the chance for repentance has been lost permanently. If there is remaining doubt as to whether, in Josephus's mind, the destruction of the temple eliminates atonement or severs divine-human ties, we do well to consult Josephus's lengthy treatment of the destruction of the *first* temple and its aftermath (*Ant.* 10.84–11.113). There, in his creative recasting of 2 Kings, 2 Chronicles, Jeremiah, and Daniel, we find no indication whatsoever that the people are left without the ability to reconcile with God by living righteous lives. To the contrary, God's merciful care remains in evidence, and is bestowed on Daniel and other righteous exiled Jews. Soon enough, at the predicted moment, Cyrus allows the Jews to return and rebuild (11.1–7).

Josephus, the Rabbis, and Apocalyptic

As we have seen, Josephus precedes the rabbis in concluding that the destruction of the second temple is a divine punishment for transgression, brought about by a divinely-empowered Roman Empire. Josephus also precedes the rabbis in recognizing that the lamentable events of his own day are a repeat performance, playing out once again the drama experienced in Jeremiah's day and recorded in scripture. Finally, we have seen that Josephus precedes the rabbis in fostering a realistic memory of the past. He describes a glorious but human structure, one that was built, in part, by rather sinful leaders. This realistic memory of the past suggests—but does not demonstrate—that Josephus also preceded the rabbis in hoping for a rebuilt temple that would closely resemble the one that was lost.

It is with regard to Josephus's hopes and memories that we find the greatest degree of contrast with apocalyptic literature, despite his interest in and reverence for Daniel's precise predictions (10.267). The books of *2 Baruch* and *4 Ezra* do not praise the temple of old, and look forward to a future very different from the past (see esp. 4 Ezra 10.25–27 and *2 Bar.* 4.1–6, 32.1–5).[103] Yet we should not push the contrast between Josephus and apocalyptic too far, for Josephus and the visionaries shared a great deal. The apocalyptic seers, too, interpreted the destruction of the second temple covenantally (4 Ezra 9.27–37; *2 Bar.* 13.8–9, 78.2–79.4). Moreover, the artifice of pseudepigraphy serves to emphasize that the events of 70 CE follow the biblical pattern, to say nothing of having been predicted by biblical figures—just as we found, generally, in Josephus. Indeed, it would appear that practically all extant Jewish literature interpreting the catastrophe of 70 CE—Josephan, apocalyptic, and rabbinic—agrees on these few, not insignificant points: the destruction was orchestrated by God, to punish a sinful people, in a way that recalls earlier catastrophes, especially that of 586 BCE. So the destruction of the second temple plays out a biblical drama for a second time. General agreement on such core issues among a wide array of texts, written right after the destruction and much later, seems hardly to testify to any great theological crisis. The well-attested answer is the expected one. This chorus of theological consensus is not the sound of a religion shattering.

Essenes, Sadducees, and 70 CE

In the introduction to his widely used and eminently readable translation of the Dead Sea Scrolls, Geza Vermes offers the following explanation for the disappearance of the Essenes (which Vermes associates with the Roman destruction of Qumran in 68 CE):

> Essenism is dead. The brittle structure of its stiff and exclusive brotherhood was unable to withstand the national catastrophe which struck Palestinian Judaism in 70 CE. Animated by the loftiest of ideals and devoted to the observance of "perfect holiness," it lacked the plaint strength and the elasticity of thought and depth of spiritual vision which enabled rabbinic Judaism to thrive and flourish. And although the Teacher of Righteousness clearly sensed the deeper obligations implicit in the Mosaic Law, he was without the genius of Jesus the Jew who succeeded in uncovering the essence

of religion as an existential relationship between man and man and man and God.[104]

This rich passage is fascinating in many respects. In part, it summarizes the results of Vermes's other scholarly projects, particularly insofar as the historical Jesus relates to rabbinic sources.[105] But what matters for our concerns is the supposition that Essene ideology was religiously unable to withstand, let alone respond to, the catastrophe of 70 CE—it was too stiff to adapt; too strict to survive. Its disappearance is explained by its inadequacies, which in turn made room for better things.

John Trever, who was among the first scholars to encounter the Dead Sea Scrolls, reached similar conclusions:

> The vitality of the Qumran organization and faith, though sufficient to perpetuate the community for almost 200 years, was apparently inadequate to survive the final cataclysmic destruction meted out by the "Sons of Darkness," the Romans. Such a reversal of their belief concerning the end of the age was too severe a blow to their neatly ordered faith, and it was shattered. The vitality of Christians, on the other hand, sustained by a dynamic faith focused on God (whom they found revealed in the living presence of the resurrected Christ), could not be destroyed by the most heinous connivings of Roman persecutors.[106]

There are important historical—and moral—differences between the approaches represented in these excerpts. Tellingly, Vermes passionately defends the legitimacy of post-70 CE rabbinic Judaism. Trever implicitly criticizes all Judaism in his condemnation of the Essenes, and grudgingly concedes (only in a note) the survival of a "less rigid" Pharisaic Judaism.[107] But the common denominator between Trever and Vermes is disturbing enough: the successful survival of a religious tradition is taken as prima facie evidence of its quality; the disappearance of a tradition proves its failure.

This isn't academic history at all. It's blatant religious supersessionism, laced with a lethal dose of social Darwinism. To say—especially after 1945—that the violent obliteration of any particular historical religious community is to be explained by some inadequacy in the destroyed community's theology seems particularly insensitive, to say the least. One might as well suggest that Armenian Christianity in Asia Minor was religiously inadequate, or that Polish Judaism was just too stiff or rigid. We no longer blame victims—at least not in polite company. We shouldn't blame the victims of the ancient past either.

Leaving moral concerns aside, the fact of the matter is that the historical arguments for the disappearance of the Essenes right after 70 CE are just as invalid as the arguments for the shattering of Judaism in general. Our sources tell us less than we would hope, so some scholars fill in the blanks with what modern analogies or ideologies would suggest should have happened. But our sources tell us more than nothing, and it behooves us to attend carefully to what they do say. As Martin Goodman has emphasized, practically everything we know about the Essenes (and the Sadducees, too) comes from writers who write after 70 CE (Josephus included). Virtually all of these writers speak *as if* these groups are still around. Of course, Josephus himself speaks of the temple in the present tense in *Apion* (e.g., 2.193–98)[108]—decades after its destruction—so we cannot put too much stock in grammatical time. But it remains of significance that no writer before Epiphanius of Salamis (in the fourth century CE) refers to the disappearance of the Sadducees, Essenes, or other schools or sects (*Panarion* 19.5.6–7; 20.3.1–4).[109] The discovery of the *Damascus Document* in the Cairo Genizah is certainly an intriguing clue for the survival of Essenes, as well as other striking terminological and conceptual similarities between the second temple sectarian literature and that of the medieval Karaites.[110] But other explanations, such as late antique and early medieval manuscript discoveries near Jericho, can account for such similarities without presuming the survival of sectarians/Essenes into the Middle Ages.[111] But we certainly cannot continue to assume that the sectarians all disappeared in 70 CE either.[112]

Writing in the decade following the demise of Qumran, Josephus describes the suffering of the Essenes during the war against Rome in heroic terms:

> The war with the Romans tried their souls through and through by every variety of test. Racked and twisted, burnt and broken, and made to pass through every instrument of torture, in order to induce them to blaspheme their lawgiver or to eat some forbidden thing, they refused to yield to either demand, nor ever once did they cringe to their persecutors or shed a tear. (153) Smiling in their agonies and mildly deriding their tormentors, they cheerfully resigned their souls, confident that they would receive them back again. (*War* 2.152–53)

We have discussed some aspects of this passage previously. Josephus's brief report on Essene martyrdom likely alludes to 4 Maccabees and proves his familiarity with, though not his enthusiasm for, martyrological tendencies among predestruction Judaism.[113] What matters for present purposes is that after describing the sufferings of the Essenes in the war, the passage continues, explaining that their belief in immortality encourages and sustains them—all as if their school still exists (*War* 2.154–58). Had Josephus thought that the Essene decision to submit to martyrdom resulted in their complete or even nearly complete disappearance, he might have shaped this account differently. To be sure, he does not say explicitly that some Essenes survived the war. But the passage does support those who would shift the burden of proof: we ought not to take it as a given that the Essenes were *all* martyred. As Goodman has argued, it falls on those who claim that the Essenes disappeared right after 70 CE to prove their case.[114] At the same time, however, the passage quoted above also puts the lie to any claims that the disappearance of the Essenes—whenever it happened—resulted from their brotherhood being too "stiff" or their theology having become too "shattered." The Qumran sectarians had read Jeremiah; the theologically similar Essenes likely knew the biblical story, too. Josephus's Essenes were proficient in prophecy, and their theodicy included the doctrine of immortality. And quite possibly, the Essenes had determined that the temple was divinely rejected before its destruction (see *Ant.* 18.19).[115] Exactly what question asked in 70 CE couldn't be adequately answered by an Essene? If the Essenes did fail to survive the war, the most likely cause—the only cause our meager sources suggest—is that the Romans happened to kill a great many of them.

The disappearance of Sadducaism is often explained by virtue of the fact that a priestly, aristocratic group tied to the temple would not have been able to withstand the destruction in 70 CE.[116] Of course, it doesn't help matters that virtually all of our ancient sources—and too many of our modern ones, as we have observed already—are aligned against the Sadducees, viewing the group as boorish, rude, rich, rigid, stringent, or even—in Lauterbach's memorable wording—"blind slaves to the letter of the Law."[117]

Josephus says little about the Sadducees during the war. The latest Sadducee he mentions is the high priest Ananus, who is remembered in *Antiquities* for killing James, the brother of Jesus (20.199–200). But Josephus does speak of the Sadducees in *War* and *Antiquities* as if they still exist as one of Judaism's three philosophical schools. And rabbinic sources occasionally speak of Sadducees in the present tense too (e.g., *m. Niddah* 4.2).[118] Goodman's claim for a shift in the burden of proof applies here as well: we ought not to assume that the Sadducees disappeared immediately. But what really matters for present purposes is not to argue in favor of Sadducean persistence but to argue against any claim that their theology was inadequate to the tasks at hand after 70 CE. What was said earlier applies here as well: Sadducees who knew the biblical story would have had no difficulty reaching the general conclusions everyone else did. But there are some ways, quite possibly, in which Sadducean theology might have been particularly well adapted to respond to the crisis. Josephus tells us that the (presumably predestruction) Sadducees "removed God beyond not merely the commission, but the very sight of evil" (*War* 2.164). This is not at all dissimilar to the notion of God hiding his face (Deut. 31.17–18), which is expressed in a number of rabbinic traditions sometimes taken as responses to the destruction (e.g., *Genesis Rabbah* 36.1 [ed. Theodor/ Albeck 1:334]).[119] As we discussed in chapter 2, Josephus's description of the Sadducees' belief in free will is related to their belief in earthly justice (*War* 2.165), with the implication that humans suffer on earth in accordance with the wickedness they perpetuate. Whatever one thinks of such beliefs, it would be unwise to think them inadequate to the challenges of 70 CE. Indeed, for what little modern analogies are worth, it is notable that the "free will defense" plays a prominent role in modern Jewish attempts to account for the Shoah: radical earthly evil can be understood as the dangerous corollary to unrestricted human freedom.[120] If such thinking has precedents in classical Jewish thought, the earliest best bets may well be Sirach 15.11–20 and Josephus's description of the Sadducees. Be that as it may, we ought not to downplay the potential power of Sadducean theology to respond to 70 CE. The Sadducees' disappearance, too—whenever it occurred—will have to be explained by other factors.[121]

Considering one possible explanation for these developments allows us to identify yet one more similarity between Josephus and the rabbis. In his classic article reconsidering the "significance of Yavneh," Shaye Cohen suggested that the disappearance of sectarianism and the rise of rabbinic Judaism can be explained, in part, by the rabbinic willingness to foster "a society which tolerates disputes without producing sects."[122] Some aspects of Cohen's argument are problematic: his use of the term "pluralism" may seem anachronistic to some, and it may well be a stretch to say that the rabbis accepted the existence of "conflicting truths."[123] More likely, the rabbis were just not sure how to figure out which claim was *the* truth. Be this as it may—and granting the fact that we really do not know when the sects disappeared, let alone why—it is important to point out two essential points relating to Josephus's testimony regarding Jewish diversity and unity. While Josephus's evidence is often understood (for good reasons, as argued throughout this book) as accurately describing the pre-destruction theological diversity of ancient Judaism, it is also important not to forget that Josephus's descriptions of ancient Jewish diversity are themselves composed after the destruction. And his testimony regarding diversity is balanced, as we have also observed, with an interest in consensus. Josephus's *Antiquities* in particular emphasizes the unity of Jewish history, while finding a legitimate place for limited diversity within the Jewish polity. The later work *Against Apion*, as we have noted, focuses on the other side of this coin: by apologetically describing and perhaps thereby attempting to reinforce a Jewish consensus. So *if* the eventual disappearance of sectarianism is to be explained—at least in part—by rabbinic efforts to negotiate both the recognition of differences and the forging of consensus, we may do well to recognize that Josephus's various works struggle with the similar tensions, perhaps pointing in similar directions.

Theodicy, Plausibility, Skepticism, and Crisis

In his classic book *The Sacred Canopy*, Peter Berger discusses the challenges posed by theodicy in relation to the "world-maintenance" functions of religion. Leaving aside functionalism (to say nothing of the problematic secularization theories that even Berger himself subsequently abandoned), *Sacred Canopy* provides some helpful conceptual terminology and comparisons that shed light on the kind of problem we have been considering in this chapter. Berger describes the "plausibility structure" of a religious society—the societal institutions and leadership whose existence represents, legitimates, and, in turn, reinforces the religious worldview in question. If these supporting pillars are pulled out, the entire structure can collapse:

> Thus, for example, the religious world of pre-Columbian Peru was objectively and subjectively real as long as its plausibility structure, namely, pre-Columbian Inca society, remained intact.... Conversely, when the conquering Spaniards destroyed this plausibility structure, the reality of the world based on it began to disintegrate with

terrifying rapidity. Whatever may have been his own intentions, when Pizarro killed Atahualpa, he began the destruction of a world of which the Inca was not only the representative but the essential mainstay. By his act, he shattered a world, redefined reality and consequently redefined the existence of those who had been "inhabitants" of this world....Much of the history of Peru, and of Latin America generally, since then has been concerned with the consequences of this world-shattering catastrophe.[124]

Reading this passage, one might wonder, for a moment, whether the destruction of the temple in 70 CE would have shattered Judaism's plausibility structure.

But there are important differences between the model Berger describes and the Jewish experience in 70 CE. First and foremost, Berger's approach to Peruvian history is on sounder footing precisely because he is seeking a theoretical model to explain events we know occurred. Inca society did collapse; what remains of its religion is rocks. So historians can safely dispute whether the shattering of this religious world contributed to the demise of this society. The collapse of Judaism in 70 CE, however, is a hypothesis that finds support in a few references to postdestruction apostasy, a supposed sudden decline in Jewish literary production, and an imagined theological crisis—sometimes informed, in turn, by a misguided, indeed false, historical analogy.

The fact is that we really don't know what Jewish society as a whole experienced in the wake of 70 CE. Seth Schwartz and others conjure scant evidence for mass apostasy—but there is probably just as much (again, scant) evidence for the abandonment of Judaism before 70 CE as after—to wit, Tiberius Julius Alexander and Saul/Paul of Tarsus.[125] For all we know of the dates of our various extant texts, it is within the realm of possibility that Jewish literary production *increased* in the wake of 70 CE, at least in comparison to previous decades. And for all the talk of religious crisis, the fact remains that there is very little evidence of unanswerable religious doubt in the wake of 70 CE. Yes, 4 Ezra asks hard questions—but he answers them. To be sure, Adiel Schremer and others are not entirely off the mark in finding echoes of skeptical views in rabbinic sources. But three important caveats must be taken into consideration before we conjure images of religious crisis. First, a good number of the rabbinic sources questioning God's justice are focused not on the vicissitudes of history broadly speaking but on smaller, though harrowing, losses, such as the death of a child (e.g., *b. Qiddushin* 39b; *y. Hagigah* 2.1, 77b).[126] Second, we can find just as many texts poignantly questioning divine justice among sources written long before the destruction of the second temple. A full catalogue is not possible here, but we can note Sirach 5.4–8 and 16.17–23, which are explicit attempts to counter such views, to say nothing of the books of Ecclesiastes and Job, which articulate such doubt—and do so without any explicit connection to historical catastrophes. It would appear that rather sophisticated contemplations of personal and communal theodicy were well advanced by the first century CE.[127] Finally, the most important point of all is the one that Josephus drives home repeatedly, in both *War* and *Antiquities*: the destruction of the second temple, as horrific as it was, is not an event that Judaism couldn't explain. It had happened before, as told and explained by 2 Kings, Jeremiah, Ezekiel, and 2 Chronicles.

Conclusion

We should not belittle the suffering that Jews in rebel areas of Judea and Galilee suffered at the hands of the Romans: many Jews were killed, and many others were tortured, raped, abused, plundered, and sold into slavery (even if Josephus's numbers are exaggerated).[128] Certainly, many Jewish lives were shattered by these events, just as lives were disrupted or cut short by the various wars and catastrophes that beset the Jewish people throughout the period, from the destruction of the first temple through the Antiochene persecution, and down through the revolts in Israel and the Diaspora that succeeded 70 CE. But the wrecking of lives does not lead, necessarily, to the shattering of a religion. Contrary to the assertions of Bokser, Kirschner, Schremer, Schwartz, and others cited earlier, Judaism—be it Pharisaic, rabbinic, apocalyptic, or other—was not shattered by the destruction of the temple (or, for that matter, by the fall of Betar). Judaism contained within itself—indeed, within its canonical texts—all the key ideas that would eventually appear in the assorted Jewish explanations of the tragedy: the destruction was a predicted, precedented, divinely orchestrated punishment for the people's transgressions. There was no difficulty reaching this conclusion, and we can with justification understand it as dictated by ancient Jewish common sense.[129] After all, practically every extant ancient Jewish source reaches the exact same conclusion, for the destruction of the second temple is precisely what it sounds like: the second time this has happened. On these core issues— and even regarding some lesser, but still significant details, too—the rabbis, the apocalyptic seers, and Josephus all agree. But for some reason, the Josephan evidence is largely overlooked in scholarly discussions of these matters.

Scholarly understandings of the Jewish response to 70 CE would do well to put Josephus's works right at the center. Instead of imagining pervading gloom and mass apostasy, Josephus's works would guide us to appreciate the viability of Jewish covenantal theology, especially its power to withstand and respond to calamities that had already befallen the Jewish people once before. Josephus's works model the way other Jews—contemporary apocalyptic seers and later rabbis among them—will see the events of the first century CE as playing out biblical history for a second time. God retains his control of the world, and the Romans rule—for now—only by divine permission. Jewish tradition remains in force for the present, and there is hope for a better future. Of course, if we did have historiographic evidence that testified to mass apostasy and grave unanswerable questions, then we would do well to decenter Josephus's works. But his works have been sidelined not by competing ancient evidence but by a contemporary scholarly *mirage*. Of course, as we have argued throughout this book, and as we will reiterate and elaborate in our conclusion, Josephus's evidence concerning ancient Jewish theology has a great deal to contribute to current scholarly constructions of ancient Judaism, whether in relation to understanding what happened before the destruction or after.

Conclusion

OVER THE COURSE of this book, we have focused our attention on two interrelated data sets: Josephus's accounts of theological disputes among the Pharisees, Sadducees, and Essenes, and his own personal theological observations and inclinations. We have seen that his evidence regarding the schools is, on the whole, both internally consistent and externally confirmable. His descriptions of Essene theology reasonably match what we find among the sectarian Qumran scrolls. His descriptions of Sadducean theology reasonably match what we find among wisdom writers (especially Ben Sira), as well as the evidence regarding Sadducees from the New Testament and even some rabbinic sources. His descriptions of Pharisaic theology generally align with rabbinic traditions, as well as the descriptions of the group's beliefs found, once again, in the New Testament. To be sure, Josephus's accounts are brief, and therefore simplified and even at times exaggerated. Moreover, they are composed in the Greek language, infused with Hellenistic philosophical terminology—at times tinged with classical literary allusions—all in the effort of reaching audiences quite different from the groups he describes. Nevertheless, the accounts find a great deal of verification and encounter very little disconfirmation. Josephus was, as we observed in chapter 2, a good teacher, whose descriptions navigate among the conflicting concerns of accuracy, brevity, and clarity, without sacrificing too much of the first for either of the latter. Even when probed for their nuances—for example with regard to the efforts to balance fate and free will or the differences between immortality and reembodiment—Josephus's accounts often emerge as remarkably on target.

These characteristics—internal consistency and external verifiability—also pertain to Josephus's personal theological testimony. In agreement with his claim (*Life* 12) to have adopted the Pharisaic outlook as his own, his views are on the whole Pharisaic, in line with the way he describes this school's outlook. Josephus, too, balances fate and free will by subordinating the former to divine providence, not unlike the so-called Middle Platonists. He believes in immortality (like the Pharisees and Essenes) and looks forward to a future reembodiment (like the Pharisees but unlike the Essenes). While Josephus knew of and even respected martyrdom (particularly among the Essenes), he did not advocate it. Nor did he advocate suicide. He indeed depicted Eleazar ben-Yair as speaking of a seemingly assured incorporeal afterlife in order to exhort his followers to kill themselves and their kin. Yet Josephus's own (and rather Pharisaic) afterlife hopes were more materialistic, and balanced by fears of postmortem punishment.

Like the Pharisees he describes, Josephus values not only the Mosaic laws but admittedly subsequent rulings as well. He attributes authority to law and tradition equally, without prejudice, and without great concern for assigning given laws to one category or the other. He made no effort to justify new rulings scripturally. Nor did he allow the possibility that rulings were ever or could ever be changed by post-Mosaic prophets. Intriguingly, his reaction to the destruction of the temple is comparable to the later rabbinic one—just as we might expect a Pharisaic response to be as well. In short, Josephus's theological views do in fact align with those of the Pharisees (again, as he describes them). This, of course, is precisely what his own testimony about his allegiance would have us believe (*Life* 12).

This is not to say, of course, that Josephus's works are always reliable, or that his historical narratives should be accepted as truth until disconfirmed. This book is not meant to be a general plea for Josephan accuracy. As granted throughout, Josephus's accounts of various historical events— such as the Masada episode or his surrender at Jotapata—are notoriously suspicious, to say the least. We have also largely set aside his problematic (and unverifiable) effort to establish the independent existence of a rebellious "fourth philosophy." As a general rule, this book is aligned with and builds on the current literary turn in Josephan studies: Josephus is a creative author whose works can only be fully understood when his literary and ideological interests are taken into account. But as we have seen, his descriptions of Jewish scholastic debates are a distinct data set, one that can best be evaluated in light of his own rather consistent theologizing, as well as the wealth of comparable ancient Jewish theological material at our disposal. I have argued for the general reliability of Josephus's accounts of Jewish theological matters precisely because I find this material to be both intelligible and reasonably confirmable. Perhaps some readers will believe that I have been too credulous. But if so, the next step will have to be to argue against the correlations and comparisons I have suggested. Still, I believe that the understanding of Josephus's own theology—as a Pharisee by his terms—should prove of value to even the most literary-minded of scholars. After all, this facet of my argument, whether convincing or not, rests less on external comparisons and more on the methods espoused by literary-minded readers of Josephus. In fact, because literary readings of Josephus depend on understanding his own views, I hope that this project has contributed something toward that effort as well.

Be that as it may, this book is addressed primarily to those who engage in the work of reconstructing the history of ancient Judaism. I believe that the observations and verifications we have traced here suggest that scholars ought to recenter Josephus's evidence when trying to understand better the nature and contours of the religio-theological diversity in Josephus's day. Indeed, as intimated in chapter 1 and demonstrated in chapters 2–5, a renewed focus on Josephus's testimony challenges a number of regnant assumptions regarding the study of ancient Judaism. In what follows, we review the more salient general observations regarding each of these matters.

Decentering the Law-Centered Approach

The claim that Jewish religious practice played some role in the development and solidification of ancient Jewish sectarian dispute is undeniable and—when put this way—well nigh irrefutable, whether on grounds of evidence or logic. But many scholars make much stronger claims, suggesting that disputes regarding law are the primary and perhaps even the only significant factor in causing sectarian strife and determining sectarian identity. To be sure, a good portion of rabbinic literature and a significant portion of the Qumran texts deal with matters of law. And Jesus and his contemporaries quite likely disputed over matters of law as well. I certainly do not wish to suggest that disputes concerning, for instance, purity or the temple were insignificant.

It is the denial of significance to theological disputes that this book seeks to counter. Josephus is our most important source for the attribution of distinct views to namable groups of ancient Jews. And as we have seen, he gives pride of place to matters of theology in identifying the nature of these groups. To a large degree, his data are confirmable. Both the New Testament and rabbinic sources concur that disputes among the Pharisees and Sadducees concerned matters of theological concern, such as life after death. In fact, every avenue of evidence we have concerning the Sadducees—Josephus, the New Testament, rabbinic sources, even patristic sources—concur, for instance, that the denial of what we could call a beatific afterlife was a key defining feature of Sadducaism.

Even Josephus's testimony as to the fate and free will dispute is largely confirmable. These accounts are not, I have argued, the creation of some philosophic fancy. The brief reports do more than fill up small spaces in Josephus's oeuvre, and are more than incidental to Josephus's interests. His accounts of these disagreements reflect sincere, verifiable disputes among ancient Jews, going back at least to the time of Ben Sira. And Josephus's reports about these disputes—though briefer than we might wish—demonstrate his own reasonable understanding of the rather complicated issues at stake. Even if we refuse to associate Josephus's Essenes with the sectarian scrolls or the Sadducees with the wisdom tradition, the contrast between the *Community Rule* and the Wisdom of Ben Sira *proves*—to the degree proof is possible within our capacity to demonstrate anything about ancient Judaism—that ancient Jews understood the problem of fate and free will, and argued about it. Moreover, the contours of the debate were precisely the ones Josephus lays out: some Jews struggled to separate God from all evil, while others struggled to defend God's unlimited, all-powerful control over human affairs (including evil action). Others struggled with the paradoxes required to find a balance between these conflicting positions. Even Josephus's confusions—particularly about the nature of Jewish compatibilism—are both forgivable and, moreover, meaningful, for some of the same misunderstandings and paradoxes are in evidence in later rabbinic literature as well. But Josephus may well be less paradoxical—or contradictory—than many have assumed. He was, like the Pharisees, a compatibilist who subordinated fate to providence: all occurs under divine providence, but only some events are fated. Once we understand Josephus's campatibilism as a partial determinism, then most, if not all, of the claimed contradictions in his works on these themes diminish significantly. Even his report (in *Apion* 2.180–81) that all Jews believed in providence can be squared with his description of the Sadducees as denying fate (but not providence).

To be sure, the presence of legal disputes among the various groups cannot be denied. Indeed, some documents (e.g., 4QMMT) do indicate that legal disputes played some role in sectarianism. But 4QMMT aside, it is important to recognize that the relative proportion of theologically-oriented literature over legally-oriented literature in the pre-Mishnaic period is yet another confirmation of the thesis of this book. There is halakhic literature at Qumran—but even if we are being generous, it is difficult to claim that the material of halakhic significance takes up even one-third of the nonbiblical corpus.[1] The books of Leviticus and Deuteronomy are well represented among the Qumran finds. But so are Genesis, Isaiah, and the Psalms—to say nothing of the many other nonlegal biblical books that are rather well represented.[2] Even if we include *Jubilees*, the percentage of halakhic documents would again be about one-third or less. There surely are more scientific ways to run these numbers, but there's no way they can be finagled to support a claim that the halakhic literature outweighs the material whose concerns are more theological, be it wisdom, hymnic, or prophetic.

In this respect, the *total* evidence from Qumran mirrors what we find elsewhere. After all, within the vast majority of second temple literature preserved outside Qumran—including Apocrypha, Pseudepigrapha, and other surviving works such as Philo and Pseudo-Philo—theological reflection outweighs halakhic decision-making, by some significant measure. To be sure, this literature was preserved by Christians, not Jews. What evidence do we have that *Jews* shared these priorities of preservation? It bears remembering that the Hebrew Bible itself—a canon settled in the late second temple period at the earliest—contains relatively little legal material when measured for size against the remainder. What evidence do we have that second temple Jews prioritized law over all else? Little, at most; perhaps none at all. This, of course, is exactly what Josephus suggests: both legal and theological disputes occurred—but if anything, there may have been more of the latter.

I will immediately grant that numbers aren't everything, and may mean little. Moreover, the dichotomy played here between halakhic and theological documents is false, for halakhic texts can have theological concerns, just as theological ones can have legal concerns. But if the law-centered theory is supported neither by what the ancient sources say about the schools nor by the numerical preponderance of surviving evidence from the late second temple period, where then can its support be found? Given all the verifications we have found for the approach that puts Josephus's testimony in the center, it is difficult to understand how the "law-centered" theory can continue to be maintained, at least as currently formulated.

Theology and Crisis in the Study of Ancient Judaism

We have argued passionately—and, I hope, clearly—that Josephus's testimony seriously limits the capacity to claim that the destruction of the temple in 70 CE left the Jews of that time in a deep *theological* crisis. Numerous Jewish lives were lost, and many living survivors suffered grievously. The event was traumatic, to be sure, but it was not unprecedented. The theological questions raised by the destruction were ones that were already answered, quite clearly, in biblical sources. It is, therefore, mistaken to assume that Judaism or the Jewish people were shocked into silence or otherwise unable to respond. Moreover, postdestruction theological probing did not threaten any particular belief structure that we can identify: Sadducaism and Essenism, too, could have answered the questions posed, and in practically all the same ways—with perhaps some variation—that Josephus and the later rabbis did. The disappearance of the Sadducees and Essenes as groups—whenever that took place—must be explained by factors other than the alleged shattering of their theological systems.

In some respects, the arguments of chapter 5 were presaged by those of chapter 3, when we noted that Josephus's works provide little support to those who would claim that the development of beliefs in resurrection and immortality have something to do with particular historical crises, such as the persecutions and martyrdoms that preceded the Maccabean revolt. A number of scholars, as I have noted, have already discredited (or even disavowed) this theory, based in part on the pre-Maccabean date of 1 *Enoch*, as demonstrated by the Qumran finds. It is to be hoped that a growing number of scholars will also desist from assuming that the Sadducees denied immortality because their wealth rendered the belief unnecessary—as if money provided a shield against illnesses, accidents, or attackers. As argued in chapter 3, it is imperative to reckon with the fact that Josephus views the disputes regarding afterlife as both age-old and ongoing. He does not give us any reason to believe that afterlife beliefs developed or changed in response to any historical crisis. Indeed, if anything, his works suggest that he believes the relation between afterlife beliefs and social crisis or status runs the other way. Beliefs in life after death can encourage martyrdom, and comfort those who risk death fighting against the odds. So it is not that social crises bring about theological development; but certain theological beliefs may encourage particular types of responses to a given crisis. Josephus may or may not be correct in this regard. But there's certainly no reason to think, whether from Josephus or any other ancient Jewish evidence, that afterlife beliefs gained a stronger hold in Israel because of the Maccabean crisis or any other particularly challenging event.

On a related side note, Josephus's testimony is also more important than has been generally realized for those who wish to consider the early history of Jewish martyrdom. Josephus was certainly aware of Jewish martyrs (especially, he tells us, among the Essenes). It also appears that he was familiar with at least one Jewish martyrological text (4 Maccabees). While some scholars have endeavored to establish that Jewish martyrdom is a postdestruction, Christian phenomenon, Josephus's works demonstrate conclusively that Jewish martyrdom cannot be overlooked or downplayed in our reconstructions of the late second temple period. Here, too, Josephus helps us see that certain ideas may in fact predate the events currently believed to have brought them about.

My last observation on this theme is a more general one. For all the talk of theologies shattered by crisis or doctrines developing in the wake of distinct historical challenges, it is important to drive home the point that Josephus's silence on any such dynamic matches the fact that neither our ancient Jewish evidence nor any sound theoretical modeling would provide any good reason to think that Jewish theology in antiquity developed or shattered in direct relation to any particular historical events known to have taken place during that period. We simply do not have enough evidence to reconstruct the history of theological development in ancient Judaism. And we do not know enough about how and why beliefs develop in general to allow us to fill in the gaps in our evidence. Facing this uncertainty, scholars have taken to the crisis-development model. But the very notion of a theological crisis in the wake of catastrophe appears to be, as argued previously, an imposition of a distinctly modern concept onto the past—and a concept that is not entirely true, even about the present, to put it mildly. What is unlikely to be true is even less likely to be helpful.

The Zadokites and Sectarianism

Alongside the law-centered approach, another popular theory suggests that second temple period sectarianism began to flourish in the wake of the Maccabean revolt as a direct result of the break in high priestly descent, from Zadokites to Hasmoneans. This, too, is a theory that finds little confirmation in Josephus, and even less in other sources. As for Josephus, he notes various disruptions and changes in priestly succession and practice—and of all the issues that seem to bother him, it is the late second temple period deposition of priests (whether Zadokite or not) that he singles out as a notably problematic practice. None of these commotions, however, are connected in any clear way to the rise of sectarian disputes. In the one instance that Josephus relates that Pharisees accuse a high priest of illegitimate ancestry, Zadokite descent is not the issue, and the accusation is presented more as an effect of sectarian strife than its cause (*Ant.* 13.288–92).

Because Josephus hardly addresses the issue of Zadokite descent, we cannot know for certain why the issue was unimportant to him. It is of course possible that his own Hasmonean ancestry plays a role here, but he hardly refrains from criticizing these Jewish priests and kings. Moreover, it is not as if we find other sources isolating the Zadokite descent issue either. So despite Josephus's possible motive, there still remains no credible evidence of a coverup. But a more likely explanation for Josephus's approach emerges in light of our analysis, and it may help explain a great deal beyond his own view. As argued in chapter 4, Josephus allows no place for post-Mosaic prophetic legislation. This can be seen most conspicuously in the way he glosses over the reference in 1 Maccabees 4.46 to a specific legal problem that would be solved by a future prophet (*Ant.* 12.318). But his reluctance to allow prophets to legislate can also be seen in his consistent understanding of prophets as predictors and his glossing over of the biblical prophets' teachings and precepts. In line with all this, he says nothing about Ezekiel's priestly laws—and it is Ezekiel 40–48 that serves as the prophetic-legal basis for the concerns with Zadokite priestly lineage. So Josephus's lack of interest in Zadokite descent is perfectly commensurate with his approach to prophetic law in general. We would suggest that this is the likely reason he gives little credence to Ezekiel's Zadokite concerns: without legitimating post-Mosaic prophetic legislation, there is no basis for excluding non-Zadokite priests from priestly offices.

But if Josephus's lack of interest in the issue reflects his views of law and prophecy, perhaps we should assume, then, that the issue of Zadokite descent was in fact more important than he allows? Have we simply uncovered another motivation for Josephus to downplay this issue? We must indeed be alert to the possibility that Josephus has altered the historical record in line with his own ideology. But with regard to this particular issue, there is little reason to suspect that he is concealing something from us. After all, the theory that the break in high priestly Zadokite descent mattered a great deal is a scholarly chimera. There are no sources that clearly tell us that sectarianism emerged or developed in relation to the shift from Zadokite descent. Even the Qumranic concerns with Zadokite priests (in the plural, and possibly understood metaphorically) as prominent members of the community tell us very little about a Zadokite lock on the high priesthood in the late second temple period. And those texts, like *Pesher Habakkuk* and 4QMMT, that do criticize high priestly morality or cultic practices also say nothing about Zadokite descent. The emphasis on Zadokite descent is, in fact, partially based on a selective and flawed reading of Josephus. Some point to the placement of *Antiquities* 13.171–73, which suggests that sectarian disputes were apparent already during the time of Jonathan the Hasmonean. Some point to Josephus's references to the chain of priestly descent that went ostensibly unbroken from Zadok to the Maccabean era (*Ant.* 20.224–51). But none can point to anything that resembles a smoking gun. And a fuller reading of Josephus suggests that there is little reason to draw any connection between the rise of the groups he describes (or the ideas he attributes to them) and dynastic shifts in the priesthood.

Indeed, a careful reading of Josephus against the full backdrop of evidence we have concerning the priesthood, sectarianism, and disputes regarding the nature and development of Jewish law may help us understand better why Zadokite descent—possibly understood metaphorically—mattered at Qumran more than elsewhere. Josephus was likely not alone in accepting the legitimacy of non-Zadokite Aaronides and opposing the legitimacy of post-Mosaic prophetic legislation. The legal basis for Zadokite dominance, after all, comes not from Leviticus but Ezekiel. The later rabbis exhibit no particular interest in Zadokite priests, and various rabbinic sources are, as noted, wary of prophetic legislation or even justifying legal positions by appeal to prophetic texts. Since the Pharisees and Sadducees all participated in the cult throughout the second temple period, both groups must have accommodated non-Zadokite priests as well. It is, I believe, no coincidence that the only group we can identify as having some Zadokite concerns—the Qumran sect—is also the only one we know to have given great authority to post-Mosaic prophetic legal revelation. To be sure, Josephus does not spell all this out. But this reading of Josephus in light of the available evidence is, I believe, a stronger one than those that argue (or simply assume) that the break in Zadokite descent gave rise to sectarian strife.

Despising the Sadducees—And Even the Essenes

One problematic trope in current scholarship extends not from ignoring Josephus but from misusing him. He derides the Sadducees as rude, boorish, and out of touch, and too many scholars seem inclined to follow suit. After all, his hostility is taken up by the later Christian and Jewish traditions, both of which come to adopt beliefs in the afterlife, over or against any earlier Sadducean opposition. Although modern scholars are not necessarily advocates for the afterlife, they find in Josephus's reports about the Sadducees other things to oppose, be it literalism, conservatism, or aristocratic airs. As a result, the Sadducees still come out looking bad— much more often than they should. At the same time, the revered wisdom tradition—presented by scholars such as James Crenshaw as a forerunner of a modern-looking thoughtful skepticism—is typically severed from the Sadducean group. This phenomenon has some reasonable justification, and may or may not reflect anti-Sadducean biases. But separating wisdom from the Sadducees certainly reinforces these biases, by standing in the way of one quite reasonable way to reevaluate Sadducean theology in a more positive light. Doing so also prevents appreciating the Sadducees as one very likely late second temple period heir of the wisdom tradition.

While Josephus was rather taken by the Essenes, many scholars are less convinced that this group exhibits ideals that could be appealing. Of course, this really should not matter at all—and for the most part, scholars do remain fascinated by Essenes, without evaluating their religiosity one way or another. But distinct criticisms of the Essenes do emerge now and then, particularly when it comes to explaining their disappearance. Here too, scholars sometimes let the rhetoric get away from them, suggesting that the eclipse of the Essenes was in some way fitting, reflecting their stringent refusal to adapt to new circumstances or their stunned inability to explain the Jewish defeat.

Of course, one problem with all this is that we have no idea when the Essenes disappeared, let alone why. But there is a greater problem, similar to those observed with regard to the Sadducees: scholars have not been careful enough to separate evidence from judgment, explanation from evaluation. Most scholars today—though not all, unfortunately—have ceased from uttering prejudicial words against ancient Jews in general or Pharisees in particular. In part, this is no doubt due to the efforts of those who revere or respect those who are considered—or who consider themselves—the descendants of these ancient Jews and Pharisees. But those ancient Jewish groups who have no clear heirs in the present world—the Sadducees and Essenes—have not typically faired as well among scholars. To be sure, those who dislike Judaism in general will often say sordid things about the Sadducees, and at least these judgments, pernicious as they are, can be easily accounted for. But how then to explain the animus against the Sadducees and even Essenes by generally nonhostile or even Jewish scholars? This is not a manifestation of anti-Semitism, but an unfortunate response to it. Scholars like Louis Finkelstein and Jacob Lauterbach—who struggled mightily to rehabilitate the evaluation of Pharisees (and Jews)—often did so at the expense of the Sadducees. These scholars allowed that there were, in fact, ancient Jews who manifested the traits that Gentiles disliked among Jews, whether these were related to backwardness, stinginess, or stringency. But those dislikable ancient Jews were the Sadducees. The Pharisees, Finkelstein and Lauterbach assured us, were something altogether different. So the anti-Semites of their day were not entirely wrong—they were just off target. Generations later, the academic rehabilitation of the Pharisees is largely complete. Anti-Judaism is largely absent from the academy. Yet the derogation of the Sadducees endures, with less thought than is now needed.

To be clear, I am not suggesting that scholars suspend all judgment. Scholars need not and should not forgive Herod's murderous sins. Nor should we, as I have argued, let the Masada "defenders" be presumed innocent. As described by Josephus, their actions were not just suicidal but murderous, too. Neither Pharisees nor Sadducees should be let off the hook either. The issue here is not about suspending judgment; it is about applying that judgment fairly, and without prejudice. When scholars struggle to explain the disappearance of a given group by suggesting that the group's unappealing qualities made that disappearance well nigh inevitable, the rest of us should be wary. Such analyses could well be religious advocacy, albeit under the disguise of scholarly argument. Of course we must grant one concession: scholars who denigrate the Sadducees cannot be accused of downplaying Josephus.

Few doubt that theology was important to Josephus. I have argued here that Josephus was correct to tell us that theology was important to ancient Jews—more important, perhaps, than other issues focused on by scholars today. I have also argued here that Josephus was largely correct in the way he characterized these ancient Jewish theological disputes. This in turn justifies, I hope, the greater attention we have paid here to Josephus's own theology, particularly when it comes to understanding Jewish religious disagreement and evaluating the Jewish response to the destruction of the temple in 70 CE.

That said, it must be emphasized that it is not my hope—or the thesis of this book—that law-centered approaches be replaced with theologically centered ones. I have not argued and will not argue that sectarianism emerged as a result of arguments concerning the afterlife or fate. If the rise of ancient Jewish sectarianism cannot be explained by theological disagreements, by halakhic disputes, or by the break in the Zadokite dynasty, what, then, is the reason it emerged? Frankly, I have no idea. Although I am sure this answer will fail to satisfy many, I would urge caution on these questions. After all, we know neither when the various schools arose nor when they disappeared. How can we explain a phenomenon we have not yet been able to circumscribe? Perhaps some day we will be able to understand the emergence and disappearance of ancient Jewish sectarianism better, whether by discovering new sources or finding fuller historical analogies than the ones elaborated heretofore. In the meantime, I believe we are best off asking questions we can answer and framing our analyses around the sources we have, trying to understand them more fully. This would put us in a better position than some current scholarship, which has downplayed our most important source, and filled in gaps with guesswork and inference.

We who study second temple period Judaism—and who teach it to undergraduate, graduate, and even public audiences—must reckon with the possibility that theology was as important to ancient Jews as Josephus, our greatest source, says it was. This will require many of us to spend a bit more time studying and teaching Josephus than we have previously— something that will become even easier when the Brill Josephus Project comes to completion. But we may also need to think more carefully about theology in general. Instead of assuming that theological development occurs in relation to historical crises, or that certain doctrines can be tied to given social classes or castes, we need to develop better analogies and more nuanced models. Scholars of ancient Judaism can make a good start here, by measuring the ample evidence regarding ancient Jewish theological dispute and development against these or other assumptions. Scholars of religion in general will need to help, too. Those of us who strive to explain texts and traditions that clearly were concerned with divine providence, human freedom, the afterlife, and theodicy could use a little less complaining about the ostensibly dangerous presence of theologians in the academy and a little more help understanding the historical

222 JOSEPHUS AND THE THEOLOGIES OF ANCIENT JUDAISM

development of religious beliefs and their relation to historical developments and social differentiation.

To be clear, I do not want to deny the possibility that there could be some truth to the charges, raised by Wiebe, Fitzgerald, and others, that the discipline of religious studies continues to be unduly influenced by unacknowledged theological biases and interests. Indeed, I believe I have, in my own way, argued the same point, albeit on a smaller scale. My previous work called attention to the continued impact of Christian and Jewish religious biases on the understanding of cultic matters. This project discerns contemporary Jewish ideas lurking behind the "law-centered" approach and the presumption that Judaism shattered after 70 CE. Even so, there are some serious problems with the general, common accusation of theological bias in the study of religion. First, the prevalent interest in theological biases strikes me as selective: surely there are other ideologies, commitments, and preconceptions—intellectual, political, national, gender-related, "Western," and what-have-you—that have also impacted the study of religion in discernable, but not yet fully acknowledged, ways. But the bigger problem is that the theoreticians' selective interest in the dangers presented by theological biases have left the field insufficiently equipped to handle the kinds of problems we have addressed in this book. Certainly the study of ancient Judaism in particular would be helped if the situation were different.

Be this as it may, we scholars of ancient Judaism cannot blame the discourse of religious studies for the disparities in the ways our own source materials are studied. We ourselves are responsible for the nature of our subfield, and we have the means to change how we study and teach our texts, should we be convinced that we should consider such changes. It is my sincere hope that this book has contributed something of value to the understanding of Josephus and ancient Jewish religion. It is also my hope that this endeavor can contribute to the effort of finding a better, more secure place for the academic study of religious thought, at least within the study of ancient Judaism, if not within the study of religion in general.

Appendix: Essenes and Resurrection According to Hippolytus

HAVING SURVEYED JOSEPHUS's accounts of the schools' beliefs regarding afterlife, we must turn at last to consider the related evidence preserved in the *Refutation of All Heresies* (also known as the *Elenchos* or the *Philosophumena*), widely attributed to Hippolytus of Rome (c. 175–236 CE).[1] Book 9 of this work—preserved in a single medieval manuscript discovered in a Mount Athos monastery in 1841 or 1842—includes discussions of the Essenes, Pharisees, and Sadducees, with the Zealots/Sicarii thrown in for good measure (9.18.1–9.30.8). There can be no doubt that the *Refutation* 9.18.2–9.29.3 is quite closely related to the schools passage in *Jewish War* 2.119–66—the similarities in style and content are often so close that some textual relationship must exist. But the *Refutation* differs from *Jewish War* in no small measure, particularly insofar as the patristic work consistently attributes to the Essenes and Pharisees not only the belief in immortality but also the belief in bodily resurrection (9.27.1–9.28.5). Similarly, the Sadducees are described as denying not only immortality but also resurrection (9.29.1–3).[2] So two important, related questions arise. How can the relationship between the *Refutation* and *Jewish War* best be explained? And is it possible that *Refutation* independently preserves historically reliable information, which could mean that the Essenes believed not only in immortality but also resurrection?

Scholarship on these matters goes back to the decades following the discovery of the *Refutation*. But we can safely begin our discussion nearly a century later, with the classic treatment of Morton Smith, who argued that the best (and, in his view, only) way to explain the similarities and differences between the two works is to suppose that both made independent use of pre-Josephan source material—not unlike the common view that Matthew and Luke made independent use of a hypothetical Q. Where

Josephus consistently Hellenized his version of this material, the patristic author consistently edited the same pre-Josephan material in light of later Jewish and Christian piety.[3] Smith continues to have his followers, particularly among scholars eager to associate Qumranic texts on resurrection with the classical accounts of the Essenes.[4] But a number of problems have led scholars (later including even Smith himself) to consider other possibilities.[5] Christoph Burchard, for instance, defended what had been the more prevalent view, that the *Refutation* is based directly on *Jewish War*.[6] Measuring Smith against Burchard—and finding both wanting—Albert Baumgarten rejected Smith's hypothetical pre-Josephan common source and suggested instead that the *Refutation* made use of an intermediate source that revised the account of the schools from *Jewish War* in light of a pro-Pharisaic *tendenz*.[7] Among the important points scored by Baumgarten is the recognition that Josephus worked with sources rather freely, as Shaye Cohen demonstrated.[8] For Baumgarten, this clearly "undermines the possibility that Josephus and Hippolytus drew on the same source and produced versions which agree so remarkably."[9]

But not all have been convinced that an intermediate source is the best explanation of the problems we face. Roland Bergmeier, perfectly at home with elaborate source-critical efforts, nonetheless rejects the idea that Hippolytus made use of anything other than *Jewish War* 2, even as Josephus himself used other sources in compiling his own account.[10] Steve Mason—ever eager to defend the literary integrity of Josephus's works—rejects the approaches of Smith and Bergmeier, arguing (convincingly) that the Josephan passages are substantially "his creation," even if sources were used.[11] Mason cites Baumgarten's hypothesis primarily as an added caution against using the patristic source in the effort of discerning what might have been Josephus's source material—an endeavor Mason views as largely hopeless.[12] Coming full circle, Elledge has recently defended Smiths's hypothesis and the relative accuracy of the *Refutation*, at least insofar as resurrection is concerned, arguing that changing references from resurrection to immortality is more in keeping with Josephus's concerns than the reverse procedure (replacing immortality with resurrection) would be characteristic of Hippolytus.[13]

Anyone wishing to get a good handle on these debates is wise to be wary. Much of the scholarship just surveyed is problematically piecemeal: much attention has been paid to the *Refutation's* evidence concerning the Essenes. A bit less has been paid to the Pharisees; even less to the Zealots, and virtually none at all (of course) to the Sadducees. If we are convinced by Mason that evidence from Josephus must be evaluated in light of Josephus's full literary efforts, certainly we can settle for no less regarding the *Refutation* either. Although a detailed treatment of the *Refutation*'s complete account of Jews and Judaism remains a desideratum, we are fortunate to have a number of works treating the *Refutation* as a whole, prominent among them Miroslav Marcovich's introduction to his critical edition of the work, as well as the monograph of Jaap Mansfeld.[14] Tellingly, both of these authorities believe that the *Refutation* 9 is based on *Jewish War* 2.[15] And both agree that key differences between *Jewish War* and *Refutation* can be explained in light of Christian apologetic concerns, ones characteristic of *Refutation* as a whole.[16]

Solving these thorny problems lies beyond the contours of this book, and far beyond the capabilities of its author. But we need not fully account for the origin and nature of the *Refutation*'s description of ancient Judaism. We simply must consider this question: What are the chances of recovering historically reliable information from the *Refutation* in those cases where it differs from *Jewish War*? This question can be answered. And the answer is that the chances are minute.

The first point to raise here is that chronology works against the possibility, and in a number of ways. First, the (generally accepted) author of the *Refutation*, Hippolytus of Rome, lived in the late second/early third century CE—roughly contemporary with Judah the Prince and the publication of the Mishnah. If scholars are generally skeptical about using rabbinic sources for the construction of early Jewish history, surely that skepticism should be applied equally to patristic sources—especially ones whose authorship (and therefore date) remains hypothetical, even if widely accepted.[17] But beyond that, book 9 of the *Refutation*—indeed, the bulk of the work—is extant only in a single fourteenth-century manuscript. Even if we accept Hippolytus's authorship of this material, we cannot always be certain that our lone, late manuscript is uncorrupted.[18]

The second point that militates against relying on the *Refutation* over against *Jewish War* is the fact that in many cases, the differences between the two can only be explained by positing that the patristic source has confused the matters at hand. Two twofold examples will suffice: In *Refutation* 9.26.1–4, we are told that the Zealots are to be equated with the Sicarii, and that the single binomial group constitutes one of four divisions of the Essenes. These Zealots-Sicarii are characterized by their refusal to use image-bearing coins or pass through gates adorned with statues, as well as their willingness to kill those who refuse to circumcise. Although

Martin Hengel, for instance, finds here information that is "remarkable" and "important,"[19] Smith previously better described this passage as a "mishmash of misinformation evidently concocted from misunderstood reports."[20] Similarly, in *Refutation* 9.29.4 we are told that the Sadducees were especially prevalent in Samaria and canonized only the Law, not the Prophets or the other writings. Clearly, the *Refutation* is here conflating Sadducees and Samaritans—further evidence of misinformation and misunderstanding.[21]

A third factor arguing against making much use of Hippolytus is the fact that a good many differences between *Refutation* and *Jewish War* can be explained as pious Christianizations—or even scripturalizations—of Josephus. For instance, the *Refutation* speaks not infrequently of the Law and the Prophets (9.22.2, 9.30.5, 9.30.6; see also e.g., 7.38.2, 8.19.1, 10.20.2), using the twofold referent found not in Josephus but, frequently, in the New Testament (e.g., Matt. 5.16; Luke 16.16, 24.44; see prologue to Ben Sira). As a second example, *Refutation* 9.24.1–2 interpolates into Josephus's description of Essene ethics (*War* 2.139) the practice of praying for enemies (compare Matt. 5.44//Luke 6.28). Added to the catalogue of Pharisaic beliefs in *Refutation* 9.28.4 is the school's adherence to traditions relating to ritual purity, in line with Mark 7.1–23 (//Matt. 15.1–20). The Sadducean denial of immortality (*Refutation* 9.29.1–3) seems expanded in light of Ben Sira, with the understanding that one's immortality comes through progeny (Sir. 30.4–5, 40.19, 44.13–15).[22] *Refutation* 9.30.4 includes, in its general description of ancient Jewish theology, references to the Sadducean denial of angels and spirits, in agreement with Acts 23.8.[23] Given all this, it is certainly safe to wonder whether the references in the *Refutation* to resurrection regarding the Pharisees and Sadducees are inspired by Acts 23, as well as Mark 12.18–27 (//Matt. 22.23–33//Luke 20.27–40). The Essenes would have become believers in resurrection, too, by virtue of their association with the Pharisees, and opposition to the Sadducees.[24]

Many mysteries remain, perhaps the most enduring being the overall nature of Hippolytus's description of the ancient Jewish schools of thought. Baumgarten expressed surprise at the account's "pro-Pharisaic" nature and hypothesized an intermediate pro-Pharisaic revision of Josephus to account for this. But the *Refutation* can be equally described as "pro-Essene" (Zealots-Sicarii aside), or indeed, at least through 9.30.4, simply "pro-Jewish."[25] Even the account of the Sadducees is rather positive (or rather neutral). Most noticeably, Hippolytus shortens or eliminates Josephus's nastier comments about this group (9.29.3, see *War* 2.166).[26] But on top of that, Hippolytus brings God back into the description of Sadducean libertarianism, eliminating the possibility that readers would think the Sadducees were atheists in any sense. To prevent any confusion of the two, the *Refutation* clearly differentiates the Sadducean theistic rejection of fate (9.29.1–3) with the Epicureans' denial of both fate and providence (1.22.3).[27] More generally, the *Refutation* is enamored of Jewish antiquity (10.30.1–10.31.1) and convinced that Greco-Roman philosophy is both more recent and, wherever correct, derivative (10.31.1–10.32.5). Although the Jews' law is superseded when Jesus appears on earth (10.33.10–17), Jews past and even present are described as observing their God-given law with care and integrity (9.30.3–4; 10.33.10). Presumably, Hippolytus's sympathy for the Jews and their law is directly related to his antipathy toward various "Gnostic" groups that deride the demiurge, misinterpret Jewish scriptures, and view the Jews—and, therefore, "orthodox" Christians as well—as utterly fooled (see, e.g., 5.20.1–5 on Sethians; 5.23.1–3 on Justinus; 6.9.1–6.10.2, 6.19.1 on Simon; 7.28.1–7 on Saturnilus; 7.32.1–8 on Carpocrates).[28] The Jews, rather, revere the real God in authentic, but outdated, ways. For these and perhaps other reasons that would emerge from a fuller analysis, the *Refutation* is a world away from the *Adversus Judaeos* literature of Chrysostom or even Augustine.[29]

The question we must return to is this: is it more likely that Josephus altered a source so as to speak of immortality alone, or is it more likely that Hippolytus altered Josephus's accounts to make them speak of resurrection?[30] That Josephus is inclined to speak of immortality of the soul is unquestionable. Moreover, we know that another contemporary Jewish writer did precisely the same thing: the author of 4 Maccabees consistently eliminated references to resurrection in his own expansive retelling of the martyrdoms recorded in 2 Maccabees 6–7. Nonetheless, I am persuaded by the work of Jaap Mansfeld that the author of the *Refutation* consistently added references to resurrection into his account, and with regard not only to the Pharisees and Essenes but also to the Stoics (1.21.5) and Heraclitus (9.10.6).[31] And just as the Sadducees are made into deniers of resurrection (9.29.1–2), so the *Refutation*'s Epicureans deny not only immortality but bodily resurrection as well (1.22.4–5). Clearly, the author of the *Refutation* had both the will and the way to alter his written sources, especially when the matter concerned Christian doctrines such as resurrection. No one working on Hellenistic philosophy would rely on Hippolytus's accounts to suggest that Stoics or Heraclitus believed in bodily resurrection. So although we can determine, from the New Testament and rabbinic sources, that Hippolytus happens to be correct about the Pharisees, we should be wary of assuming, without clear confirmatory evidence, that Hippolytus is also necessarily correct on this score regarding the Essenes.

Notes

CHAPTER 1

1. For discussions of the historical development of religious studies as an emerging discipline and its fraught interrelationships with theological institutions, concerns, and presuppositions, see Hart, *University Gets Religion*, and Wiebe, *Politics*, esp. 3–50. For an assessment somewhat more sympathetic to the theological legacy in religious studies, see J. Z. Smith, "Tillich['s] Remains."

2. Notable among these are Weber, *Sociology of Religion* (e.g., chs. 9 and 10 on theodicy and salvation); Berger, *Sacred Canopy* (esp. ch. 3, again on theodicy), and Douglas, *Natural Symbols*, ch. 7 (on the problem of evil).

3. See, for example, Fitzgerald, *Ideology*, and Wiebe, *Politics*. Despite the generalized titles of these works, both authors focus their critiques of religious studies on the dangers posed by (Christian) theological biases in particular. Indeed, note the subtitle of Wiebe's book: *The Continuing Conflict with Theology in the Academy*.

4. See, e.g., Wellhausen, *Pharisees*, 13.

5. Schechter, *Aspects*, and Moore, *Judaism*.

6. See, for example, the brief but telling comments by Gillman, *Doing Jewish Theology*, x, 119–127.

7. Any biographic sketch of Josephus begins with Josephus's autobiography, *Life*, on which see Mason, *Life of Josephus* (BJP 9), xiii–liii. The brief sketch above is drawn from Josephus's account, but by no means summarizes it.

8. On Josephus's priestly lineage, in addition to *Life* 1–7, see, e.g., *War* 1.3, 3.352, and *Ant.* 16.187. On Josephus's Hasmonean ancestry, see *Life* 2, on which see Mason, *Life of Josephus* (BJP 9), 6–7 nn. 14–17, and D. Schwartz, *Flavius Josephus*, 63 n. 4.

9. Josephus's claims about his youth and education (*Life* 8–12) are no doubt self-serving, establishing his credentials among his Greco-Roman readers (Mason, *Life of Josephus* [BJP 9], 12–21, esp. nn. 56–60, 66, 75) and, possibly, positioning

himself as aligned with the Pharisees for the sake of some gain within the Roman Jewish community (Cohen, *Josephus*, 144–151; but see Mason, *Life of Josephus* [BJP 9], 21 n. 91, and *Flavius Josephus on the Pharisees*, 325–356; further discussion later in this chapter). But while we can be annoyed by Josephus's bragging, we ought not assume his claims are entirely false either—he clearly was indeed both talented and knowledgeable.

10. Surveys of Josephus's literary works are legion. Particularly helpful surveys include Attridge, "Josephus and His Works," and Mason, *Josephus and the New Testament.* Among classic surveys, Thackeray's *Josephus: The Man*, remains valuable. Samuel Krauss, "Josephus," in Singer, *Jewish Encyclopedia*, 7:274–281, remains of interest as an early Jewish scholarly appreciation of Josephus and his works.

11. On *War* in particular, see Cohen, *Josephus*, Mason, *Josephus, Judea*, 45–68, and Rajak, *Josephus.*

12. For some speculations on how the Aramaic original of *War* may have differed from the later, expanded Greek version we now have, see Hata, "Is the Greek Version." For a more careful assessment, see Rajak, *Josephus*, 174–184.

13. On *Antiquities*, see Attridge, *Interpretation*, and Mason, introduction to *Judean Antiquities.*

14. On *Life*, see Mason's introduction to *Life of Josephus* (BJP 9); see xv–xix for the arguments dating *Life* to (c.) 95 CE. Against this more prevalent view, and granting that the outer "shell" of *Life* was authored late in Josephus's life, D. Schwartz has recently proposed that the core of *Life* preserves memoirs composed by Josephus as early as 68–69 CE (Schwartz, *Flavius Josephus*, 4–5). For a recent general assessment of the nature and purpose of *Life* (with a helpful review of previous scholarship) see P. Stern, "*Life of Josephus*," esp. 88–93.

15. On *Against Apion*, see Barclay's introduction to *Against Apion* (BJP 10), xvii–lxxi; on the date of *Apion*, see xxvi–xxviii.

16. Josephus refers, in *Ant.* 1.25, 29, 20.268, and elsewhere, to his desire to write a four-volume work on Jewish customs. If he composed the work as intended, it is now lost. Possibly (but doubtfully) *Against Apion* constitutes the results of these efforts. See Feldman's note d on *Ant.* 20.268 (in LCL ad loc.), and Feldman, *Judean Antiquities 1–4* (BJP 3), 10 n. 34.

17. The most thorough treatments of the intended audiences of Josephus's works are Mason's; see *Josephus, Judea*, 45–68 (on the audience for *War*), and "'Should Any Wish to Enquire Further'" (on *Antiquities*). More briefly, see Mason's Introduction to *Aniquities 1–4* (BJP 3), xxvii–xx and Mason, *Life of Josephus* (BJP 9), xix–xxi. Mason maintains throughout that the interested Roman, Gentile audience is Josephus's primary and intended readership, and the evidence Mason presents in favor of this view includes Josephus's own claims about his intent (e.g., *War* 1.3, 6; *Ant.* 1.5; 20.262) as well as the basic information he supplies throughout that would be known to Jews but not to Gentiles (e.g., *Ant.*

1.33, 128–129). This basic Judaic information was clearly necessary so as not to preclude a Gentile audience; its presence, therefore, cannot be understood to deny the intent of a Jewish audience, too. Educated Greek-reading Jews in the Roman diaspora were not likely as ignorant of Roman history as Greco-Romans were of Jewish history. On the question of audience(s) as related to the matter of literacy and the nature of publication, see Huitink and Henten, "Publication."

18. See, e.g., Price, "Provincial Historian," and see S. Schwartz's brief critique of Mason's approach in *Were the Jews*, 83 n. 7 (and see Schwartz's fuller argument presented throughout *Josephus and Judaean Politics*, 29–30, 57, 136, 140–141, 170–208, 213). To be fair, while Mason rhetorically emphasizes Josephus's *intent* to reach a Gentile audience, he does not deny that Jewish readers were (if secondarily) of interest (see, e.g., *Josephus, Judea*, 47). Feldman goes further, arguing that Josephus's apologetic concerns are directed not only toward Gentiles, but toward Jews as well (*Josephus's Interpretation*, 49–50, 132–162). In my view, the evidence in favor of an intended Jewish readership, in addition to the intended Roman one, includes the extensive theological overlays of *War* and *Antiquities* (which will concern us throughout this book). For the case in favor of an intended Jewish readership, in dialogue with Mason, see Ehrenkrook, *Sculpting Idolatry*, 13–16; Olson, *Tragedy, Authority*, 40–49, and (with regard to *War*) Brighton, *Sicarii*, 43–47. See also Huitink and Henten, "Publication," who allow that Josephus's readership was likely geographically and ethnically diverse.

19. On the importance of this passage for evaluating Josephus's intended Jewish readership, see Brighton, *Sicarii*, 44–45.

20. On the possibility that Talmudic rabbis were influenced (directly or indirectly) by Josephus's works, see Kalmin, *Jewish Babylonia*, 43–60, 75–80, 149–172. On *Josippon*, a medieval Hebrew work derived from Latin manuscripts of *Antiquities*, *War* (via *Hegesippus*), the books of the Maccabees, and other sundry apocrypha, see Flusser, *Josippon*, and "*Josippon*, a Medieval Hebrew Version of Josephus," 386–397. For a brief survey of the vicissitudes of historical consciousness (and historical works) among the Jewish people, see Yerushalmi, *Zakhor*.

21. For brief discussions of the Jewish accusations against Josephus (and their enduring impact on the memory of Josephus), see, e.g., Thackeray, *Josephus: The Man*, 2, 50, and (more recently) Mason, *Josephus and the New Testament*, 24–27. Regardless of Josephus's behavior during the war, his enduring commitment to Judaism and the Jewish people is difficult to deny; see, e.g., Rajak, *Josephus*, 185–222; for a briefer recent assessment of Josephus's enduring Jewish loyalty, see Ehrenkrook, *Sculpting Idolatry*, 180. The Jewish theology articulated in Josephus's works will of course constitute one of our main themes.

22. Briefly, on Jewish and Christian attitudes toward Josephus, see Thackeray, *Josephus: The Man*, 2–3, 20–21. For the Christian reception of Josephus, see Hardwick, *Josephus as an Historical Source*, and Schreckenberg, "Josephus in

Early Christian Literature." For a survey of medieval Christian (and Jewish) versions, see Leoni, "Translations and Adaptations."

23. The Josephan accounts of John the Baptist (18.116–119) and James the Just (20.200) appear to be largely, if not entirely, authentic. However, medieval Christian scribes surely doctored the passage that speaks of Jesus (*Ant.* 18.63–64; the so-called *testimonium flavianum*), identifying him as "the Christ." On these passages, see (briefly) Thackeray, *Josephus: The Man*, 125–153, and (more fully) Meier, *Marginal Jew*, 1:56–88. Further Christianizations of Josephus can also be seen in a number of the Slavonic "additions" to *Jewish War* (see, e.g., additions 7, 9, 11, 12, 13, 20, and 21–23 in the appendix to the LCL edition of *War*). On the Slavonic version of *Jewish War*, see Leeming and Leeming, *Josephus' Jewish War* (especially the lengthy introduction by N. A. Meščerskij) as well as Leeming, "*Josephus slavonice,*" and Bickerman, *Studies*, 2:832–859. Moving even further along the same Christianizing trajectory evident in the *testimonium* and the Slavonic *War*, William Whiston, in an appendix to what remains the most popular (i.e., readily available) English translation of Josephus's works, defended the antiquity of all three (Greek) passages in *War* concerning John, Jesus, and James and took them as proof that the Jewish historian became an Ebionite or Nazarene (see dissertation 1 in any full edition of Whiston's 1736 translation).

24. J. N. Simchoni's Hebrew translation of *War* was published 1923–28. Abraham Schalit's Hebrew translation of *Antiquities* began to appear in 1944, with the last published volume appearing in 1963. Both have been repeatedly reprinted, though not necessarily widely distributed.

25. In America, Christian publishers continue to predominate over the distribution of Josephus's works, with the exception of the Penguin edition of Josephus's *Jewish War*.

26. See Mason's comments in his series preface that opens each volume of the Brill Josephus Project. For other surveys of recent achievements, see Bond, "New Currents" (to 2000), and Rajak's preface to the second (2002) edition of her 1983 study *Josephus*.

27. See, in particular, Mason, *Josephus, Judea*, 7–44, 103–137, and *Josephus and the New Testament*, 7–31. James McLaren's *Turbulent Times* is also of enduring importance in part for demonstrating how some scholarly reconstructions of first-century Judean history are more indebted to Josephus than scholars generally realize.

28. For a review of classic scholarship on the authenticity of documents presented by Josephus see Feldman, "Select Critical Bibliography of Josephus," esp. 374–376.

29. So, e.g., Schiffman, *From Text to Tradition*, 170.

30. On the contradictions between *War* and *Life*, see Cohen, *Josephus*, and Mason, *Life of Josephus* (BJP 9), xxvii–xxxiv.

31. Among the more influential scholars, Mason is particularly skeptical; see *Josephus, Judea*, 217–279; see esp. 229 for Mason's characterization of the passages as conventional, vague, perfunctory, and, simply, relatively unimportant for understanding Josephus (let alone ancient Judaism). See also "What Josephus Says," 446: with regard to Essene prophecy (*War* 2.159), Mason avers that "it seems pointless to apply theological rigour to a rhetorical historian." For the more common dismissal of Josephus's philosophical descriptions of the sects, see Feldman, "Torah and Greek Culture," 67, and Moore, "Fate and Free Will." Among scholarly works taking a more sanguine view, see Flusser, *Judaism*, 1:214–257, and 2:221–231.

32. See, again, Feldman, *Josephus's Interpretation*, 132–162.

33. For Pharisaic allegiance, particularly in *Antiquities* and *Life*, see Cohen, *Josephus*; see also Rajak, *Josephus*, 33–34, 224–225. For a critical survey of scholarship on this issue up until 1991, see Mason, *Flavius Josephus on the Pharisees*, 325–341.

34. So, especially, Mason, *Flavius Josephus on the Pharisees*, 325–341; on *Ant.* 17.41–45 see 260–280.

35. See Feldman, "Torah and Greek Culture," 48–59, discussed more fully in chapter 4.

36. Mason, *Flavius Josephus on the Pharisees*, 330–339.

37. Mason, *Flavius Josephus on the Pharisees*, 334–335.

38. On Josephus and his sources, especially with regard to Josephus's intellectual development (measured in terms of classical and Jewish sources utilized), see S. Schwartz, *Josephus and Judaean Politics*, 22–57, 223–232.

39. So, e.g., Moore, "Fate and Free Will."

40. Cohen, *Josephus*, 24–66; compare, more briefly, McLaren, *Turbulent Times*, 49–51.

41. Mason, *Flavius Josephus on the Pharisees*, 176–177, 207–211, 306–307.

42. Mason, *Judean War 2* (BJP 1b), esp. 87–90.

43. Consider, for example, Josephus's adaptation of *Letter of Aristeas*, in *Antiquities* 12.12–118, on which see Cohen, *Josephus*, 34–35. Then imagine the situation if we were trying to reconstruct *Aristeas* from Josephus—we would have no idea, for example, that the letter contains an extended discourse on the symbolic value of Jewish rituals laws. Still, many scholars remain convinced that Josephus drew heavily on written sources with regard to his descriptions of the schools in general, and of the Essenes in particular. Further discussions of Josephus's account of the Essenes can be found later this chapter; see the appendix for a consideration of the relationship between Josephus's and Hippolytus's accounts of the Essenes.

44. On the lack of such studies in previous scholarship, see Mason, *Josephus, Judea*, 69–70, 103–104; see 70–102, 105–137 for Mason's own literary approach to matters such as Josephus's audience and use of irony. See also McLaren, *Turbulent Times*, for suggestions on how to attend to Josephus as a writer while still making use of his writings in the effort of historical reconstruction.

45. See, e.g., Mason, *Josephus, Judea*, 7–44, 103–137, and *Josephus and the New Testament*, 7–31.

46. On "school" as a preferred translation for αἵρεσις, see Mason, *Flavius Josephus on the Pharisees*, 125–128. We will follow this advice for the most part, though when describing the simultaneous existence of multiple schools of thought, the term "sectarianism" remains of use. The bibliography on Josephus's "three schools" passages is legion. Mason's *Flavius Josephus* is among the most helpful treatments (esp. 120–177, 196–212, 281–308); while this work focuses in the Pharisees, the other schools are discussed, too, as a matter of course. A more recent helpful survey (focusing on the rhetorical function of the passages in Josephus's works) is Haaland, "What Difference."

47. As we will see in chapter 3, there is some dispute regarding the precise afterlife beliefs that Josephus ascribes to the Pharisees and Essenes, and the adoption here of the general locution ("life after death") reflects this. Clearly, both groups believe *at least* in the immortality of the soul (*War* 2.154, 163). Some scholars see intimations of reincarnation in *War* 2.163 (e.g., Thackeray's note a in LCL; see Beall, *Josephus' Description*, 105–106). Others find intimations of resurrection, revivification, or reembodiment. See, e.g., Elledge, *Life after Death*, 48–51; other literature will be cited in chapter 3, where we hope to clarify the terminological problem, too.

48. This passage—along with the parallels in *Antiquities*—will be scrutinized more fully in chapter 2.

49. The former translation ("boorish") of the Greek ἀπηνεῖς in *War* 2.166 is Thackeray's (in LCL); the latter ("uncouth") is Mason's (in *Judean War 2* [BJP 1b]).

50. On the strange—and seemingly random—placement of this passage within Josephus's paraphrase of 1 Maccabees 12, see Sievers, "Josephus, First Maccabees, Sparta." Sievers's argument militates against using this passage as evidence that the three groups thrived as such during Jonathan's day—a view that is fundamental to many classic formulations of the "Essene hypothesis" (e.g., Cross, *Ancient Library*, 100–110, and Vermes, *Complete Dead Sea Scrolls*, 46–53).

51. On the killing of kinsmen in *Ant.* 18.5, see LCL ad loc. n. 4 to the Greek text and note b to the translation (but compare Niese, *Flavii Iosephi*, 4:140–141, on *Ant.* 18.5). On Judas's innovations—and the "fourth philosophy in general"—in light of Josephus's general approach to tradition and change, see chapter 4.

52. As Joan Taylor points out ("Philo of Alexandria," 4) Josephus obviously does not intend to equate the Pythagoreans with the Essenes: after all, the Pythagoreans were vegetarians, but Josephus does not claim that the Essenes were. On Pythagoras's alleged knowledge of, and reverence for, Jewish traditions, see *Against Apion* 1.162–165.

53. On this passage, see Mason, *Life of Josephus* (BJP 9), 15–21.

54. We will examine this text and probe the Sadducee/Epicurean comparison in chapter 2.

55. Regarding the latter, it is possible that Josephus describes John as being from the town of Essa; see Mason, *Judean War 2* (BJP 1b) to *War* 2.567, esp. 384 n. 3396, and "What Josephus Says," 428.

56. E.g., Feldman, "Torah and Greek Culture," 67, and Moore, "Fate and Free Will." C. D. Elledge, for instance, helpfully speaks in this regard of Josephus's "apologetic translation" (*Life after Death*, 3, 45, 81–82).

57. See Appelbaum, "'The Idumeans' in Josephus," for a very helpful (and cautionary) look at Josephus's stereotyping of this particular ethnic group.

58. So, e.g., Cohen, *Josephus*; for a contrary view see Mason, *Flavius Josephus on the Pharisees*, esp. 339–341.

59. On providence in *Antiquities* in particular, see Attridge, *Interpretation*, and chapter 2 here.

60. See, e.g., Mason, *Flavius Josephus on the Pharisees*, 97–106; see further chapter 4 here.

61. Generally, see Price, "Some Aspects."

62. This presumption is more often assumed than argued, and more often defended than discussed. For one very partial discussion focused on the Dead Sea Scrolls, see Ullmann-Margalit, *Out of the Cave*, 135–146.

63. M. Smith, "Dead Sea Sect," 360.

64. Note, e.g., Schiffman, *Halakhah*, and J. Baumgarten, *Studies*.

65. Sussmann, "History of the Halakha," 40, 61–62, and "Appendix 1," 196. It is hardly clear, however, that 4QMMT is in fact a founding document of the sect. For alternate readings of 4QMMT, see Fraade, *Legal Fictions*, 69–91, and Grossman, "Reading 4QMMT."

66. Schiffman, *Qumran and Jerusalem*, 5; see also 121–122, 139, 143–144. Note, too, Schiffman's rather dismissive comments regarding Josephus's originality and veracity in *From Text*, 170–171.

67. Shemesh, *Halakhah*, 1–2; Sussmann, "History of *Halakha*," 40, 61–62, and "Appendix 1," 196); Shemesh and Werman, "Halakhah at Qumran," 104. For A. Baumgarten's discussion of his earlier and revised views, see his essay "'But Touch the Law and the Sect Will Split,'" which further develops ideas presented in *Flourishing*, 75–80, identifying legal disagreement as one symptom, but not the cause, of sectarian strife. In both works, Baumgarten also points out that the number of identifiable sects can exceed the number of distinct positions on some key legal questions. Baumgarten's earlier law-centered view is in evidence elsewhere in *The Flourishing*, to wit the practice-centered discussions of sectarian identity. Baumgarten's revised view is not, however, a turn toward Josephus's theological schema. Baumgarten's revised view recognizes (1) that there were often more groups than legal options in specific sectarian disputes, and (2) that sociological factors will determine when or whether legal disputes lead to rifts or compromises.

68. Heger, *Cult as the Catalyst*, 4; Heger diverges from this consensus only insofar as he argues that disputes regarding cultic practices in particular gave rise to sectarian strife (*Cult as the Catalyst*, 7–8).

69. See, for example, Gillman, *Doing Jewish Theology*, x, and Gordon Tucker's introduction to Heschel, *Heavenly Torah*, xxi–xxii. Heschel's *Heavenly Torah* itself also takes on this theme (see esp. 1–45). On a more personal level, see also Susannah Heschel's pertinent reminiscences in Donnelly and Pawlikowski, "Lovingly Observant."11. There were, of course, important exceptions—Solomon Schechter and George Foot Moore in the early twentieth century, and Urbach and Sanders in the later twentieth century.

70. Douglas, *Purity and Danger* and *Natural Symbols*; see also J. Z. Smith, *Drudgery Divine*.

71. Examples abound, so two will suffice here: Charles's preface to *Book of Enoch*, vi: "as a whole, Orthodox Judaism still confesses and still champions the one-sided Judaism, which came into being after the Fall of Jerusalem in 70 AD., a Judaism lopped in the main of its spiritual and prophetic side and given over all but wholly to a legalistic conception of religion." See also Wellhausen, *Pharisees*, p. 13, who speaks of a "wretched yoke of intellectualism"—not among early Christians, of course.

72. Indeed, note Schiffman's discussion, *Qumran and Jerusalem*, 3–5, and compare Heger, *Cult as the Catalyst*, 1–8, 17 (and esp. the comments on p. 4, quoted earlier and cited in n. 68).

73. J. Baumgarten, "Sadducean Elements," 32.

74. See, e.g., Neusner's 1995 summary statement, "Four Approaches to the Description of Rabbinic Judaism," which appears (among other places) in *Rabbinic Judaism*, 1–27.

75. See, e.g., Neusner, *Judaism*, esp. 25–37, which overlooks Josephus even when comparing the Mishnaic response to 70 CE to what can be found in the late first-century apocalypses 2 *Baruch* and 4 Ezra.

76. See, e.g., Mason, *Josephus, Judea*, 239–279, and see also his more popular article "Did the Essenes." Mason frequently credits Neusner as a methodological model: see, e.g., Mason, *Josephus, Judea*, 185, 329–331, and "Revisiting Josephus's Pharisees," 22.

77. Again, see, e.g., Neusner, *Rabbinic Judaism*, esp. 7–23.

78. S. Schwartz, *Imperialism*, 108–109; see also esp. 15–16, 175 (where he speaks of Judaism "shattered"). We will take a closer look at Schwartz's approach to 70 CE in chapter 5.

79. Bokser, "Rabbinic Responses," 61; Goldenberg, "Destruction," 198; Kirschner, "Apocalyptic and Rabbinic Responses," 28–29, 44–45. For a discussion of the (modernist Jewish) supersessionistic elements of some approaches, see Klawans, *Purity, Sacrifice*, 203–211, and chapter 5 here.

80. See Klawans, "Josephus, the Rabbis, and Responses to Catastrophes," 283-289.

81. Goldenberg, "Destruction," mentions Josephus on p. 197; but he moves quickly to speak of mass apostasy and despair (198–199). S. Schwartz, of course, cannot be accused of overlooking Josephus in general. Why he thinks Josephus's evidence matters so little for evaluating Jewish religious responses to 70 CE is unclear; see fuller discussion in chapter 5 here.

82. See, e.g., Cross, *Ancient Library*, 100–110, and Vermes, *Complete Dead Sea Scrolls*, 50–53, 63 n. 1.

83. For a helpful (and creative) analysis of the biblical traditions concerning this figure, see Hauer, "Who Was Zadok"; for a more recent review, see Olyan, "Zadok's Origins."

84. See Klawans, *Purity, Sacrifice*, 94–97, for fuller discussion (and additional bibliography) concerning aspects of Ezekiel's program that were not put into practice in the second temple period.

85. Geiger, *Urschrift*, 20–38; *Judaism and Its History*, 99–103.

86. E.g., Kohler, "Sadducees," in Singer, *Jewish Encyclopedia*, 10:630–633; Finkelstein, *Pharisees*, 1:80, 2:835, and Schürer, *History*, 2:405–407. See also—with some qualification—Meyer, "Σαδδουκαῖος," esp. 36–43, and Sanders, *Judaism*, 25–26.

87. E.g., Gafni, "Historical Background," 12, and Schiffman, *From Text*, 108. See also Meier, *Marginal Jew*, 3:394–395, 450–452 n. 23.

88. See, in addition to works of Cross and Vermes cited above, Eshel, *Dead Sea Scrolls*, 33, 55, 60, and Schiffman, *Qumran and Jerusalem*, 81–83, 100–101. Eshel (p. 33) even suggests that the "Teacher of Righteousness" (*Moreh ha-Zedeq*) was a Zadokite. Although this approach to Qumran literature is common, it is not universal. Among the doubters (beside the present writer) is Collins, *Beyond the Qumran Community*, 46–48, 51.

89. Boccaccini, *Roots of Rabbinic Judaism*, 43–72, 151–163. Fidelity toward Zadokite descent also plays a prominent role in Rachel Elior's depictions of the "secessionist" priesthood; see Elior, *Memory and Oblivion*, 29–30, 49–52, 115–130, and *Three Temples*, 1–28, 165–231.

90. See Sievers, "Josephus, First Maccabees, Sparta," but compare (briefly) Mason, *Josephus, Judea*, 232 n. 32.

91. See Mason, *Flavius Josephus on the Pharisees*, 285.

92. Indeed, in chapter 4 we will come to understand better why Josephus would have rejected Ezekiel's prophecies regarding legal change in this respect.

93. For further references to the Aaronide priesthood, see *Ant.* 2.216, 3.188–192, 4.63–66, 8.228, 9.224, 20.225–226, 235. The only passage that gives real priority to Zadok is the list of priests who served in the first temple, which begins with Zadok (10.151–153). But Zadok goes unmentioned when Josephus summarizes the history of the second temple high priesthood (20.224–251). As Lester L. Grabbe (among others) has noted, it is not at all certain that Onias was a Zadokite; see *Judaic Religion*, 145. Yet Josephus—who does, to be sure, trace

his own descent to the Hasmoneans (*Life* 1–2)—stops short of stating explicitly what so many have inferred: that the end of the Zadokite priesthood gave rise to a sectarian crisis among Jews. So there are two distinct levels of ambiguity here: (1) it is not known for certain that the Zadokite line continued down, unbroken, to Onias III, and (2) even if it did, that does not necessarily mean the breaking of the line caused a particular crisis.

94. On the conflicted appointment of Phannis, see Thoma, "High Priesthood in the Judgment of Josephus," 213–214. Thoma suggests here that the priest chosen by lot was, in fact, a Zadokite, and that Josephus opposed this appointment *for that reason.* While this is a possible understanding of what occurred, it is not a necessary one. Compare VanderKam, *From Joshua to Caiaphas,* 487–490.

95. See Mason, *Flavius Josephus on the Pharisees,* 213–245, where it is recognized that in this case, source-critical questions are inescapable; see *b. Qiddushin* 66a, where the same charge is raised against Alexander Jannaeus.

96. See *Avot de-Rabbi Natan* A 5, B 10 (ed. Schechter 13a–b), see discussion in Le Moyne, *Les Sadducéens,* 113–117. For the Karaite tradition, see Nemoy, "Al-Qirqisānī's Account," 326, and discussion in Le Moyne, *Les Sadducéens,* 137–141.

97. Epiphanius, *Panarion* 14.2.1 (ed. F. Williams 36–37) also puts greater weight on the simpler connection between the name "Sadducee" and the Hebrew word for righteousness (*zedeq*).

98. Ginzberg already recognized this, and speculated that CD refers to a priest in the days of Josiah (*Unknown Jewish Sect,* 21, 68); Ginzberg then goes further to identify this Zadok with the Teacher of Righteousness (211, 219–220).

99. See A. Baumgarten, "Zadokite Priests," and Kugler, "Priesthood," esp. 97–100.

100. It is possible, of course, that the group was not celibate; it is equally possible (if not more possible) that Zadokite descent was not taken literally. The real problem concerns those reconstructions—like Cross's and Vermes's—that presume both a celibate sect and a literal concern with Zadokite descent.

101. This understanding was suggested already by Ginzberg, *An Unknown Jewish Sect,* 15; for more on this passage, see Grossman, "Priesthood as Authority," esp. 126–128.

102. See Olyan, "Ben Sira's Relationship," esp. 270–277, which argues that neither the figure Zadok nor Zadokite descent were of any particular interest to Ben Sira. Note especially Sir. 50.13, which refers to "all the sons of Aaron." On the reference to Zadokites in Sir. 51.12i (which is a subsequent addition to the book), see Olyan, "Ben Sira's Relationship," 275–276.

103. On 4QMMT in this regard, see Kister, "Studies in 4Miqsat Ma'aseh ha-Torah," esp. 323, and nn. 20–21.

104. Schofield and VanderKam, "Were the Hasmoneans Zadokites?"

105. It has recently been argued—adding yet another level of ambiguity—that a number of the first-century high priests (such as those belonging to the house of Annas, including Joseph Caiaphas) were in fact Zadokites; see Bond, *Caiaphas* 24, 35, 149–153. Although she approaches the matter of Zadokite descent differently than I have, Bond's analysis confirms the larger claims being made here: that disputes concerning Zadokite descent were not of enormous consequence to the history of late second temple Judaism, and that our sources say precious little about the matter.

106. Geiger, *Urschrift*, esp. 100–158, 200–230. For a fuller treatment of Geiger's assessment of ancient Judaism in its nineteenth-century German and Jewish context, see S. Heschel, *Abraham Geiger*, esp. 76–105. On Geiger's view of the Essenes in particular, see 93, 172–173.

107. See, e.g., Geiger, *Judaism and Its History*, 102–103, 123–124.

108. Of course, it was Josephus himself who blamed the Sadducean high priest Ananus for the death of James (*Ant.* 20.197–203). Going one step further than even the New Testament, Jean Le Moyne blames the Sadducees for Jesus's death; see Le Moyne, *Les Sadducéens*, 403–404.

109. For a brief survey of the rabbinic sources on the Sadducees, see Porton, "Sadducees," 892–895; on the problems pertaining to the fluidity of the terms referring to Sadducees, Boethusians, sectarians, and Epicureans in rabbinic manuscripts, see Le Moyne, *Les Sadducéens*, 97–102.

110. See Kalmin, *Jewish Babylonia*, 149–166; Kalmin reviews the Babylonian traditions concerning the Sadducees, arguing both for a (possibly indirect) dependence on Josephus and an increasing negativity toward the group in Babylonian (over Palestinian) Talmudic sources.

111. Finkelstein, *Pharisees*, esp. 2:637, 2:753. For similar views, see also, e.g., Baron, *Social and Religious History*, 2:35–38; Geiger, *Judaism and Its History*, 102–103; Herford, *Effect*, 8–9; Lauterbach, *Rabbinic Essays*, 38–39, 48, 51–52, 95–96; Simon, *Jewish Sects*, 24–27; Tcherikover, *Hellenistic Civilization*, 263–264, 494 n. 44, and Zeitlin, *Rise and Fall*, 1:176–187. For a fuller catalogue of anti-Sadducean statements by modern scholars, see Meier, *Marginal Jew*, 3:466–467 n. 73.

112. See the previous note for examples regarding the Sadducees. For a detailed survey of the description of Pharisees as "democratic" by reform-oriented Jewish scholars, see D. Schwartz, *Studies*, 57–80.

113. Goodman, *Ruling Class*, 79. The entire passage is quoted—and assessed favorably—by Richardson, *Herod*, 253. See the important qualifications to such views introduced by Segal, *Life after Death*, 377. The Sadducees have had their defenders, of course; see in particular Sanders, *Judaism*, 337–339.

114. See, among other studies, Elledge, *Life after Death*; Levenson, *Resurrection*, and Segal, *Life after Death*; also note the revised reprint of Nickelsburg, *Resurrection, Immortality*, as well as the additional literature surveyed in Elledge, "Future Resurrection."

115. See, in particular, Boccaccini, *Middle Judaism*, and, more recently, *Roots of Rabbinic Judaism*. Going back earlier, one must also note Sanders, *Paul*.

116. So, e.g., Nickelsburg, *Resurrection, Immortality*, Sanders, *Paul*, and Winston, *Ancestral Philosophy*. Sanders makes up for the deficiency of his 1977 work in his later *Judaism: Practice and Belief*, which makes substantial use of Josephus. Another recent work that gives serious attention to Josephus's theological descriptions of the schools is Meier, *Marginal Jew*, vol. 3, esp. 289–613.

117. See especially Boccaccini, *Beyond the Essene Hypothesis* and *Roots of Rabbinic Judaism*; see also *Middle Judaism*.

118. On the law-centered approach operating throughout ancient Jewish history, see Schiffman, *Qumran and Jerusalem*, 4–5; on comparisons between 70 CE and 1945, see, e.g., Bokser, "Rabbinic Responses," and further examples cited and discussed in chapter 5 here.

119. The question of causation of these disputes is beyond the interests of this study and beyond, in my view, the confines of what our sources can help us determine.

120. Recent helpful surveys of the Sadducees include Porton, "Sadducees," Regev, "Sadducees," and Stemberger, "Sadducees."

121. On Ananus ben Ananus the high priest (identified as a Sadducee in *Ant.* 20.199), see VanderKam, *From Joshua to Caiaphas*, 476–482. The only other individual explicitly identified by Josephus as a Sadducee is an otherwise unknown Jonathan who persuaded John Hyrcanus to incline toward the Sadducees, against the Pharisees (*Ant.* 13.289–296); see discussion in VanderKam, *From Joshua to Caiaphas*, 297–304.

122. Kohler, "Sadducees," in Singer, *Jewish Encyclopedia*, 10:632; see also Geiger, *Urschrift*, 131–132.

123. See, for example, Crenshaw, "Problem of Theodicy," 55; Di Lella, "Conservative and Progressive Theology," 140; Meyer, "Σαδδουκαῖος," 49, and (more recently) Segal, *Rebecca's Children*, 46–47, and *Life after Death*, 254–255 (both discussing primarily Ben Sira 14.16–19). Compare also Boccaccini, *Roots of Rabbinic Judaism*, 134–150, read along with the chart on p. xii. Boccaccini sees Ben Sira as aligned with the Zadokite priesthood and (along with other works) leading toward later Sadducaism. Le Moyne, too, discusses Ben Sira in *Les Sadducéens*, 67–73, deeming it a pre-Sadducean work. Compare the comments of Baumbach, "Sadducees in Josephus," 175, with regard to Ben Sira 15.11–20, to be discussed in chapter 2. Baumbach follows (and cites) Leszynsky, *Die Sadduzäer*, 172–175; Leszynsky, notoriously, identified a large percentage of ancient Jewish works as Sadducean, including 1 Maccabees (175–176) and *Jubilees* (179–237) among others, so his judgment with regard to Ben Sira does not result from any specific interest in the wisdom tradition. William Horbury has suggested that Wisdom of Solomon in part serves to attribute views to Israel's king that are characteristically Pharisaic, thereby

countering the fact that other wisdom works would support views that have come to be associated with the Sadducees; see "Christian Use," 195–196.

124. Sadducees remain unmentioned in two standard introductions to wisdom: Crenshaw, *Old Testament Wisdom* and Murphy, *Tree of Life*. The Sadducees are mentioned in passing (but tangentially) by Horsley, "Wisdom and Apocalypticism," 223, and by Snaith, "Ecclesiasticus," 178. Perdue mentions Sadducees as Hellenized aristocrats in *Wisdom Literature*, 174–175, 220, 343.

125. Crenshaw, for instance, focuses on skepticism in his discussion of wisdom's legacies (*Old Testament Wisdom*, 229–250). Perdue, Scott, and Wiseman, *In Search of Wisdom*, contains essays on apocalyptic and the Gospels (canonical and non-), including *Gospel of Thomas* and Q.

126. For general information on the wisdom tradition and ample bibliography, see Crenshaw, *Old Testament Wisdom*, and Murphy, *Tree of Life*.

127. On wisdom at Qumran, see Goff, "Recent Trends."

128. So, Origen, *Contra Celsum* 1.49 and Hippolytus, *Refutation of All Heresies*, 9.29.4. See Stemberger, "Sadducees," 436.

129. So already Moore, *Judaism*, 1:68. Not entirely unrelated is the narrower question of whether the Sadducees would have accepted Daniel (with its reference to immortality in 12.1–3) as canonical. For some brief comments on the issue, see Segal, *Life after Death*, 281.

130. See, e.g., Crenshaw, *Old Testament Wisdom*, 24–25, 229, 243–247. Compare Boccaccini, *Roots of Rabbinic Judaism*, 103–111, who lists "sapiential Judiasm" among the opponents of what he calls "Zadokite Judaism." Boccaccini believes that a rapprochement between the two develops with works such as Tobit and Ben Sira (113–150; see the chart on xii).

131. On the issues surrounding the identification of wisdom Psalms, for example, see Crenshaw, *Old Testament Wisdom*, 187–194, and Murphy, *Tree of Life*, 103–104, 221, 270–273. For a fuller discussion see Crenshaw, "Wisdom Psalms," Kuntz, "Reclaiming," and Crenshaw's response to Kuntz ("Gold Dust"). My own sense of this debate is that Crenshaw's narrow definitions of wisdom literature may help isolate better those documents that truly represent the creations of Israel's wisdom sages (see also Crenshaw, "Method"). But at the same time, Crenshaw's narrow definitions preclude grappling with *syntheses*, which of course need not be produced by wisdom sages per se. So the presence of "nonwisdom elements" in the Josephus story (see Crenshaw, "Method") may support the argument that the story was not composed by wisdom sages; but the presence of such elements does not argue against the claim that the incorporation of the story into the Pentateuch represents early moves to synthesize wisdom and Torah. The common claim that Ben Sira represents the first synthesis of wisdom and Torah (e.g., Crenshaw, *Old Testament Wisdom*, 155) is an artifice, built on stringent definitions that exclude earlier synthetic efforts (e.g., the Joseph story, Pss. 34 and 37) from the discussion.

132. Josephus speaks of the wisdom books (presumably) only in a very general way in *Against Apion* 1.40: "the remaining four books contain hymns to God and precepts [ὑποθήκας] for everyday life" (see also *Ant.* 7.166 and 8.126). S. Schwartz develops a sustained comparison between Josephus and Ben Sira in *Were the Jews*, 45–109. Schwartz comments on the broader question of Josephus's relation to the wisdom tradition in general in *Josephus and Judaean Politics*, esp. 46–47, 55.

133. On Josephus's account of Solomon, see Feldman, *Josephus's Interpretation*, 570–628; on Solomon's wisdom see esp. 579–598; see 97–106 on Josephus's general approach to praising the wisdom of biblical heroes. According to Feldman, Josephus's general goal is to counter calumnies (such as that offered by Apion; see *Apion* 2.135) to the effect that Jews never produced great wise men as did the Greeks.

134. See, e.g., Von Rad, *Wisdom*, 267–284. On the wisdom-apocalyptic connection in modern scholarship, see DiTommaso, "Apocalypses," 374–381. Saldarini, interestingly, considers Ben Sira (briefly) with regard to the scribes (*Pharisees, Scribes, and Sadducees*, 254–260).

135. See, e.g., Crenshaw, *Old Testament Wisdom*, 229–250. The stark contrasts between Ben Sira and the Wisdom of Solomon (disagreeing, as they do, on issues that also separated Sadducees from Pharisees) should be enough to prove that the wisdom tradition had multiple heirs in the late second temple period.

136. On this understanding of this passage, see Baumbach, "Sadducees in Josephus," 178, and Le Moyne, *Les Sadducéens*, 42. Contrast *Ant.* 18.16 with 18.12: the Pharisees accept the teachings of *their* teachers.

137. The literature on the Pharisees is, of course, vast. Neusner and Chilton's recent collection, *In Quest of the Historical Pharisees*, includes reviews of relevant scholarship (both recent developments and also classical benchmarks) as well as treatments of the major texts and issues; see also Neusner's bibliographical reflections in *Rabbinic Traditions*, 3:320–368. Many "law-centered" approaches also assume a rather direct connection between Pharisees and rabbis, though obviously with legal matters being the main point of comparison (see, e.g., Shemesh, *Halakhah*). For questions concerning Josephus and the Pharisees, see Mason, *Flavius Josephus on the Pharisees*, as well as Mason, "Revisiting Josephus's Pharisees," and Grabbe, "Pharisees: A Response to Steve Mason."

138. Compare, for instance, Neusner, *From Politics to Piety* (which traces the linear connection) with Neusner, *Judaism* (which downplays the Pharisees, recognizing a broader social range of contributors to rabbinic Judaism). For another well-known important work, this one emphasizing both continuity (from Pharisees to Rabbis) and change (primarily in response to the destruction of the temple), see Cohen, "Significance of Yavneh."

139. See, Klawans, *Impurity and Sin*, esp. 92–93 (and the literature cited there) on method for using tannaitic sources; see 146–150, and *Purity, Sacrifice*, 234–241, for my tentative efforts to reconstruct Pharisaic views reflected in gospel traditions by comparison with later tannaitic sources. An earlier, helpful, treatment of the methodological challenges when using rabbinic sources for the study of first-century Judaism is Sanders, *Paul*, 59–84. A clear statement of Neusner's approach can be found in Neusner, *Rabbinic Judaism*, 1–27. For a general symposium on the broader question of using rabbinic sources for historical purposes, see the articles collected by Neusner and Avery-Peck in *Judaism in Late Antiquity* (vol. 3, pt. 1: *Where We Stand*).

140. See S. Schwartz, *Josephus and Judean Politics*, which builds on earlier arguments to this effect by Cohen, Neusner, and M. Smith.

141. Mason, "Pharisaic Dominance," 367–371; see also Mason, *Flavius Josephus on the Pharisees*, and *Josephus, Judea*, 185–215.

142. For discussion of the possibilities see Mason, *Judean War 2* (BJP 1b), 132 n. 1006, and *Flavius Josephus on the Pharisees*, 129–131.

143. So, e.g., Mason, "Pharisaic Dominance," esp. 371.

144. To be precise, it is Pollion who is consistently identified as a Pharisee, and Samaias is referred to as his disciple. Presumably, the disciple of a Pharisee would also be a Pharisee; see Mason, *Flavius Josephus on the Pharisees*, 262. On the other hand, even rabbinic sources, with their fondness for discipleship, can urge caution: according to *Avot de-Rabbi Natan* A 5, B 10 (ed. Schechter 13a–b), the Sadducees and Boethusians were founded by Zadok and Boethus—two disciples of Antigonus of Sokho.

145. See, e.g., Feldman, "Identity of Pollio." These particular identifications, however, were rejected by Neusner, *Rabbinic Traditions*, 1:5.

146. This, famously, was the method employed by Neusner in his earlier efforts to catalogue Pharisaic traditions in rabbinic literature (e.g., *From Politics to Piety* and *Rabbinic Traditions*).

147. For a fuller treatment of each of the individual figures explicitly identified as Pharisees by Josephus or other prerabbinic sources, see Sievers, "Who Were the Pharisees?"

148. See, e.g., Neusner, *Rabbinic Judaism*, 1–27.

149. I am thinking here of Heschel, *Heavenly Torah*; the three original Hebrew volumes appeared in 1962, 1965, and 1990.

150. The standard introductions to the scrolls (VanderKam and Flint, *Meaning*; Vermes, *Complete*) cover the basics of the Essene hypothesis and the history of the discussion. One of the fullest articulations remains Beall, *Josephus' Description*. For helpful analytic surveys of Josephus's accounts of the Essenes see Rajak, *Jewish Dialogue*, 219–240, and Mason, "What Josephus Says."

151. See Ullmann-Margalit, *Out of the Cave*, for a history of the Essene hypothesis and a philosophical analysis of its staying power.

152. See, e.g., A. Baumgarten, "Who Cares," and Golb, *Who Wrote*.

153. See Ullmann-Margalit, *Out of the Cave*, 19–20.

154. Mason has published his arguments in a number of places. Important, larger discussions include *Josephus, Judea*, 239–279; "What Josephus Says," and *Judean War 2* (BJP 1b), esp. 84–131. For a briefer, popular treatment—one that is also helpful and in some ways revealing—see Mason, "Did the Essenes." Some of these works are cited approvingly in Elior, *Memory and Oblivion*, 38 n. 21.

155. Principally, see Atkinson and Magness, "Josephus's Essenes." See also Collins, *Beyond the Qumran Community*, 122–165; Collins accepts a number of Mason's methodological points regarding Josephus, but still determines that the Essene hypothesis is more likely than any alternative.

156. Cross, *Canaanite Myth*, 331–332; for critical discussions of this passage, see Ullmann-Margalit, *Out of the Cave*, 38, and Golb, *Who Wrote*, 89–90.

157. Cross, *Canaanite Myth*, 334–342.

158. Wise, "Dating The Teacher."

159. Magness, *Archaeology of Qumran*, 47–72.

160. See, e.g., VanderKam and Flint, *Meaning*, 239–254 ("branch," 250).

161. So, e.g., Sanders, "Dead Sea Sect," 41–42; Collins, *Beyond the Qumran Community*, 2–3, 122, 209; Ullmann-Margalit, *Out of the Cave*, 21.

162. The most elaborate source-critical approach to the Essene passage in particular is Bergmeier, *Die Essener-Berichte*. Mason's arguments against source-critical approaches to Josephus's descriptions of the schools (including the Essenes) strike me as definitive; see, especially, *Judean War 2* (BJP 1b), esp. 87–90, and compare Collins's helpful discussion, *Beyond the Qumran Community*, 133–142.

163. Mason, *Josephus, Judea*, 258–261, 278–279; *Judean War 2* (BJP 1b), e.g., 93–95, 101 n. 773, 102 n. 777, 107 nn. 812, 817, 108–109 n. 830, etc.

164. Mason, *Judean War 2* (BJP 1b), 91.

165. Mason, "What Josephus Says," 423–424.

166. Mason, *Judean War 2* (BJP 1b), 117–118 n. 901; "Did the Essenes," 62–63; see, e.g., Atkinson and Magness, "Josephus's Essenes," 326–329.

167. Mason, "What Josephus Says," 430, 450; see *Judean War 2* (BJP 1b), 94–95: "The new covenanters represent a mentality completely at odds with the aristocratic, Greek-cultured, statesmen-like values of Josephus and the others who so admiringly describe Essenes." For James's classic descriptions of the "healthy-minded" and the "sick souls" see lectures 4–7 of *Varieties of Religious Experience*.

168. Without reference to William James, compare Klawans, "Purity in the Dead Sea Scrolls," esp. 394–396; coincidentally, James's essay on free will ("Dilemma of Determinism") proves helpful in understanding ancient Jewish views of free will. In addition to chapter 2 here, see Klawans, "Dead Sea Scrolls."

169. James, *Varieties of Religious Experience*, 387 (lecture 8).

170. Note also M. H. Gottstein's earlier attempt to make use of the "twice-born" concept to differentiate Josephus's Essenes from the scrolls ("Anti-Essene Traits," 146). Gottstein, however, attempted to distinguish between the "twice-born" Essenes whom Josephus describes and what he calls the "annual-birth" type envisioned in 1QS 2.19. The basis of Gottstein's distinction is unclear, but standard usage of the "twice-born" category requires differentiation from a "once-born" category. Still, it is interesting that both Gottstein and Mason have made use of the "twice-born" category to argue against the Essene hypothesis, with one (Gottstein) finding the "twice-born" among Josephus's Essenes and the other, by implication, finding the "twice-born" at Qumran.

171. Mason, *Judean War 2* (BJP 1b), 105–106, esp. n. 804, and "What Josephus Says," 437–438. Though by the logic of the example discussed previously, perhaps the prohibition in the *Temple Scroll* should be taken as evidence that the sectarians were indeed sun worshipers?

172. See Beall, *Josephus' Description*, 52–54.

173. In addition to the material noted by Mason in the notes to *Judean War 2* (BJP 1b), see M. Smith, "Helios."

174. On the cosmic temple in Josephus, Philo, and other writings, see Klawans, *Purity, Sacrifice*, 111–128.

175. As noted, with regard to the Essenes, already by Ginsburg, *Essenes*, 9, 69–70.

176. See Mason, *Josephus, Judea*, 272.

177. So, e.g., Feldman's note d to *Ant.* 18.18, in LCL ad loc.; Taylor, "Philo of Alexandria," 8–9; Rajak, *Jewish Dialogue*, 231–234; Vermes and Goodman, *Essenes*, 19.

178. For further parallels among ancient sources to Philo's and Josephus's attitudes toward women, see Mason, *Judean War 2* (BJP 1b), 100 n. 758.

179. See Rajak, *Jewish Dialogue*, 225.

180. For fuller comparisons between Josephus and Philo on the Essenes, see Taylor, "Philo of Alexandria," and Mason, *Judean War 2* (BJP 1b), 91–92, as well as the notes ad loc. to Josephus's descriptions of the Essenes.

181. Cohen, *Josephus*, 24–66; see, e.g., Mason, *Judean War 2* (BJP 1b), 87.

182. See Wolfson, *Philo*, 1:435–441.

183. See Taylor, "Philo of Alexandria," for a recent review of Philo's evidence about the Essenes, and see especially her conclusion (27–28) for the case against "the quarrying of snippets" in the absence of "a clear knowledge of his language, rhetoric and his works as a whole."

CHAPTER 2

1. For a survey of scholarship on fate and free will in Josephus, see Mason, *Flavius Josephus on the Pharisees*, 384–398. One classic treatment remains Moore, "Fate and Free Will." Another important study, though less well known, is Flusser,

"Pharisees and the Stoic Sages," translated in Flusser, *Judaism*; my citations of this article, when the technical vocabulary involved requires it, refer to both the Hebrew original and the English translation.

2. Josephus's description of the Pharisaic and Sadducean positions in *War* 2.162–166 is echoed and expanded in the *Refutation Against All Heresies,* generally attributed to Hippolytus (also known as the *Philosophumena* or *Elenchos*). See especially *Refutation* 9.28.3–29.4. The *Refutation*'s adaptation of *Jewish War's* description of the Jewish schools is discussed in the appendix; I argue there that it is highly unlikely that the *Refutation* preserves historically reliable material, apart from what is taken directly from Josephus.

3. For an alternative translation with notes, see Thackeray, "Josephus's Statement."

4. See Sievers, "Josephus, First Maccabees, Sparta," who argues for a rather random insertion of the passage at this point. Haaland ("What Difference," 271–272) suggests that the description of the philosophical schools meaningfully complements the preceding description of alliances with Rome and Sparta (*Ant.* 13.163–170). Having described the Jewish political achievements of the era, Josephus moves naturally to describe the era's Jewish philosophical achievements.

5. So, e.g., Moore, "Fate and Free Will," who asserts that Josephus likely, and rather mindlessly, copied them from the writings of Herod's court historian, Nicolaus of Damascus—a person presumably more familiar with, and sympathetic to, Greek philosophy than Jewish theology.

6. So, e.g., Mason, *Judean War 2* (BJP 1b), 132 n. 1007, who suggests that the view attributed to the Pharisees in *War* 2 is the same as the view attributed to the Essenes in subsequent passages. We will return to this issue later in this chapter.

7. So, e.g., Schiffman, *Qumran and Jerusalem*, 3–5, discussed in chapter 1.

8. So, e.g., Winston, *Ancestral Philosophy*, which reprints various essays treating determinism and free will in ancient Jewish thought, without nary a mention of Josephus's evidence. See also Winston, *Wisdom of Solomon*, 46–58.

9. So, e.g., Flusser, "Pharisees and the Stoic Sages."

10. For general discussion and definitions of these terms as used in religious studies and theology, see Kees W. Bolle, "Fate," in Eliade, *Encyclopedia of Religion*, 5:290–297. For Hellenistic definitions, see Moore, "Fate and Free Will," and (especially) Bobzien, *Determinism*, esp. 16–58. The contemporary philosophic discussion of these matters is also influenced (but not determined) by the Hellenistic definitions; for a brief survey of the modern philosophical issues, addressed to the general reader, see Pink, *Free Will*. Many other definitions of fate could be offered; it is common, for instance, to speak of "fate" when translating *miqreh* in Ecclesiastes (e.g., Eccles. 2.14; see Machinist, "Fate"). But when considering the fate/free will paradox, one must utilize a definition of fate that

impacts on free will. We will observe, however, usages of "fate" more in line with the usage of Ecclesiastes, with the meaning "destiny."

11. See, again, Moore, "Fate and Free Will," and Flusser, "Pharisees and the Stoic Sages." Note again that C. D. Elledge helpfully speaks (with regard to evidence concerning life after death) of Josephus's "apologetic translation" (*Life after Death*, 3, 45, 81–82). Of course, the employment of descriptive terminology from more or less related discourses is something that modern scholars do as well, as when scholars speak of halakhah at Qumran (against which see Meier, *Marginal Jew*, 4:63–66 n. 62).

12. See Ileana Marcoulesco, "Free Will and Determinism," in Eliade, *Encyclopedia of Religion*, 5:419–421.

13. See Dewey D. Wallace, Jr., "Free Will and Predestination," in Eliade, *Encyclopedia of Religion*, 5:422–427.

14. For a brief statement of this doctrine, see Calvin, *Institutes*, 3.21.1. Calvin refers to the doctrine as "Eternal Election, by which God has predestined some to salvation, others to destruction."

15. On Josephus's use of "fortune" (τύχη) in *War* see Michel and Bauernfeind, *De Bello Judaico*, 2:2, 212–214 (excursus 18), and see further discussion later in this chapter.

16. On Josephus's belief in divine providence, see, in particular, Attridge, *Interpretation*, 71–107.

17. On these passages, see Reider, *Book of Wisdom*, 35, 167–168; Winston, *Wisdom of Solomon*, 265; Hadas, *Third and Fourth Books*, 23, 118, 213. See also Attridge, *Interpretation*, 75–76, 158–159.

18. See discussion in Wolfson, *Philo*, 1:328–330, 2:283–285, 2:292–294, 2:450–452; see also Attridge, *Interpretation*, 158–159, and Dillon, *Middle Platonists*, 166–168.

19. See Kraabel, "Pronoia at Sardis," for a general discussion; for the inscriptions from Sardis, see Kroll, "Greek Inscriptions," esp. inscriptions 16, 21–23, 58, 66; and see inscriptions 12, 17, 19, 20, 24 (as restored).

20. So, e.g., Mason, *Josephus, Judea*, 226; see further discussion later in this chapter.

21. On the identification of fate with providence, see Bobzien, *Determinism*, 13, 44–47; on the distinction in later Greek thought, see 411; compare Attridge, *Interpretation*, 156–158.

22. On astrological fate as a partial determinism see Bobzien, *Determinism*, 13, and Barton, *Ancient Astrology*, 52–63, 71–78 (who distinguishes between astrology and "fatalism"). On Middle Platonist approaches, which subordinate fate to providence, see Dillon, *Middle Platonists*, 208–211, 294–298, 320–326, and "Plutarch and Second Century Platonism," 225–226 (Plutarch, who lived 46–120 CE, was a younger contemporary of Josephus). On Gnostic ideas within these currents, see Williams, *Rethinking "Gnosticism,"* 202–208. I acknowledge

Williams's more general point—articulated also by King (*What Is Gnosticism*)—questioning the accuracy and utility of the terms "Gnostic" and "Gnosticism." Of course, the term "Gnostic" still has its defenders, too (e.g., M. Meyer, *Gnostic Discoveries*, 38–43). Until a suitable alternative becomes widely accepted, comparative analyses like this one will have to proceed using standard, more widely recognizable terminology.

23. On the usage and meaning of the term "compatibilism" in modern philosophy, see Pink, *Free Will*, esp. 18–19, 43–72, 109–110. For a more thorough review of the terms and issues with regard to Stoic philosophy, see Bobzien, *Determinism*, 16–58.

24. See, for example, Roy, *How Much*, 13–25, and Feinberg, "God Ordains all Things," 19–43. As we will see, the debate among contemporary evangelical Christians, as reflected in these two works (for instance), is in some respects comparable to the debate among ancient Jewish schools.

25. See, e.g., Rudavsky, *Time Matters*, 95–148 (on medieval Jewish thought), and Duhaime, "Determinism," 194 (on ancient Jewish thought).

26. So, e.g., Duhaime, "Determinism," 196; see further the literature surveyed and cited later.

27. It could therefore be argued that philosophic terms should not be used at all in discussions of the theological disputes. But the invention of further vocabulary for the various overlapping concepts is unlikely to help clarify these matters. And as we will see, it will prove helpful, despite the differences, to compare ancient and modern philosophical systems to the theological ones that characterized ancient Judaism. Besides, philosophic terms have been used with regard to the Jewish theological debates since the time of Josephus. So we do well to work with philosophical vocabulary to the extent this is possible, and indicate as necessary how the terms' nuances change in disparate contexts.

28. For the view of apocalyptic as deterministic, see, e.g., Russell, *Method and Message*, 230–234, and Von Rad, *Wisdom*, 278–282; for the understanding of Ecclesiastes as deterministic (even predeterministic), see, e.g., Crenshaw, *Ecclesiastes*, 92–93, and Hengel, *Judaism and Hellenism*, 141; see Von Rad, *Wisdom*, 143, 264–265.

29. See, e.g., Von Rad, *Wisdom*, 267–284; for further analysis and bibliography, see DiTommaso, "Apocalypses (Part II)," 374–381.

30. See Fox, *Time to Tear Down*, 191–217; compare also the comparisons (and contrasts) drawn between Ecclesiastes and the Stoics in Gammie, "Stoicism and Anti-Stoicism," esp. 183–185.

31. See Helberg, "Determination of History," for a full discussion, and esp. 285 n. 32 for a list of scholars who have asserted (with less clarity than Helberg) that Daniel's determinism is partial. See also DiTommaso, "Apocalypses (Part II)," 384–390.

32. For a brief survey of predestination in the scrolls, see Lange, "Wisdom." On the *Thanksgiving Hymns*, see Merrill, *Qumran and Predestination*, 16–23, and Mansoor, *Thanksgiving Hymns*, 55–57.

33. In general, Josephus exhibits restraint with regard to angels, as we will have occasion to observe again in the next chapter; see Feldman, *Josephus's Interpretation*, 212–213.

34. We part here from Skehan and Di Lella, who translate the Hebrew of MS B (יצרו) as "his free choice." They are correct to argue (*Wisdom of Ben Sira*, 271–272) that the concept of human freedom is expressed in this passage, especially insofar as the decision to do good or bad is presented in vv. 15–16, and separated from God's control in vv. 11–12. But their translation is misleading if it is taken to suggest the presence in this passage of a technical vocabulary akin to what we find in Hellenistic philosophical texts.

35. Translation of Sirach here and throughout follows Skehan and Di Lella, *Wisdom of Ben Sira*; on this passage, see 267–275.

36. Curiously, Philo (*Every Good Man* 84) states that the Essenes believe that "the deity is the cause of all good, but of no evil," which seems rather similar to Sirach 15.11–13 and the Sadducean view, as described by Josephus. Compared to Josephus, Philo says relatively little about Essene theology. And, as noted in the previous chapter, what little Philo does say (as here) seems to express also Philo's own views (see Wolfson, *Philo*, 1:435–446). Unlike Josephus, Philo exhibits little interest in the free will problem per se (the issues come up, to be sure, but the problem as such is not addressed head on, as in Josephus). So while *Every Good Man* 84 confirms that some Jews struggled to separate God from evil, the brief notice does not pose insurmountable challenges to the ongoing comparison between theology of Josephus's Essenes and that of the sectarian Dead Sea Scrolls—which of course separate God from wickedness by attributing evil more directly to the powers of darkness. An additional interesting—but only partial—parallel to Ben Sira's (and the Sadducees') separation of God from evil is the striking assertion in *Wisdom* 1.13 that God did not create death. On this passage, see Reider, *Book of Wisdom*, 56–57, and Winston, *Wisdom of Solomon*, 107–108.

37. Mason, *Judean War 2* (BJP 1b), 132 n. 1007; *Josephus, Judea*, 231–232.

38. For an earlier defense of Josephan consistency regarding his account of the Pharisaic view, see Whiston's note b to his translation of *Antiquities* 13.172. Mason's fuller account of the differences between *War* 2 and *Ant.* 13 in *Flavius Josephus on the Pharisees* (esp. 204–205) is more nuanced, accounting for the similarities and differences with regard to both fate and free will.

39. As was discussed more fully in chapter 1, we are not interested in presenting a systematic account of rabbinic theology, or even a general description of the rabbinic approach(es) to fate and free will. We are also not interested in dating rabbinic texts or individual rabbinic traditions. Rabbinic sources will be used here

for the purposes of illuminating and evaluating the plausibility of Josephus's
descriptions of ancient Jewish theologies.

40. See, for example, Finkelstein, *Pharisees*, 1:252–253, as well as Thackeray's note d
to Josephus, *War* 2.163 (in LCL ed.) and L. H. Feldman's note 3 to *Antiquities* 18.13
(in LCL ed.). See also (though with qualifications) Mason, *Judean War 2* (BJP
1b), 133 n. 1010. The most recent, thorough effort to associate the *Avot* passage
with Josephus's Pharisees is Hultgren, "Rabbi Akiba on Divine Providence."
Hultgren's effort to associate Josephus's Pharisees with a toned-down rabbinic
determinism is not without merit; but the effort is undermined by his reluctance to make full sense of Josephus's accounts of the Sadducean and Essene
positions, especially with regard to humans' freedom to do otherwise (in compatibilist and libertarian positions) and God's implication in evil (in compatibilist and determinist positions; see, for example, the brief comments offered
at 123 n. 50). In my view, the Josephan discussions of fate and free will can only
be understood when all three positions are fully explicated; and only when all
three positions are mapped out can one best see where Josephus's view is to be
located.

41. Such is the translation of Danby, *Mishnah*, 452; we also follow here Danby's versification, but note that the versification of this tractate varies considerably. The
passage is translated similarly by, among others, Taylor, *Sayings*, 59; Herford,
Ethics, 88; Hertz, *Sayings*, 61; Neusner, *Mishnah*, 660–661; see also Albeck,
Shishah Sidre Mishnah, 4:367 (where the passage is explained in this manner)
and 4:497 (where Akiba's view is compared to the Pharisees explicitly). Despite
this near unanimity, there is some evidence for an alternative understanding of
the passage.

42. Precisely speaking, the statement is anonymous. The attribution to R. Akiba
results from carrying over the attribution from a previous statement (3.14),
even though this passage lacks the tractate's common way of connecting one
statement to another (the phrase "He used to say"—see 3.15 and 3.17). See the
comments offered by Gordon Tucker in Heschel, *Heavenly Torah*, 216 n. 27. Of
course, even if the attribution to R. Akiba were unambiguous, the historical
reliability of the attribution would still remain questionable. Throughout this
book, attributions of statements to named authorities will be noted, under the
assumption that this data is potentially useful for analytic purposes and in any
event helpful heuristically for those who are familiar with rabbinic literature.
For what it is worth, a similar (but not identical) statement is attributed to R.
Eliezer, the son of Yosi the Galilean, in *Avot de-Rabbi Natan* B 44 (ed. Schechter
62a).

43. See Tucker's comments in Heschel, *Heavenly Torah*, 209, and Winston, *Ancestral
Philosophy*, 53–54.

44. This tradition (along with some parallels, and in comparison to Josephus's
Pharisees), will be discussed more fully later.

45. In addition to works cited in previous notes, see, e.g., Kohler, "Pharisees," in Singer, *Jewish Encyclopedia*, 9:664–665. Compare the more thorough treatment in Urbach, *Sages*, 255–285. Though Urbach understands *m. Avot* 3.16 as advocating freedom of choice (256–260), he compiles other evidence for the varied compromise positions articulated in rabbinic sources.

46. Note that the interpretation that follows differs considerably from my earlier briefer consideration of this passage in "Josephus on Fate," 80.

47. The murder of Aristobulus: *Ant.* 15.50–56; the murder of Mariamme: 15.232–239; the proposed mass murder on Herod's death: 17.178–181.

48. Translation largely follows LCL, but modified in light of the discussion in Mason, *Flavius Josephus on the Pharisees*, 141–142.

49. Some interpreters are led astray here, thinking that Josephus means to say that the debate about fate and free will is elaborated in the Law (see, e.g., Mason, *Flavius Josephus on the Pharisees*, 142, and see LCL ad loc., note d, which points not back to Josephus's paraphrase of the Torah but forward to Josephus's discussion of the beliefs of the Pharisees in *Ant.* 18.12–15). To be sure, the debate about fate and free will is not elaborated in the Law. But Josephus clearly believes that the Law's "philosophy" involves human freedom and moral responsibility, along with God's caring guidance: see *Ant.* 1.1–26, and fuller discussion later in this chapter.

50. Contra, e.g., Mason, *Judean War 2* (BJP 1b), 132 n. 1007, who associates Josephus's position with the Essene one (see also Mason, *Josephus, Judea*, 232).

51. Urbach, *Sages*, 257–258, 802–803 n. 11; the possibility of this sense was also discussed by Taylor, *Sayings*, 59 n. 28 and 160, though his translation, as noted, reads "foreseen." Taylor also collects evidence from medieval manuscripts and commentaries preserving the alternate reading "all is set forth" (צפון). See Taylor, *Appendix to Sayings*, 122, 152. Needless to say, the interpretation of *m. Avot* 3.16 often coincides with the philosophic view of the interpreter. Maimonides's direct commentary on the passage understands it in the sense of foresight, in line with his deterministic (and/or compatibilistic) view. See Maimonides's comment to *Avot* 3.16 ad loc. (ed. Qafih 4.284–285) and see the philosopher's seemingly libertarian assertions in chapter 8 of his "Eight Chapters" introducing *m. Avot* (ed. Qafih 4.260–466). Maimonides's determinism is expressed especially in *Guide of the Perplexed* 2.48 (trans. Pines, 2:409–412). On Maimonides's approach to fate and free will, see Sokol, "Maimonides." Sokol's understanding of Maimonides's approach to fate and free will is not all that different from the early Stoic view, as will be discussed later.

52. Translation follows Wright, "Psalms of Solomon."

53. See, for example, Finkelstein, *Pharisees*, 1:251–253; Maier, *Mensch und freier Wille*, 264–350. See, however, Charlesworth's (editorial) assessment in Wright, "Psalms of Solomon," 642, which articulates the more generally accepted approach today: "It is unwise to label these psalms as either Pharisaic or Essene."

54. Perhaps the best known rabbinic assertion of human freedom is *Sifre Deut.* secs. 53–54 (on Deut. 11.26–27; ed. Finkelstein, 120–122). We also know, of course, that other rabbinic traditions move in the other direction, toward a more certain determinism: consider, for example, the saying attributed to R. Hanina bar Hama in *b. Hullin* 7b: "A person does not bruise a finger below, unless it be announced concerning him on high, for it is said (Prov. 20.24), 'a person's steps are decided by the Lord.'" This and other deterministic rabbinic traditions are collected and discussed in Urbach, *Sages*, 276–281.

55. Sanders, *Paul*, 263.

56. Merrill, *Qumran and Predestination*, 45; see also 16, 58.

57. Schuller, "Petitionary Prayer," 39–43.

58. Schuller, "Petitionary Prayer," 45.

59. Duhaime, "Determinism."

60. In addition to the works cited in previous notes, see e.g., Jassen, "Religion," 11; Mason, *Flavius Josephus on the Pharisees*, 333–334, and Meier, *Marginal Jew*, 3:326–327, 409–410. This view is not unanimous, however. Martone ("Qumran and Stoicism," 619) states that the sect's strict determinism "left no room for human freedom."

61. So, e.g., Merrill, *Qumran and Predestination*, 16, 45, 58; Ringgren, *Faith of Qumran*, 109–111, and Sanders, *Paul*, 265.

62. See, e.g., Meyer, "Σαδδουκαῖος," 46; see discussion in Baumbach, "Sadducees in Josephus," 175, and see further literature cited there.

63. On the Sadducees' purported atheism as relating to Josephus's biases, see Baumbach, "Sadducees in Josephus," 175. Flusser suggests that Josephus let himself get carried away by his philosophical comparison, exaggerating the Sadducean view; see "Pharisees and the Stoic Sages," 321–324 (*Judaism*, 2:224–227), and see Flusser, "Josephus on the Sadducees." So, too, Meier, *Marginal Jew*, 3:410–411. Stemberger (*Jewish Contemporaries*, 70) suggests that Josephus is simply mistaken.

64. This insight derives from an observation drawn by Sarah J. Chandonnet, who perspicaciously asked in class about Josephus's Sadducees on reading (in Vermes's English translation) CD 1.3–4 and 2.8–9, which speak of God hiding his face from a sinful Israel.

65. On Josephus's anti-Sadducean views, see Baumbach, "Sadducees in Josephus," 175–178, and Mason, *Judean War 2* (BJP 1b), 134 n. 1014; compare Stemberger, *Jewish Contemporaries*, 5–20.

66. Winter, "Ben Sira and the Teaching," 315–318; so also Flusser, "Pharisees and the Stoic Sages," 320 n. 7 (*Judaism*, 2:224 n. 7).

67. See, e.g., Hengel, *Judaism and Hellenism*, 1.141; M. Segal, *Sefer Ben Sira*, 29; Von Rad, *Wisdom*, 250, 266–268, and Winston, *Wisdom of Solomon*, 49–50, and *Ancestral Philosophy*, 35–43.

68. See, e.g., Moore, *Judaism*, 1:454–459.

69. See Winston, *Wisdom of Solomon*, 46–58, who compares Qumran, Sirach, and rabbinic literature to the compatibilist position of the Hellenistic Stoic philosophers; this is also the broad thrust of Winston's essay on the subject, as collected in *Ancestral Philosophy*, esp. 11–56. Winston's commentaries and essays are inspiring, especially insofar as they exhibit depth in both ancient Jewish and Hellenistic philosophical sources. We have already noted, however, that Winston's work gives little attention to Josephus's tripartite typology of the ancient Jewish schools.

70. So, e.g., Flusser, "Pharisees and the Stoic Sages," 320 n. 7 (*Judaism*, 2:224 n. 7); M. Segal, *Sefer Ben Sira*, 29; Winston, *Ancestral Philosophy*, 18, 47–48; Winter, "Ben Sira and the Teaching."

71. Of course, believers in double predestination equate predestination with election: see, e.g., Calvin, *Institutes*, 3.21.1. But unless one believes that all ancient Jews were Calvinists, we cannot impose—consciously or unconsciously—a Calvinist elision of this distinction on our ancient Jewish sources.

72. For this understanding of Sirach, see Skehan and Di Lella, *Wisdom of Ben Sira*, 395–401.

73. See, for example, Roy, *How Much*, 34–72, which discusses the two examples noted here, among many others. See also Boettner, *Reformed Doctrine*, 42–46. Boettner follows and expands on Calvin, *Institutes*, 1.8.8 (ed. McNeill 1:87–88).

74. In the Hellenistic world, the accuracy of divination and astrology was also seen as evidence for the truth of determinism; see Bobzien, *Determinism*, 87–96. It is imperative, however, to refrain from reversing the equation: neither practitioners of nor believers in astrology or divination are necessarily determinists. Astrology can operate with the assumption that only certain events (e.g., times of birth or death) are fated. See Bobzien, *Determinism*, 13, for a definition of astrological fate as distinct from (and more limited than) causal determinism. See also Stuckrad, "Jewish and Christian Astrology," 3–5.

75. See, however, *Ant.* 18.22, which, rather unclearly, compares the Essenes with the some of the Dacians—perhaps ones called "Ctistae." On the text-critical issues with this passage, see Feldman's comments in LCL ad loc., and the discussion in Beall, *Josephus' Description*, 121–122 (see Niese, *Flavii Iosephi*, 4:144, on *Ant.* 18.22).

76. So, e.g., Begg and Spilsbury, *Judean Antiquities 8–10* (BJP 5), 315 nn. 1181–1182; Feldman, *Josephus's Interpretation*, 192; Mason, *Judean War 2* (BJP 1b), 134 nn. 1014–1015; Mason, *Life of Josephus* (BJP 9), 16–17 n. 72; Mason, *Josephus, Judea*, 225–226, 230.

77. Compare Stemberger, *Jewish Contemporaries*, 69–70.

78. As implied in Mason, *Flavius Josephus on the Pharisees*, 141.

79. Compare Barclay, *Against Apion* (BJP 10), 270–271 nn. 704, 707, 711; see in chapters 4 and 5 here for further observations on the relation between *Apion* and *Antiquities*.

80. That Josephus's use of the term "providence" here in place of "fate" is intended can be confirmed by the fact that he brings up "fate" once in *Against Apion*, in the context of making light of Zeus being left at the mercy of fate (in the Zeus-Apollo myth, as Josephus retells it; *Apion* 2.245).

81. See, for example, Ringgren, *Faith of Qumran*, 109–110; Sanders, *Paul*, 263–264; Duhaime, "Determinism," 195–196; Jassen, "Religion," 11.

82. For the difference, as it pertains to the philosophical debates, see Bobzien, "Inadvertent Conception," 134.

83. A number of writers have correctly recognized that theological determinism differs, by necessity, from some philosophical counterparts. See Moore, "Fate and Free Will," 379, and Flusser "Pharisees and the Stoic Sages," 318–319 (*Judaism*, 2:221–222).

84. Calvin, *Institutes*, 2.4.1–8. The comparison between Calvinist predestination and the Dead Sea sect is developed further in Klawans, "Dead Sea Scrolls."

85. See, for instance, Boettner, *Reformed Doctrine*, 208–227, and compare Roy, *How Much*, 13–16.

86. See, for example, Ringgren, *Faith of Qumran*, 123; Sanders, *Paul*, 262–263; Duhaime, "Determinism," 196; Jassen, "Religion," 11; for a more thorough discussion, see Schuller, "Petitionary Prayer."

87. Compare Boettner, *Reformed Doctrine*, 214–218, and Calvin, *Institutes*, 2.4.7.

88. These and other examples are discussed by Schuller, "Petitionary Prayer," 40–41; see also Martone, "Qumran and Stoicism."

89. Among the most helpful are Flusser, "Pharisees and the Stoic Sages," and Urbach, *Sages*, 255–285.

90. Steve Mason is among the few scholars who recognize the distinction developed here (*Flavius Josephus on the Pharisees*, 203–205, 297). Mason follows, in part, Maier, *Mensch und freier Wille*, 13–20. What is presented in what follows, however, differs somewhat from both Mason's and Maier's understandings of the distinction. Hultgren, "Rabbi Akiba on Divine Providence," 124–131, also recognizes the distinction, apparently without building on those who had recognized this distinction previously.

91. It must also be noted that there are many rabbinic traditions that do not closely match either of the two compatibilist views described by Josephus. As Urbach noted in his treatment long ago, the rabbinic traditions preserve the record of "a multifaceted struggle, extending over generations of sages, which cannot be summarized in a dictum by one or another scholar—not even the formulation of Josephus" (*Sages*, 284).

92. On this passage, see Mason, *Flavius Josephus on the Pharisees*, 120–177.

93. On this passage, see Mason, *Flavius Josephus on the Pharisees*, 281–308; compare Thackeray, "On Josephus's Statement."

94. On this term—and the text-critical problems associated with this particular reading, as opposed to κρίσις—see Mason, *Flavius Josephus on the Pharisees*,

141–142, 295. On the term in Stoic philosophy in general, see Salles, *Stoics on Determinism*, 54–61. While Feldman in LCL, ad loc., and Thackeray, "On Josephus's Statement," prefer κρᾶσις, Niese preferred κρίσις (*Flavii Iosephi*, 4:141, on *Ant.* 18.13). Mason demonstrates in his discussion (295) that the same general sense of "blending" or "balancing" can be teased out of either reading.

95. The Soncino translation (ed. I. Epstein), which has been utilized here and subsequently, follows the text of the traditional printed editions. Variants preserved in the manuscripts will be noted here only when directly relevant to the issue at hand.

96. See Urbach, *Sages*, 807 n. 51, and H. Freedman's note ad loc. to *B. Shabbat* 104a in the Soncino translation. Urbach himself (*Sages*, 272–273) correctly rejects this understanding of the passage. Other rabbinic traditions do come closer to separating God from evil in some fashion; see, for example, the statement attributed to R. Eleazar in *Genesis Rabbah* 3.6 (ed. Mirkin 1:23–24; ed. Theodor/Albeck 1:23) and to R. Yohanan in *Midrash Tanhuma, Tazria*, sec. 9 (ed. Buber 20b [sec. 12]), to the effect that God's name is not mentioned in direct relation to evil. But as Urbach correctly observes (*Sages*, 274–275), the rabbinic fear of dualism trumps the desire to separate God from the creation of and role in evil.

97. Manuscript traditions preserve further variants on the two possible attributions preserved in the standard printed edition. See Rabbinovicz, *Diqduqe Soferim*, ad loc., and compare also MS Jerusalem Yad ha-Rav Herzog 1, easily accessible via the Jewish National and University Library's Online Treasury of Talmudic Manuscripts, http://jnul.huji.ac.il/dl/talmud/index.htm. The variants to the tradition itself preserved in the manuscripts and noted by Rabbinovicz are not significant for our concerns.

98. See *Mekilta de-Rabbi Ishmael, Va-Yassa* 1 (ed. Lauterbach 2:95–97; ed. Horovitz/Rabin 157–158); *Ba-Hodesh* 2 (ed. Lauterbach 2:203; ed. Horovitz/Rabin 208).

99. See Thackeray, "On Josephus's Statement," which paraphrases *Ant.* 18.13 to the effect that fate goes halfway to meet the person who proceeds with virtuous intent.

100. On this passage, see Mason, *Flavius Josephus on the Pharisees*, 196–212; Martin, "Josephus' Use," and Penner, "Fate."

101. See also *b. Megillah* 25a and *b. Niddah* 16b. A similar, anonymous, tannaitic tradition—quoting Prov. 22.5—is preserved in *b. Ketubot* 30a.

102. The translation, again, follows Soncino. The text of traditional printed edition has been compared to MS Vatican 111, available via the Online Treasury of Talmudic Manuscripts.

103. In line with the general imprecision in treating Pharisaic and rabbinic compatibilism, Feldman cites *b. Berakhot* 33b and *b. Niddah* 16b as near parallels to *Ant.* 18.13 (see LCL ed. ad loc.).

104. For textual notes and variants, see Rabbinovicz, *Diqduqe Soferim*, ad loc., and compare also MS Jerusalem Yad ha-Rav Herzog 1, Online Treasury of Talmudic

Manuscripts, http://jnul.huji.ac.il/dl/talmud/index.htm. The passage quoted continues with the tradition attributed to Rab Huna or R. Eleazar, quoted in the previous section.

105. See *Mekilta de-Rabbi Ishmael, Neziqin* 4 (ed. Lauterbach 3:35; ed. Horovitz/ Rabin 262); *b. Shabbat* 32a; *Sifre Deut.*, sec. 229 (on Deut. 22.8; ed. Finkelstein 262).

106. On Philo's approach to free will, see Wolfson, *Philo*, 1:424–462; on this passage in particular, see 1.438–441, esp. n. 37. For Wolfson, this passage demonstrates Philo's willingness to see God's providential role in certain instances of human transgression. Against Wolfson—but without reference to *Spec. Laws* 3.120–123 in particular—see Winston, *Ancestral Philosophy*, 135–150. While Winston views Philo as essentially deterministic, I am more convinced by Wolfson that Philo allows for a meaningful free will; see also Dillon, *Middle Platonists*, 166–168. It may be worth noting that John Calvin was also aware of the predeterministic implications of Exodus 21.13 (*Institutes*, 1.16.6; 1.18.3), though his interpretation of the passage is more straightforward than that of Philo or *b. Yevamot*: God's control extends to otherwise inexplicable accidents as well.

107. The argument here works as follows: Manasseh was born three years after his father Hezekiah's illness (2 Kings 21.1). This, therefore, can be seen as support for R. Akiba: Hezekiah's allotted years must have originally included his living long enough to father Manasseh—how else could a prophet living before Hezekiah have predicted the birth of Josiah (Manasseh's grandson)? Therefore, Hezekiah was always intended to live long enough to father Manasseh; these years were first taken from him, and then restored, in accordance with R. Akiba's view. According to the rabbis (in the concluding lines of the passage) it is the eventual birth of Josiah that is predetermined, not his being the grandson of Manasseh. Therefore, Josiah's birth could have come about in another way, had Hezekiah's additional years never been given to him.

108. The text of the traditional edition has been compared to MS Vatican 111, available via the Online Treasury of Talmudic Manuscripts.

109. See also *b. Mo'ed Qatan* 18b. The translation of *b. Sotah* 2a here follows Soncino (ed. Epstein) and the text of the traditional printed edition, which has been compared to MS Vatican 110, Online Treasury of Talmudic Manuscripts. Once again, the variants are not significant for our concerns.

110. In my own experience teaching texts related to these themes, I find that most students instinctively think of themselves as libertarians, especially as far as their moral decisions are concerned (see Pink, *Free Will*, 1–21). But when the discussion shifts from moral quandaries to human relationships, it is surprising to me how many students suddenly open their minds to a partial determinism. They do so when faced with the alternative that they were unaided by God in their romantic relationships. Partial determinism—what

we are calling here "type 2" Jewish compatibilism—has not disappeared from Christian and Jewish heirs of the Pharisees, especially when it is understood in light of the ideas expressed in Tob. 6.18.

111.   Mason, *Flavius Josephus on the Pharisees*, 204–205.

112.   Flusser, "Pharisees and the Stoic Sages," 327–329 (*Judaism*, 2:230–231); compare Spilsbury, "Flavius Josephus on the Rise and Fall," 8: "It becomes clear from these passages [on the schools] that Josephus writes without philosophical precision."

113.   See especially Inwagen, "Argument for Incompatibilism."

114.   See especially Moore, "Fate and Free Will," in comparison with Bobzien, *Determinism*, 16–58.

115.   Flusser, "Pharisees and the Stoic Sages," and Mason, *Flavius Josephus on the Pharisees*, 132–152. On the relationship between Josephus, his writings, and the fortunes of the Stoics in Rome see Haaland, "Josephus and the Philosophers."

116.   By many accounts, the truly pivotal work on Stoic determinism is Bobzien, *Determinism*. For a briefer treatment (with praise for Bobzien's work) see Frede, "Stoic Determinism." See also Salle, *Stoics on Determinism*, and the earlier but still important treatment by Sharples ("Soft Determinism").

117.   Translation of Cicero here and later follows, with slight modifications, Sharples's edition. I have also consulted the LCL edition (translation by H. Rackham). For discussions of the passage, see Bobzien, *Determinism*, 316–317, and Sharples, *Cicero*, 185–188. On this text as a possible background to Josephus's tripartite typology, see Penner, "Fate," 15–17, who follows (and cites) Mason, introduction to *Judean Antiquities*, xxxi.

118.   See, e.g., Pines, "Platonistic Model," against which see Flusser, "Josephus on the Sadducees."

119.   On Cicero's presentation of Stoic compatibilism, see Bobzien, *Determinism*, 236–238, 255–271.

120.   On the cylinder and cone analogy in Cicero and other ancient accounts, see Bobzien, *Determinism*, 257–271; Frede, "Stoic Determinism," 192–200; Salles, *Stoics on Determinism*, 39–49, and Sharples, *Cicero*, 191–193.

121.   On this phrase in Stoic thought—and how it differs from freedom—see Bobzien, *Determinism*, 276–290, 330–345.

122.   This is the key point that is missed in Hultgren, "Rabbi Akiba on Divine Providence," 125–126, 143: it is insufficient to point to the cone and cylinder analogies and to suggest that the Pharisaic (and/or Akiban) position argues that God (or fate) "prompts" a response without "determining" the outcome. The Stoic view described by Cicero does allow some accounting for responsibility, but it does not allow any real place for a freedom to do otherwise. But as we will see, Josephus's Pharisees—and Josephus himself—both clearly believe in a human freedom that allows one to choose between good and evil (which would be, in Cicero's analogy, the ability to choose to roll or spin).

123. Translation follows Long and Sedley, *Hellenistic Philosophers*, 1:386; compare the translation and discussion in Bobzien, *Determinism*, 346–351.

124. Bobzien, *Determinism*, 358–412, and "Inadvertent Conception." Some aspects of Bobzien's interpretation of the history of Stoic compatibilism are questioned by Salles, *Stoics on Determinism*, 69–89.

125. See Dennett, *Elbow Room*, 2, for this author's memorable approach to Stoic compatibilism, which includes a paraphrase of an account of Stoic compatibilism drawn from Hippolytus. The original passage (*Refutation* 1.21.2) reads "When a dog is tied to a cart, if it wants to follow, it is pulled and follows, making its spontaneous act coincide with necessity; but if it does not want to follow it will be compelled in any case. So it is with people too" (trans. Long and Sedley, *Hellenistic Philosophers*, 1:386). Yet Dennett also has strong words (and arguments) against those, in his view, overly concerned with the question of whether one "could have done otherwise" (131–152).

126. See, for instance, *On Human Nature*, by Nemesius (bishop of Emesa), chapter 35 (105.6–106.13) quoted and discussed in Bobzien, *Determinism*, 358–370; see also 298–301, which pits Chrysippus's compatibilism against modern philosophical objections, where it is found wanting. We have already mentioned Inwagen, "Argument for Incompatibilism," who argues that compatibilism is nonsense. A largely similar dispute is manifest in contemporary Christian theological discussions. As noted, Feinberg, "God Ordains All Things," 19–43, articulates what he calls a "compatibilist" position while defending a Calvinist approach to predestination. Compare, however, the objections of Norman Geisler and Bruce Reichenbach, in their responses to Feinberg, in Basinger and Basinger, *Predestination and Free Will*, 45–48 (Geisler), 49–55 (Reichenbach). Both maintain that the compatibilist position effectively denies any place for a meaningful degree of freedom.

127. Here especially is where the present treatment parts company with Mason, *Flavius Josephus on the Pharisees*, 203–205, 297, who equates the position Josephus attributes to the Pharisees in *War* 2 and *Ant.* 18 ("type 1") with Chrysippean compatibilism.

128. The two-sidedness of Josephus's conception of free will is also in evidence in *Ant.* 16.395–404 (discussed above), which explicitly considers Herod's alternate choices: to exile his sons or to imprison them (16.401).

129. Bobzien, *Determinism*, 398 n. 87; see also Sharples, "Soft Determinism," 267–268.

130. Bobzien, *Determinism*, 290–291, 300–301, 396–397, 411–412, and also "Inadvertent Conception." See also Salles, *Stoics on Determinism*, 78–81, who questions some aspects of Bobzien's account of this history. Salles (*Stoics on Determinism*, 63–68) also compares Stoic arguments (especially Chrysippus) with modern philosophic ones (especially Harry Frankfurt).

131. See, e.g., Duhaime, "Determinism."

132. So, e.g., Flusser, "Pharisees and the Stoic Sages," 326–329 (*Judaism*, 2:228–231).

133. This observation should not be understood to suggest that the sectarians were necessarily influenced by Stoicism in any direct way. Indeed, the likelihood of this is small, and the evidence to support such a claim is entirely lacking. See further Martone, "Qumran and Stoicism." It is worth noting— along with Martone (621)—that among Hellenistic philosophical schools, Stoicism stands out by the fact that so many of its major figures came from the eastern Mediterranean; see Sedley, "School," esp. 8–9, 22–23. Quite possibly, then, Qumran and Stoicism were similarly influenced in their strict determinism by other eastern Mediterranean cultural influences, such as Babylonian astrology (see Martone, "Qumran and Stoicism," 621–622). For a more confident assertion of the influence of Hellenistic philosophy on second temple period Jews and Jewish literature, see Winston, *Ancestral Philosophy*, 11–32.

134. Compare the similarly compatibilist positions taken in Feinberg, "God Ordains All Things," 13–25.

135. Although this point is rarely made explicitly, it emerges clearly from the definitions of determinism offered in many philosophic works (see, e.g., Bobzien, *Determinism*, 33–58, and Pink, *Free Will*, 13). For many philosophic discussions, both ancient and modern, if determinism is only partially true, then it is partially false, in which case it as generally defined is simply false.

136. Mason, *Flavius Josephus on the Pharisees*, 155.

137. See Hultgren, "Rabbi Akiba on Divine Providence," for a different approach to some of the same material (see esp. 131–134). Hultgren is correct to associate Josephus's view with that of Josephus's Pharisees; and Hultgren is correct to identify deterministic elements in Josephus's position. But in my view, the benefits of Hultgren's effort to describe Josephus's view (and the Pharisaic view) as "determinist" is undercut by the fact that the analysis does not engage (or supply vocabulary to describe) the full range of options on the question described by Josephus. As I will argue the benefit of describing Josephus's view as compatibilist rests precisely on the resulting ability to differentiate Josephus's and the Pharisaic view(s) from the stricter determinism he ascribes to the Essenes (to say nothing of the stricter determinism associated with many philosophers).

138. On this passage, see esp. Begg and Spilsbury, *Judean Antiquities 8–10* (BJP 5), 265–266, 313–317, and Vermes, "Josephus' Treatment," esp. 160.

139. On the term "αὐτομάτως" (10.278), see Begg and Spilsbury, *Judean Antiquities 8–10* (BJP 5), 315–316 n. 1185. See also *Ant.* 4.47, for a similar contrast between a world guided by providence as opposed to a world operated automatically; see Feldman, *Judean Antiquities 1–4* (BJP 3), 344 n. 115. Yet Josephus recognizes elsewhere that providence can operate so that things happen

automatically—meaning without human effort. Such "automatic" phenomena include, in *Antiquities*, uncultivated plants (e.g., *Ant.* 1.46, of plants in the Garden of Eden; *Life* 11, with regard to Bannus's diet), and, in *War*, accidental occurrences (*War* 1.373, 3.100–101). The miraculous can also seem accidental (Red Sea: *Ant.* 2.347; the auspicious opening of the temple gates: *War* 6.293–295). The rejection of "automatism" as a general principle in the passage above is, as Josephus explicitly intends, a critique of the Epicurean denial of providence. But Josephus is not here articulating a general agreement with Stoic determinism either (so, e.g., Attridge, *Interpretation*, 98 n. 1, who differentiates Josephus from Stoic views, contra Feldman, *Judean Antiquities 1–4* (BJP 3), 344 n. 115, who links Josephus with the Stoics).

140. In this respect, Josephus's view is not unlike that of the rabbis in *b. Yevamot* 49b–50a, discussed earlier: the prophecy of Josiah's birth must be fulfilled, but there could have been more than one way of reaching that goal. Indeed, Josephus's image of God exercising constant, ongoing guidance is also rather similar to the way William James concludes his famous essay "Dilemma of Determinism." Quite unlike the predestinarians who appeal to predictive prophecy to demonstrate the fixed course of all human decisions, James concludes his essay by appealing to the analogy of a chess game between a master and a novice. Without knowing which moves the novice will make, the true master maintains, nonetheless, complete control of the game, modifying his own plan to bring about his victory. As far as the world is concerned, therefore, James states: "The creator's plan of the universe would thus be left blank as to many of its actual details, but all possibilities would be marked down. The realization of some would be left absolutely to chance.... Other possibilities would be *contingently* determined; that is their decision would have to wait till it was seen how the matters of absolute chance fell out. But the rest of the plan, including its final upshot, would be rigorously determined once for all. So the creator himself would not need to know *all* the details of actuality until they came.... Of one thing, however, he might be certain: and that is that his world was safe, and that no matter how much it might zig-zag, he could surely bring it home at last" (182).

141. Note also *Ant.* 17.345–355, where Josephus sees the fulfillment of Archelaus's and Glaphyra's portent-laden dreams as evidence of divine justice and foresight (354: προμηθείᾳ; this term used of God's foresight also in 4.185). Josephus also sees here a proof of immortality, presumably because the living Glaphyra dreamt of the deceased Archelaus; see Gray, *Prophetic Figures*, 63–64. On dreams of the deceased and beliefs in immortality see Segal, *Life after Death*, 207–208, 326–330.

142. See, e.g., Attridge, *Interpretation*, 156–158; Feldman, *Josephus's Interpretation*, 194–195; Mason, *Flavius Josephus*, 141–142, and Spilsbury, "Flavius Josephus on the Rise and Fall," 7–9.

143. On the equation of fate and providence, see, e.g., Ralph Marcus's note g to *Ant.* 13.172 (LCL ad loc.) and Feldman's note d to *Ant.* 18.13 (also in LCL ad loc.). See also Finkelstein, *Pharisees,* 1.195–196; Hultgren, "Rabbi Akiba on Divine Providence," 132; Mason, *Josephus, Judea,* 226; Spilsbury, "Flavius Josephus on the Rise and Fall," and Stuckrad, "Jewish and Christian Astrology," 22–28. For one attempt to identify some differences—with regard to "fortune," too— see Michel and Bauernfeind, *De Bello Judaico,* 2:2, 212–214 (excursus 18).

144. See, e.g., Roy, *How Much,* 34–71; see Calvin, *Institutes,* 1.8.7–8.

145. So, e.g., Attridge, *Interpretation,* 156. Without accounting for free will, Spilsbury uses the terms "preordained" ("Flavius Josephus on the Rise and Fall," 7) and "predetermination" (8) with regard to Josephus's understanding of history.

146. See also Calvin, *Concerning the Eternal Predestination,* 10.1–15 (trans. Reid: 162–185).

147. See Bobzien, *Determinism,* 44–47.

148. On the superiority of providence to fate in middle Platonism, see Dillon, *Middle Platonists,* 80–88, 166–168, 208–211, 320–326. (For what it is worth, a number of the key figures discussed by Dillon emerged from the eastern Mediterranean, including Antiochus of Ascalon, Eudorus of Alexandria, and Philo of Alexandria.) On the Gnostic prioritization of (higher) providence over fate, see Williams, "Higher Providence, Lower Providences, and Fate," and also *Rethinking "Gnosticism,"* 202–208. As Williams explains, the issue is rendered more complicated when some thinkers imagine multiple providences; but fate in these Gnostic and middle Platonist schemes is always subordinated to a higher providence.

149. *Contra,* e.g., Begg and Spilsbury, *Judean Antiquities 8–10* (BJP 5), 315 nn. 1181–1182; Feldman, *Josephus's Interpretation,* 192; Mason, *Life of Josephus* (BJP 9), 16–17 n. 72; Mason, *Josephus, Judea,* 225–226, 230.

150. The fullest analysis of *pronoia*/providence in *Antiquities* remains Attridge, *Interpretation,* 71–107. In both works, Josephus uses the word with regard not only to divine providence but also to careful human planning. Indeed, in *Antiquities,* virtually every worthy Israelite leader exhibits such foresight (e.g., Joseph: 2.86; Moses: 5.4; see Attridge, *Interpretation,* 71–72 n. 2). Philo, too, used the term with regard to both God (e.g., *On Creation* 9) and humans (e.g., *Posterity of Cain* 11).

151. On this passage, see Attridge, *Interpretation,* 67–70.

152. In *War* in particular, Josephus finds evidence of providential justice in coincidences: Aristobulus's blood was spilled where Antigonus was slain (1.82), and the massacre at Caesarea took place on the same day as the massacre of a Roman garrison (2.457). Of course, Josephus will also note the coincidence— this one "fated"—that the destruction of the second temple occurred on the same day as that of the first (6.250, 267).

153. See Attridge, *Interpretation*, 99–104.

154. We will return to Josephus's prophetic self-conception when we consider his response to the destruction of the temple more fully, in chapter 5.

155. On the Greco-Roman and Jewish backgrounds for and parallels to this passage, see Michel and Bauernfeind, *De Bello Judaica*, 2:2, 186–188 (excursus 14).

156. On this understanding of "fortune" in Josephus, see Cohen, "Josephus, Jeremiah, and Polybius," 371–375; compare Price, "Provincial Historian," 116–117. On "fortune" in general in *War* see Michel and Bauernfeind, *De Bello Judaico*, 2:2, 212–214 (excursus 18). On Josephus's approach to Rome's rise (and eventual fall), see Spilsbury, "Flavius Josephus on the Rise and Fall."

157. So, e.g., *Ant.* 8.409, 412, 419 in Whiston, Ralph Marcus (LCL), and Begg and Spilsbury (BJP 5); Moore had it better ("Fate and Free Will," 388–389), translating the term as "Must-be," capitalized so as to emphasize the term's function as a synonym for God.

158. See *Ant.* 8.307, which is the fourth and final usage of the term (in this form) in *Antiquities*; see also 7.383.

159. Attridge, *Interpretation*, 101–102, esp. n. 2; see also Feldman, *Josephus's Interpretation*, 195–197.

160. Quite possibly, Josephus's decreased use of the term "fate" in his later works reflects a greater recognition on his part of the confusions the term engenders; see Attridge, *Interpretation*, 156–158. It is equally possible that *War*'s greater use of the term reflects the fact that it reaches is climax with the fulfillment of the predicted and, eventually, fated destruction (see further discussion later in this chapter).

161. Josephus also speaks of "fortune" when certain people meet their ends (e.g., *War* 5.548).

162. The juxtaposition of "fate" and "providence" in *War* 4.622 is, for some scholars, the smoking gun, so to speak, that proves Josephus's general identification of fate and providence (e.g., Feldman, *Josephus's Interpretation*, 194–195; Spilsbury, "Flavius Josephus on the Rise and Fall," 8–9). Josephus clearly thought that the fulfillment of predicted events is the overlap between providence and fate. But overlap is not identity, and Josephus does not view *all* events as predicted, or therefore predetermined by fate.

163. On conditional fate (if A, then by necessity, B) in Middle Platonism, see Dillon, *Middle Platonists*, 320–326. For a simple reference to the concept, see Tacitus, *Annals* 6.22. For a fuller discussion, see Sharples, "Alexander of Aphrodisias." For a somewhat similar approach—but in relation to biblical, not philosophical parallels—see Cohen, "Josephus, Jeremiah, and Polybius."

164. See Price, "Josephus and the Dialogue," 189, who argues that this appeal was "mistaken, or in vain" since the destruction was already fated. But if fate is subordinate to providence, as we have argued, then there's no reason to believe that genuine repentance would have been of no use.

165. Price, "Some Aspects," 114–115, correctly recognizes the difficulty of discerning precisely *when* God decided to destroy the temple (see also "Josephus and the Dialogue," 186–188). The distinction we have suggested between providence and fate as well as the possible conditionality of fate would solve some of the other difficulties and contradictions Price discerns ("Some Aspects," 114–119).

166. According to *Antiquities*, God is similarly implicated in Saul's murder of the priests of Nob. On the one hand, Josephus condemns the act as an example of Saul's murderous character (6.262–268). On the other hand, Josephus follows scripture to the extent of understanding the event as a fulfillment of the foretold judgment of Eli's house, for the sins of his sons (*Ant.* 6.261; see also 1 Sam. 2.27–36).

167. Compare William James's reference ("Dilemma of Determinism," 182, quoted in note 140) to the "zig-zags" that may occur under divine providence.

168. Remarkably, this legend is echoed in rabbinic sources, too: see *b. Ta'anit* 23a and *Leviticus Rabbah* 35.10. This tradition will come up again in chapter 4.

169. See Mason, *Judean War 2* (BJP 1b), 289–290 n. 2354, and 305 n. 2472, for further references to Rome's fortune. On God granting power to the Romans, see Cohen, "Josephus, Jeremiah, and Polybius." And see further chapter 5 here.

170. On "dramatic reversals" as a motif in *Antiquities*, see Attridge, *Interpretation*, 92–98. On reversals in *War*, see Mason, *Judean War 2* (BJP 1b), 74 n. 688 (with regard to *War* 2.113). On sudden change as a motif of the wisdom tradition, see my discussion of the Sadducean approach to reward and punishment in the next chapter.

171. Note also the case of Gedaliah (*Ant.* 10.155–172), which is more complicated than the others, for Josephus squarely lays part of the blame on Gedaliah himself, who ignored warnings and let himself get drunk; see Begg, "Gedaliah Episode," esp. 29–33.

172. Some have questioned Mariamme's innocence: see, e.g., Ilan, *Integrating Women*, 105–115. Even so, Josephus believes that Herod's suffering came about, in part, as a result of this crime (*Ant.* 15.240–246).

173. Ironically, in *Antiquities* (20.199–200), the perpetrator of James's murder is the very same Ananus who is himself murdered, along with his fellow priest Jesus, in *War*.

174. Although Josephus did not put the matter in quite these terms, one aspect of his theodicy would be the "free will" defense: some bad things that happen to righteous people are the results of evil decisions made by wicked people.

CHAPTER 3

1. The literature on ancient Jewish views of the afterlife is legion. I will make particular use here of two recent general works: Levenson, *Resurrection,* and

Segal, *Life after Death*. Also instructive are many of the essays in Avery-Peck and Neusner, *Judaism in Late Antiquity 4: Death, Life-After-Death*. For a review of recent scholarship on this topic, with some focus on Segal's work in particular, see Elledge, "Future Resurrection," esp. 397–402 (on Segal). For its catalogue of primary sources, Cavallin, *Life after Death*, remains of value. On afterlife in Josephus, Elledge, *Life after Death*, is essential reading. Also quite helpful is Sievers, "Josephus and the Afterlife."

2. On noble deaths in ancient Judaism in general—and Josephus in particular—see Droge and Tabor, *Noble Death*.

3. See, briefly, D. Schwartz's notes to 2 Macc. 7.22 and 28 in Coogan, *New Oxford Annotated*, 1614. See more fully his commentary: *2 Maccabees*, 296–319, and esp. 312–313. Also helpful is the treatment of the two texts in Elledge, *Life after Death*, 15–19 (2 Macc.), 147–152 (4 Macc.). Even more fully, see Henten, *Maccabean Martyrs*.

4. The current scholarly consensus—quite reasonably—views 4 Maccabees as a direct literary expansion of 2 Maccabees 6–7 (as opposed to hypothesizing an independent common source for the two texts). On the traditional (but false) attribution of 4 Maccabees to Josephus, see, e.g., Hadas, *Third and Fourth Books*, 113–115.

5. See, briefly, Elledge, *Life after Death*, 27–28 (on Wisdom), 29–30 (on Philo), 41–44 (on rabbinic literature). More fully on Philo, see Goodenough, "Philo on Immortality," and Wolfson, *Philo*, 1:360–426. Further treatments of rabbinic literature will be cited subsequently.

6. The phrase "intimations of immortality"—also the title of a poem by William Wordsworth—is used by both Segal (*Life after Death*, 3) and Levenson (*Resurrection*, 82).

7. Segal, *Life after Death*, 145–146. Returns from the brink of death are also alluded to in various psalms (e.g., Ps. 18.1–20//1 Sam. 22.1–21 and Jonah 2.3–8). See Levenson, *Resurrection*, 35–66.

8. See Segal, *Life after Death*, 124–131. For an alternate take on the implications of the séance at Endor, compare Levenson, *Resurrection*, 52–54, and 245–246 n. 26.

9. For this term, and for helpful survey of early Israel's attitude toward death, see Mendenhall, "From Witchcraft to Justice," 69.

10. Further on biblical attitudes toward death and Sheol, see Droge and Tabor, *Noble Death*, 53–84 (esp. 67); Segal, *Life after Death*, 134–138; compare Levenson, *Resurrection*, 35–66.

11. Levenson, *Resurrection*, 67–81.

12. Levenson, *Resurrection*, 245–246 n. 26.

13. On Enoch and Elijah, see Levenson, *Resurrection*, 99–103; compare Segal, *Life after Death*, 154–156.

14. Levenson, *Resurrection*, 78.

15. Josephus, for one, seems to believe that all three figures ascended upon their deaths (Enoch: *Ant.* 1.85; Moses: *Ant.* 4.326; Elijah: *Ant.* 9.28); see Begg, "'Josephus's Portrayal,'" responding (correctly) to Tabor, "Josephus's Portrayal."

16. See Segal, *Life after Death*, for discussions of Israelite and ancient Jewish beliefs in the context of Egyptian, Mesopotamian, Iranian, and Hellenistic trends.

17. For a recent review of Jewish burial practices in the second temple period, see Magness, *Stone and Dung*, 145–180. On the (not so simple) relationship between burial practices and afterlife beliefs see Fine, "Note on Ossuary Burial"; Magness, *Stone and Dung*, 151–155; and further literature cited in these works. For a classic (but somewhat dated) effort to correlate the archaeological and literary (including rabbinic) evidence see Meyers, *Jewish Ossuaries*, esp. 73–92, which discusses the theology of secondary burial.

18. The now classic formulation of this argument is Nickelsburg, *Resurrection*, first printed in 1972 (references are to the 2006 expanded edition, which, along with additional newer material still includes the entire original edition essentially unchanged); see the introduction to the revised edition, esp. 5–6.

19. Generally, see Levenson, *Resurrection*, 181–200. For a discussion of recent scholarship concerning the "social dynamics" of resurrection beliefs, see Elledge, "Future Resurrection," esp. 395–406.

20. On immortality in *1 Enoch*, see Segal, *Life after Death*, 272–281.

21. Levenson, *Resurrection*, 80–81, 216.

22. On the afterlife in Josephus, see Elledge, *Life after Death*; Elledge's study has proven extremely useful to this analysis. Our conclusions, however, are more sanguine than Elledge's, at least with regard to the relative accuracy of Josephus's accounts of the schools.

23. As was noted in the previous chapter, Josephus sees Glaphyra's fulfilled dream as a proof of immortality presumably because she dreamt of the deceased Archelaus; see Gray, *Prophetic Figures*, 63–64. On dreams of the deceased and beliefs in immortality see Segal, *Life after Death*, 207–208, 326–330.

24. Not all treatments of afterlife in ancient Judaism consider the Sadducean view. For reviews of these traditions, see Segal, *Life after Death*, 367, 376–377; Elledge, *Life after Death*, is among the studies that does not treat the Sadducees. While treatments of Sadducees are legion, treatments that offer something meaningful regarding the group's denial of the beatific afterlife are fewer. Among the more helpful treatments of the Sadducees' view of the afterlife are Le Moyne, *Les Sadducéens*, and Stemberger, "Sadducees."

25. Steve Mason has recently argued that the author of Luke-Acts may have read (or, more precisely, heard) Josephus's works in Rome in the late first century; see *Josephus and the New Testament*, 251–295, and *Josephus, Judea*, 329–373. This could account for a number of intriguing parallels between the two sources, including particularly the familiarity of Luke-Acts with early Jewish rebels not mentioned anywhere else other than Josephus (Acts 5.36–37; see *War* 2.118,

261–263, and *Ant.* 18.4–10, 20.97–98, 102; Acts, however, confuses the chronology). Another intriguing point of connection will be pointed out later in our treatment of sacrilegious murders (see Acts 6.8–7.60). If indeed the author of Luke-Acts read/heard Josephus's works, then we cannot readily use these texts in the effort to confirm Josephus's account of the historical record. Yet in this particular case, Acts 23.8 is only a partial parallel at best. To be sure, it would be characteristic of Acts to change a reference to immortality into a reference to resurrection, especially since Luke follows Mark in attributing to the Sadducees a belief in resurrection. But Josephus does not speak of angels or spirits as subjects of scholastic discussion (as we will see later); and the dispute about resurrection/immortality is attested elsewhere. Therefore, Acts 23.8 does not seem to be dependent on Josephus in any respect.

26. See, e.g., *b. Menahot* 37a, where a sage asks about the placement of phylacteries on a two-headed person, or *b. Pesahim* 10a, which discusses increasingly convoluted scenarios beginning with a mouse, a piece of bread, and a house that has already been cleaned for Passover.

27. The strange scenario depicted here recalls in some respects the plight of Sarah in the book of Tobit, whose first seven husbands died at the hands of the demon Asmodeus (3.7–15). We will turn to other tales of seven dead brothers later.

28. On these passages—and in defense of their historical value—see Meier, *Marginal Jew*, 3:431–444.

29. For a litany of rabbinic attempts to root resurrection in the Torah, see *b. Sanhedrin* 90a–92b. As in Mark 12.18–27 (and parallels), some of the rabbinic arguments "prove" afterlife or immortality in general more than resurrection in particular; but all are phrased as proofs of resurrection.

30. According to Meier (*Marginal Jew*, 3:423–424), the passage intends that resurrected bodies will be celibate (and in that sense angel-like) but physical and human nonetheless.

31. Of course, it is possible that Acts is wrong on this score; see Meier, *Marginal Jew*, 3:407–409, 475 n. 110. On Josephus's general lack of interest in angels, as evidenced by his consistent reduction (but not elimination) of their biblical role in his *Antiquities*, see Feldman, *Josephus's Interpretation*, 212–213. See also Vermes, "Josephus' Treatment," 165, who notes Josephus's elimination of angels from his retelling of the Daniel stories (compare, e.g., *Ant.* 10.213–215 and Dan. 3.1–30, esp. 3.25, 28).

32. Again see Meier, *Marginal Jew*, 3:431–444.

33. See Le Moyne, *Les Sadducéens*, 40–41, following Leszynsky, *Die Sadduzäer*, 19.

34. On the soul (and the term נפש) in the Hebrew Bible, see Segal, *Life after Death*, 142–145, and Barr, *Garden of Eden*, esp. 36–45.

35. Compare the curse Josephus depicts Titus uttering for those who deny the immortality that awaits the deceased warrior (*War* 6.46): the deniers deserve to die of disease, with body and soul alike confined to the tomb.

36. Notably, in *Ant.* 6.332, Samuel is called up from "Hades." See *War* 2.156 and 165.

37. See, e.g., Goodman, *Ruling Class*, 79; Segal, *Life after Death*, 367–368, 376–377 (compare 169); Simon, *Jewish Sects*, 27; Wellhausen, *Pharisees*, 45–47.

38. On Karaite beliefs in resurrection, see Lasker, *From Judah Hadassi*, 248–262. The Samaritans, too, came to believe in resurrection, even without Daniel as part of their canon; see Dexinger, "Samaritan Eschatology."

39. Baron, *Social and Religious History*, 2:39, describes the Sadducean view as rationalist and worldly.

40. On the afterlife traditions concerning the Pharisees, see especially Elledge, *Life after Death*, 48–51, 59–63, and Mason, *Flavius Josephus on the Pharisees*, 156–170, 297–300.

41. On rabbinic afterlife beliefs, see Segal, *Life after Death*, 596–638.

42. Elledge, *Life after Death*, 3, 45, 81–82; compare Mason, *Flavius Josephus on the Pharisees*, 161–170.

43. H. St. J. Thackeray, LCL ad loc., note a to *War* 2.163. See also Mason, *Judean War 2* (BJP 1b), 133 n. 1012. But see Thackeray, *Josephus: The Man and the Historian*, 97, which speaks more clearly of Josephus's belief in a "return to bodily existence of souls of the good."

44. L. Feldman, LCL ad loc., to *Antiquities* 18.14. More fully, see Mason, *Flavius Josephus on the Pharisees*, 169–170.

45. Elledge, *Life after Death*, 49–51, 59–63, 129–130; see also Sanders, *Judaism*, 301.

46. For a general survey of reincarnation in world religions (including India and ancient Greece), see J. Bruce Long, "Reincarnation," in Eliade, *Encyclopedia of Religion*, 12:265–269. On Greek ideas of the afterlife in general (including reincarnation), see Segal, *Life after Death*, 204–247; on Greek ideas in relation to Josephus's accounts, see Mason, *Flavius Josephus on the Pharisees*, 161–170.

47. See Elledge, *Life after Death*, 49–50, and the literature cited there.

48. Elledge, *Life after Death*, 43, 50, 94; the quoted phrase is the concluding formula for a blessing to be recited on waking up in the morning.

49. Elledge, *Life after Death*, 49–51, 59–63, 129–130.

50. On Paul's view of resurrection, see Segal, *Life after Death*, 399–440; on this passage, see esp. 428–431.

51. The tradition preserved in *b. Sanhedrin* 90b (bottom) reads as follows: Queen Cleopatra asked R. Meir, "I know that the dead will revive, for it is written, 'And they [i.e., the righteous] shall blossom forth out of the city [Jerusalem] like the grass of the earth' (Ps. 72.16). But when they arise, shall they arise naked or in their garments?" He replied, "You may deduce [the answer] by an *a fortiori* argument from a wheat grain: if a grain of wheat, which is buried naked, sprouts forth in many robes, how much more so the righteous, who are buried in their raiment!"

52. For some intriguing observations concerning this process, with particular attention to 1 Cor. 15.35–49, see Smith, "Transformation by Burial."

53. See also Mason, *Judean War 2* (BJP 1b), 133 n. 1012 (on *War* 2.163), and Barclay, *Against Apion* (BJP 10), 296–297, esp. nn. 890–891 (on *Apion* 2.218).
54. On Josephus's discussions of Essene afterlife beliefs, see Collins, "Essenes and the Afterlife"; Elledge, *Life after Death*, 57–59, and Nickelsburg, *Resurrection*, 206–209.
55. On this passage, see Beall, *Josephus' Description*, 105–108; Elledge, *Life after Death*, 57–59, and Mason, *Judean War 2* (BJP 1b), 123–128.
56. For discussions of Platonic afterlife ideas and their eventual impact on Judaism, see Droge and Tabor, *Noble Death*, 17–51, and Segal, *Life after Death*, 224–237.
57. See, e.g., Beall, *Josephus' Description*, 105–108; on Hellenism in late second temple Judean society see, e.g., Hengel, *"Hellenization" of Judaea*, and Levine, *Judaism and Hellenism*, 46–93.
58. See, in great detail, Puech, *La Croyance*.
59. Again, e.g., Puech, *La Croyance*, 2:703–762; see further in the appendix.
60. For helpful brief treatments of these texts, see Collins, *Apocalypticism*, 124–128, and Elledge, *Life after Death*, 23–26. For fuller treatments see Puech, *La Croyance*, 2:605–616 (4Q385), 627–692 (4Q521). The editio princeps of 4QPseudo-Ezekiel (4Q385–388, 391) is Dimant, *Qumran Cave 4, XXVI* (DJD 30), 7–88; the editio princeps of 4QMessianic Apocalypse (4Q521) is Puech, *Qumrân Grotte 4, XVIII* (DJD 25), 1–38.
61. Dimant, *Qumran Cave 4, XXVI* (DJD 30), esp. 10–14 (on 4Q385); Puech, *Qumrân Grotte 4, XVIII* (DJD 25), 3–6 (on 4Q521).
62. So, e.g., Dimant and Flint, *Qumran Cave 4, XXVI* (DJD 30), 13–14, 31–37. So also Elledge, *Life after Death*, 24–26; Puech, *La Croyance*, 2:612–616, and, more briefly, VanderKam and Flint, *Meaning*, 245–246.
63. See Puech, *La Croyance*, 2:627–692; it is the last Qumran text Puech covers, and he treats it last to seal his argument.
64. Elledge, *Life after Death*, 26.
65. Vermes, *Complete Dead Sea Scrolls*, 89.
66. Collins, *Apocalypticism*, 128; Collins also dispenses economically with the possible but problematic suggestion that the Qumran burials are suggestive of the sect's afterlife beliefs (*Apocalypticism*, 123–124).
67. Popović, "Bones, Bodies, and Resurrection," esp. 238–239.
68. Translations of 1QH here and subsequently largely follow Vermes, *Complete Dead Sea Scrolls*; versification follows Stegemann and Schuller, *Qumran Cave 1, III: 1QHodayot* (DJD 40).
69. On immortality (as opposed to resurrection) in the *Thanksgiving Hymns*, see Collins, *Apocalypticism*, 119–123; Licht, *Thanksgiving Scroll*, 50; Mansoor, *Thanksgiving Hymns*, 84–89. For an alternate view, see Nickelsburg, *Resurrection*, 179–193. There are passages in these hymns that may refer to some form of resurrection (albeit, unlikely a bodily one). See, e.g., 1QH 14.32–33, 37, 19.15; these and similar passages are discussed briefly in Collins, *Apocalypticism*, 121–122.

70. See, for example, Beall, *Josephus' Description*, 105–108, and Collins, *Apocalypticism*, 110–129; both associate Qumran with the Essenes in some way, and believe that the sect believed in immortality, but not resurrection. Reviewing the same passages, Elledge (*Life after Death*, 19–23) agrees that they speak more clearly of immortality than resurrection. Elledge's overall conclusion, though, is more circumspect, as he gives more weight to the 4Q passages discussed here (*Life after Death*, 23–26).

71. Taken as a whole, these passages also constitute a strong counterargument to those who maintain that the Qumran sectarians were living a realized eschatology, believing that angels—or even the divine presence—lived among them. For examples of such views, see Ringgren, *Faith of Qumran*, 148–151, and compare Nickelsburg, *Resurrection*, 181–206. For a different approach to this question, see Klawans, "Purity in the Dead Sea Scrolls," esp. 394–398.

72. Thackeray (in LCL) translates the Greek text's ὡς as "confidently," in place of "as if," as here. Mason follows LCL in eliding ὡς and supplying "knowing," though Mason puts "knowing" in brackets. Whiston reads "as"; so too Elledge, *Life after Death*, 58. This translation is to be preferred, for as the following passage makes clear (*War* 2.154–158, discussed in the previous section), the martyrs were motivated not by a firm belief that they would get their souls back, but that their souls would live on elsewhere.

73. On this passage, see Mason, *Judean War 2* (BJP 1b), 121–123; compare (with greater emphasis on comparison to Qumran) Beall, *Josephus' Description*, 102–104. On Essene suffering, see also Philo, *Every Good Man*, 89–91; on the comparison of this passage with *War* 2.152–153, see Rajak, *Jewish Dialogue*, 235. Without regard to the Essenes in particular, Tacitus described the Jews in general as willing to submit to tortures or risk death on the battlefield, believing a better life awaits them elsewhere (*Histories* 5.5.3). See Stern, *Greek and Latin Authors*, 2:41–43, and Elledge, *Life after Death*, 56.

74. Beall, *Josephus' Description*, 104; but note Josephus's report of a post-70 CE persecution in Antioch: *War* 7.50–53.

75. Commenting on the words translated here as "twisted," "tormented," and "yield," Mason points out (*Judean War 2* [BJP 1b], 122 n. 931): "These same words are concentrated, along with others graphically depicting endurance under torture, in 4 Maccabees (στρεβλ- ["twisted"] 7:4, 14; 8:11, 13, 24; 9:17, 22; 12:3, 11; 14:12; 15:14, 24, 25; αἰκι- ["torment"] 1:11; 6:9, 16; 7:4; 14:1; 15:19; ὑπομένω- ["endure"] 1:11; 5:23; 7:9, 22; 9:8, 30; 15:30; 16:17, 22; 17:4, 12, 17, 23), a fact that seems to highlight Josephus' debt to this work." See also nn. 933–934.

76. Compare the discussion of later Gnostic ideas in King, *What Is Gnosticism*, 209–211.

77. On this passage generally, see Elledge, *Life after Death*, 64–67; more generally (and with a focus on the version in *Antiquities*), see Begg, "Ruler or God."

78. Although the teachers—and therefore their teachings—are sometimes identified as Pharisees (e.g., Sanders, *Judaism*, 385), Josephus himself does not make this connection explicit (Mason, *Josephus, Judea*, 193). While their popularity and expertise in the laws (1.648) calls to mind Josephus's subsequent description of the Pharisees (2.162), the teachers' call to immortality in order to risk death evokes the same sentiments expressed in Josephus's description of the Essenes.

79. There is an expanded version of this speech preserved in the Slavonic: see addition no. 7 in the appendix to the LCL edition of *Jewish War*; compare Leeming and Leeming, *Jewish War*, 228–229, and N. A. Meščerskij's comments (ad loc.), in Leeming and Leeming, *Jewish War*, 652. On the likelihood that these additions reflect later Christian piety, see Elledge, *Life after Death*, 67 n. 60, and Bickerman, *Studies*, 2:843–844. With regard to the Slavonic edition of the sophists' encouragement of the youths, the Christianizing is patent: the Slavonic version imagines the teachers appealing to the examples of Eleazar and the seven brothers (2 Macc. 6–7). The story is retold in *Ant.* 17.149–167, though there the rebels are motivated simply by the promise of a noble death (we will return to this passage in our discussions of noble death in this chapter, and of Herod's crimes in the following chapter).

80. Some have claimed that book 7 is later addition to the work; see, e.g., S. Schwartz, "Composition." For a discussion of the issues and arguments in favor of the structural and thematic unity of *War*, see Brighton, *Sicarii*, 33–41, who builds on Mason's methods and approach (on the structure and unity of *War*, see Mason, *Josephus and the New Testament*, 66–68).

81. On the afterlife aspects of the Masada narrative, see Elledge, *Life after Death*, 69–73. The historicity of the Masada story and the relation between the archaeological and historiographical record need not detain us. The issues—both methodological and ideological—are complicated, and literature is vast; for recent reviews of the historical data with helpful bibliography, see (in addition to Elledge), Brighton, *Sicarii*, 93–140, and Chapman, "Masada in the Twenty-First Century." Two older studies of enduring importance are Ladouceur, "Josephus and Masada" and Stern, "Suicide of Eleazar ben Jair." For arguments in favor of the historicity of the event as recorded by Josephus, see Brighton, *Sicarii*, 129–131, and compare Chapman, "Masada." For a skeptical view, see Cohen, "Masada." For a review of the religious and political implications of the Masada narrative—and their impact on Israeli and Jewish society in general (and Yigael Yadin in particular), see Ben Yehudah, *Masada Myth*, and Zerubavel, *Recovered Roots*, 60–78.

82. On the ideologies articulated in the first speech—especially the refusal to submit to Rome—as motivations for the suicides, see Stern, "Suicide of Eleazar ben Jair."

83. In addition to the notes in LCL ad loc., see Ladouceur, "Masada: A Consideration," Luz, "Eleazar's Second Speech," Michel and Bauernfeind, *De Bello Judaico*, 2:2,

276–278 (excursus 24), and Stern, "Suicide of Eleazar ben Jair," 376–378. Stern notes, among other texts, Philo's discussions of Indian suicidal behavior: *On Abraham* 182–183 and *Every Good Man Is Free* 96.

84. Michel and Bauernfeind, *De Bello Judaico*, 2:2, 276–278 (excursus 24), esp. 277.

85. There is one more instance where Josephus depicts a leader encouraging his followers to risk death, with the hope of securing immortality: Titus's speech in advance of the costly conquest of the Antonia Fortress (*War* 6.46–49). Like Eleazar, Titus, too, appeals to an unembodied afterlife, without concern for postmortem punishments. On this speech, see Elledge, *Life after Death*, 73–75, and Michel and Bauernfeind, *De Bello Judaico*, 2:2, 162–163 (excursus 12).

86. Again, the historicity of these events need not detain the discussion here. On Josephus's speech against suicide in relation to the Masada story, see Elledge, *Life after Death*, 67–69; Gray, *Prophetic Figures*, 44–52; Kelley, "Cosmopolitan Expression," 271–273, and Ladouceur, "Masada: A Consideration." Weitzman, too, develops some interesting contrasts between Josephus's own view and the suicidal behavior he also describes (*Surviving Sacrilege*, 138–157, and "Josephus on How to Survive").

87. Elledge, *Life after Death*, 73; see also Brighton, *Sicarii*, 119–129; Droge and Tabor, *Noble Death*, 94–96, and Kelley, "Cosmopolitan Expression," 272; for a fuller discussion of the concept (and its Platonic background) see Droge and Tabor, *Noble Death*, 21–22, 31–35.

88. For Josephus in praise of the noble death, see Droge and Tabor, *Noble Death*, esp. 86–96, and compare Elledge, *Life after Death*, 117–127. Henten, "Noble Death," allows Josephus greater ambiguity (but without providing categorical clarification). On the suicides of Masada as "martyrs" (or at least comparable to them) see, e.g., Brighton, *Sicarii*, 118, 128, 133, 135; Droge and Tabor, *Noble Death*, 3; compare 91–94; Goodblatt, "Suicide in the Sanctuary," 28–29 (note subtitle: "Traditions of Priestly Martyrdom"); Segal, *Life after Death*, 383–384. See also Flusser, *Judaism*, 2:76–110 (translated by Azan Yadin as "The Martyrs of Masada," for the slightly more ambiguous Hebrew *harugey Metzadah*); note, however, that Flusser's argument in the end distinguishes between martyrs (righteous persons who die for the sins of others) and the Masada suicides, who (he argues) atoned for their own sins through suicide.

89. So, e.g., Droge and Tabor, *Noble Death*.

90. The typology that follows was developed independently of that presented in Tomes, "Heroism." Tomes's first two categories ("warriors" and "martyrs") are similar to the first two categories identified here, though his third ("pre-emptive suicide") is not. Because Tomes develops his categories primarily from 1 and 2 Maccabees, his typology does not serve to illustrate the contrasts between these books and Josephus, especially insofar as our second and third categories are concerned.

91. We will return, in the next chapter, to the legal implications of this decision.

92. On Josephus's use of 1 Maccabees, see Cohen, *Josephus*, 44–47; for a synoptic comparison of the sources of this era (particularly 1 Maccabees, *War*, and *Antiquities*), see Sievers, *Synopsis*.

93. See Feldman, *Josephus's Interpretation*, 461–489 (on Samson), and 509–536 (on Saul).

94. So, e.g., Henten, "Noble Death," 207; note also the view Josephus attributes to Titus: "valor is only deserving of the name when coupled with forethought and a regard for one's security" (*War* 5.316).

95. See discussion of the value of the term, despite its lack of appearance in Jewish sources, in Rajak, *Jewish Dialogue*, 99–103; Rajak cites 4 Macc. 16.16 (διαμαρτυρίας) as one possible anticipation of the later Christian usage. Rajak's approach, in my view, is more persuasive (and more helpful for our purposes) than Bowersock, *Martyrdom and Rome*, 7–13.

96. Studies of martyrdom frequently focus on the internal structure of the trial or confrontation; particularly helpful among such analyses are Henten, *Maccabean Martyrs*, and Rajak, *Jewish Dialogue*, 99–133. These studies have, in turn, influenced Brighton (*Sicarii*, 17–18). Others, focusing on later rabbinic and patristic material, may highlight other structures or criteria (e.g., Boyarin, *Dying for God*, esp. 95–96). This typology is not meant to replace more intricate internal structures identified by these and other scholars. Our goal, rather, is to facilitate a broader comparison (and contrast) among various types of noble deaths in second temple literature in general, and Josephus in particular; for that purpose I believe the typology will prove helpful. For the same reason, those studies that downplay the Maccabean material are of less help for our purposes; see, e.g., Bowersock, *Martyrdom and Rome*, 7–13; Boyarin, *Dying for God*, 93–95, 187–189, nn. 6, 11, and Shepkaru, *Jewish Martyrs*, 19–33. The importance of Josephus's evidence for this issue was earlier recognized by Weitzman, "Josephus on How to Survive," 230.

97. On this dynamic—martyrdom bringing about God's mercy—see, briefly, D. Schwartz's notes to 2 Macc. 7.38 in Coogan, *New Oxford Annotated*, 1614–1616; see more fully D. Schwartz's commentary: *2 Maccabees*, 270–319, esp. 272–273, 298–299, 317.

98. Shepkaru ("From After Death to Afterlife") attempts to sever the connection between afterlife hopes and martyrdom, but the argument—which requires sidelining much of the evidence we are reviewing here—is not convincing (see Shepkaru, *Jewish Martyrs*, 6–33, and compare D. Schwartz, "Review of *Jewish Martyrs*"). Clearly, some second temple period Jewish sources believed Jews were motivated to give up their lives in part by their beliefs in afterlife. At the same time, as we have seen, some ancient Jews questioned afterlife altogether. As we will soon see, others questioned whether a martyrological (or suicidal) death would result in such a postmortem blessing.

99. Hadas, *Third and Fourth Books*, 121–122, 181; Weitzman, *Surviving Sacrilege*, 140–143.

100. See D. Schwartz's comments on 2 Macc. 14.37–46 in Coogan, *New Oxford Annotated*, 1630; see more fully D. Schwartz's commentary: *2 Maccabees*, 487–491. As noted by Schwartz (*2 Maccabees*, 317), the brief account of Taxo and his seven sons (*Assumption of Moses* 9.1–7) also follows the basic pattern: the righteous die, calling out for revenge (9.7), and then divine judgment of the wicked soon follows (10.1–10). Tomes, "Heroism" attempts to carve out an independent category of "pre-emptive suicides"—but in my view, the heroic redemptive suicides (like Razis) are more like martyrdoms; the nonheroic or less heroic suicides are something else altogether (as we will see later).

101. The disciples of the two teachers are also remembered as facing death happily: *War* 1.653. Josephus, too, asserts that he would have faced death happily, had that proven necessary (3.382). For further examples—usually related to warrior deaths—see Mason, *Judean War 2* (BJP 1b), 123 n. 940. According to some rabbinic traditions, Rabbi Akiba endured his martyrdom with a smile; see, e.g., *y. Berakhot* 9.5, 14b (see, without the smile, *b. Berakhot* 61b). For a brief discussion of this motif with Christian parallels, see Boyarin, *Dying for God*, 107–108.

102. So Mason, *Judean War 2* (BJP 1b), 122 n. 931, quoted earlier in note 75; this has important ramifications for questions concerning the date of 4 Maccabees, suggesting that the book was completed before Josephus's *Antiquities*. Although some recent studies prefer a later date (e.g., Bowersock, *Martyrdom and Rome*, 7–13, 77–81), some noted authorities argued for a pre-70 CE date (e.g., Bickerman, *Studies*, 1:266–271, and Hadas, *Third and Fourth Books*, 95). Mason's observations counter Shepkaru's argument that Josephus was entirely unfamiliar with the Maccabean martyrs (*Jewish Martyrs*, 41–52, esp. 43); Josephus's testimony is not considered by Bowersock.

103. Compare Weitzman, *Surviving Sacrilege*, 155–156; as Weitzman points out, Josephus may also be interested here in discouraging suicidal (i.e., rebellious) behavior.

104. In the *Antiquities* account, the teachers encourage their disciples to action not with an appeal to immortality, but with a more classic promise of everlasting fame (*Ant.* 17.152–154; see also 1 Macc. 9.10)—but while the teachers' names are recorded by Josephus, the names of the disciples, ironically, are not.

105. On these stories, see Shepkaru, *Jewish Martyrdom*, 48–50.

106. Curiously, this passage is devoid of the sentiment that the martyrs happily endure death.

107. On martyrdom in rabbinic literature see Shepkaru, *Jewish Martyrs*, 66–106; compare Boyarin, *Dying for God*. Neither of these works, however, deals adequately with the second temple material. Boyarin's main focus is the rabbinic (and patristic material); Shepkaru's focus is the rabbinic and (Jewish) medieval material.

108. On the traditions concerning the martyrdoms of rabbinic sages, see Shepkaru, *Jewish Martyrs*, 73–90; see 107–140 for the medieval elaborations of these rabbinic tales.
109. On the disparate versions of this legend in rabbinic literature, see G. Cohen, *Studies*, 39–60, and Shepkaru, *Jewish Martyrs*, 69–73.
110. On these traditions, see Shepkaru, "From After Death," 26–27.
111. See Weitzman, *Surviving Sacrilege*, 155–157, and (more fully) "Josephus on How to Survive."
112. The food laws, of course, are a cause célèbre for martyrdom in 2 and 4 Maccabees, as well as (for the Essenes) in *War* 2.152.
113. See also *b. Pesahim* 25a–b, *b. Yoma* 85b, and discussion in Shepkaru, *Jewish Martyrs*, 97–104.
114. On this passage, see Kalimi, "Murder in Jerusalem."
115. On this passage, see Williamson, "Historical Value" (though the historical arguments per se are of little material significance for the present argument); see also Cohen, "Alexander and Jaddus," 61–62, who draws a contrast between this incident and the Roman destruction of the temple, for the Persians are eventually punished for their desecration of the temple. But see chapter 5 here for intimations of what Josephus expects will happen to Rome.
116. See Ralph Marcus's note g in LCL ad loc., and appendix B at the end of the volume, for an argument that Artaxerxes III is meant; the timing of the event—whether it happened or not—makes no difference for our concerns.
117. On Onias as a prophet (but without reference to the pattern we are discussing) see Gray, *Prophetic Figures*, 145–147.
118. Josephus is somewhat equivocal in this case, allowing that Herod Antipas had practical reasons to fear sedition. We will turn back of Josephus's account of John in chapter 4.
119. Note here the subsequent narrative on the unjust execution of James (*Ant.* 20.197–203), though fewer elements of the pattern are in evidence in Josephus's telling of this tale. But see Inowlocki, "Did Josephus Ascribe," where it is speculated (based on Origen, *Contra Celsum* 1.47) that Josephus's story of James may have originally included more elements of the pattern we have been tracing here.
120. See Mason, *Josephus and the New Testament*, 66–68.
121. These priestly figures are treated much less positively in Josephus's later work *Antiquities* (e.g., 20.197–203). See Cohen, *Josephus*, esp. 150–151, 156–158, 184–187.
122. On the role played by the Idumeans in these crimes—and Josephus's stereotyping of this group—see Appelbaum, "'The Idumeans' in Josephus."
123. Josephus has more to say about the relationship between the Jews' sacrilegious crimes—including the defilement of the temple—and the destruction of the temple; we will consider this theme further in chapter 5.

124. For echoes of the Zechariah tale in rabbinic literature, see, e.g., *y. Ta'anit* 4.6, 69a; *Lamentations Rabbah, proem* 23 (ed. Buber 10b–11a); *Lamentations Rabbah* 4.13 (ed. Buber 75a); *Pesikta de-Rab Kahana* 15.7 (ed. Mandelbaum 1:257–258); these legends are discussed briefly in Klawans, *Purity, Sacrifice, and the Temple,* 184, and will be mentioned again in chapter 5). For a story of priestly murder in the sanctuary—one that leads to its divinely ordained destruction—see, e.g., *t. Yoma* 1.12, discussed in *Purity, Sacrifice, and the Temple,* 182–184. For another echo of the Zechariah episode, see *Lives of the Prophets* 23.1–2.

125. We have noted Mason's arguments that the author of Luke-Acts was familiar with Josephus's works. The adoption by Luke-Acts of the "murder in the sanctuary" motif may be another important parallel with Josephus.

126. See further Kalimi, "Murders of the Messengers," and "Murder of the Prophet."

127. So, e.g., Brighton, *Sicarii,* 118, 128 133, 135; Droge and Tabor, *Noble Death,* 3, see also 91–94; Goodblatt, "Suicide in the Sanctuary," 28–29 (note subtitle: "Traditions of Priestly Martyrdom"); Segal, *Life after Death,* 383–384. Within Orthodox Jewish circles in particular, there have been discussions about the status of the deaths of Masada in light of rabbinic/halakhic norms, with differing opinions offered. In the wake of the Masada excavations, a lively discussion took place in the journal *Tradition* (published by the Orthodox Rabbinical Council of America). See, for example, Hoenig, "Sicarii" (who opposes viewing Masada as a martyrdom on halakhic grounds), and Shapiro, "In Defense," esp. 39–41 (which accepts the Masada suicides as halakhic martyrdoms). The discussion among Orthodox rabbis and scholars continues in this journal; see *Tradition* 11.3 (1970), 12.1 (1971), 13.2 (1972), and subsequent issues.

128. Contrast the results of the martyrdoms of 2 and 4 Maccabees—these martyrs become, as Henten puts it, "saviors of Jewish people" (the appropriate subtitle of his book *Maccabean Martyrs*).

129. On this passage, see Brighton, *Sicarii,* 50–53; as Brighton observes, Josephus does not explicitly credit Judas with founding the Sicarii, and Judas does not introduce the dagger-wielding tactic for which they became known. But Josephus does claim that Eleazar of Masada was descended from Judas (*War* 7.253).

130. On these passages see Brighton, *Sicarii,* 53–64, 84–87, and 96–104. Ben-Yehuda laments that the Passover massacre of women and children at Ein Gedi (*War* 4.398–405) receives less attention than it should in popular and scholarly treatments of Masada; see *Masada Myth,* e.g., 13, 57, 79, 204.

131. For this comparison, see Brighton, *Sicarii,* 128; Brighton does, however, point out levels of irony in this comparison, for the sinful suicides of Masada were wholly unlike the righteous Razis. True martyrdoms are not ironic.

132. On Josephus's tendency to display balance in his moral assessments of heroic figures, see Mason, introduction to *Judean Antiquities,* xxxii–xxxiv. See also

Feldman, *Josephus's Interpretation*, 461–489 (on Samson) and 509–536 (on Saul).

133. The massacre at Nob—with heroic priests murdered at a sanctuary—shares many elements with the sacrilegious murders described here, but with one essential difference: Josephus follows the biblical account, which presents the massacre at Nob as a fulfillment of the prophetic condemnation of Eli's house, and therefore as a just punishment for the priests' inherited guilt (*Ant.* 6.261, following 1 Sam. 2.27–36). See further Begg, "Massacre of the Priests."

134. See further examples and discussion in Droge and Tabor, *Noble Death*, 86–90, and Henten, "Noble Death," 203–207. Henten is correct to be less certain than Droge and Tabor that Josephus views these deaths as noble or heroic.

135. Examples include the defeats at Gamala (*War* 4.78–80) and Jericho (4.435–436). For a fuller accounting see Newell, "Forms and Historical Value of Josephus' Suicide Accounts," 278–294, esp. 280–283, and 292 n. 15 for a list of cases.

136. See, e.g., *War* 1.150–151 (//*Ant.* 14.69–70) and *War* 2.49–50 (//*Ant.* 17.261–264); see fuller discussion, along with Greco-Roman parallels, in Goodblatt, "Suicide in the Sanctuary."

137. On mass suicides in Greco-Roman historiography in general, see Cohen, "Masada," 386–392, who is also rather dubious as to Josephus's credibility regarding such narratives; see also Ladouceur, "Josephus and Masada," esp. 106–109.

138. See Droge and Tabor, *Noble Death*, 89–91, following Newell, "Forms and Historical Value," esp. 280–281.

139. In favor of the historicity of ancient Jewish suicidal behavior in general, see Newell, "Forms and Historical Value," esp. 281–282.

140. Yadin, for example, famously emphasized the heroism of Masada's "defenders," despite the fact that Josephus does not depict them as actively resisting against the Romans during the siege—let alone fighting courageously to the very end. See, e.g., Yadin, *Masada*, 11–17, 193–201, 209–231; compare Ben-Yehuda, *Masada Myth*, 41–42, 57–58, 155–158, 190. Curiously, subsequent Jewish tradition and legend "corrects" this problem. The medieval Jewish version depicts the Jewish men killing their wives and children—to protect their freedom and chastity—and then going out to fight the Romans, dying bravely in a futile battle (*Josippon* 89; ed. Flusser, 429–431, see esp. 429 n. 119 and 430 n. 129). This "memory" of Masada fighters seems to have been behind Isaac Lamdan's famous poem "Masada," published in the 1920s (see Zerubavel, *Recovered Roots*, 60–78). According to Roskies, Lamdan's poetic image of fighting to the last was the single most important literary inspiration for the Warsaw Ghetto uprising (*Literature of Destruction*, 357–358).

141. See the marginalia in LCL ad loc. to *War* 2.470.

142. So Flusser, *Judaism*, 2:76–110.

143. See, e.g., Ben-Yehuda, *Masada Myth*, 9, 45–46: compare 201–204.

144. On Tacitus's surprise at the Jewish reluctance to expose children, see Stern, *Greek and Latin Authors*, 2:41; Weitzman also views Josephus's Masada narrative as intended to appeal to his Roman readers (*Surviving Sacrilege*, 144–155; "Josephus on How to Survive," 233–239).

145. On irony in the works of Josephus in general, see Mason, *Josephus, Judea*, 69–102; on irony in *War* in general and the Masada narrative in particular, see Brighton, *Sicarii*, 15, 21, 23–29, 112, 125–129. Brighton correctly identifies levels of irony in the Masada story, suggesting that Josephus intends Jews and Romans to read the story differently (see Brighton, *Sicarii*, 41–47, on the question of a Jewish and Gentile audience for *War*). But unlike Brighton, I don't believe that Josephus intended his Jewish readers to understand the Masada narrative as a martyrdom (see 137). For an alternative interpretation of the Masada episode's meanings to Jewish and Roman audiences, see Kelley, "Cosmopolitan Expression."

146. That rebellion is suicide: see Chapman, "Masada," esp. 100; that suicide is a fitting punishment for killing kin: see Kelley, "Cosmopolitan Expression," 261–273; Ladouceur, "Josephus and Masada," 95–113, and "Masada: A Consideration."

147. See further Ladouceur, "Josephus and Masada," 95–113. The guilt of the Masada rebels in Josephus's eyes is not usually overlooked, but it is frequently underplayed; so, e.g., Droge and Tabor, *Noble Death*, 95–96. For a fuller discussion of the artificially cleansed reputation of the Zealots/Sicarii in popular and scholarly works on Masada, see Ben-Yehuda, *Masada Myth*.

CHAPTER 4

1. See Feldman, *Judean Antiquities 1–4* (BJP 3), 7–8 n. 22, for a brief treatment, emphasizing biblical precedents for Josephus's statements to this effect (e.g., Deut. 4.2, 12.32). For a fuller account that looks to Greco-Roman parallels for Josephus's assertions of textual fidelity, see Inowlocki, "'Neither Adding nor Omitting Anything.'"

2. The fullest review of Josephus's legal positions now is Nakman, "Halakhah," which as of this writing remains an unpublished dissertation, though one made readily available to scholars for download from the PACE website maintained by Steve Mason. Nakman argues that Josephus by and large agrees with later rabbinic law; but Nakman recognizes the importance of those instances where Josephus disagrees with later rabbinic law, agreeing instead with sectarian or other legal sources.

3. Feldman, "Torah and Greek Culture," 48–59 (quote from p. 48). Feldman here follows, among others, Kohler, who understood Josephus (and/or his priestly

source) as representing "a middle stage between Sadducaism and Pharisaism" ("Halakik Portions," 70). But see also Feldman, *Judean Antiquities 1–4* (BJP 3), 397 n. 572, where Feldman repeats, without explicitly endorsing or criticizing, Revel's suggestion ("Some Anti-traditional Laws," 294) that Josephus's divergences from rabbinic halakhah result from the mature historian in Rome forgetting the learning of his youth in Jerusalem. Compare the more recent, similar, assessment by Nakman, "Halakhah," 310–319. Schalit viewed the matter similarly, but phrased it more positively, as Josephus remembering some of the learning of his youth (*Flavii Josephi*, 1:xli; see xxxix).

4. Mason, *Flavius Josephus on the Pharisees*, 99–100. See also Barclay, *Against Apion* (BJP 10), 283 n. 797 (on 2.199) and 286 n. 815 (on 2.202); among possible parallels to *Apion* 2.199, Barclay points to *Sentences of Pseudo-Phocylides* 186.

5. Mason, *Flavius Josephus on the Pharisees*, 97–106 (quote from p. 99).

6. Regev and Nakman, "Josephus and the Halakhah." Compare, more fully, Nakman, "Halakhah," esp. 168–169, 319–323. Although Josephus's halakhic agreements with *Jubilees* are relatively rare, Josephus may well have been familiar with this work, considering the rather large number of *aggadic* similarities/dependencies: see Halpern-Amaru, "Flavius Josephus and *The Book of Jubilees*." It cannot be established, however, that Josephus was familiar with *The Temple Scroll*; see Altshuler, "On the Classification of Jewish Laws."

7. Regev and Nakman, "Josephus and the Halakhah," 420.

8. Briefly, see Mason, *Josephus, Judea*, 198–199; for a fuller treatment with examples of assorted combinations, see *Flavius Josephus on the Pharisees*, 96–106, 230–245. For examples in *Life* see Mason, *Life of Josephus* (BJP 9), 14 n. 64. On Josephus's use of "law" and "custom" (ἔθος) in particular, see Wilson, *Luke and the Law*, esp. 6–10. For a fuller survey of Josephus's references to ancestral traditions per se, see Schröder, *Die "väterlichen Gesetze."* As Schröder correctly observes—and as I will demonstrate further—Josephus's usage does not distinguish clearly between biblical and postbiblical laws (*Die "väterlichen Gesetze,"* e.g., 31, 38). Schröder's analysis is limited, however, by his focus on one particular set of terms, and his reluctance to understand Josephus's usages (and their interchangeability) in light of contemporary and later Jewish understandings of these matters; see D. Goldenberg, "Review of Bernd Schröder," as well as the analysis below.

9. So, e.g., Rajak, *Josephus*, 33–34, 224–225; see fuller discussion in chapter 1 above.

10. See Mason, *Flavius Josephus on the Pharisees*, esp. 103–105, 373–374 (and see his critical review of prior scholarship, 325–341). Mason also points to Josephus's antipathy toward Pharisaic political machinations, as expressed in passages such as *Ant.* 17.41–45 (to be discussed below). Schröder, *Die "väterlichen Gesetze"* (esp. 159–199), also emphasizes Greco-Roman analogues to Josephus's usage of "ancestral laws," thereby mitigating any claims for a distinctive Pharisaic allegiance (see also 113–120).

11. For a paradigmatic example of this effort (providing ample bibliography), see Shemesh, *Halakhah*.

12. For a paradigmatic example of this effort (providing ample bibliography), see Meier, *Marginal Jew*, vol. 4.

13. I discuss more fully the challenges inherent in evaluating the novelty or radicality of Jesus' halakhic views in "Prohibition of Oaths and 'Contra-scriptural *Halakhot*.'"

14. On this passage, see Mason, *Flavius Josephus on the Pharisees*, 213–245; for a full comparison with *War* 1.54–69, see esp. 214–230. For a brief, but interesting, discussion of this incident in light of Hasmonean diplomatic efforts, see Weitzman, *Surviving Sacrilege*, 44–54.

15. Mason, *Flavius Josephus on the Pharisees*, 219–221; for a fuller comparison of the Talmudic and Josephan traditions, see Kalmin, *Jewish Babylonia*, 53–59, 160–164, as well as Geller, "Alexander Jannaeus."

16. The explanatory phrase "[in scripture]" is supplied by the LCL translator (Ralph Marcus); see discussion later in this chapter.

17. See Mason, *Flavius Josephus on the Pharisees*, 230–245. To be sure, the Talmudic discussion of the matter (b. *Qiddushin* 66a) also grapples with the impact of the events for the teaching and preservation of (what the rabbis refer to as) "Written" and "Oral" Torah. But as noted, Sadducees per se remain unmentioned in the Talmudic account. Moreover, the difference between Written and Oral Torah is mentioned not in the Hebrew material (written in a neobiblical style) but in later glosses on the tradition, written in classic Talmudic Aramaic idiom. It is possible that the Talmudic discussion of Written and Oral Torah here has been influenced by Josephus's editorial additions to his version of the story (see Kalmin, *Jewish Babylonia*, 162–164). But Mason is likely correct that the "original" Jewish tale, did not include or concern this aspect of the Pharisee-Sadducee disagreement.

18. Mason, *Flavius Josephus on the Pharisees*, 244–245.

19. Translation here based on Feldman's (LCL) but modified in light of the translation and fuller discussion provided in Mason, *Flavius Josephus on the Pharisees*, 288–293.

20. On this passage (and the implied connection between respecting elders and respecting tradition), see Mason, *Flavius Josephus on the Pharisees*, 288–293, and Saldarini, *Pharisees, Scribes and Sadducees*, 112–115.

21. On *War* 1.571, see Mason, *Flavius Josephus on the Pharisees*, 116–119; on *Ant.* 17.41–45 see 260–280. On the (poor) relations between Herod and the Pharisees in general, see Richardson, *Herod*, 254–256. On Pheroras's wife's attraction to Pharisaism, see Ilan, *Integrating Women*, esp. 23–25.

22. See discussion of this in Mason, *Flavius Josephus on the Pharisees*, 275–278.

23. Mason, *Flavius Josephus on the Pharisees*, 278–280.

24. On Queen Alexandra's attraction to Pharisaism, see Ilan, *Integrating Women*, esp. 21–23 (see 100–105 on Josephus's general portrait of Alexandra).

25. On the Pharisaic and Essene opposition to Herod's loyalty oath, see Richardson, *Herod,* 237–238, 254–258.

26. On the *tevul yom* as reflected in rabbinic sources and the Dead Sea Scrolls, see Schiffman, "Pharisaic and Sadducean Halakhah."

27. Finkelstein long ago speculated that the *eruv* was among the Pharisaic leniencies making them popular among the poorer classes: see *Pharisees,* 1:137. Sanders more recently followed suit: see *Judaism,* 335, 425. On CD 11.7–9 as paralleling the Sadducean position, see Regev, *Sadducees,* 59–66. For an alternative assessment of the relationship between rabbinic and second temple sources on this matter, see Fonrobert, "From Separatism to Urbanism."

28. On Mark 7 and Matthew 15, see Meier, *Marginal Jew,* 4:342–477; on the terminological relationships among the New Testament, Josephan, and rabbinic sources, see A. Baumgarten, "Pharisaic Paradosis."

29. For a fuller evaluation of the New Testament evidence on the Pharisees, see Meier, *Marginal Jew,* 3:289–288.

30. See, e.g., J. Baumgarten, *Studies,* 13–35; Feldman, "Torah and Greek Culture," and Safrai, *Literature of the Sages,* esp. 35–60.

31. Mason, *Josephus Flavius on the Pharisees,* 240–245; Fraade, *Legal Fictions,* 365–379, esp. 370–378; see Sanders, *Judaism,* 420–424.

32. See Goodman, "Note on Josephus," 17–18, Neusner, *Rabbinic Traditions,* 2:163–165, and Mason, *Josephus Flavius on the Pharisees,* 240–245. Among other earlier authorities, Mason cites J. Epstein, *Introduction,* 2:697.

33. See Sanders, *Judaism,* 421–424.

34. See J. Baumgarten, *Studies,* 19–23.

35. On Pharisaic *exegesis,* see below. On "accuracy" among the Pharisees—and as a self-designation for Josephus's approach to history (e.g., *War* 1.9, 7.454–455; *Ant.* 20.260)—see Mason, *Flavius Josephus on the Pharisees,* esp. 75–79, 89–96, 108–115.

36. See, e.g., Lauterbach, *Rabbinic Essays,* 79, 84, 91–112. Others who assert that Pharisees engaged in exegetical activity include Neusner, *Rabbinic Traditions,* 3.39–43, Kugel, *Early Biblical Interpretation,* 63–71; Sanders, *Jewish Law,* 127–128. Some of these, as well as other examples, are cited by Mandel, "Scriptural Exegesis," 20–21 n. 4.

37. On the antiquity of simple midrashic exegesis, see Halivni, *Midrash, Mishnah,* 18–37; on legal exegesis at Qumran, see below.

38. For further elaboration of these tensions between midrash and nonscriptural tradition, see Halivni, "Reflections," and A. Yadin, "4QMMT, Rabbi Ishmael," esp. 133–140.

39. See, e.g., Werman, "Oral Torah vs. Written Torah(s)," esp. 180–193, which is helpful in drawing the conceptual distinction between the duality of the Oral/Written Torah and the singularity of midrashic approaches. Werman's speculative historical reconstructions are, however, overly confident.

40. Mandel, "Scriptural Exegesis."

41. On this phrase in rabbinic sources, see Hayes, "*Halakhah le-Moshe mi-Sinai.*"

42. On *Avot* as the Mishnah's first apology, see (e.g.) Neusner, *Introduction*, 571–573.

43. This is not to suggest that we can backdate given Mishnaic traditions by appeal to Josephus's evidence without additional specific parallels among verifiably ancient sources (e.g., New Testament or Qumran).

44. See Goodman, "Note on Josephus," and Mason, *Flavius Josephus on the Pharisees*, 240–245.

45. Lauterbach, *Rabbinic Essays*, 23–24, 38–39.

46. Baron, *Social and Religious History*, 2:36 (for the term "literal" see 2:38).

47. E.g., Simon, *Jewish Sects*, 25–26; Tcherikover, *Hellenistic Civilization*, 263–264; Zeitlin, *Rise and Fall*, 1:185–186. For an effective rebuttal, see Meier, *Marginal Jew*, 3:375 n. 123, 405–406, 462–463 n. 60.

48. Some patristic sources (e.g., Hippolytus *Refutation* 9.29.4, discussed in the appendix) suggest that the Sadducees canonized only the Torah. This is now widely recognized as a misunderstanding of *Ant.* 13.297 and/or a confusion of the Sadducees with the Samaritans (see, again, Hippolytus *Refutation* 9.29.4).

49. See Grabbe, "Law, the Prophets" (on the state of the canon in the second temple period), as well as Ulrich, *Dead Sea Scrolls and the Origins* (on the canon as well as the state of the various biblical texts and text-traditions).

50. On the force of some such claims in antiquity, see Inowlocki, "'Neither Adding nor Omitting Anything.'"

51. And even if he did, we would still have to wonder how to take the claim. As noted, Josephus claims that he will neither add to nor subtract from the biblical record (*Ant.* 1.17; *Apion* 1.42). Yet Josephus does both, repeatedly, as any reader of *Antiquities* can quickly realize. See (briefly) Feldman, *Judean Antiquities 1–4* (BJP 3), 7–8 n. 22, and (for a fuller assessment) Inowlocki, "'Neither Adding nor Omitting Anything.'"

52. Urbach long ago surmised that the Sadducees consciously engaged in exegetical activity; see *Halakhah*, 93–108 (esp. 105–108, which translates Urbach, "Derashah," 180–182). Endorsed by Halivni (*Midrash, Mishnah*, 19), this view has been taken up again by Schremer, "'[T]he[y] Did Not Read,'" 113–117, and Shemesh, *Halakhah*, 95–96.

53. Shemesh, *Halakhah*, esp. 15–20. For similarly binary approaches to the halakhic history of second temple Judaism, see D. Schwartz, "Law and Truth" (opposes rabbinic "nominalists" with Qumranic/Sadducean "realists"), and Schremer, "'[T]he[y] Did Not Read.'" In the latter, Schremer distinguishes between a text-based Sadducean/Qumranic approach and a tradition-based Pharisaic/rabbinic approach.

54. See Shemesh, *Halakhah*, 1–3. Shemesh, however, downplays the binary elements of Geiger's project, preventing him from seeing the degrees of continuity we identify here.

55. See, e.g., Geiger's discussion of the books of the Maccabees in *Urschrift*, 200–230 (1 Macc. as Sadducean, 2 Macc. as Pharisaic). On Geiger's scant attention to the Essenes, see S. Heschel, *Abraham Geiger*, 93, 172–173.

56. Geiger, *Urschrift*, 127–134 (on Josephus's mistaken views), 134–158 (on halakhic disputes between the two groups), and esp. 133–134 (that the Sadducees, too, maintained and taught nonscriptural traditions). See Feldman's note a to *Ant.* 18.16, which cites *m. Makkot* 1.6 as a basis for demonstrating Sadducean acceptance of nonscriptural decrees.

57. So, e.g., Schiffman, *Reclaiming the Dead Sea Scrolls*, 75–76, 87–89; *Qumran and Jerusalem*, 34.

58. So, e.g., Shemesh, *Halakhah*, 13–19.

59. Shemesh, *Halakhah*, esp. 5, 72–74, 80; see 90 (on Sadducean stringency). Shemesh cites, and to a certain degree follows, Schremer, "'[T]he[y] Did Not Read,'" 113–114. Goodman also noted Pharisaic conservatism in "Note on Josephus."

60. Shemesh, *Halakhah*, esp. 96, 105–106.

61. A. Baumgarten, *Flourishing*, 77–78; see "'But Touch the Law,'" 305–307.

62. See, in particular, Regev, "Were the Priests all the Same?" Regev identifies various Sadducean laws unparalleled at Qumran (161–164) as well as contradictions between the Qumran texts and laws identified as Sadducean in rabbinic literature (164–169). Regev also argues that the Sadducees would have followed a lunisolar calendar, not the 364-day calendar known from Qumranic texts such as 4QMMT (169–177).

63. See Shemesh, *Halakhah*, 18–19.

64. On the general contrast between the "hidden" and "revealed" things at Qumran, see also 1QS 5.11–12, 8.11–16. On the prophetic/revelatory powers of the Teacher of Righteousness, see, in addition to the CD passage, 1QpHab 2.6–10 and 6.14–7.5. For a brief but informative discussion, see Flusser, *Judaism*, 1:293–298. For a fuller, more recent, review, see Tzoref, "'Hidden' and the 'Revealed'."

65. On this figure at Qumran, see Shemesh and Werman, "Hidden Things and Their Revelation," 418–425, and Wieder "'Law-Interpreter' of the Sect." For a brief survey of views on this figure—and his relationship to the Teacher of Righteousness—see Collins, *Beyond the Qumran Community*, 34–39.

66. On rabbinic and Qumranic understandings of this verse (and these terms), see Shemesh and Werman, "Hidden Things and Their Revelation." See also Wieder, *Judean Scrolls*, 53–94.

67. On the Teacher as an inspired exegete, compare Wieder, *Judean Scrolls*, 86–87; on the Interpreter as a figure on par with Moses, see "'Law-Interpreter' of the Sect" (and note the addenda and corrigenda to "The 'Law-Interpreter' of the Sect" in the 2005 reprint of *Judean Scrolls*, 437–439). That the sectarian "hidden things" include doctrinal as well as legal matters see Flusser, *Judaism*, 1:293–298.

68. See Wieder, *Judean Scrolls*, 77–79.

69. On the contrast between exegetical and revelatory authority at Qumran, see, e.g., Fraade, *Legal Fictions*, 145–167, and Shemseh and Werman, "Halakhah at Qumran." Shemesh and Werman also introduce the helpful category of "explicit exegesis" (esp. 119–123). For a survey of the exegetical methods and forms employed at Qumran, see Bernstein and Koyfman, "Interpretation of Biblical Law." For a general survey suggesting similarities and differences between rabbinic midrash and Qumranic exegesis, see Mandel, "Midrashic Exegesis."

70. On the *Temple Scroll* as lacking the characteristics of explicit exegesis (namely the clear differentiation of the verse from its interpretation, as in rabbinic midrash or Qumranic *pesher*), see Shemseh and Werman, "Halakhah at Qumran," esp. 110–119.

71. See Shemesh, *Halakhah*, 39–71. On the possibly polemical/antisectarian intent of the rabbinic approach, see Mandel, "Midrashic Exegesis," Schremer, "'[T]he[y] Did Not Read,'" and Shemesh and Werman, "Hidden Things and Their Revelation."

72. Though hardly ignored by scholarship, this issue has received less attention than others, perhaps because debate is not among the issues addressed head-on in the legal material from Qumran. Meier appropriately gives the issue pride of place toward the beginning of his extensive discussion of Jesus and Jewish law (*Marginal Jew*, 4:31–35). A fuller review (one of the few not cited by Meier) is Bar-Kochva, *Judas Maccabaeus*, 474–493 (an appendix entitled "Defensive War on the Sabbath according to the Books of the Maccabees"). Bar-Kochva's discussion is detailed and well annotated, though he advocates a rather surprising position, doubting the possibility that "mainstream" Jews really opposed defensive warfare on the Sabbath even in the pre-Maccabean era (see esp. 477, 492–493). The most recent review is Nakman, "Halakhah," 272–281. Also of note is Goren, "Fighting on Sabbath." Although not annotated in any academic sense, this informed survey of the issue by the first chief rabbi of the Israel Defense Forces includes many helpful readings of a wide range of primary sources on our topic. The same holds for the posthumously published, unannotated manuscript by Nikiprowetzky, "Le Sabat et les armes."

73. For an attempt to narrow down the contours of Josephus's legal position on the matter, see especially Nakman, "Halakhah," 272–281.

74. So Rashi on Josh. 6.15; see also *y. Shabbat* 1.7, 4a–b; see Goren, "Fighting on the Sabbath," 149–155, and Sivan, *Between Woman*, 102–106.

75. So, e.g., Meier, *Marginal Jew*, 4:32–33, and Sivan, *Between Woman*, 105–106.

76. Bar-Kochva, *Judas Maccabaeus*, 476.

77. Bar-Kochva, *Judas Maccabaeus*, 476. On Sabbath at Elephantine, see Porten, *Archives from Elephantine*, 122–133; for other Jewish military activity in the Persian period, see *Ant.* 12.148–153.

78. On sacrificial aspects of holy war ideology see Niditch, *War in the Hebrew Bible*, 28–55; see also Klawans, *Purity, Sacrifice*, 64–65, and the literature cited there.

79. See, e.g., *t. Eruvin* 3(2).7; *Sifre Deut.*, sec. 203 (on Deut. 20.19; ed. Finkelstein 238–239); *y. Shabbat* 1.7, 4a–b; *b. Shabbat* 19a. Curiously, the more "permissive" ruling is often attributed to Shammai. On these traditions, see Ben-Shalom, *School of Shammai*, 89–94. Accepting these traditions over Josephus's testimony, Ben-Shalom concludes (93) that even elective, offensive warfare was permitted in the post-Maccabean era.

80. As Albeck recognized long ago (*Das Buch der Jubiläen*, 11), the passage makes no distinction between offensive and defensive warfare, and therefore clearly intends to prohibit all fighting on the Sabbath; see Bar-Kochva, *Judas Maccabaeus*, 493 n. 44.

81. As Finkelstein surmised, *Jubilees* 50.12–13 is directed against the policies of the Maccabees ("Book of Jubilees," 51).

82. See Bar-Kochva, *Judas Maccabaeus*, 481–484 (on 1 Macc.) 484–492 (on 2 Macc.); see Goren, "Fighting on Sabbath," 158–162. As Bar-Kochva points out, it is not altogether clear that the martyrs in these instances are opposed to fighting on the Sabbath per se. It is conceivable that these pietists would have responded passively even when attacked during the week (see *Judas Maccabaeus*, 482–484). Of course, since we are led to believe that they all perished, there's no way we—or even our ancient authors—could know these martyrs' motivations and limitations. But the Hasmonean response, according to 1 Maccabees is crystal clear: defensive fighting when necessary will no longer be considered a violation of the sanctity of the Sabbath.

83. E.g., Geiger, *Urschrift*, 219–226.

84. As Bar-Kochva points out (*Judas Maccabaeus*, 477), the case of Joshua's conquest of Jericho is by far the most straightforward biblical justification for warfare—even of an offensive sort—on the Sabbath. Curiously, however, the precedent is not appealed to until the rabbinic period.

85. Bar-Kochva, *Judas Maccabaeus*, 477–481.

86. The Agatharchides passage is "quoted" a second time in different form in *Apion* 1.209–210, also to the effect that Jews do not fight on the Sabbath. On the Agatharchides passage, see also Stern, *Greek and Latin Authors*, 1:104–109. Bar-Kochva (*Judas Maccabaeus*, 477–481), reads these passages in a rather restricted way, in order to support his claim that "normative" Jews did not in fact oppose defensive warfare on the Sabbath (see Nakman, "Halakhah," 278–279). The historical (or halakhic) question, however, is not our concern here; whether historically correct or not, Josephus was persuaded that the opposition was real and that the Maccabees needed to change the prevalent practice.

87. See Cohen, *Josephus*, 44–47, and Gafni, "Josephus and I Maccabees," 116–131. As noted in the previous chapter, I am persuaded that Josephus was aware of and possibly alludes to 4 Maccabees when describing Essene martyrdom in *War*

2.152–153; see Mason, *Judean War 2* (BJP 1b), 122 n. 931, and my fuller discussion in chapter 3.

88. Some historians doubt the accuracy of this report. As Ben-Shalom points out (*School of Shammai*, 91–92, esp. n. 93), it is notable that Josephus, perhaps still drawing on earlier sources, refers to the Sabbath as a fast day (14.66). Ben-Shalom follows earlier scholars in his belief that the widespread references to Jewish fasting on Sabbath were mistaken. For a more recent review, which takes reports of Jewish sabbatical fasting more seriously, see Diamond, *Holy Men*, 121–127. See also Marcus's note d ad loc. in the LCL translation, which precludes the possibility that the Day of Atonement is meant.

89. Meier has already called attention to the remarkable use of "Law" in this case; see *Marginal Jew*, 4:35.

90. In *Jewish War* 2.390–394, Josephus imagines that Agrippa II spoke of the Sabbath when attempting to persuade the rebels to lay down their arms. Josephus's Agrippa presents his listeners with a stark choice: either they will follow their Sabbath customs, leaving themselves open to an easy defeat, as in the time of Pompey; or they will break the ancestral laws and anger the deity. Clearly, the rebels picked the second option. This passage exhibits some terminological inconsistencies, referring to Sabbath observance as "customary" (ἔθη) in 2.392 and the permission to fight defensive war only as an "ancestral law" (πάτριον νόμον) in 2.393. But the passage is less remarkable than *Ant.* 14.63, since (1) it does not speak of "the Law," and (2) *War* only lays out what the Jewish practice is (see also 1.146); the book has not described the origin of the practice as *Antiquities* does. Whether the historical Agrippa would have been concerned with the Sabbath in this way is another question altogether. We will note later, in relation to our discussion of Herod, what Josephus elsewhere says about Agrippa's breaking of Jewish laws and customs.

91. The references to Jewish rebellious activity on the Sabbath may not pertain to the legal question at hand, at least in Josephus's view, since Josephus views the war, in retrospect, as sinful of itself and therefore not a legitimate act of self-defense. In his view, the desecrations of holy times are but one example of the sacrilegious behavior of the rebels, as we will see more clearly in the next chapter.

92. On these and other such documents in Josephus, see Olson, *Tragedy, Authority*, 200–204. The accounts of military exemptions in *Antiquities* may not pertain to the legal matter at hand either. The Maccabean policy pertains, it would appear, to fighting against those who would attack the Jews on the Sabbath day. It is not at all clear whether Jews in general—or, at least, Josephus himself—would have believed that the Maccabean policy permitted Jews to fight on the Sabbath, even in defense, on behalf of Rome or other militias, beyond Jewish territory, when not defending Jewish communities, institutions, or way of life. So nothing in these documents necessarily contradicts Josephus's own testimony or opinion

on the matter: in his view, Jewish defensive warfare has been deemed permissible since the Maccabean period.

93. Geiger (*Urschrift*, 216–226) however, surmised that 1 Maccabees articulated the Sadducean position, while 2 Maccabees articulated the Pharisaic view (opposing defensive warfare); see Bar-Kochva, *Judas Maccabaeus*, 484. Accepting the rabbinic traditions attributed to Shammai as historically pivotal—and Pharisaic—Ben-Shalom (*School of Shammai*, 89–94) believes the Pharisaic view was more permissive than 1 Maccabees or Josephus.

94. See Nakman, "Halakhah," 168.

95. Generally, on Josephus's portrait of Nehemiah, see Feldman, *Studies*, 489–499.

96. See Feldman, *Judean Antiquities 1–4* (BJP 3), 402–403 nn. 612–615.

97. Generally, see Nakman, "Halakhah," 307–308.

98. See Sievers, *Synopsis*, 69–71 to conveniently compare 1 Macc., 2 Macc. and *Ant.* on the establishment of the Festival of Lights; see 141–142 for the passages on Nicanor's Day. This day is also listed in *Megillat Ta'anit* (13 Adar): see Noam, *Megillat Ta'anit*, 118–119, 298–302.

99. None of these festivals is noted in any of the calendrical materials from Qumran; nor is there any unambiguous evidence of Esther or 1 Maccabees at Qumran. Briefly, see VanderKam and Flint, *Meaning*, 260, as well as 450 n. 4, which notes that Purim would have, problematically, fallen on a Sabbath in the Qumranic 364-day calendar. For a fuller account of the data regarding Purim and Esther at Qumran, see Kalimi, "Book of Esther." Even Talmon, who finds echoes of the book of Esther among various scrolls, concludes that the festival of Purim—like Hanukkah—would have been "beyond the pale" at Qumran; see Talmon, "Book of Esther," esp. 267.

100. So, e.g., Gafni, "Josephus and 1 Maccabees," 118–119. For the view that Josephus believes in the continuation of predictive prophecy in his own day, see Gray, *Prophetic Figures*, 7–34.

101. See Gray, *Prophetic Figures*, 35–79.

102. See fuller discussion of this matter in chapter 2. This is not to say, of course, that everything prophets predict is destined to come about: sometimes, as we have seen, repentance can avert the dire decree (e.g., *Ant.* 8.418).

103. Perhaps the one exception would be the fact that Josephus does follow scripture in describing the prophet and judge Samuel as facilitating the dramatic change from aristocracy to monarchy (*Ant.* 6.32–94). But of course, Samuel is not understood to be legislating a new practice, but instituting one allowed for in the Mosaic law (*Ant.* 4.223–24; compare Deut. 17.14–20). It is also notable that Josephus imagines that difficult cases would be appealed to the "high priest, the prophet, and the council of elders" (*Ant.* 4.218; compare Deut. 17.8–13). The prophet's role here is curious (and, along with the reference to the council, an addition to scripture). Clearly, however, Josephus

does not intend for the prophet alone to solve the matter, but to participate in the priestly, aristocratic deliberations. On this passage, see Feldman, *Judean Antiquities 1–4* (BJP 3), 410–411 nn. 667–669. For some general observations on Josephus's approach(es) to aristocracy, monarchy, and priestly rule, see D. Schwartz, "Josephus on the Jewish Constitutions."

104. Generally, on Josephus's portrait of Ezra, see Feldman, *Studies*, 473–488. As Feldman points out, Josephus is at pains to downgrade Ezra, certainly in comparison to the later rabbinic tradition, but even in comparison to his source 1 Esdras, presumably to preserve Moses's status as the greatest prophet and legislator of the Jewish people.

105. For a fuller accounting of second temple period prophets in Josephus, see Gray, *Prophetic Figures*, esp. 112–163.

106. The effort to separate prophets from law is also in evidence in rabbinic literature: see, e.g., Sifra, *be-Huqotai* Perek 13, on Lev. 27.34 (ed. Weiss 115b). Of course, opposing or more nuanced views of the subject are preserved as well, for example the suggestion that prophets could—but only temporarily—override Torah law; see, e.g., *Sifre Deut.*, sec. 175, on Deut. 18.15 (ed. Finkelstein 221); see also *b. Yevamot* 102a, *b. Avodah Zarah* 36a. One famous *aggadic* tradition even claims that the prophets progressively *reduced* the number of commandments from Moses's 613 until Habakkuk (2.4) sums it all up singularly: "the righteous shall live by faith" (*b. Makkot* 23b–24a). Generally, see Urbach's classic essay, "Halakhah and Prophecy," some points of which are summarized in *Sages*, 300–302. Also of note is Shemesh, *Halakhah*, 39–71; though insightful, this treatment is characteristically (and problematically) binary, distinguishing between rabbinic dependence on exegesis and sectarian dependence on revelation.

107. On Essene prophecy in Josephus, see Beall, *Josephus' Description*, 109–111, and Gray, *Prophetic Figures*, 80–111.

108. On the literary and archaeological evidence for this structure, see Richardson, *Building Jewish*, 165–179; for a helpful survey of Josephus's testimony with speculative comparisons to Qumran, see Hayward, "Jewish Temple at Leontopolis."

109. Possibly, Josephus here prefigures the later rabbinic reluctance to derive law from prophetic texts; see, e.g., *b. Hagigah* 10b, and the fuller discussion in Urbach, "Halakhah and Prophecy," esp. 12–19.

110. On the "ambiguous oracle" in *War* 6.312, see Michel and Bauernfeind, *De Bello Judaico*, 2:2, 190–192 (n. 149 and excursus 15). On the general issue of predicting the destruction before the fact, see chapter 5 here.

111. For a particularly skeptical view, see Sanders, *Judaism*, 280–284. For a more moderate assessment, allowing for some truth with significant distortion, see Goodman, *Ruling Class*, 93–96.

112. Perhaps the most trusting assessment is Hengel, *Zealots*, esp. 76–145; but see also Goodblatt, *Elements*, 88–107, who places Josephus's fourth philosophy and their "God-alone" politics within the context of priestly, theocratic ideologies.

113.   There is a text-critical problem in 18.9. LCL (following Niese) reads "innovation" (καίνισις), while various manuscripts yield other readings and marginal corrections (see Niese, *Flavii Iosephi*, 4:141, on *Ant.* 18.9). While the text is clearly corrupt, perhaps beyond repair, the general sense however is clear, as Josephus continues to criticize Judas for his new and therefore problematic philosophy (18.9, 24–25).

114.   On the preference of aristocracy over monarchy, see also, e.g., *Ant.* 6.26, 84, 268.

115.   For more on these issues, see D. Schwartz, *Studies*, 102–116; on Gentiles and the temple generally, see Hayes, *Gentile Impurities*, 34–37, 59–63.

116.   The same holds true for an additional example, mentioned in chapter 1: the selection, by lot, of Phannis (Phinehas), son of Samuel, as high priest after the Zealot takeover of the temple (*War* 4.147–161). Josephus tells us that the Zealots appealed to an "ancient custom" (ἔθος ἀρχαῖον), though he himself views this as a pretext. Josephus's opposition is based, again, not on any appeal to scripture, but on an appeal to customary practice (4.153–154).

117.   Josephus also criticizes other Jewish rulers for breaking Jewish customs, notably Agrippa II (see, e.g., *Ant.* 20.211–218), and of course the Hellenizing high priest Menelaus (*Ant.* 12.240–241).

118.   On Herod's temple-building project, see Netzer, *Architecture*, 137–178, and Richardson, *Herod*, 185–186, 245–249. On the project as architecturally (and, therefore, religiously) "innovative" (especially with regard to the structure and layout of the outer courts) see Richardson, *Herod*, 245–247, and more fully, *Building Jewish*, 271–298. Josephus, however, doesn't remark on these matters as changes to "law" or "custom."

119.   Herod's religious behavior has been reviewed recently by Gideon Fuks and Eyal Regev; see Fuks, "Josephus on Herod's Attitude," and Regev, "Herod's Jewish Ideology." Both are more interested in the historical Herod than the writer Josephus—and neither set out to use the material as we will here, to illumine Josephus's legal theory.

120.   In both *War* (1.204–211) and *Ant.* (14.158–184), Josephus relates that Herod, while serving as governor of Galilee, stood trial for violently pursuing a band of brigands. Fuks takes this as his first example of Herod's violation of ancestral customs (*War* 1.209) or "the law" (*Ant.* 14.167); see "Josephus on Herod's Attitude," 238–239. But this instance is much less clear than the cases we will discuss. The trials Josephus describes appear rather politically motivated (to say the least), and the legal issues are rather murky to boot: would a governor really be prevented by Jewish law or custom from taking a police action against armed bandits? Of course, once he becomes king, Herod will continue to pursue brigands, as at Arbel (*War* 1.304–313; *Ant.* 14.420–430). On Herod and the brigands, see Richardson, *Herod*, 250–252.

121. Fuks, "Josephus on Herod's Attitude," and Regev, "Herod's Jewish Ideology," present two very different evaluations of Herod. Fuks, focusing on Josephus's criticisms, emphasizes the king's willingness to break Jewish law when it suited him. Regev struggles to exonerate Herod, at least to a certain extent. To do so, Regev expands the scope to take into account the marriages Herod arranged for his family members (often to Jews) as well as archaeological remains (e.g., ritual baths at Herodian structures), which he believes "show that Herod maintained ritual purity in his private life" (211). Regev also gives greater weight to Herod's speeches in Josephus's works, which Regev attributes to Nicolaus of Damascus (213). For a reasonably evenhanded treatment of Herod's religious policies and convictions, see Richardson, *Herod*, 183–186, 240–261. On Herod's architectural talent and practicality, see Netzer, *Architecture*, 306.

122. Aristobulus quickly becomes a victim of Herod's murderous rage, whereupon Ananel is then restored to the priesthood (*Ant.* 15.50–56). Herod will later depose other high priests, such as Simon, son of Boethus, whose daughter (also one of Herod's wives) was allegedly involved in a plot against the king (*Ant.* 17.78). Generally on Herod and the priesthood, see Richardson, *Herod*, 241–247. For more of what little we know about the high priesthoods of Aristobulus (III), Ananel, Simon, son of Boethus, and others who served under Herod, see VanderKam, *From Joshua to Caiaphas*, 394–416. On Josephus and the priesthood, see also Thoma, "The High Priesthood in the Judgment of Josephus."

123. Herod will also not be the last to depose priests. His descendant Agrippa II was a particularly active deposer of high priests, though Josephus makes no effort to criticize Agrippa's practice on legal grounds. While some of these depositions are for cause, others may be more capricious. When Ishmael, son of Phabi, is detained in Rome, Agrippa (reasonably) appoints Joseph (Kabi), son of Simon (*Ant.* 20.195–196). He is removed shortly thereafter, to be replaced by Ananus, son of Ananus (20.197–198). This priest is then deposed for cause, after he has executed James (*Ant.* 20.199–203). Ananus's successor, Jesus, son of Damnaeus, is then deposed in favor of Jesus, son of Gamaliel, and this leads to priestly feuds, contributing to the city's strife and eventual downfall (20.213–214). This Jesus is then deposed in favor of Mathias, son of Theophilus (20.223). On all these priests, see VanderKam, *From Joshua to Caiaphas*, 463–486. Without reference to the deposition of priests per se, Josephus does disapprove of Agrippa's policies regarding other cultic matters. Josephus criticizes as contrary to custom (πάτριον) Agrippa's construction of a room with a view overlooking the temple; *Ant.* 20.189–191, but see n. 5 (and note e) to LCL ad loc., and see Niese, *Flavii Iosephi*, 4:308. In addition, when Agrippa permits certain classes of Levites to don linen robes and others are permitted to join in the singing of hymns (20.216–218),

Josephus points out that all this was in violation of the "national laws" (τοῖς πατρίοις νόμοις; 20.218; but again note the text-critical problem: "laws" is omitted in some mss; see n. 1 to LCL ad loc., and see Niese, *Flavii Iosephi*, 4:313, ad loc.).

124. Rabbinic sources, for what it is worth, recall that many high priests were deposed in the late second temple period; see, e.g., *b. Yoma* 9a, and fuller discussion in Klawans, *Purity, Sacrifice*, 178–180. Rabbinic literature also recognized that purity concerns could require appointing interim high priests to serve in the event the duly appointed priest became temporarily ineligible. Although these stand-ins later step aside for the duly appointed high priest, they still retain a special sanctity above regular priests, in line with the principle that "one ascends in holiness, but does not descend" (*b. Yoma* 12b–13a; *b. Megillah* 9b).

125. Fuks, "Josephus on Herod's Attitude," 239.

126. On Herod's building projects in general, see Netzer, *Architecture*, and Richardson, *Herod*, 174–215; on his cultural projects (such as theaters and stadia) in particular, see Netzer, *Architecture*, 277–281, and Richardson, *Herod*, 186–188.

127. Fuks, "Josephus on Herod's Attitude," 239–240; on these structures, see Richardson, *Herod*, 184–185.

128. Josephus holds Agrippa II to account for similar construction projects (*Ant.* 20.211–212).

129. See also *Ant.* 15.365, which presumably indicates that Herod's temple to Caesar at Paneion was understood as a violation of Jewish customs and piety.

130. Fuks, "Josephus on Herod's Attitude," 241–242.

131. It is not clear that Herod intended for the eagle to be understood as an idolatrous affront. A defender of Herod, in his own day or in Josephus's, could point to the temple's official currency (shekels of Tyre) for an instance of tolerated eagle imagery. For more on this incident, see (briefly) Richardson, *Herod*, 15–18, and more fully, Begg, "Ruler or God." For some observations regarding this incident in light of other "aniconic" narratives in *Josephus*, see Ehrenkrook, *Sculpting Idolatry*, 112–113, 166–171.

132. On the imprecise relationship between Herod's violations and Josephus's understanding of the Second Commandment, prohibiting idolatry (Exod. 20.4; *Ant.* 3.91), see Ehrenkrook, *Sculpting Idolatry*, 69–81; see also 144–145, 183–184.

133. So, for instance, Fuks ("Josephus on Herod's Attitude," 242–244) makes note of Herod's participation in official cultic ceremonies at Rome (*War* 1.285, *Ant.* 14.388), and the sacrifices offered preceding the war against the Nabateans (*War* 1.380; *Ant.* 15.147). But since Josephus offers no criticism of these behaviors, reviewing them will not illumine our subject, which is Josephus's traditional-legal grounds for criticizing Herod.

134. Fuks, "Josephus on Herod's Attitude," 240–241.

135. For more on the minutiae of this legal matter, see Feldman, *Judean Antiquities 1–4* (BJP 3), 440–442, esp. nn. 896–901. As Revel observed long ago ("Some Anti-traditional Laws," 296–297) Josephus's paraphrase differs in some ways from later rabbinic tradition, agreeing in some ways with later Karaite rulings.

136. So Schröder, *Die "väterlichen Gesetze."*

137. On the fluidity and complexity of these categories in rabbinic literature and subsequent interpretive literature, see Roth, *Halakhic Process*, 13–48.

138. On developments and disagreements regarding this category, see Hayes, "Halakhah le-Moshe mi-Sinai."

139. And see the "Al ha-Nissim" prayer: "therefore they established these eight days of Hanukkah, for giving thanks and praise to [God's] holy name."

140. If anything, we can continue to point out similarities: Josephus's description of Pharisaic legal "accuracy" (*War* 1.110, 2.162) may be compared to, and illumined by, his own claims to accurately present the history of his people (*War* 1.9, 7.454–455; *Ant.* 1.17, 20.260). Just like the Pharisees he describes, Josephus's own approach to scripture is something other than a straightforward re-presentation of biblical material, despite his promises neither to add nor subtract (*Ant.* 1.17, 20.260). For some interesting observations on the relationship between Josephus's assertions of textual fidelity and his claims of historical accuracy (but without reference to the Pharisees), see Inowlocki, "'Neither Adding nor Omitting Anything,'" esp. 52–54.

141. For the fullest analysis of Josephus's specific *halakhot*, see Nakman, "Halakhah," who as we have noted argues that a good number of Josephus's rulings cohere with rabbinic/Pharisaic law.

142. Alone among the New Testament writers, Luke (in both Luke and Acts) also speaks not only of Jewish laws but also of Jewish customs (e.g., Luke 1.9, Acts 6.14), apparently using the terms interchangeably; see Wilson, *Luke and the Law*, esp. 1–11. We have noted various echoes of Josephus in Luke-Acts, and this may well be another. Some scholars have utilized distinctions between law and custom in the service of explaining why early Christians maintained some Jewish practices, even while breaking with "the Law." The analysis above would caution against the argument that first century Jews in general (or Luke in particular) understood a clear difference between custom and law. See Klawans, review of *Torah in the New Testament.*

143. The precise understanding of this passage has long been disputed: do the Essenes bar themselves from entering the temple, or are they barred by the temple authorities? And can this passage be understood in light of Qumranic criticisms of the second temple? See, in addition to Feldman's notes a, b, and c, ad loc. to the LCL translation, A. Baumgarten, "Josephus on Essene Sacrifice," J. Baumgarten, *Studies*, 57–74, and the discussion in Klawans, *Purity, Sacrifice*, 161–168 (with additional references cited there).

144. See our fuller discussion of Essene morning prayers in chapter 1.

145. Discussions of this matter are legion. See, among many other treatments, Beall, *Josephus' Description*, 38–42, 111–112, 120 (on Josephus and Philo vis-à-vis the Qumran scrolls) and Mason, *Judean War 2* (BJP 1b), 98–100 (for a very different assessment of Josephus vis-à-vis Qumran). On the celibacy of Essenes in Philo, see Taylor, "Philo of Alexandria," 20–26. On Pliny's testimony, see Mason, *Judean War 2* (BJP 1b), 92–93, and Stern, *Greek and Latin Authors*, 1:465–481.

146. See Feldman, *Judean Antiquities 1–4* (BJP 3), 37 n. 255; Feldman does not draw a connection between this omission and Josephus's praise of the Essenes.

147. For a sound and thorough treatment of the historical value of the New Testament sources in relation to Josephus and other evidence, see Meier, *Marginal Jew*, 2:19–233. The (briefer) classic treatment by Thackeray remains of interest as well: *Josephus: The Man and the Historian*, 131–133.

148. For my understanding of John's baptism vis-à-vis ritual and moral purification, see *Impurity and Sin*, 138–143.

149. On the phrase "good man" (18.117) see Feldman's n. 3 and note c to the LCL edition ad loc.; see also Thackeray, *Josephus: The Man and the Historian*, 132–133. Even if the phrase is a pious emendation of later Christian scribes, the general tenor of Josephus's report is entirely positive.

150. Klawans, *Impurity and Sin*, 139–140.

151. See also *War* 2.162, as discussed in Mason, *Judean War 2* (BJP 1b), 132 n. 1006.

152. For echoes of Pharisaic power in the New Testament, see Mason, "Pharisaic Dominance." We have commented briefly on the Pharisee-rabbi connection in the Introduction; see further, chapter 5.

153. The same sentiment is echoed in Philo (*Special Laws* 1.67) as well as *Sifre Deut.*, sec. 354 (ed. Finkelstein 416) and *Numbers Rabbah* 18.8 (ed. Mirkin 10:196). For further references, see Feldman, *Judean Antiquities 1–4* (BJP 3), 399 n. 583. A partial parallel—without reference to the single temple—appears in *2 Baruch* 48.24, as noted already by Kohler, "Halakik Portions," 71–72. Kohler understands these passages in light of Josephus's critique of the Leontopolis temple, discussed earlier.

154. For the view that *Apion* stands apart from *Antiquities* (with the former based largely on Alexandrian pamphlets), see S. Schwartz, *Josephus and Judaean Politics*, 21, 52–53, 108. For readings that allow a greater unity of thought (and originality) in Josephus's works, see Barclay, *Against Apion* (BJP 10), xxii–xxvi, and Barclay's notes ad loc. to the sections of *Apion* discussed here. See also Rajak, *Jewish Dialogue*, 195–217, and Spilsbury, "*Contra Apionem*." Note, however, Haaland's recent argument (in "Josephus and the Philosophers of Rome") that *Apion* downplays philosophical aspects in Judaism as a response to antiphilosophical turns taken in contemporary Roman society. Focusing on politics, D. Schwartz discerns a diasporic, post-70 CE perspective emerging in Josephus's later works, especially in *Apion* ("Josephus on the Jewish Constitutions").

155. Barclay, *Against Apion* (BJP 10), 270–271, nn. 704, 707, 711.
156. On shared descent and history as a theme in *Apion*, see Barclay, *Against Apion* (BJP 10), lvi, and "Constructing Judean Identity," 102–104.
157. In addition, Feldman discerns various instances where Josephus's reworkings of biblical narrative serve to emphasize either the importance of Jewish unity or the dangers of civil strife. See generally *Josephus's Interpretation*, 140–143; see also, e.g., 531 (on Esther), and *Studies*, 316–321 (discussing Jehoshaphat).
158. And the Essenes are indeed criticized for their relation to the temple (*Ant.* 18.19), as noted.
159. The juxtaposition of foreign "customs" (τῶν πατρίων) with Jewish "law" (τὸν νόμον) is simply another example of the terminological flexibility displayed by Josephus in all his discussions of these issues.
160. Cohen, "History and Historiography," 7–8.
161. Compare Barclay, *Against Apion* (BJP 10), 270–271 nn. 704, 707, 711.
162. Barclay, *Against Apion* (BJP 10), 272 n. 716.
163. On this motif in *War* especially, see Rajak, *Josephus*, 65–77.
164. The juxtaposition is not entirely unlikely: as we noted, some (e.g., S. Schwartz, "Composition") have maintained that book 7 of *War* was written rather late— around the same time as *Apion*.
165. We can even suggest a modern analogue for comparative purposes: Solomon Schechter (1847–1915). Without denying the significant disputes regarding Jewish practice in his day (which ranged from radical Reform to ultra-Orthodoxy), Schechter staked out a middle-of-the road position under the banner of "Catholic Israel," by which he intended to describe what he viewed as the consensus position: accepting moderate changes to Jewish norms while bestowing legitimacy on customs as practiced (even over the authority of printed legal codes). See Schechter, *Studies in Judaism*, xviii–xx. Proponents of other views would, of course, either reject Schechter's claim to represent the majority or deny the legitimacy of appealing to customary practice and consensus instead of halakhic codes or legal experts. Neither Josephus nor Schechter was acting as a dispassionate historian when making the claims that certain positions were popular enough to represent the consensus view. They were, rather, participating in the debates of their day.
166. See, again, Cohen, "History and Historiography," Haaland, "Josephus and the Philosophers of Rome," and D. Schwartz, "Josephus on the Jewish Constitutions."

CHAPTER 5

1. For a sampling of the objections, see, e.g., Jaffee, *Early Judaism*, 16–20. Boccaccini, *Middle Judaism*, also does not recognize 70 CE as a turning point, albeit without much discussion of this matter per se.

2. Seth Schwartz, *Imperialism*, esp. 15–16, 108–110, 175.

3. Schwartz, *Imperialism*, 109. The excerpt quoted is extracted from a fuller argument about the relative marginality of rabbinic culture during the first centuries CE. For the most part, Schwartz's *Imperialism* speaks of the near eclipse of Jewish society in the aftermath not only of the destruction of the temple (in 70) but also the failure of the Bar Kochba rebellion (135 CE). Moreover, Schwartz generally roots his argument in archaeological more than literary data. A full consideration of Schwartz's work would take this discussion well beyond the interests of this book. What matters for our concerns, however, is the fact that Schwartz, in the statement quoted here, speaks of a shattered *religion* (not society) in the wake of 70 (not 135), and the support for this is found not in archaeology, but in 4 Ezra, which was composed *before* the Bar Kochba rebellion. Schwartz may well root other parts of his argument in archaeological data, but "panic," "despair," and "gloom" can only be found in literary evidence. It is therefore appropriate to align *this aspect* of Schwartz's work with that of Bokser (cited rather favorably in Schwartz, *Imperialism*, 108–109 n. 12) as well as others who speak of the shattering of Judaism in the wake of 70 CE.

4. Goldenberg, "Destruction," 198,

5. Schremer, "'The Lord Has Forsaken,'" 189, see also 198. In this article, Schremer helpfully identifies various rabbinic sources that recognize and attempt to counter doubts concerning God's providence. He then attempts to argue that these sources testify to a "spirit of despair among Palestinian Jews, which was one of the results of the military defeats of Palestinian Jewry in its wars against Rome" (198; see also 189). Yet as Schremer recognizes (184–185 n. 6), few of the sources he discusses explicitly relate to the events in question (70 and 135 CE), and fewer can reliably be dated to the period in question (185–186 n. 10). He therefore admits that the existential crisis he speaks of is "reconstructed" (196). Schremer also overlooks or downplays prerabbinic (and predestruction) denials of earthly divine justice (e.g., Ecclesiastes) as well as rabbinic denials that are predicated on personal concerns, such as those regarding the death of a child, a phenomenon that will be noted again later in this chapter.

6. See especially Bokser, "Rabbinic Responses to Catastrophe." Compare also "*Ma'al* and Blessings over Food," and "Wall Separating God and Israel."

7. For a fuller critical assessment of Bokser's interpretation of these particular traditions and their parallels, see Klawans, *Purity, Sacrifice*, 203–211.

8. See Bokser, "Rabbinic Responses," esp. 59–61; compare Bokser, "*Ma'al* and Blessings over Food," 570–571. For a similar approach to the book of Lamentations, see M. Moore, "Human Suffering," esp. 537. Without explicit reference to the Holocaust, both Robert Kirschner and Shaye J. D. Cohen have described an initial shock followed (after centuries) by a gradual acceptance. See Cohen, "Destruction," 18–19, and Kirschner, "Apocalyptic and Rabbinic Responses," 27–28, 45–46; see also Mandel, "Loss of Center," 17–18.

9. Various aspects of Bokser's analogy are problematic. For further critical observations, see Klawans, *Purity, Sacrifice*, 203–204.

10. Goodman, *Rome and Jerusalem*, 427–428; Price, "Josephus and the Dialogue," 181; Schiffman, *From Text to Tradition*, 162. Even as he criticizes the supposition that 70 CE created a crisis, Cohen accepts Bokser's comparison to the Holocaust with regard to a delayed response; see Cohen, "Temple and the Synagogue," esp. 314–316.

11. Pearson, *Gnosticism, Judaism*, 50–51. Pearson is not certain that Jewish Gnosticism began in the wake of 70 CE; but his discussion does draw the modern parallel, even citing the work of Richard Rubenstein (discussed later in this chapter).

12. See especially Neusner, "Implications of the Holocaust," esp. 301–302, and (more recently) *Israel after Calamity*, esp. 10, 110–111.

13. Neusner, "From History to Religion," esp. 104–106.

14. Key selections from these writers, with helpful annotations and bibliographies, can be found in Katz, Biderman, and Greenberg, *Wrestling with God*; for key statements on the present theme, see 415–416 (Rubenstein), 499–500 (I. Greenberg)

15. E.g., Morgan, *Holocaust Reader*, esp. 1–7, and see 79–89.

16. See, R. Rubenstein, "Fall of Jerusalem," and I. Greenberg, "Cloud of Smoke, Pillar of Fire," and "Third Great Cycle of Jewish History," both reprinted with annotations in Katz, Biderman, and G. Greenberg, *Wrestling with God*, esp. 507 and 527. I. Greenberg and Rubenstein were preceded by earlier writers such as Ignaz Maybaum, who spoke already in 1949 of the destruction of European Jewry as a third *"Hurban"*; see Katz, Biderman, and G. Greenberg, *Wrestling with God*, 401–408.

17. For fuller argumentation and bibliography, see Klawans, "Josephus, the Rabbis and Responses to Catastrophes."

18. Katz, *Holocaust in Historical Context 1*, 76–80. Note also the important differences in the events' aftermaths: the destruction of European Jewry was followed by the devastating defeat of Nazi Germany, the Nuremberg trials, and the establishment of the state of Israel. The destruction of the second temple was not followed by any such reversal, although Jews continued to live in the land of Israel.

19. See, e.g., Katz, *Holocaust in Historical Context I*, which maintains the uniqueness of the Holocaust even when compared to the experience of Armenians in World War I and Cambodians in the 1970s. For a fuller variety of perspectives see the essays collected in Rosenbaum (ed.), *Is the Holocaust Unique?*

20. See, e.g., Halivni, *Breaking the Tablets* esp. 28–31.

21. See Roskies, *Literature of Destruction*, 3–12 (Roskies's Introduction), 381–564 (anthology of responses to Holocaust, written during the Holocaust), and Diner, *We Remember*, 1–149, which chronicles early American Jewish efforts

to commemorate the Holocaust. See also the materials in Morgan, *Holocaust Reader*, 19–77.

22. See, e.g., Diner, *We Remember*, 150–215, which chronicles the American Jewish community's prodigious postwar efforts on behalf of the survivors. For a moving account of the efforts of the survivors themselves, see Mankowitz, *Life between Memory and Hope*.

23. See the sources collected, translated, and discussed in Katz, Biderman, and Greenberg, *Wrestling with God*, 11–201.

24. E.g., Heschel, *Man is Not Alone*, 150–157; reprinted with introduction and annotations in Katz, Biderman, and G. Greenberg, *Wrestling with God*, 376–380. For a review of traditional approaches to the Holocaust that do not assert that the victims were sinful, see Pinchas Peli, "Borderline: Searching for a Religious Language of the *Shoah*." in Katz, Biderman, and G. Greenberg, *Wrestling with God*, 244–262.

25. On the early, traditional, theological responses, see G. Greenberg's comments in Katz, Biderman, and Greenberg, *Wrestling with God*, 11–26. On intellectual versus other responses to the catastrophe, see for instance, the comments of Shalom Rosenberg, "Holocaust: Lessons, Explanation, Meaning," excerpted and translated in Katz, Biderman, G. Greenberg, *Wrestling with God*, 332–349, esp. 335–336.

26. See Berger, *Sacred Canopy*, esp. 53–80, 78–79. According to Berger, this earthquake as well as World War I raised greater questions (among Christians) regarding theodicy than did the "immeasurably greater horrors of World War II" (78; see also 160–161).

27. Kant, "On the Failure of All Attempted Philosophical Theodicies." See, in this respect, Seeskin, *Jewish Philosophy*, 174, 197–202.

28. See, e.g., Robert Gordis, "Cruel God or None," and Michael Wyschogrod, "Faith and the Holocaust," both reprinted with annotations in Katz, Biderman, and G. Greenberg, *Wrestling with God*, 455–461 and 490–496. See also Neusner, "Implications of the Holocaust," 303. Indeed, the idea that a child's death could shatter one's belief in providence is recognized already in rabbinic sources (e.g., *b. Qiddushin* 39b; *y. Hagigah* 2.1, 77b). It also figures prominently in modern discussions of theodicy that do not focus on the Holocaust per se, such as Kushner, *When Bad Things Happen*.

29. Indeed, within circles fostering traditionalist views of the Pentateuch, the Holocaust is even believed to have been predicted: see, e.g., Drosnin, *Bible Code*, 40–43, 105–107.

30. Beer, "Destruction of the Second Temple."

31. Price, "Some Aspects." See also Magness, "Arch of Titus," esp. 215–216, who follows Price in some respects in recognizing the value of Josephus's works as evidence for the contemporary Jewish theological response to 70 CE.

32. Goodman, "Sadducees and Essenes," 352. Even more recently, Kenneth R. Jones has spoken of a "supposed religious crisis" after 70 CE in *Jewish Reactions*, 271.

33. Cohen, "Temple and the Synagogue," 314, and n. 60, which refers to statements by George Foot Moore, Willhelm Bousset, Heinrich Graetz, and Israel Abrahams.

34. Herford, "Effect," 17. Compare Margolis and Marx, *History*, 205, and Schechter, *Aspects*, 299 n. 3.

35. The redaction of the *Fourth Sibylline Oracle* is commonly dated to about 80 CE, for it speaks of the destruction of Jerusalem by Rome (115–129) and the subsequent eruption of Vesuvius in 79 CE (130–134) as recent events. The work's antitemple polemic (6–11, 27–30) and baptismal ritual (165–170), however, suggest a Jewish-Christian (or Christian?) provenance or redaction; see Collins, "Sibylline Oracles, Book 4." For a more recent review, defending the Jewish authorship of the *Fourth Sibylline Oracle* (as well as the *Fifth Sibylline Oracle*), see Jones, *Jewish Reactions*, 36–38, 173–243.

36. See Rajak, "Josephus and Justus of Tiberias."

37. On the permeability of these boundaries, see in particular Boyarin, *Border Lines*.

38. For brief treatments of the Christian response to the destruction, see Goldenberg, "Destruction," 197–198, and Neusner, "Emergent Rabbinic Judaism," 41–43. On the Christian (especially Markan) belief that Jesus predicted the temple's demise, see Kloppenborg, "*Evocatio Deorum.*" For a classic Christian understanding of the destruction—one that exemplifies also the Christian use of Josephus—see Eusebius, *Ecclesiastical History*, esp. 3.5.1–3.10.11. On Eusebius's use of Josephus in this regard, see Hardwick, *Josephus as an Historical Source*, 80–90, 100–101, 117, 123–125 (see 59–66 on Origen's use of Josephus).

39. Wisdom of Solomon is dated by some to the reign of Caligula; see, e.g., Winston, *Wisdom of Solomon*, 20–25. For arguments questioning the undue precision of this approach and suggesting an earlier date see, e.g., Horbury, "Christian Use," 183–185. For a modern defense of the traditional claim that *Megillat Ta'anit* is Pharisaic in origin, see Noam, *Megillat Ta'anit*, esp. 19–22.

40. Compare the observations offered by Richard Kalmin, in his argument countering the hypothesis that the shift from attributed to anonymous discourse in the Babylonian Talmud can be explained by persecutions in the Persian period. He observes—with reference to the modern experience—that there is very little reason to believe that persecution would necessarily have a negative impact on literary production. See *Redaction of the Babylonian Talmud*, 93–94.

41. Neusner, *Judaism*, 37; compare "Implications of the Holocaust," 301–302.

42. Kirschner, "Apocalyptic and Rabbinic Responses."

43. But see Beer, "Destruction of the Second Temple," and Price, "Josephus and the Dialogue" and "Some Aspects."

44. For an interesting discussion on the impact of the Holocaust on one Josephus scholar in particular, see D. Schwartz, "On Abraham Schalit."

45. For our purposes, it suffices to compare Josephus with the latter rabbis, without arguing that the later rabbis were influenced by the writings of the earlier historian. On the latter possibility, see Kalmin, *Jewish Babylonia*, esp. 43–60, 75–80, 149–172.

46. For a general review, see Price, "Some Aspects."

47. Rajak, *Josephus*, 65–77. Whether Josephus's account of the revolt's origins is true or not is not really our concern here; for a critical review, see McLaren, *Turbulent Times*.

48. See Rajak, *Josephus*, 78–103.

49. We have discussed *War*'s account of the murders of Ananus and Jesus in chapter 3; see *Ant.* 20.197–203, where Ananus is described much less favorably. Yet even while the depictions of personalities change, the same overall dynamic pertains in *Antiquities*, with the destruction blamed on Jewish murderous transgressions (20.165–166).

50. As was discussed in chapter 2, we cannot necessarily identify the precise instant when the scale was tipped, but the general dynamic is clear enough.

51. See, in addition to our discussion in chapter 2, Cohen, "Josephus, Jeremiah, and Polybius," 371–375; Price, "Provincial Historian," 116–117, and Spilsbury, "Flavius Josephus on the Rise and Fall." See also M. Stern, "Josephus and the Roman Empire."

52. Josephus allows a contrary voice to emerge, however; in his excursus on the Roman military, he asserts that Roman victories depend on the soldiers' valor, not fortune (*War* 3.71, see also 3.100).

53. It is famously unclear how much of Josephus's reports on these matters can be trusted, and to what degree *Jewish War* is influenced by Flavian patronage. For a skeptical approach see Cohen, *Josephus*, esp. 232–242; for a more trusting approach see Rajak, *Josephus*, 185–222.

54. As observed, for instance, by Halpern-Amaru, "Land Theology."

55. As argued by Spilsbury, "God and Israel in Josephus."

56. For a catalogue of rabbinic sources on the destruction, see Neusner, *How Important*. Differing from his previous works on the theme, Neusner, *How Important*, denies that the destruction caused any great theological crisis and downplays the novelty of the rabbinic approach (see xxiii–xxvii, 287–310). Some echoes of Neusner's older views remain, however. With regard to *m. Rosh ha-Shanah* 4.1–4, he still speaks of a "liturgical crisis" in the aftermath of the destruction (4–6, 39–40). With regard to the Mishnah's silence regarding 70 CE, Neusner still speaks of *"denial, denial, denial"* (299, italics in original). Without considering the Josephan parallels, Neusner also still insists on dating the rabbinic approach to the third century CE, based on the generally accepted dates of the completed early rabbinic documents (303–305). Finally, although he does not place the Holocaust front and center in *How Important* (in contrast to, e.g., *Israel after Calamity*) Neusner does suggest that the image of divine

weeping (170–177, quoting *Lamentations Rabbah, proem* 24) is the one original rabbinic idea that could serve as a modern helpful response to the Shoah (see also 285).

57. See also *Lamentations Rabbah* 1.5 (ed. Buber 33a–b); *Avot de-Rabbi Natan* A 6, B 13 (ed. Schechter 16a–b); compare Josephus, *War* 6.193–213. The rabbis elsewhere speak of cannibalism in Jerusalem during the famine (see Lam 2.20), but typically these traditions are speaking more specifically of the destruction of the first temple; see, e.g., Sifra *be-Huqotai, perek* 6.3 (ed. Weiss 112a); *Lamentations Rabbah* 1.16 (ed. Buber 43a–b).

58. A number of rabbinic traditions (*y. Ta'anit* 4.6, 69a; *Lamentations Rabbah, proem* 23 [ed. Buber 10b–11a]; *Lamentations Rabbah* 4.13 [ed. Buber 75a]; *Pesikta de-Rab Kahana* 15.7 [ed. Mandelbaum, 1:257–258]) elaborate on the biblical account of the murder of the priest Zechariah (2 Chron. 24.20–22). In the previous chapter, we observed that this biblical narrative was remembered by Josephus and the New Testament, and likely served as a literary/theological model for later murder stories. The rabbinic traditions focus on the destruction of the first temple, but they merit mention here as they make the claim that the murder of the innocent priest, judge, and prophet took place not only in the temple but also on the Sabbath and the Day of Atonement. Therefore, these rabbinic traditions not only parallel Josephus in echoing the Zechariah narrative but also constitute general parallels to Josephus's accounts of internecine bloodshed on holy days; see *War* 5.100–105 (which speaks of bloodshed in the temple on Passover); and see 2.449–456 (massacre of Roman garrison on the Sabbath); 4.97–105 (John of Gischala uses the Sabbath as a cover for escape), and 4.398–405 (the Sicarii enact their Passover massacre at Ein Gedi).

59. For further analysis of these tales (with bibliography) see Klawans, *Purity, Sacrifice,* 182–184.

60. For a fuller discussion of these particular parallels, see D. Schwartz, "KATA TOYTON TON KAIPON." On priestly greed in Josephan, rabbinic, and Christian memory, see Klawans, *Purity, Sacrifice,* 178–185, 225–231. Again, on echoes of Josephus in the Babylonian Talmud, see *Jewish Babylonia,* esp. 43–60, 75–80, 149–172. For an earlier discussion of rabbinic sources as they relate to Josephus's works, see Cohen, *Josephus,* 253–260.

61. On the ben Zakkai legends (e.g., *b. Gittin* 56a–56b; *Avot de-Rabbi Natan* A 4, B 6–8 [ed. Schechter 10a–12b]; *Lamentations Rabbah* 1, to Lam. 1.5 [ed. Buber 33a–35a]), see Alon, *Jews, Judaism,* 269–313; Neusner, "In Quest," and J. Rubenstein, *Talmudic Stories,* 138–175.

62. See fuller discussion of this contrast in Klawans, *Purity, Sacrifice,* 186. Note also the rabbis' express interest in the (moral) defilement of the land, while Josephus is primarily interested in the defilement of the sanctuary. On Josephus's relative lack of interest in the sanctity (or defilement) of the land of Israel, see Halpern-Amaru, "Land Theology."

63. On Josephus's own sadness, see *War* 1.11–12; 5.19–20, 566; 6.111, 267–268. On the people's lamentation leading up to and following the destruction, see (e.g.) 2.455, 649; 4.128; and 6.274 (though in the last instance, interestingly, the people keep on fighting after lamenting that the temple was already destroyed!).

64. Eshel, "Josephus' View on Judaism without the Temple," esp. 232–233.

65. This sentence paraphrases S. Schwartz, *Imperialism*, 175; for a similar assertion of mass despair and apostasy after 70 CE, see Goldenberg, "Destruction," 198.

66. For brief observations on this point, see Rajak, *Josephus*, 170–171. According to Feldman, the parallels Josephus sees between the two destructions impact on Josephus's creative recasting, in *Antiquities*, of the account of the first destruction. See Feldman, *Studies*, 442–444 (on Jehoiachin); 444 n. 5 and 452 (on Nebuchadnezzar), and 463, 468–472 (on Gedaliah).

67. So Jer. 52.12; see Thackeray's note a to *War* 6.250, ad loc. in the LCL edition, and see *b. Ta'anit* 29a for the rabbinic treatment of the discrepancies between Jeremiah and 2 Kings with regard to the traditional Jewish observance of the 9th of Av.

68. On Josephus's accounts of predestruction signs and prophecies, see Gray, *Prophetic Figures*, 57–58, 123–125, 158–163, and (briefly) Rajak, *Josephus*, 192–194. For a discussion of Josephus's accounts of such omens in light of contemporary Greco-Roman efforts to instill courage (or fear), see Weitzman, *Surviving Sacrilege*, 118–136.

69. A vaguer prediction is put in the mouth of Moses (*Ant.* 4.314; see Rajak, *Josephus*, 212, and Barclay, *Against Apion* [BJP 10], 279 n. 769). As Feldman notes (*Judean Antiquities 1–4* [BJP 3] 470 n. 1097), Josephus diverges from Deut. 28.15–68 by asserting that Moses predicted the destruction of not just one but multiple sanctuaries. Josephus's extrapolation, however, is possibly based on the plural "sanctuaries" (מקדשיכם) in a different curse-passage from the Pentateuch, Lev. 26.31 (MT; so, too, LXX; but compare Samaritan Pentateuch, which refers to a singular sanctuary). Note also that *Antiquities* 4.314, unlike Deut. 28.15–68, imagines the people's future return, which again finds a basis in Lev. 26.40–45.

70. On the ambiguity of the oracle predicting the destruction in *War* 6.312, see Michel and Bauernfeind, *De Bello Judaico*, 2:2, 190–192 (n. 149 and excursus 15).

71. Stern, *Greek and Latin Authors*, 2:1–93, esp. 60–62.

72. See Kloppenborg, "*Evocatio Deorum*," who allows the possibility that the earliest versions of these predictions can be dated prior to the temple's destruction in 70 CE.

73. See Cohen, "Josephus, Jeremiah, and Polybius," and Daube, "Typology in Josephus." On Josephus's self-understanding as a prophet in general, see Feldman, *Josephus's Interpretation*, 56–61, and Gray, *Prophetic Figures*, 35–79.

74. For the claim that Josephus saw himself—in part—as a latter-day Daniel, see Gray, *Prophetic Figures*, 74–77; Mason, "Josephus, Daniel, and the Flavian House," and Feldman, *Josephus's Interpretation*, 629–657. On Josephus and

the book of Daniel, see Vermes, "Josephus' Treatment." Feldman observes
that Josephus recognizes biblical predecessors of himself in a variety of
characters, including (in addition to Jeremiah and Daniel) Joseph, Esther,
Mordecai, and Gedaliah. See Feldman, *Studies*, 463 (for the general observation), and 463–472 (on Gedaliah). The parallels Josephus sees between himself and any biblical characters are of interest; the parallels between figures
from the generation of the destruction and its aftermath (Jeremiah, Gedaliah,
and Daniel) are for our purposes more important in underscoring the degree
to which Josephus understood the events of his own day as following a biblical
pattern.

75. Rajak *Josephus*, 170–171.
76. See Neusner's comment on the tradition's ambiguity in this respect in *How
    Important*, 224. Various traditions discussed throughout Neusner's book are
    determined to be similarly ambiguous.
77. See Milikowsky, "Notions of Exile, Subjugation and Return," esp. 293.
78. On the rabbinic understanding of the departure of the Divine Presence from a
    defiled sanctuary, see Klawans, *Impurity and Sin*, 127–134.
79. E.g., Neusner, *How Important*, 153, 187, 253, and, more thoroughly, Tropper,
    "Yohanan ben Zakkai."
80. For a survey and analysis of the relevant rabbinic traditions, in light of second
    temple and Greco-Roman literature, see Raviv, "Talmudic Formulation of the
    Prophecies."
81. See, esp., Neusner, *Judaism*.
82. Cohen, "Jacob Neusner, Mishnah, and Counter-Rabbinics," esp. 57–58. It seems
    now that Neusner agrees with Cohen; see Neusner, *How Important*, 287–310.
83. This important comparison was noted earlier by Vermes, "Summary," 296;
    see also (without comparison to rabbinic literature) Barclay, *Against Apion* (BJP
    10), 279 n. 769. On the roles that literary descriptions of the Jewish temple
    could play in the Greco-Roman world, both before and after the destruction, see
    Weitzman, *Surviving Sacrilege*, 79–95.
84. For a fuller discussion of this point, especially with regard to rabbinic literature
    and a differing perspective at Qumran, see Klawans, *Purity, Sacrifice*, 187–198.
    On the realistic nature of rabbinic hopes for the future, see 199–211.
85. E.g., Momigliano, *Essays on Ancient and Modern Judaism*, 67–78. For a review
    of this trend in scholarship, see Bilde, "Josephus and Jewish Apocalypticism,"
    36–39.
86. See Spilsbury, "Josephus on the Burning of the Temple," esp. 317–322, and
    "Flavius Josephus on the Rise and Fall," 15–20. See also Bilde, "Josephus and
    Jewish Apocalypticism," 52–55; Mason, "Josephus, Daniel, and the Flavian
    House," and Price, "Josephus and the Dialogue," 192–194. As Mason points out
    ("Josephus, Daniel, and the Flavian House," 172), by identifying the Romans
    with Daniel's fourth kingdom (*Ant.* 10.276), the eventual demise of Rome is

clearly implied. On Josephus's future hopes—but without reference to Daniel—see Weitzman, *Surviving Sacrilege*, 94–95, 151–155.

87. For a survey of such traditions, see Lee, *New Jerusalem*; see also (with additional bibliography) Klawans, *Purity, Sacrifice*, 128–144. On the temple in 4 Ezra, see Lichtenberger, "Zion and the Destruction of the Temple." On the temple in *2 Baruch*, see F. Murphy, "Temple."

88. E.g., *Pesikta de-Rab Kahana* 18.6 (ed. Mandelbaum 1:299–300).

89. For example, the measurements for the temple supplied in Mishnah Tractate *Middoth*—while not entirely in agreement with Josephus—are by no means extraordinary or beyond what Jerusalem's physical landscape would easily allow.

90. For a fuller discussion, see Klawans, *Purity, Sacrifice*, 199–211.

91. Goodman, *Rome and Jerusalem*, 427–428.

92. For a survey of Jewish and Roman reactions to 70 CE (violent and otherwise), see Goodman, *Rome and Jerusalem*, 424–487. On eschatological or apocalyptic ideology underpinning the Bar Kokhba revolt, see, e.g., Neusner, "Emergent Rabbinic Judaism," and Schäfer, "Bar Kokhba and the Rabbis."

93. See Bilde, "Josephus and Jewish Apocalypticism."

94. See Schäfer, "Bar Kokhba and the Rabbis."

95. So, correctly, Kirschner, "Apocalyptic and Rabbinic Responses," 27–32. One particularly notable parallel between rabbinic and apocalyptic literature concerns the shared tradition that the temple priests returned their keys to God in advance of the temple's demise; see *2 Bar.* 10.18, and compare *Leviticus Rabbah* 19.6, on Lev. 15.25 (ed. Margulies 1:436); *Avot de-Rabbi Natan* A 4, B 7–8 (ed. Schechter 11a–b, 12b); *b. Ta'anit* 29a.

96. See, e.g., Alon, *Jews in Their Land*, 50–52; Goldenberg, "Broken Axis," 872–873; Neusner, "Emergent Rabbinic Judaism," 36, 46–47, and *How Important*, 31. For a survey of the rabbinic approach to atonement in the context of a broader study of ancient Judaism, see Sanders, *Paul*, esp. 157–180. For a classic discussion on the rabbinic view regarding (nonsacrificial) atonement, see Schechter, *Aspects*, 293–343.

97. For related traditions regarding sacrificial and nonsacrificial atonement, without reference to Yohanan ben Zakkai, see (e.g.) *Pesikta de-Rab Kahana* 24.5 (ed. Mandelbaum 2.352–354); *Leviticus Rabbah* 7.2 (on Lev. 6.2, ed. Margulies 1:150–153); *b. Rosh ha-Shanah* 18a; *b. Sukkah* 49b.

98. See, for instance, the fifth and sixth blessings of the daily *'amidah*. See Elbogen, *Jewish Liturgy*, esp. 42.

99. See *m. Yoma* 8.1–8, which contains various traditions attributed to postdestruction sages, discussing ritual atonement and the requirement to seek forgiveness (from people harmed and from God), with the cumulative effect being that atonement remains accessible to the Jewish people.

100. *Genesis Rabbah* 41(2).3, on Gen. 14.1 (ed. Theodor/Albeck 1:407); *Leviticus Rabbah* 11.7, on Lev. 9.7 (ed. Margulies 1:237); *Lamentations Rabbah* 4.22 (ed. Buber 77b).

101. In this I agree with Bokser, "Rabbinic Responses," 38–39.
102. It is generally agreed that (nonsacrificial) penitential prayers were significant to various ancient Jewish groups long before the destruction of the second temple. Further important examples include Bar. 1.15–3.8 and the Prayer of Manasseh (see also 2 Chron. 33.11–13), and note the advice on the matter in Sirach 17.24–29 and 18.12–14. For a variety of scholarly approaches to a number of key texts, see Boda, Falk, and Werline, *Seeking the Favor of God*, vols. 1 and 2.
103. On the temple in 4 Ezra, see Lichtenberger, "Zion and the Destruction of the Temple." On the temple in 2 Baruch, see F. Murphy, "Temple." For a more thorough (and very recent) review of these apocalyptic works as reactions to 70 CE, see Jones, *Jewish Reactions*, 39–77 (4 Ezra) and 79–109 (2 Baruch).
104. Vermes, *Complete Dead Sea Scrolls*, 25; on the Roman destruction of Qumran, see (briefly) Magness, *Archaeology*, 61–62.
105. Vermes's published autobiography, *Providential Accidents*, chronicles his personal trajectory through the boundaries of Jewish and Christian milieus, and sheds a great deal of light on this scholar's lifelong commitment to uncovering similarities between Judaism and Christianity. On his professed commitment to a personal, "existential" version of Judaism, see 169–170.
106. Trever, *Dead Sea Scrolls*, 186; see the fuller discussion, "Lessons from Differences," 181–187.
107. Trever, *Dead Sea Scrolls*, 235 n. 8: "It was the less rigid and more broadly focused faith of some Pharisees which managed to survive Roman oppression and eventuate in modern Judaism." But compare the implied criticisms of traditional Judaism in the following barbs tossed explicitly at the Qumran sect (*Dead Sea Scrolls*, 181): "If devotion to the law, a particular interpretation of Scripture, purity in thought and deed, piety, personal denial and rigid discipline were major prerequisites for divine favor and nurture, certainly the Qumran community should have continued to thrive." And on 187: "A faith centered in the 'traditions of men' will die, but a faith that unleashes in humanity the Spirit of God cannot be destroyed."
108. See Barclay, *Against Apion* (BJP 10), 279 n. 769.
109. Goodman, "Sadducees and Essenes," esp. 347–350; see Goodman, "Religious Variety," which suggests that the temple's disappearance made it easier for the various groups to ignore each other. For further arguments regarding the persistence of the Essenes (and possible echoes of this persistence in rabbinic literature) see Burns, "Essene Sectarianism."
110. For terminological and conceptual similarities between Qumran and Karaite literature see Wieder, *Judean Scrolls*. For discussions of the possible ways Qumran sectarians could have left a mark on later Karaite literature, see Astren, "Dead Sea Scrolls," and Erder, "Karaites." Long before the discovery of the scrolls, Geiger argued that the Karaites were the heirs of the Sadducees; see, e.g., *Judaism and Its History*, 262–268.

111.   So, e.g., Erder, "Karaites," 141. On these early medieval Jewish manuscript discoveries, see Astren, "Dead Sea Scrolls," esp. 111–115 (see also 122–123: Astren is more cautious than Erder when it comes to identifying any particular route of Qumran to Karaite influence). Of course, as Astren notes (p. 108), even if the Essenes did not persist into the Middle Ages, that doesn't mean they disappeared in 70 CE. For an entirely different account of Essene influence after 70 CE (refracted through Christianity and Christian sources down to Protestant and even Marxist heirs) see Flusser, *Judaism and the Origins*, 193–201, esp. 201: "The Essene social message is not dead: it lives on in both Christian and secular movements." The contrast with Vermes's judgment of the Essenes and their influence is particularly salient, though Flusser's conjectures are not necessarily sounder than Vermes's assertions.

112.   Moving in the opposite direction from the perspectives just surveyed, but allied in the effort of shifting focus away from 70 CE, Wise has suggested that the Qumran movement largely dissipated long *before* the temple's destruction—this would explain the lack of reference to first-century CE historical events in sectarian documents. See "Dating the Teacher," esp. 85.

113.   See discussion in chapter 3.

114.   Goodman, "Sadducees and Essenes," 355.

115.   On the criticisms of the temple offered at Qumran, with reference to the Essene material as well, see Klawans, *Purity, Sacrifice*, 145–174. For the suggestion that the Essenes in particular were well situated to weather the storm of 70 CE, see Burns, "Essene Sectarianism," esp. 268–272. Indeed, some scholars have even taken to suggesting that the Essene/sectarian rejection of the temple paved the way for later Jews to live successfully without it; see Magness, "Arch of Titus," 211, and (especially) Fleischer, "On the Beginnings of Obligatory Jewish Prayer."

116.   E.g., Herford, "Effect," 4; Margolis and Marx, *History*, 205; Schiffman, *From Text*, 167, Schürer, *History*, 2:414. Yet as Goodman points out ("Sadducees and Essenes," 350–351), the Essenes may have been even more institution-centered than the Sadducees. On the related question of the persistence of the priesthood after 70 CE, see Alexander, "What Happened."

117.   Lauterbach, *Rabbinic Essays*, 38–39.

118.   Goodman, "Sadducees and Essenes," 349–350.

119.   See, e.g., Schremer, "'The Lord Has Forsaken,'" 192–193, for a discussion of such traditions (without recognizing the predestruction Sadducean precedent). We have already noted the role this metaphor plays in post-Holocaust thought.

120.   Among writers whose works are included in Katz, Biderman, and Greenberg, *Wrestling with God*, the following are among those who at least take seriously the free will defense: Pinchas Peli (256–257), Alexander Donat (280), Moshe

Unna (289), Yehudah Bauer (294), and Robert Gordis (493–494). Of course, the noncanonical Sadducean and Sirachian precedents are not discussed in these works.

121. As noted, Geiger long ago surmised a connection between the medieval Karaites and the earlier Sadducees; see *Judaism and Its History*, 262–268. Again, for our purposes, there is no need to accept such arguments as anything more than a caution against presuming that Jewish sectarianism ceased shortly after 70 CE.

122. Cohen, "Significance of Yavneh," 29; some aspects of this approach have been endorsed by A. Baumgarten, *Flourishing*, 194–195.

123. Cohen, "Significance of Yavneh," 47; for a fuller discussion of rabbinic "polysemy" see Fraade, *Legal Fictions*, 427–475.

124. Berger, *Sacred Canopy*, 45–46.

125. And decades later, according to rabbinic legends, Elisha ben Abuya (*Aher*) will abandon Judaism—but for reasons other than the destruction of the temple (e.g., *y. Hagigah* 2.1, 77b, explaining *Aher*'s apostasy as resulting from the death of a virtuous child).

126. Schremer grants this point ("'The Lord Has Forsaken,'" 187): "Without any doubt, such theological stances can be embraced by any person, at any time, without any specific relation to concrete historical reality." In my view, Schremer's parenthetical concession, read in light of the above analysis, unravels his entire argument regarding a post-70 CE theological crisis.

127. See also Berger, *Sacred Canopy*, 53–80, with respect to the ability of religions to respond to the vicissitudes of history with developed theodicies.

128. For Josephus's numbers of dead and prisoners, see *War* 6.420–432. On his hyperbolic imprecision with numbers, see (with regard to a different matter entirely) Thackeray's note c to 3.245–246 in the LCL ed. ad loc.

129. Contra S. Schwartz, *Imperialism*, 110, esp. n. 17. Schwartz's appeal to Clifford Geertz's understanding of "common sense" seems off the mark to me. Berger's *Sacred Canopy*, as discussed, provides a more relevant theoretical frame.

CONCLUSION

1. The first section of Vermes's *Complete Dead Sea Scrolls* is entitled "Rules" and takes up less than one-third of the book's pages—of course, this rough calculation assigns the hortatory sections of the *Damascus Document* and the *Community Rule* to the halakhic side. Even adding the calendrical material to the halakhic side does not substantially change the outcome of this unscientific experiment.

2. The basic numbers are readily available in textbooks, such as VanderKam and Flint, *Meaning*, 154–181.

APPENDIX: ESSENES AND RESURRECTION ACCORDING
TO HIPPOLYTUS

1. For a general survey of this work, see Marcovich, *Hippolytus*, 1–51. For the Greek text of *Refutation*, the modern edition by Marcovich as well as the classic edition by Wendland have been consulted (Wendland has, among other enduring values, a fuller term-index). Various translations are to be found; the classic translation by Legge has the advantage of using the same numbering system (for chapters and paragraphs) later adopted by both Wendland and Marcovich.

2. Josephus's and Hippolytus's passages on life after death are discussed in Elledge, *Life after Death*, 82–99, and printed in synopsis form (in English translation only) 163–167. A fuller synopsis of the Greek text can be found in Puech, *La Croyance*, 2:763–769. The annotated synopsis provided by Smith ("Description," 293–313) is also quite helpful, though the format is cumbersome—and covers only the passages concerning the Essenes.

3. Smith, "Description," esp. 288–289.

4. E.g., VanderKam and Flint, *Meaning*, 245–246; Puech, *La Croyance*, 2:703–762, and Elledge, *Life after Death*, 93–97.

5. For surveys of scholarship since Smith, see Collins, "Essenes and the Afterlife," Elledge, *Life after Death*, 82–99 and, more briefly, Mason, *Judean War 2* (BJP 1b), 87–90. On Smith's recanting, under the influence of Cohen, see Smith, "Helios," 211–12 n. 24.

6. Burchard, "Die Essener bei Hippolyt."

7. A. Baumgarten, "Josephus and Hippolytus." A similar approach was advocated earlier by Zeitlin, "Account." See also Hardwick, *Josephus as an Historical Source*, 51–57, 106, 111, and following Zeitlin in some respects, reaching conclusions similar to Baumgarten's.

8. See Cohen, *Josephus*, 24–66.

9. Baumgarten, "Josephus and Hippolytus," 6.

10. Bergmeier, "Die Drei jüdischen Schulrichten."

11. Mason, *Judean War 2* (BJP 1b), 84–87. So also Rajak, *Jewish Dialogue*, 230–231.

12. Mason, *Judean War 2* (BJP 1b), 87–90.

13. Elledge, *Life after Death*, 93–97, esp. 94; see Smith, "Description," 284.

14. Marcovich, *Hippolytus*, 1–51; Mansfeld, *Heresiography*.

15. Mansfeld, *Heresiography*, esp. 48–49, 239, 319–320, 325; Marcovich, *Hippolytus*, 8, 27; see also 50. Both describe Hippolytus's method as plagiarism: see, e.g., Mansfeld, *Heresiography*, 325, and Marcovich, *Hippolytus*, 36, 50.

16. See Mansfeld, *Heresiography*, esp. 48–49, 319–320, 325; compare Marcovich, *Hippolytus*, 35–38, 49–51. Granting that Hippolytus frequently plagiarizes, Marcovich, in this particular case, allows for an indirect usage, suggesting an intermediate Christianized version of *Jewish War* (Marcovich, *Hippolytus*, 27). Mansfeld argues forcefully that no intermediate source is necessary: Hippolytus

directly plagiarized Josephus, interpolating here and deleting there, in accordance with his apologetic concerns (see esp. 319–320, 325).

17. In defense of Hippolytus's authorship, see Marcovich, *Hippolytus*, 8–17. The primary doubter is Pierre Nautin; see, e.g., "Hippolytus."

18. Marcovich, *Hippolytus*, 7–8.

19. Hengel, *The Zealots*, 70–73.

20. Smith, "Description," 282–283.

21. An additional curiosity concerns the assertion that some of the Essenes would not even get out of bed on the Sabbath (9.25.2). It is possible that this is an accurate account of an authentic stringency, based perhaps on Exodus 16.29 (see Schiffman, *Halakhah at Qumran* 97). That Essenes or other Jews really remained bedridden on Sabbath seems unlikely, and one wonders what confusions lay behind this interpolation.

22. The conceptual connection with all three verses is strong; the terminological connection is closest with Sirach 30.4.

23. These are the most salient instances. Other (possible) examples of "scripturalizations" include *Refutation* 9.26.2, with the reference to the Zealots killing the uncircumcised based perhaps on 1 Macc. 2.46 (see also 2.26), and *Refutation* 9.29.2, with the reference to animals and humans suffering the same fate based perhaps on Eccles. 3.19–21. A fuller analysis would likely yield additional examples.

24. Curiously, Pythagoras (1.2.11) is described as believing in immortality and reincarnation—but not resurrection.

25. See Elledge, *Life after Death*, 92, who speaks of the account as an *apologia pro Judaeos*—until the end of 9.30.4.

26. Hippolytus's evaluation of the Sadducees (confused, let us recall, with the Samaritans) is particularly surprising in light of the hostility toward the Sadducees to be found among the New Testament, Josephus, and even the rabbis. Curiously, the Slavonic *War* also glosses over most of Josephus's barbs against the Sadducees; see Leeming and Leeming, *Josephus' Jewish War*, 258.

27. The *Refutation*'s description of the Pharisaic view on fate and free will is curious: Although the text follows *War* 2.162–163, the description of Pharisaic compatibilism is much more in line with *Ant.* 13.172, to the effect that the school upheld a partial determinism, assigning certain matters to fate, others to people themselves; yet God (not fate) is the ultimate cause of all. This matter, too, is worthy of a fuller analysis. I strongly suspect that the *Refutation*'s alteration of Josephus's description of the Pharisees is meant to differentiate the Jewish school's position from that of the Stoics (just as *Refutation* 9.29.1–3 differentiates the Sadducees from the Epicureans, as described in 1.22.1–2). While the *Refutation*'s Stoics (as described in 1.21.1–2) identify God, providence, and fate, the Pharisees in *Refutation* 29 clearly place God above fate.

28. Hippolytus's accounts of various Gnostic traditions are discussed throughout Pearson, *Ancient Gnosticism*; it bears noting that Pearson is rather skeptical of the relative value of Hippolytus's accounts of Gnostic traditions, not only when compared to the Nag Hammadi corpus, but even when compared to other Patristic writers such as Irenaeus (e.g., 52, 98, 135, 143).

29. For a brief survey of Christian *Adversus Judaeos* literature and recent scholarship on these texts, see Stroumsa, "From Anti-Judaism to Antisemitism."

30. Elledge, *Life after Death*, 94.

31. See Mansfeld, "Resurrection Added," as well as Mueller, "Heterodoxy and Doxography," 4354–4357.

Bibliography

Abegg, Martin G. *Qumran Sectarian Manuscripts: Qumran Text and Grammatical Tags.* Accordance QUMRAN, version 2.9. Altamonte Springs, Fla.: OakTree Software, 2008.

Albeck, Chanoch. *Das Buch der Jubiläen und die Halacha.* Bericht der Hochschule für die Wissenschaft des Judentums in Berlin 47. Berlin: Hochschule für die Wissenschaft des Judentums, 1930.

Albeck, Chanoch, ed. *Shishah Sidre Mishnah.* 6 vols. Jerusalem: Bialik Institute, 1952–58.

Alexander, Philip S. "What Happened to the Jewish Priesthood after 70?" In *A Wandering Galilean: Essays in Honour of Seán Freyne,* edited by Zuleika Rodgers, with Margaret Daly-Denton and Anne Fitzpatrick McKinley, 5–33. JSJSup 132. Leiden: Brill, 2009.

Alon, Gedaliah. *The Jews in Their Land in the Talmudic Age.* Translated by Gershon Levi. Cambridge, Mass.: Harvard University Press, 1989.

Alon, Gedaliah. *Jews, Judaism, and the Classical World.* Translated by Israel Abrahams. Jerusalem: Magnes Press, 1977.

Altshuler, David. "On the Classification of Judaic Laws in the *Antiquities* of Josephus and the Temple Scroll of Qumran." *AJSR* 7–8 (1982–83): 1–14.

Appelbaum, Alan. "'The Idumeans' in Josephus' *The Jewish War.*" *JSJ* 40.1 (2009): 1–22.

Astren, Fred. "The Dead Sea Scrolls and Medieval Jewish Studies: Methods and Problems." *DSD* 8.2 (2001): 105–123.

Atkinson, Kenneth, and Jodi Magness. "Josephus's Essenes and the Qumran Community." *JBL* 129.2 (2010): 317–342.

Attridge, Harold W. *The Interpretation of Biblical History in the "Antiquitates Judaicae" of Flavius Josephus.* Harvard Dissertations in Religion 7. Missoula, Mont.: Scholars Press, 1976.

Attridge, Harold W. "Josephus and His Works." In *Jewish Writings of the Second Temple Period: Apocrypha, Pseudepigrapha, Qumran Sectarian Writings, Philo, Josephus,* edited by Michael Stone, 185–232. CRINT II.2. Assen: Van Gorcum, 1984.

Avery-Peck, Alan J., and Jacob Neusner, eds. *Judaism in Late Antiquity.* Pt. 4. *Death, Life-after-Death, Resurrection and the World-to-Come in the Judaisms of Late Antiquity.* Leiden: Brill, 1999.

Barclay, John M. G. *Against Apion: Translation and Commentary.* Edited by Steve Mason. BJP 10. Leiden: Brill, 2007.

Barclay, John M. G. "Constructing Judean Identity after 70 CE: A Study of Josephus's *Against Apion.*" In *Identity and Interaction in the Ancient Mediterranean: Jews, Christians, and Others: Essays in Honour of Stephen G. Wilson,* edited by Zeba A. Crook and Philip A. Harland, 99–112. Sheffield, England: Sheffield Phoenix Press, 2007.

Bar-Kochva, Bezalel. *Judas Maccabaeus: The Jewish Struggle against the Seleucids.* Cambridge: Cambridge University Press, 1989.

Baron, Salo Wittmayer. *A Social and Religious History of the Jews.* 16 vols. New York: Columbia University Press, 1952–83.

Barr, James. *The Garden of Eden and the Hope of Immortality.* Minneapolis: Fortress, 1992.

Barton, Tamsyn. *Ancient Astrology.* London: Routledge, 1994.

Basinger, David, and Randall Basinger, eds. *Predestination and Free Will: Four Views of Divine Sovereignty and Human Freedom (John Feinberg, Norman Geisler, Bruce Reichenbach, Clark Pinnock).* Downers Grove, Ill.: IVP Academic, 1986.

Baumbach, Günther. "The Sadducees in Josephus." In *Josephus, the Bible, and History,* edited by Louis H. Feldman and Gohei Hata, 173–195. Detroit: Wayne State University Press, 1989.

Baumgarten, Albert I. "But Touch the Law and the Sect Will Split: Legal Dispute as the Cause of Sectarian Schism." *Review of Rabbinic Judaism* 5.3 (2002): 301–315.

Baumgarten, Albert I. *The Flourishing of Jewish Sects in the Maccabean Era: An Interpretation.* Leiden: Brill, 1997.

Baumgarten, Albert I. "Josephus and Hippolytus on the Pharisees." *HUCA* 55 (1984): 1–25.

Baumgarten, Albert I. "Josephus on Essene Sacrifice." *JJS* 45.2(1994): 169–183.

Baumgarten, Albert I. "The Pharisaic *Paradosis.*" *HTR* 80.1 (1987): 63–77.

Baumgarten, Albert I. "Who Cares and Why Does It Matter? Qumran and the Essenes, Once Again!" *DSD* 11.2 (2004): 174–190.

Baumgarten, Albert I. "The Zadokite Priests at Qumran: A Reconsideration." *DSD* 4.2 (1997): 137–156.

Baumgarten, Joseph M. "Sadducean Elements in Qumran Law." In *The Community of the Renewed Covenant: The Notre Dame Symposium on the Dead Sea Scrolls,* edited by Eugene Ulrich and James VanderKam, 27–36. Notre Dame, Ind.: University of Notre Dame Press, 1994.

Baumgarten, Joseph M. *Studies in Qumran Law.* SJLA 24. Leiden: Brill, 1977.

Beall, Todd S. *Josephus' Description of the Essenes Illustrated by the Dead Sea Scrolls.* Society for New Testament Studies Monograph Series 58. Cambridge: Cambridge University Press, 1988.

Beer, Moshe. "The Destruction of the Second Temple in Early Jewish Thought." In *The Jews in the Hellenistic-Roman World: Studies in Memory of Menahem Stern,* edited by Isaiah M. Gafni, Aharon Oppenheimer, and Daniel R. Schwartz, 437–451. Jerusalem: Zalman Shazar Center for Jewish History, 1996.

Begg, Christopher T. "The Gedaliah Episode and Its Sequels in Josephus." *Journal for the Study of the Pseudepigrapha* 6.12 (1994): 21–46.

Begg, Christopher T. "'Josephus's Portrayal of the Disappearances of Enoch, Elijah, and Moses': Some Observations." *JBL* 109.4 (1990): 690–693.

Begg, Christopher T. *Judean Antiquities 5–7*. Edited by Steve Mason. BJP 4. Leiden: Brill, 2001.

Begg, Christopher T. "The Massacre of the Priests of Nob in Josephus and Pseudo-Philo." *Estudios Bíblicos* 55 (1977): 171–198.

Begg, Christopher T. "Ruler or God? The Demolition of Herod's Eagle." In *The New Testament and Early Christian Literature in Greco-Roman Context: Studies in Honor of David E. Aune*, edited by John Fotopoulos, 257–286. Leiden: Brill, 2006.

Begg, Christopher T., and Paul Spilsbury. *Judean Antiquities 8–10*. Edited by Steve Mason. BJP 5. Leiden: Brill, 2005.

Ben-Shalom, Israel. *The School of Shammai and the Zealots' Struggle against Rome* [Hebrew]. Jerusalem: Yad Ben-Zvi, 1993.

Ben-Yehuda, Nachman. *The Masada Myth: Collective Memory and Mythmaking in Israel*. Madison: University of Wisconsin Press, 1995.

Berger, Peter L. *The Sacred Canopy: Elements of a Sociological Theory of Religion*. New York: Anchor Books, 1969.

Bergmeier, Roland. "Die drei jüdischen Schulrichtungen nach Josephus und Hippolyt von Rom: Zu den Paralleltexten Josephus, *B.J.* 2,119–166 und Hippolyt, *Haer.* IX 18,2–29,4." *JSJ* 34.4 (2003): 443–470.

Bergmeier, Roland. *Die Essener-Berichte des Flavius Josephus: Quellenstudien zu den Essenertexten im Werk des Jüdischen Historiographen*. Kampen, Netherlands: Kok Pharos, 1993.

Bernstein, Moshe J., and Shlomo A. Koyfman. "The Interpretation of Biblical Law in the Dead Sea Scrolls: Forms and Methods." In *Biblical Interpretation at Qumran*, edited by Matthias Henze, 61–87. Grand Rapids, Mich.: Eerdmans, 2005.

Bickerman, E. J. *Studies in Jewish and Christian History: A New Edition in English Including "The God of the Maccabees."* 2 vols. Edited by Amram Tropper. With an introduction by Martin Hengel. Ancient Judaism and Early Christianity 68. Leiden: Brill, 2007.

Bilde, Per. "Josephus and Jewish Apocalypticism." In *Understanding Josephus: Seven Perspectives*, edited by Steve Mason, 35–61. JSPSup 32. Sheffield, England: Sheffield Academic Press, 1998.

Bobzien, Susanne. *Determinism and Freedom in Stoic Philosophy*. Oxford: Clarendon, 1998.

Bobzien, Susanne. "The Inadvertent Conception and Late Birth of the Free-Will Problem." *Phronesis* 43.2 (1998): 133–175.

Boccaccini, Gabriele. *Beyond the Essene Hypothesis: The Parting of the Ways between Qumran and Enochic Judaism*. Grand Rapids, Mich.: Eerdmans, 1998.

Boccaccini, Gabriele. *Middle Judaism: Jewish Thought 300 BCE to 200 CE.* With a foreword by James H. Charlesworth. Minneapolis: Fortress, 1991.

Boccaccini, Gabriele. *Roots of Rabbinic Judaism: An Intellectual History, from Ezekiel to Daniel.* Grand Rapids, Mich.: Eerdmans, 2002.

Boda, Mark J., Daniel K. Falk, and Rodney A. Werline, eds. *Seeking the Favor of God.* Vol. 1. *The Origins of Penitential Prayer in Second Temple Judaism.* EJL 21. Atlanta: Society of Biblical Literature, 2006.

Boda, Mark J., Daniel K. Falk, and Rodney A. Werline, eds. *Seeking the Favor of God.* Vol. 2. *The Development of Penitential Prayer in Second Temple Judaism.* EJL 22. Atlanta: Society of Biblical Literature, 2007.

Boettner, Loraine. *The Reformed Doctrine of Predestination.* Philipsburg, N.J.: Presbyterian and Reformed Publishing Company, 1932.

Bokser, Baruch M. "*Ma'al* and Blessings over Food: Rabbinic Transformation of Cultic Terminology and Alternative Modes of Piety." *JBL* 100.4 (1981): 557–574.

Bokser, Baruch M. "Rabbinic Responses to Catastrophe: From Continuity to Discontinuity." *PAAJR* 50 (1983): 37–61.

Bokser, Baruch M. "The Wall Separating God and Israel." *JQR* 73.4 (1983): 349–374.

Bond, Helen K. *Caiaphas: Friend of Rome and Judge of Jesus?* Louisville, Ky.: Westminster John Knox, 2004.

Bond, Helen K. "New Currents in Josephus Research." *Currents in Research: Biblical Studies* 8 (2000): 162–190.

Bowersock, Glen W. *Martyrdom and Rome.* Cambridge: Cambridge University Press, 1995.

Boyarin, Daniel. *Border Lines: The Partition of Judaeo-Christianity.* Philadelphia: University of Pennsylvania Press, 2004.

Boyarin, Daniel. *Dying for God: Martyrdom and the Making of Christianity and Judaism.* Stanford: Stanford University Press, 1999.

Brighton, Mark Andrew. *The Sicarii in Josephus's "Judean War": Rhetorical Analysis and Historical Observations.* EJL 27. Atlanta: Society of Biblical Literature, 2009.

Buber, Salomon, ed. *Midrash Echah Rabbah.* Vilna: Romm, 1899.

Buber, Salomon, ed. *Midrash Tanhuma.* Vilna: Romm, 1885.

Burchard, Christoph. "Die Essener bei Hippolyt: Hippolyt, *Ref.* IX 18, 2–28, 2 und Josephus, *Bell.* 2, 119–161." *JSJ* 8.1 (1977): 1–41.

Burns, Joshua Ezra. "Essene Sectarianism and Social Differentiation in Judaea after 70 CE." *HTR* 99.3 (2006): 247–274.

Capes, David B., April D. DeConick, Helen K. Bond, and Troy A. Miller, eds. *Israel's God and Rebecca's Children: Christology and Community in Early Judaism and Christianity, Essays in Honor of Larry W. Hurtado and Alan F. Segal.* Waco, Tex.: Baylor University Press, 2007.

Cavallin, Hans Clemens Caesarius. *Life after Death: Paul's Argument for the Resurrection of the Dead in I Cor 15.* Coniectanea biblica: New Testament Series 7. Lund: Gleerup, 1974.

Chapman, Honora Howell. "Masada in the 1st and 21st Centuries." In *Making History: Josephus and Historical Method*, edited by Zuleika Rodgers, 82–102. JSJSup 110. Leiden: Brill, 2007.

Charles, R. H. *The Book of Enoch, or 1 Enoch: Translated from the Editor's Ethiopic Text, and Edited with the Introduction, Notes and Indexes*. 2nd ed. Oxford: Clarendon, 1912.

Cohen, Gerson D. *Studies in the Variety of Rabbinic Cultures*. JPS Scholars of Distinction Series. Philadelphia: Jewish Publication Society, 1991.

Cohen, Shaye J. D. "Alexander and Jaddus According to Josephus." *AJSR* 7–8 (1982–83): 41–68.

Cohen, Shaye J. D. "The Destruction: From Scripture to Midrash." *Prooftexts* 2.1 (1982): 18–39.

Cohen, Shaye J. D. "History and Historiography in the Against Apion of Josephus." *History and Theory* 27.4 (1988): 1–11.

Cohen, Shaye J. D. "Jacob Neusner, Mishnah, and Counter-Rabbinics: A Review Essay." *Conservative Judaism* 37.1 (1983): 48–63.

Cohen, Shaye J. D. *Josephus in Galilee and Rome*. Columbia Studies in the Classical Tradition 8. Leiden: Brill, 1979.

Cohen, Shaye J. D. "Josephus, Jeremiah, and Polybius." *History and Theory* 21.3 (1982): 366–381.

Cohen, Shaye J. D. "Masada: Literary Tradition, Archaeological Remains, and the Credibility of Josephus." *JJS* 33.1–2 (1982): 385–405.

Cohen, Shaye J. D. "The Significance of Yavneh: Pharisees, Rabbis, and the End of Jewish Sectarianism." *HUCA* 55 (1984): 27–53.

Cohen, Shaye J. D. "The Temple and the Synagogue." In *The Cambridge History of Judaism*, vol. 3, *The Early Roman Period*, edited by William Horbury, W. D. Davies, and John Sturdy, 298–325. Cambridge: Cambridge University Press, 1999.

Collins, John J. *Apocalypticism in the Dead Sea Scrolls*. London: Routledge, 1997.

Collins, John J. *Beyond the Qumran Community: The Sectarian Movement of the Dead Sea Scrolls*. Grand Rapids, Mich.: Eerdmans, 2010.

Collins, John J. "The Essenes and the Afterlife." In *From 4QMMT to Resurrection: Mélanges qumraniens en homage à Émile Puech*, edited by Florentino García Martínez, Annette Steudel, and Eibert Tigchelaar, 35–53. STDJ 61. Leiden: Brill, 2006.

Collins, John J. "The Sibylline Oracles, Book 4." In *The Old Testament Pseudepigrapha*, edited by James H. Charlesworth, 2 vols., 1:381–389. Garden City, N.Y.: Doubleday, 1983.

Colson, F. H., and G. H. Whitaker, eds. and trans. *Philo of Alexandria*. 10 vols., with 2 supp. volumes translated by Ralph Marcus. LCL. Cambridge, Mass.: Harvard University Press, 1929–62.

Coogan, Michael D., ed., with Marc Z. Brettler and Pheme Perkins, associate eds. *The New Oxford Annotated Bible, New Revised Standard Version with Apocrypha: Fully Revised Fourth Edition*. New York: Oxford University Press, 2010.

Crenshaw, James L. *Ecclesiastes: A Commentary.* Old Testament Library. Philadelphia: Westminster, 1987.

Crenshaw, James L. "Gold Dust or Nuggets? A Brief Response to J. Kenneth Kuntz." *CBR* 1.2 (2003): 155–158.

Crenshaw, James L. "Method in Determining Wisdom Influence upon 'Historical' Literature." *JBL* 88.2 (1969): 129–142.

Crenshaw, James L. *Old Testament Wisdom: An Introduction.* 3rd ed. Louisville, Ky.: Westminster John Knox, 2010.

Crenshaw, James L. "The Problem of Theodicy in Sirach: On Human Bondage." *JBL* 94.1 (1975): 47–64.

Crenshaw, James L. "Wisdom Psalms?" *Currents in Research: Biblical Studies* 8 (2000): 9–17.

Cross, Frank Moore. *The Ancient Library of Qumran.* 3rd ed. Minneapolis: Fortress, 1995.

Cross, Frank Moore. *Canaanite Myth and Hebrew Epic: Essays in the History of the Religion of Israel.* Cambridge, Mass.: Harvard University Press, 1973.

Danby, Herbert. *The Mishnah: Translated from the Hebrew with Introduction and Brief Explanatory Notes.* Oxford: Oxford University Press, 1933.

Daube, David. "Typology in Josephus." *JJS* 31.1 (1980): 18–36.

Dennett, Daniel C. *Elbow Room: The Varieties of Free Will Worth Wanting.* Cambridge, Mass.: MIT Press, 1984.

Dexinger, Ferdinand. "Samaritan Eschatology." In *The Samaritans,* edited by Alan D. Crown, 266–292. Tübingen: Mohr Siebeck, 1989.

Diamond, Eliezer. *Holy Men and Hunger Artists: Fasting and Asceticism in Rabbinic Culture.* New York: Oxford University Press, 2004.

Di Lella, Alexander A. "Conservative and Progressive Theology: Sirach and Wisdom." *CBQ* 28.2 (1966): 139–153.

Dillon, John. *The Middle Platonists: 80 B.C. to A.D. 220.* Rev. ed. with a new afterword. Ithaca, N.Y.: Cornell University Press, 1996.

Dillon, John. "Plutarch and Second Century Platonism." In *Classical Mediterranean Spirituality: Egyptian, Greek, Roman,* edited by Arthur Hilary Armstrong, 214–229. World Spirituality 15. New York: Crossroad, 1987.

Dimant, Devorah. *Qumran Cave 4, XXVI: Parabiblical Texts.* Pt. 4. *Pseudo-Prophetic Texts.* Partially based on earlier transcriptions by John Strugnell. DJD 30. Oxford: Clarendon, 2001.

Diner, Hasia R. *We Remember with Reverence and Love: American Jews and the Myth of Silence after the Holocaust, 1945–1962.* New York: New York University Press, 2009.

DiTommaso, Lorenzo. "Apocalypses and Apocalypticism in Antiquity (Part II)." *CBR* 5.3 (2007): 367–432.

Donnelly, Doris, and John Pawlikowski. "Lovingly Observant." Interview with Susannah Heschel. *America* 196.21 (2007): 10–13.

Douglas, Mary. *Natural Symbols: Explorations in Cosmology.* 1970. Reprint, with a new introduction, London: Routledge, 1996.

Douglas, Mary. *Purity and Danger: An Analysis of the Concepts of Pollution and Taboo.* 1966. Reprint, with a new preface, London: Routledge, 2002.

Droge, Arthur J., and James D. Tabor. *A Noble Death: Suicide and Martyrdom among Christians and Jews in Antiquity.* New York: HarperSanFrancisco, 1992.

Drosnin, Michael. *The Bible Code.* New York: Simon and Schuster, 1997.

Duhaime, Jean. "Determinism." In *The Encyclopedia of the Dead Sea Scrolls.* Edited by Lawrence H. Schiffman and James C. VanderKam, 2 vols., 1:194–198. New York: Oxford University Press, 2000.

Ehrenkrook, Jason von. *Sculpting Idolatry in Flavian Rome: (An)iconic Rhetoric in the Writings of Flavius Josephus.* EJL 33. Atlanta: Society of Biblical Literature, 2011.

Elbogen, Ismar. *Jewish Liturgy: A Comprehensive History.* 1931. Reprint, Translated by Raymond P. Scheindlin. Philadelphia: Jewish Publication Society, 1993.

Eliade, Mircea, ed. *The Encyclopedia of Religion.* 16 vols. New York: Macmillan, 1987.

Elior, Rachel. *Memory and Oblivion: The Mystery of the Dead Sea Scrolls* [Hebrew]. Jerusalem: Van Leer Institute, 2009.

Elior, Rachel. *The Three Temples: On the Emergence of Jewish Mysticism.* Translated by David Louvish. London: Littman Library of Jewish Civilization, 2004.

Elledge, C. D. "Future Resurrection of the Dead in Early Judaism: Social Dynamics, Contested Evidence." *CBR* 9.3 (2011): 394–421.

Elledge, C. D. *Life after Death in Early Judaism: The Evidence of Josephus.* WUNT 2, 208. Tübingen: Mohr Siebeck, 2006.

Epstein, Isidore, ed. *The Soncino Translation of the Babylonian Talmud.* 18 vols. London: Soncino Press, 1961.

Epstein, Jacob N. *Introduction to the Text of the Mishnah* [Hebrew]. 2 vols. 2nd ed. Jerusalem: Magnes Press, 1964.

Erder, Yoram. "The Karaites and the Second Temple Sects." In *Karaite Judaism: A Guide to Its History and Literary Sources,* edited by Meira Polliack, 119–143. Leiden: Brill, 2003.

Eshel, Hanan. *The Dead Sea Scrolls and the Hasmonean State.* Translated by David Louvish and Aryeh Amihay. Grand Rapids, Mich.: Eerdmans, 2008.

Eshel, Hanan. "Josephus' View on Judaism without the Temple in Light of the Discoveries at Masada and Murabba'at." In *Gemeinde ohne Tempel: Zur Substituierung und Transformation des Jerusalemer Tempels und seines Kults im Alten Testament, antiken Judentum und frühen Christentum,* edited by Beate Ego, Armin Lange, and Peter Pilhofer, in cooperation with Kathrin Ehlers, 229–238. WUNT 1, 118. Tübingen: Mohr Siebeck 1999.

Feinberg, John S. "God Ordains All Things." In *Predestination and Free Will: Four Views of Divine Sovereignty and Human Freedom (John Feinberg, Norman Geisler, Bruce Reichenbach, Clark Pinnock),* edited by David Basinger and Randall Basinger, 19–43. Downers Grove, Ill.: IVP Academic, 1986.

Feldman, Louis H. "The Identity of Pollio, the Pharisee, in Josephus." *JQR* 49.1 (1958): 53–62.

Feldman, Louis H. *Josephus's Interpretation of the Bible*. Hellenistic Culture and Society 27. Berkeley: University of California Press, 1998.

Feldman, Louis H. *Judean Antiquities 1–4: Translation and Commentary*. Edited by Steve Mason. BJP 3. Leiden: Brill, 2000.

Feldman, Louis H. "A Select Critical Bibliography of Josephus." In *Josephus, the Bible, and History*, edited by Louis H. Feldman and Gohei Hata, 330–448. Detroit: Wayne State University Press, 1989.

Feldman, Louis H. *Studies in Josephus' Rewritten Bible*. JSJSup 58. Leiden: Brill, 1998.

Feldman, Louis H. "Torah and Greek Culture in Josephus." *Torah U-Madda Journal* 7 (1997): 47–87.

Feldman, Louis H., and Gohei Hata, eds. *Josephus, Judaism and Christianity*. Detroit: Wayne State University Press, 1987.

Feldman, Louis H., and Gohei Hata, eds. *Josephus, the Bible, and History*. Detroit: Wayne State University Press, 1989.

Fine, Steven. "A Note on Ossuary Burial and the Resurrection of the Dead in First-Century Judaism." *JJS* 51.1 (2000): 69–76.

Finkelstein, Louis. *The Pharisees: The Sociological Background of Their Faith*. 3rd ed. With supp. 2 vols. Philadelphia: Jewish Publication Society, 1962.

Finkelstein, Louis, ed. *Sifre on Deuteronomy* [Hebrew]. 1939. Reprint, New York: Jewish Theological Seminary, 1993.

Fitzgerald, Timothy. *The Ideology of Religious Studies*. New York: Oxford University Press, 2000.

Fleischer, Ezra. "On the Beginnings of Obligatory Jewish Prayer" [Hebrew]. *Tarbiz* 59.3–4 (1990): 397–441.

Flusser, David. "Josephus on the Sadducees and Menander." *Immanuel* 7 (1977): 61–67.

Flusser, David. "*Josippon*, a Medieval Hebrew Version of Josephus." In *Josephus, Judaism and Christianity*, edited by Louis H. Feldman and Gohei Hata, 386–397. Detroit: Wayne State University Press, 1987.

Flusser, David. *The Josippon [Josephus Gorionides]: Edited with an Introduction, Commentary and Notes*. Vol. 1. *Text and Commentary* [Hebrew]. 2nd corrected ed. Jerusalem: Bialik Institute, 1981.

Flusser, David. *Judaism and the Origins of Christianity*. Jerusalem: Magnes Press, 1988.

Flusser, David. *Judaism of the Second Temple Period*. Vol. 1. *Qumran and Apocalypticism*. Edited by Serge Ruzer. Translated by Azzan Yadin. Jerusalem: Magnes Press, 2007.

Flusser, David. *Judaism of the Second Temple Period*. Vol. 2. *The Jewish Sages and Their Literature*. Edited by Serge Ruzer. Translated by Azzan Yadin. Grand Rapids, Mich.: Eerdmans; Jerusalem: Magnes Press, 2009.

Flusser, David. "The Pharisees and the Stoic Sages according to Josephus" [Hebrew]. *Iyyun* 14 (1963): 318–329 (English summary 366–367). English translation in Flusser, *Judaism of the Second Temple Period*, vol. 2, *The Jewish Sages and Their Literature*, edited by Serge Ruzer and translated by Azzan Yadin, 221–231. Jerusalem: Magnes Press, 2009.

Fonrobert, Charlotte Elisheva. "From Separatism to Urbanism: The Dead Sea Scrolls and the Origins of the Rabbinic 'Eruv.'" *DSD* 11.1 (2004): 43–71.

Fowler, Harold North, ed. and trans. *Plato, with an English Translation*. Vol. 1. *Euthyphro, Apology, Crito, Phaedo, Phaedrus*. LCL. Cambridge, Mass.: Harvard University Press, 1917.

Fox, Michael V. *A Time to Tear Down and a Time to Build Up: A Rereading of Ecclesiastes*. Grand Rapids, Mich.: Eerdmans, 1999.

Fraade, Steven D. *Legal Fictions: Studies of Law and Narrative in the Discursive Worlds of Ancient Jewish Sectarians and Sages*. JSJSup 147. Leiden: Brill, 2011.

Frede, Dorothea. "Stoic Determinism." In *The Cambridge Companion to the Stoics*, edited by Brad Inwood, 179–205. Cambridge: Cambridge University Press, 2003.

Fuks, Gideon. "Josephus on Herod's Attitude towards Jewish Religion: The Darker Side." *JJS* 53.3 (2002): 238–245.

Gafni, Isaiah. "Historical Background." In *Jewish Writings of the Second Temple Period: Apocrypha, Pseudepigrapha, Qumran Sectarian Writings, Philo, Josephus*, edited by Michael Stone, 1–31. CRINT II.2. Assen: Van Gorcum, 1984.

Gafni, Isaiah. "Josephus and I Maccabees." In *Josephus, the Bible, and History*, edited by Louis H. Feldman and Gohei Hata, 116–131. Detroit: Wayne State University Press, 1989.

Gammie, John G. "Stoicism and Anti-Stoicism in Qoheleth." *Hebrew Annual Review* 9 (1985): 169–187.

García Martínez, Florentino, and Eibert J. C. Tigchelaar, eds. *The Dead Sea Scrolls Study Edition*. 2nd ed. 2 vols. Leiden: Brill, 2000.

Geiger, Abraham. *Judaism and Its History, in Two Parts*. Translated by Charles Newburgh. New York: Bloch, 1911.

Geiger, Abraham. *Urschrift und Übersetzungen der Bibel, in ihrer Abhängigkeit von der innern Entwickelung des Judentums*. Frankfurt am Main: Verlag Madda, 1928.

Geller, M. J. "Alexander Jannaeus and the Pharisee Rift." *JJS* 30.2 (1979): 202–211.

Gillman, Neil. *Doing Jewish Theology: God, Torah and Israel in Modern Judaism*. Woodstock, Vt.: Jewish Lights, 2008.

Ginsburg, Christian D. *The Essenes: Their History and Doctrines*. London: Longman, Green, 1864.

Ginzberg, Louis. *An Unknown Jewish Sect*. Moreshet 1. New York: Jewish Theological Seminary, 1976.

Goff, Matthew. "Recent Trends in the Study of Early Jewish Wisdom Literature: The Contribution of 4QInstruction and Other Qumran Texts." *CBR* 7.3 (2009): 376–416.

Golb, Norman. *Who Wrote the Dead Sea Scrolls? The Search for the Secret of Qumran.* New York: Scribner, 1995.

Goldenberg, David M. Review of *Die "väterlichen Gesetze": Flavius Josephus als Vermittler von Halachah an Greischen und Römer*, by Bernd Schröder. *International Journal of the Classical Tradition* 8.1 (2001): 125–127.

Goldenberg, Robert. "The Broken Axis: Rabbinic Judaism and the Fall of Jerusalem." *JAAR* 45.3 supp. (1977): F 869–882.

Goldenberg, Robert. "The Destruction of the Jerusalem Temple: Its Meanings and Its Consequences." In *The Cambridge History of Judaism*, vol. 4, *The Late Roman-Rabbinic Period*, edited by Steven T. Katz, 191–205. Cambridge: Cambridge University Press, 2006.

Goodblatt, David. *Elements of Ancient Jewish Nationalism.* Cambridge: Cambridge University Press, 2006.

Goodblatt, David. "Suicide in the Sanctuary: Traditions on Priestly Martyrdom." *JJS* 46.1–2 (1995): 10–29.

Goodenough, Erwin R. "Philo on Immortality." *HTR* 39.2 (1946): 85–108.

Goodman, Martin. "A Note on Josephus, the Pharisees, and Ancestral Tradition." *JJS* 50.1 (1999): 17–20.

Goodman, Martin. "Religious Variety and the Temple in the Late Second Temple Period and Its Aftermath." *JJS* 60.2 (2009): 202–213.

Goodman, Martin. *Rome and Jerusalem: The Clash of Ancient Civilizations.* New York: Knopf, 2007.

Goodman, Martin. *The Ruling Class of Judaea: The Origins of the Jewish Revolt against Rome A.D. 66–70.* Cambridge: Cambridge University Press, 1987.

Goodman, Martin. "Sadducees and Essenes after 70 CE." In *Crossing the Boundaries: Essays in Biblical Interpretation in Honour of Michael D. Goulder*, edited by S. E. Porter, P. Joyce, and D. E. Orton, 347–356. Leiden: Brill, 1994.

Goren, Shlomo. "Fighting on the Sabbath According to the Sources" [Hebrew]. In *Sinai, Jubilee Volume*, edited by Y. L. ha-Cohen Maimon, 149–189. Jerusalem: Mosad ha-Rav Kook, 1958.

Gottstein, M. H. "Anti-Essene Traits in the Dead Sea Scrolls." *VT* 4.2 (1954): 141–147.

Grabbe, Lester L. *Judaic Religion in the Second Temple Period: Belief and Practice from the Exile to Yavneh.* London: Routledge, 2000.

Grabbe, Lester L. "The Law, the Prophets, and the Rest: The State of the Bible in Pre-Maccabean Times." *DSD* 13.3 (2006): 319–338.

Grabbe, Lester L. "The Pharisees: A Response to Steve Mason." In *Judaism in Late Antiquity*, pt. 3, vol. 3, *Where We Stand: Issues and Debates in Ancient Judaism*, edited by Jacob Neusner and Alan J. Avery-Peck, 35–47. Leiden: Brill, 2000.

Gray, Rebecca. *Prophetic Figures in Late Second Temple Palestine: The Evidence from Josephus.* New York: Oxford University Press, 1993.

Grossman, Maxine, L. "Priesthood as Authority: Interpretive Competition in First-Century Judaism and Christianity." In *The Dead Sea Scrolls as Background to*

Postbiblical Judaism and Early Christianity: Papers from an International Conference at St. Andrews in 2001, edited by James R. Davila, 117–131. Leiden: Brill, 2003.

Grossman, Maxine, L. "Reading 4QMMT: Genre and History." *RevQ* 77/20.1 (2001): 3–22.

Grossman, Maxine, L., ed. *Rediscovering the Dead Sea Scrolls: An Assessment of Old and New Approaches and Methods.*Grand Rapids, Mich.: Eerdmans, 2010.

Haaland, Gunnar. "Josephus and the Philosophers of Rome: Does *Contra Apionem* Mirror Domitian's Crushing of the 'Stoic Opposition'?" In *Josephus and Jewish History in Flavian Rome and Beyond,* edited by Joseph Sievers and Gaia Lembi, 297–316. JSJSup 104. Leiden: Brill, 2005.

Haaland, Gunnar. "What Difference Does Philosophy Make? The Three Schools as a Rhetorical Device in Josephus." In *Making History: Josephus and Historical Method,* edited by Zuleika Rodgers, 262–288. JSJSup 110. Leiden: Brill, 2007.

Hadas, Moses. *The Third and Fourth Books of Maccabees: Edited and Translated.* Jewish Apocryphal Literature. New York: Harper (for Philadelphia: Dropsie College), 1953.

Halivni, David Weiss. *Breaking the Tablets: Jewish Theology after the Shoah.* Edited and with an introduction by Peter Ochs. Lanham, Md.: Rowman and Littlefield, 2007.

Halivni, David Weiss. *Midrash, Mishnah, and Gemara: The Jewish Predilection for Justified Law.* Cambridge, Mass.: Harvard University Press, 1986.

Halivni, David Weiss. "Reflections on Classical Jewish Hermeneutics." *PAAJR* 62 (1996): 19–127.

Halpern-Amaru, Betsy. "Flavius Josephus and *The Book of Jubilees.*" *HUCA* 72 (2001): 15–44.

Halpern-Amaru, Betsy. "Land Theology in Josephus' *Jewish Antiquities.*" *JQR* 71.4 (1981): 201–229.

Hardwick, Michael E. *Josephus as an Historical Source in Patristic Literature through Eusebius.* BJS 128. Atlanta: Scholars Press, 1989.

Hart, D. G. *The University Gets Religion: Religious Studies in American Higher Education.* Baltimore: Johns Hopkins University Press, 1999.

Hata, Gohei. "Is the Greek Version of Josephus' 'Jewish War' a Translation or a Rewriting of the First Version?" *JQR* 66.2 (1975): 89–108.

Hauer, Christian E., Jr. "Who Was Zadok?" *JBL* 82.1 (1963): 89–94.

Hayes, Christine E. *Gentile Impurities and Jewish Identities: Intermarriage and Conversion from the Bible to the Talmud.* New York: Oxford University Press, 2002.

Hayes, Christine E. "*Halakhah le-Moshe mi-Sinai* in Rabbinic Sources: A Methodological Case Study." In *The Synoptic Problem in Rabbinic Literature,* edited by Shaye J. D. Cohen, 61–117. BJS 326. Providence: Brown Judaic Studies, 2000.

Hayward, Robert. "The Jewish Temple at Leontopolis: A Reconsideration." *JJS* 33.1–2 (1982): 429–443.

Heger, Paul. *Cult as the Catalyst for Division: Cult Disputes as the Motive for Schism in the Pre-70 Pluralistic Environment.* STDJ 65. Leiden: Brill, 2007.

Helberg, J. L. "The Determination of History According to the Book of Daniel, against the Background of Deterministic Apocalyptic." *Zeitschrift für die alttestamentliche Wissenschaft* 107.2 (1995): 273–287.

Hengel, Martin. *Judaism and Hellenism: Studies in Their Encounter in Palestine during the Early Hellenistic Period.* Translated by John Bowden. Minneapolis: Fortress, 1974.

Hengel, Martin. *The Zealots: Investigations into the Jewish Freedom Movement in the Period from Herod I until 70 A.D.* Translated by David Smith. Edinburgh: T. and T. Clark, 1989.

Hengel, Martin, with Christoph Markshies. *The "Hellenization" of Judaea in the First Century after Christ.* London: SCM Press, 1989.

Henten, Jan Willem van. *The Maccabean Martyrs as Saviours of the Jewish People: A Study of 2 & 4 Maccabees.* JSJSup 57. Leiden: Brill, 1997.

Henten, Jan Willem van. "Noble Death in Josephus: Just Rhetoric?" In *Making History: Josephus and Historical Method,* edited by Zuleika Rodgers, 195–218. JSJSup 110. Leiden: Brill, 2007.

Herford, R. Travers. *The Effect of the Fall of Jerusalem on the Character of the Pharisees.* London: Society for Hebraic Studies, 1917.

Herford, R. Travers. *The Ethics of the Talmud: Sayings of the Fathers.* 1925. Reprint, New York: Schocken, 1962.

Hertz, Joseph. *Sayings of the Fathers.* New York: Behrmann House, 1945.

Heschel, Abraham Joshua. *Heavenly Torah: As Refracted through the Generations.* Edited and translated by Gordon Tucker. New York: Continuum, 2007.

Heschel, Abraham Joshua. *Man is Not Alone: A Philosophy of Religion.* New York: Farrar, Strauss, and Giroux, 1951.

Heschel, Susannah. *Abraham Geiger and the Jewish Jesus.* Chicago: University of Chicago Press, 1998.

Hoenig, Sidney B. "The Sicarii in Masada—Glory or Infamy." *Tradition* 11.1 (1970): 5–30.

Horbury, William. "The Christian Use and the Jewish Origins of the Wisdom of Solomon." In *Wisdom in Ancient Israel: Essays in Honour of J. A. Emerton,* edited by John Day, Robert P. Gordon, and H. G. M. Williamson, 182–196. Cambridge: Cambridge University Press, 1995.

Horovitz, H. S., ed. *Siphre D'Be Rab, Fasciculus primus: Siphre ad Numeros adjecto Siphre zutta.* 1917. Reprint, Jerusalem: Shalem, 1992.

Horovitz, H. S., and I. A. Rabin, eds. *Mechilta D'Rabbi Ismael.* 1930. Reprint, Jerusalem: Wahrmann Books, 1970.

Horsley, Richard. "Wisdom and Apocalypticism in Mark." In *In Search of Wisdom: Essays in Memory of John G. Gammie,* edited by Leo G., Perdue, Bernard Brandon Scott, and William Johnston Wiseman, 223–244. Louisville, Ky.: Westminster John Knox, 1993.

Huitink, Luuk, and Jan Willem van Henten. "The Publication of Flavius Josephus' Works and Their Audiences." *Zutot* 6.1 (2009): 49–60.

Hultgren, Stephen. "Rabbi Akiba on Divine Providence and Human Freedom: 'Abot 3:15–16 and 'Abot de Rabbi Nathan (B) 22:13–15." *Jewish Studies Quarterly* 18.2 (2011): 107–143.

Ilan, Tal. *Integrating Women into Second Temple History*. TSAJ 76. Tübingen: Mohr Siebeck, 1999.

Inowlocki, Sabrina. "Did Josephus Ascribe the Fall of Jerusalem to the Murder of James, Brother of Jesus?" *Revue des études juives* 170.1–2 (2011): 21–49.

Inowlocki, Sabrina. "'Neither Adding nor Omitting Anything': Josephus' Promise Not to Modify the Scriptures in Greek and Latin Context." *JJS* 56.1 (2005): 48–65.

Inwagen, Peter van. "An Argument for Incompatibilism." In *Free Will*, edited by Gary Watson, 2nd ed., 38–57. New York: Oxford University Press, 2003.

Jaffee, Martin S. *Early Judaism*. Upper Saddle River, N.J.: Prentice Hall, 1997.

James, William. "The Dilemma of Determinism." In *The Will to Believe: And Other Essays in Popular Philosophy*, 145–183. 1896. Reprint, New York: Dover, 1956.

James, William. *The Varieties of Religious Experience: A Study in Human Nature*. 1902. Reprint, New York: Vintage, 1990.

Jassen, Alex P. "Religion in the Dead Sea Scrolls." *Religion Compass* 1.1 (2005): 1–25.

Jones, Kenneth R. *Jewish Reactions to the Destruction of Jerusalem in A.D. 70: Apocalypses and Related Pseudepigrapha*. JSJSup 151. Leiden: Brill, 2011.

Kalimi, Isaac. "The Book of Esther and the Dead Sea Scrolls' Community." *Theologische Zeitschrift* 60.2 (2004): 101–106.

Kalimi, Isaac. "Murder in Jerusalem Temple, the Chronicler's Story of Zechariah: Literary and Theological Features, Historical Credibility, and Impact." *RB* 117.2 (2010): 200–209.

Kalimi, Isaac. "The Murder of the Prophet Zechariah in the Gospels." *RB* 116.2 (2009): 246–261.

Kalimi, Isaac. "The Murders of the Messengers: Stephen versus Zechariah and the Ethical Values of the 'New' versus 'Old' Testament." *Australian Biblical Review* 56 (2008): 67–73.

Kalmin, Richard. *Jewish Babylonia between Persia and Roman Palestine*. New York: Oxford University Press, 2006.

Kalmin, Richard. *The Redaction of the Babylonian Talmud: Amoraic or Saboraic?* Cincinnati: Hebrew Union College Press, 1989.

Kant, Immanuel. "On the Failure of All Attempted Philosophical Theodicies." In *Kant on History and Religion*, edited and translated by Michel Despland, 283–297. Montreal: McGill-Queen's University Press, 1973.

Katz, Steven T. *The Holocaust in Historical Context*. Vol. 1. *The Holocaust and Mass Death before the Modern Age*. New York: Oxford University Press, 1994.

Katz, Steven T., Shlomo Biderman, and Gershon Greenberg, eds. *Wrestling with God: Jewish Theological Responses during and after the Holocaust*. New York: Oxford University Press, 2007.

Kelley, Nicole. "The Cosmopolitan Expression of Josephus's Prophetic Perspective in the 'Jewish War.'" *HTR* 97.3 (2004): 257–274.

King, Karen L. *What Is Gnosticism?* Cambridge, Mass.: Harvard University Press, 2003.

Kirschner, Robert. "Apocalyptic and Rabbinic Responses to the Destruction of 70." *HTR* 78.1–2 (1985): 27–46.

Kister, Menahem. "Studies in 4Miqsat Ma'aseh ha-Torah and Related Texts: Law, Theology, Language and Calendar" [Hebrew]. *Tarbiz* 68.3 (1999): 317–372.

Klawans, Jonathan. "The Dead Sea Scrolls, the Essenes, and the Study of Religious Beliefs: Determinism and Freedom of Choice." In *Rediscovering the Dead Sea Scrolls: An Assessment of Old and New Approaches and Methods*, edited by Maxine L. Grossman, 264–283. Grand Rapids, Mich.: Eerdmans, 2010.

Klawans, Jonathan. *Impurity and Sin in Ancient Judaism.* New York: Oxford University Press, 2000.

Klawans, Jonathan. "Josephus on Fate, Free Will and Ancient Jewish Types of Compatibilism." *Numen* 56.1 (2009): 44–90.

Klawans, Jonathan. "Josephus, the Rabbis, and Responses to Catastrophes Ancient and Modern." *JQR* 100.2 (2010): 278–309.

Klawans, Jonathan. "The Prohibition of Oaths and 'Contra-scriptural *Halakhot*': A Response to John Meier." *Journal for the Study of the Historical Jesus* 6.1 (2008): 33–48.

Klawans, Jonathan. "Purity in the Dead Sea Scrolls." In *The Oxford Handbook of the Dead Sea Scrolls*, edited by Timothy Lim and John J. Collins, 377–402. Oxford: Oxford University Press, 2010.

Klawans, Jonathan. *Purity, Sacrifice, and the Temple: Symbolism and Supersessionism in the Study of Ancient Judaism.* New York: Oxford University Press, 2005.

Klawans, Jonathan. Review of *Torah in the New Testament*, edited by Micahel Tait and Peter Oakes. *CBQ* 73.3 (2011): 671–672.

Klawans, Jonathan. "Sadducees, Zadokites, and the Wisdom of Ben Sira." In *Israel's God and Rebecca's Children: Christology and Community in Early Judaism and Christianity, Essays in Honor of Larry W. Hurtado and Alan F. Segal*, edited by David B. Capes, April D. DeConick, Helen K. Bond, and Troy A. Miller, 261–276. Waco, Tex.: Baylor University Press, 2007.

Kloppenborg, John S. "*Evocatio Deorum* and the Date of Mark." *JBL* 124.3 (2005): 419–450.

Kohler, Kaufman. "The Halakik Portions in Josephus' Antiquities (IV, 8, 5–43)." In *Studies, Addresses and Personal Papers*, 69–85. New York: Alumni Association of the Hebrew Union College, 1931.

Kraabel, A. Thomas. "Pronoia at Sardis." In *Te'udah XII: Studies on the Jewish Diaspora in the Hellenistic and Roman Periods*, edited by Benjamin Isaac and Aharon Oppenheimer, 75–96. Tel-Aviv: Tel-Aviv University (Ramot Publishing), 1996.

Kroll, John H. "The Greek Inscriptions of the Sardis Synagogue." *HTR* 94.1 (2001): 5–55.

Kugel, James L. *Early Biblical Interpretation*. Philadelphia: Westminster Press, 1986.

Kugler, Robert A. "Priesthood at Qumran." In *The Dead Sea Scrolls after Fifty Years: A Comprehensive Assessment*, edited by P. W. Flint and J. C. VanderKam, 2 vols., 2:93–116. Leiden: Brill, 1999.

Kuntz, J. Kenneth. "Reclaiming Biblical Wisdom Psalms: A Response to Crenshaw." *CBR* 1.2 (2003): 145–154.

Kushner, Harold S. *When Bad Things Happen to Good People*. New York: Schocken 1981.

Ladouceur, David J. "Josephus and Masada." In *Josephus, Judaism and Christianity*, edited by Louis H. Feldman and Gohei Hata, 95–113. Detroit: Wayne State University Press, 1987.

Ladouceur, David J. "Masada: A Consideration of the Literary Evidence." *Greek, Roman, and Byzantine Studies* 21.3 (1980): 245–260.

Lange, Armin. "Wisdom and Predestination in the Dead Sea Scrolls." *DSD* 2.3 (1995): 340–354.

Lasker, Daniel J. *From Judah Hadassi to Elijah Bashyatchi: Studies in Late Medieval Karaite Philosophy*. Supplements to Journal of Jewish Thought and Philosophy 4. Leiden: Brill, 2008.

Lauterbach, Jacob Z., ed. *Mekilta de-Rabbi Ishmael: A Critical Edition on the Basis of the Manuscripts and Early Editions with an English Translation, Introduction and Notes*. Philadelphia: Jewish Publication Society, 1933.

Lauterbach, Jacob Z. *Rabbinic Essays*. New York: Ktav, 1973.

Lee, Pilchan. *The New Jerusalem in the Book of Revelation: A Study of Revelation 21–22 in Light of Its Background in Jewish Tradition*. WUNT 2, 129. Tübingen: Mohr Siebeck, 2001.

Legge, F., trans. *Philosophumena: Or The Refutation of All Heresies, Formerly Attributed to Origen, but Now to Hippolytus, Bishop and Martyr, Who Flourished about 220 A.D. Translated from the Text of Cruice*. 2 vols. Translations of Christian Literature, series 1: Greek Texts. London: Society for Promoting Christian Knowledge, 1921.

Leeming, H. "*Josephus slavonice* versus *Josephus graece*: Towards a Typology of Divergence." *Slavonic and East European Review* 83.1 (2005): 1–13.

Leeming, H., and K. Leeming, eds. *Josephus' Jewish War and Its Slavonic Version: A Synoptic Comparison of the English Translation by H. St. J. Thackeray with the Critical Edition by N. A. Meščerskij of the Slavonic Version in the Vilna Manuscript Translated into English by H. Leeming and L. Osinkina*. AGJU 46. Leiden: Brill, 2003.

Le Moyne, Jean. *Les Sadducéens*. Etudes bibliques. Paris: Librairie Lecoffre, 1972.

Leoni, Tommaso. "The Text of Josephus's Works: An Overview." *JSJ* 40.2 (2009): 149–184.

Leoni, Tommaso. "Translations and Adaptations of Josephus's Writings in Antiquity and the Middle Ages." *Ostraka: Rivista di antichità* 16.2 (2007): 481–492.

Leszynsky, Rudolf. *Die Sadduzäer.* Berlin: Mayer und Müller, 1912.

Levenson, Jon D. *Resurrection and the Restoration of Israel: The Ultimate Victory of the God of Life.* New Haven: Yale University Press, 2006.

Levine, Lee I. *Judaism and Hellenism in Antiquity: Conflict or Confluence?* Seattle: University of Washington Press, 1998.

Licht, Jacob. *The Thanksgiving Scroll: A Scroll from the Wilderness of Judaea* [Hebrew]. Jerusalem: Bialik Institute, 1957.

Lichtenberger, Herman. "Zion and the Destruction of the Temple in 4 Ezra 9–10." In *Gemeinde ohne Tempel: Zur Substituierung und Transformation des Jerusalemer Tempels und seines Kults im Alten Testament, antiken Judentum und frühen Christentum*, edited by Beate Ego, Armin Lange, and Peter Pilhofer, in cooperation with Kathrin Ehlers, 239–249. WUNT 1, 118. Tübingen: Mohr Siebeck, 1999.

Long, A. A., and D. N. Sedley. *The Hellenistic Philosophers.* Vol. 1. *Translations of the Principal Sources, with Philosophical Commentary.* Cambridge: Cambridge University Press, 1987.

Luz, Menahem. "Eleazar's Second Speech on Masada and Its Literary Precedents." *Rheinisches Museum für Philologie* 126 (1983): 25–43.

Machinist, Peter. "Fate, *miqreh*, and Reason: Some Reflections on Qohelet and Biblical Thought." In *Solving Riddles and Untying Knots: Biblical Epigraphic and Semitic Studies in Honor of Jonas C. Greenfield*, edited by Ziony Zevit, Seymour Gitin, and Michael Sokoloff, 159–175. Winona Lake, Ind.: Eisenbrauns, 1995.

Magness, Jodi. "The Arch of Titus at Rome and the Fate of the God of Israel." *JJS* 59.2 (2008): 201–217.

Magness, Jodi. *The Archaeology of Qumran and the Dead Sea Scrolls.* Grand Rapids, Mich.: Eerdmans, 2002.

Magness, Jodi. *Stone and Dung, Oil and Spit: Jewish Daily Life in the Time of Jesus.* Grand Rapids, Mich.: Eerdmans, 2011.

Maier, Gerhard. *Mensch und freier Wille: Nach den jüdischen Religionspartien zwischen Ben Sira und Paulus.* WUNT 1, 12. Tübingen: Mohr Siebeck, 1981.

Main, Emmanuelle. "Les Sadducéens vus par Flavius Josèphe." *RB* 97.2 (1990): 161–206.

Mandel, Paul. "The Loss of Center: Changing Attitudes towards the Temple in Aggadic Literature." *HTR* 99.1 (2006): 17–35.

Mandel, Paul. "Midrashic Exegesis and Its Precedents in the Dead Sea Scrolls." *DSD* 8.2 (2001): 149–168.

Mandel, Paul. "Scriptural Exegesis and the Pharisees in Josephus." *JJS* 58.1 (2007): 19–32.

Mandelbaum, Bernard. *Pesikta de Rav Kahana: According to an Oxford Manuscript, with Variants from All Known Manuscripts and Genizoth Fragments and Parallel*

Passages, with Commentary and Introduction. 2 vols. New York: Jewish Theological Seminary, 1987.

Mankowitz, Zeev W. *Life between Memory and Hope: The Survivors of the Holocaust in Occupied Germany.* Cambridge: Cambridge University Press, 2002.

Mansfeld, Jaap. *Heresiography in Context: Hippolytus' "Elenchos" as a Source for Greek Philosophy.* Leiden: Brill, 1992.

Mansfeld, Jaap. "Resurrection Added: The *interpretatio christiana* of a Stoic Doctrine." *Vigiliae Christianae* 37.3 (1983): 218–233.

Mansoor, Menahem. *The Thanksgiving Hymns: Translated and Annotated with an Introduction.* STDJ 3. Leiden: Brill, 1961.

Marcovich, Miroslav, ed. *Hippolytus: Refutatio omnium haeresium.* Patristische Texte und Studien 25. New York: de Gruyter, 1986.

Marcus, Ralph. "The Pharisees in the Light of Modern Scholarship." *Journal of Religion* 32.3 (1952): 153–164.

Margolis, Max L., and Alexander Marx. *A History of the Jewish People.* Philadelphia: Jewish Publication Society, 1927.

Margulies, Mordecai, ed. *Midrash Wayyikra Rabbah: A Critical Edition Based on Manuscripts and Genizah Fragments with Variants and Notes* [Hebrew]. 3rd ed. 2 vols. New York: Jewish Theological Seminary, 1993.

Martin, Luther H. "Josephus' Use of *Heimarmene* in the *Jewish Antiquities* XIII, 171–173." *Numen* 28.9 (1982): 127–137.

Martone, Carrado. "Qumran and Stoicism: An Analysis of Some Common Traits." In *The Dead Sea Scrolls Fifty Years after Their Discovery: Proceedings of the Jerusalem Congress, July 20–25, 1997,* edited by Lawrence H. Schiffman, Emanuel Tov, and James C. VanderKam, 617–622. Jerusalem: Israel Exploration Society, 2000.

Mason, Steve. "Did the Essenes Write the Dead Sea Scrolls? Don't Rely on Josephus." *Biblical Archaeology Review* 34.6 (2008): 61–65, 81.

Mason, Steve. *Flavius Josephus on the Pharisees.* SPB 39. Leiden: Brill, 1991.

Mason, Steve. Introduction to *Judean Antiquities 1–4,* by Louis Feldman, xii–xxxvi. BJP 3. Leiden: Brill, 2000.

Mason, Steve. *Josephus and the New Testament.* 2nd ed. Peabody, Mass.: Hendrickson, 2003.

Mason, Steve. "Josephus, Daniel, and the Flavian House." In *Josephus and the History of the Greco-Roman Period: Essays in Memory of Morton Smith,* edited by Fausto Parente and Joseph Sievers, 161–191. SPB 41. Leiden: Brill, 1994.

Mason, Steve. *Josephus, Judea, and Christian Origins: Methods and Categories.* Peabody, Mass.: Hendrickson, 2009.

Mason, Steve. *Life of Josephus: Translation and Commentary.* BJP 9. Leiden: Brill, 2001.

Mason, Steve. "Pharisaic Dominance before 70 CE and the Gospels' Hypocrisy Charge (Matt 23:2–3)." *HTR* 83.4 (1990): 363–381.

Mason, Steve. "Revisiting Josephus's Pharisees." In *Judaism in Late Antiquity*, pt. 3, vol. 2, *Where We Stand: Issues and Debates in Ancient Judaism*, edited by Jacob Neusner and Alan J. Avery-Peck, 23–56. Leiden: Brill, 1999.

Mason, Steve, ed. *Understanding Josephus: Seven Perspectives*. JSPSup 32. Sheffield, England: Sheffield Academic Press, 1998.

Mason, Steve. "What Josephus Says about the Essenes in His *Judean War*." In *Text and Artifact in the Religions of Mediterranean Antiquity: Essays in Honour of Peter Richardson*, edited by Stephen G. Wilson and Michel Desjardins, 423–455. Studies in Christianity and Judaism 9. Waterloo, Canada: Wilfrid Laurier University Press, 2000.

Mason, Steve, with Honora Chapman. *Judean War 2: Translation and Commentary*. BJP 1b. Leiden: Brill, 2008.

McLaren, James S. *Turbulent Times? Josephus and Scholarship on Judaea in the First Century CE*. JSPSup 29. Sheffield, England: Sheffield Academic Press, 1998.

McNeill, John T., ed. *Calvin: Institutes of the Christian Religion*. Library of Christian Classics 20–21. 2 vols. Philadelphia: Westminster Press, 1960.

Meier, John P. *A Marginal Jew: Rethinking the Historical Jesus*. Vol. 1. *The Roots of the Problem and the Person*. New York: Doubleday, 1991.

Meier, John P. *A Marginal Jew: Rethinking the Historical Jesus*. Vol. 2. *Mentor, Message, and Miracles*. New York: Doubleday, 1994.

Meier, John P. *A Marginal Jew: Rethinking the Historical Jesus*. Vol. 3. *Companions and Competitors*. New York: Doubleday, 2001.

Meier, John P. *A Marginal Jew: Rethinking the Historical Jesus*. Vol. 4. *Law and Love*. New Haven: Yale University Press, 2009.

Mendenhall, George E. "From Witchcraft to Justice: Death and Afterlife in the Old Testament." In *Death and Afterlife: Perspectives of World Religions*, edited by H. Obayashi, 67–81. New York: Praeger, 1992.

Merrill, Eugene H. *Qumran and Predestination: A Theological Study of the Thanksgiving Hymns*. STDJ 8. Leiden: Brill, 1975.

Meyer, Marvin. *The Gnostic Discoveries: The Impact of the Nag Hammadi Library*. New York: HarperSanFrancisco, 2005.

Meyer, Rudolf. "Σαδδουκαῖος." In *Theological Dictionary of the New Testament*, edited by G. Kittel and G. Friedrich and translated by G. W. Bromiley, 10 vols., 8:35–54. Grand Rapids, Mich.: Eerdmans, 1971.

Meyers, Eric M. *Jewish Ossuaries: Reburial and Rebirth, Secondary Burials in Their Ancient Near Eastern Setting*. Biblica et orientalia 24. Rome: Biblical Institute Press, 1971.

Michel, Otto, and Otto Bauernfeind, eds. and trans. *Flavius Josephus, De Bello Judaico: Der Jüdische Krieg, Griechisch und Deutsch: Herausgegeben mit einer Einleitung sowie mit Anmerkungen versehen*. 3 vols. in 4 pts. Darmstadt: Wissenschaftliche Buchgesellschaft, 1959–69.

Milikowsky, Chaim. "Notions of Exile, Subjugation and Return in Rabbinic Literature." In *Exile: Old Testament, Jewish, and Christian Conceptions*, edited by J. M. Scott, 265–296. JSJSup 56. Leiden: Brill, 1997.

Mirkin, Moses Aryeh, ed. *Midrash Rabbah: Meforash Perush Mada'i Hadash*. 11 vols. Tel-Aviv: Yavneh, 1987.

Momigliano, Arnaldo. *Essays on Ancient and Modern Judaism*. Edited with an introduction by Sylvia Berth. Translated by Maura Masella Gayley. Chicago: University of Chicago Press, 1994.

Moore, George Foot. "Fate and Free Will in the Jewish Philosophies According to Josephus." *HTR* 22.4 (1929): 371–389.

Moore, George Foot. *Judaism in the First Centuries of the Christian Era, the Age of the Tannaim*. 3 vols. Cambridge, Mass.: Harvard University Press, 1927–30.

Moore, Michael S. "Human Suffering in Lamentations." *RB* 90.4 (1983): 534–555.

Morgan, Michael L. ed. *A Holocaust Reader: Responses to the Nazi Extermination*. New York: Oxford University Press, 2001.

Mueller, Ian. "Heterodoxy and Doxography in Hippolytus' 'Refutation of All Heresies.'" In *Aufstieg und Niedergang der römischen Welt: Geschichte und Kultur Roms im Spiegel der neueren Forschung*. Part 2, *Principat*, 36.6, edited by H. Temporini and W. Haase, 4309–4374. New York: de Gruyter, 1992.

Murphy, Frederick J. "The Temple in the Syriac *Apocalypse of Baruch*." *JBL* 106.4 (1987): 671–683.

Murphy, Roland E. *The Tree of Life: An Exploration of Biblical Wisdom Literature*. 3rd ed. Grand Rapids, Mich.: Eerdmans, 2002.

Nakman, David. "The Halakhah in the Writings of Josephus" [Hebrew]. Ph.D. diss., Department of Land of Israel Studies and Archaeology, Bar-Ilan University, 2004.

Nautin, Pierre. "Hippolytus." In *Encyclopedia of the Early Church*, edited by Angelo Di Beradino and translated by Adrian Walford, 2 vols., 1:383–385. New York: Oxford University Press, 1992.

Nemoy, Leon. "Al-Qirqisānī's Account of the Jewish Sects and Christianity." *HUCA* 7 (1930): 317–397.

Netzer, Ehud, with Rachel Laureys-Chachy. *The Architecture of Herod the Great Builder*. Tübingen: Mohr Siebeck, 2006.

Neusner, Jacob. "Emergent Rabbinic Judaism in a Time of Crisis: Four Responses to the Destruction of the Second Temple." *Judaism* 21.3 (1972): 313–327.

Neusner, Jacob. "From History to Religion." In *The Craft of Religious Studies*, edited by Jon R. Stone, 98–116. New York: Palgrave, 2000.

Neusner, Jacob. *From Politics to Piety: the Emergence of Pharisaic Judaism*. New York: Ktav, 1979.

Neusner, Jacob. *How Important Was the Destruction of the Second Temple in the Formation of Rabbinic Judaism?* Lanham, Md.: University Press of America, 2006.

Neusner, Jacob. "The Implications of the Holocaust." *Journal of Religion* 53.3 (1973): 293–308.

Neusner, Jacob. "In Quest of the Historical Rabban Yohanan Ben Zakkai." *HTR* (1966): 391–413.

Neusner, Jacob. *Introduction to Rabbinic Literature*. New York: Doubleday, 1994.

Neusner, Jacob. *Israel after Calamity: The Book of Lamentations*. Valley Forge, Pa.: Trinity Press International, 1995.

Neusner, Jacob. *Judaism: The Evidence of the Mishnah*. Chicago: University of Chicago Press, 1979.

Neusner, Jacob. *The Mishnah: A New Translation*. New Haven: Yale University Press, 1988.

Neusner, Jacob. *Rabbinic Judaism: Structure and System*. Minneapolis: Fortress, 1995.

Neusner, Jacob. *The Rabbinic Traditions about the Pharisees before 70*. 3 vols. Leiden: Brill, 1971.

Neusner, Jacob, and Alan J. Avery-Peck, eds. *Judaism in Late Antiquity*. Pt. 3, vol. 1. *Where We Stand: Issues and Debates in Ancient Judaism*. Leiden: Brill, 1999.

Neusner, Jacob, and Bruce D. Chilton, eds. *In Quest of the Historical Pharisees*. Waco, Tex.: Baylor University Press, 2007.

Newell, Raymond R. "Forms and Historical Value of Josephus' Suicide Accounts." In *Josephus, the Bible, and History*, edited by Louis H. Feldman and Gohei Hata, 278–294. Detroit: Wayne State University Press, 1989.

Nickelsburg, George W. E. *Resurrection, Immortality, and Eternal Life in Intertestamental Judaism and Early Christianity* (1972). Expanded ed. Harvard Theological Studies 56. Cambridge, Mass.: Harvard University Press, 2006.

Niditch, Susan. *War in the Hebrew Bible: A Study in the Ethics of Violence*. New York: Oxford University Press, 1993.

Niese, Benedictus. *Flavii Iosephi opera: Edidit et apparatu critico instruxit*. 7 vols. Berlin: Weidmann, 1887–95.

Nikiprowetzky, Valentin. "Le Sabat et les armes dans l'histoire ancienne d'Israël." *Revue des études juives* 159.1–2 (2000): 1–17.

Noam, Vered. *Megillat Ta'anit: Versions, Interpretation, History, with a Critical Edition* [Hebrew]. Between Bible and Mishnah. Jerusalem: Yad Ben-Zvi Press, 2003.

Olson, Ryan S. *Tragedy, Authority, and Trickery: The Poetics of Embedded Letters in Josephus*. Hellenic Studies 42. Washington, D.C.: Center for Hellenic Studies, 2010.

Olyan, Saul B. "Ben Sira's Relationship to the Priesthood." *HTR* 80.3 (1987): 261–286.

Olyan, Saul B. "Zadok's Origins and the Tribal Politics of David." *JBL* 101.2 (1982): 177–193.

Pearson, Birger A. *Ancient Gnosticism: Traditions and Literature*. Minneapolis: Fortress Press, 2007.

Pearson, Birger A. *Gnosticism, Judaism and Egyptian Christianity*. Minneapolis: Fortress Press, 1990.

Penner, Ken. "The Fate of Josephus's *Antiquitates Judaicae* 13.171–173: Ancient Jewish Philosophy in Context." *Journal of Biblical Studies* 1.4 (n.d.): 1–26.

Perdue, Leo G. *Wisdom Literature: A Theological History*. Louisville, Ky.: Westminster John Knox Press, 2007.

Perdue, Leo G., Bernard Brandon Scott, and William Johnston Wiseman, eds. *In Search of Wisdom: Essays in Memory of John G. Gammie*. Louisville, Ky.: Westminster John Knox, 1993.

Pines, Shlomo, ed. and trans. *Guide of the Perplexed*, by Moses Maimonides. 2 vols. Chicago: University of Chicago Press, 1963.

Pines, Shlomo. "A Platonistic Model for Two of Josephus' Accounts of the Doctrine of the Pharisees Concerning Providence and Man's Freedom of Action." *Immanuel* 7 (1977): 38–60.

Pink, Thomas. *Free Will: A Very Short Introduction*. Oxford: Oxford University Press, 2004.

Popović, Mladen. "Bones, Bodies, and Resurrection in the Dead Sea Scrolls." In *The Human Body in Death and Resurrection*, edited by Tobias Nicklas, Friedrich V. Reiterer, and Joseph Verheyden, in collaboration with Heike Braun, 221–242. Deuterocanonical and Cognate Literature Yearbook. Berlin: de Gruyter, 2009.

Porten, Bezalel. *Archives from Elephantine: The Life of an Ancient Jewish Military Colony*. Berkeley: University of California Press, 1968.

Porton, Gary G. "Sadducees." In *Anchor Bible Dictionary*, edited by David Noel Freedham, 6 vols., 5:892–895. New York: Doubleday, 1992.

Price, Jonathan J. "Josephus and the Dialogue on the Destruction of Jerusalem." In *Josephus und das Neue Testament: Weshselseitige Wahrnehmungen: II. Internationales Symposium zum Corpus Judaeo-Hellenisticum, 25.–28. Mai 2006*, edited by Chistfried Böttrich and Jens Herzer, with the assistance of Torsten Reiprich, 181–194. WUNT 1, 209. Tübingen: Mohr Siebeck, 2007.

Price, Jonathan J. "The Provincial Historian in Rome." In *Josephus and Jewish History in Flavian Rome and Beyond*, edited by Joseph Sievers and Gaia Lembi, 101–118. JSJSup 104. Leiden: Brill, 2005.

Price, Jonathan J. "Some Aspects of Josephus' Theological Interpretation of the Jewish War." In *"The Words of a Wise Man's Mouth Are Gracious" (Qoh 10,12): Festschrift for Günter Stemberger on the Occasion of his 65th Birthday*, edited by Mauro Perani, 109–119. SJ 32. Berlin: de Gruyter, 2005.

Puech, Émile. *La croyance des Esséniens en la vie future: Immoralité, résurrection, vie éternelle? Histoire d'une croyance dans le judaïsme ancien*. 2 vols. Paris: Librairie Lecoffre, 1993.

Puech, Émile. *Qumrân Grotte 4, XVIII: Textes hébreux (4Q521–4Q528, 4Q576–4Q579)*. DJD 25. Oxford: Clarendon, 1997.

Qafih, Joseph, ed. *Mishnah with Maimonides' Commentary* [Hebrew]. 6 vols. Jerusalem: Mosad Ha-Rav Kook, 1976–78.

Qimron, Elisha. *The Dead Sea Scrolls: The Hebrew Writings* [Hebrew]. Vol. 1. *Between Bible and Mishnah*. Jerusalem: Yad Ben-Zvi Press, 2010.

Qimron, Elisha, and John Strugnell. *Qumran Cave 4, V (Miqsat Ma'aseh ha-Torah)*. DJD 10. Oxford: Clarendon, 1994.

Rabbinovicz, Raphaelo. *Sefer Diqduqe Soferim: Variae Lectiones in Mischnam et in Talmud Babylonicum* [Hebrew]. Munich: H. Roesel, 1866–97. Reprint (2 vols.), New York: M. P. Press, 1976.

Rackham, H., ed. and trans. *De Oratore Book III together with De Fato, Paradoxica Stoicorum, De Partitione Oratoria*. LCL. Cambridge, Mass.: Harvard University Press, 1948.

Rajak, Tessa. *The Jewish Dialogue with Greece and Rome: Studies in Cultural and Social Interaction*. Leiden: Brill, 2002.

Rajak, Tessa. "Josephus and Justus of Tiberias." In *Josephus, Judaism and Christianity*, edited by Louis H. Feldman and Gohei Hata, 81–94. Detroit: Wayne State University Press, 1987.

Rajak, Tessa. *Josephus: The Historian and His Society* (1983). 2nd ed. London: Duckworth, 2002.

Raviv, Rivka. "The Talmudic Formulation of the Prophecies of the Four Kingdoms in the Book of Daniel" [Hebrew]. *Jewish Studies: An Internet Journal* 5 (2006): 1–20. www.biu.ac.il/JS/JSIJ/5–2006/Raviv.pdf.

Regev, Eyal. "Herod's Jewish Ideology Facing Romanization: On Intermarriage, Ritual Baths, and Speeches." *JQR* 100.2 (2010): 197–222.

Regev, Eyal. "Sadducees." In *New Interpreters Bible Dictionary*, edited by Katharine Doob Sakenfeld, 5 vols., 5:32–36. Nashville, Tenn.: Abingdon Press, 2009.

Regev, Eyal. *The Sadducees and Their Halakhah: Religion and Society in the Second Temple Period* [Hebrew]. Jerusalem: Yad Ben-Zvi, 2005.

Regev, Eyal. "Were the Priests All the Same? Qumranic Halakhah in Comparison with Saducean Halakhah." *DSD* 12.2 (2005): 158–188.

Regev, Eyal, and David Nakman. "Josephus and the Halakhah of the Pharisees, the Sadducees, and Qumran" [Hebrew]. *Zion* 67.4 (2002): 401–433 (English summary, xxxii).

Reid, J. K. S., ed. and trans. *Concerning the Eternal Predestination of God*, by John Calvin. Louisville, Ky.: Westminster John Knox, 1997.

Reider, Joseph. *The Book of Wisdom: An English Translation with Introduction and Commentary*. Jewish Apocryphal Literature. New York: Harper (for Philadelphia: Dropsie College), 1957.

Rengstorf, Karl Heinrich, ed. *A Complete Concordance to Flavius Josephus*. 1969–83. Study Edition in Two Volumes, Including Supplement 1: *Namenwörterbuch zu Flavius Josephus*, by Abraham Schalit. Leiden: Brill, 2002.

Revel, Bernard. "Some Anti-traditional Laws in Josephus." *JQR* 14.3 (1924): 293–301.

Richardson, Peter. *Building Jewish in the Roman East*. Waco, Tex.: Baylor University Press, 2004.

Richardson, Peter. *Herod: King of the Jews and Friend of the Romans*. Columbia: University of South Carolina Press, 1996.

Ringgren, Helmer. *The Faith of Qumran: Theology of the Dead Sea Scrolls.* Translated by Emilie T. Sander. Philadelphia: Fortress, 1963.

Rosenbaum, Alan S., ed. *Is the Holocaust Unique? Perspectives on Comparative Genocide.* 3rd ed. Boulder, Colo.: Westview Press, 2009.

Roskies, David G. *The Literature of Destruction: Jewish Responses to Catastrophe.* Philadelphia: Jewish Publication Society, 1988.

Roth, Joel. *The Halakhic Process: A Systemic Analysis.* Moreshet 13. New York: Jewish Theological Seminary, 1986.

Roy, Steven C. *How Much Does God Foreknow? A Comprehensive Biblical Study.* Downers Grove, Ill.: IVP Academic, 2006.

Rubenstein, Jeffrey L. *Talmudic Stories: Narrative Art, Composition, and Culture.* Baltimore: Johns Hopkins University Press, 1999.

Rubenstein, Richard L. "The Fall of Jerusalem and the Birth of Holocaust Theology." In *Go and Study: Essays and Studies in Honor of Alfred Jospe,* edited by Raphael Jospe and Samuel Z. Fishman, 223–240. Washington, D.C.: B'nai B'rith Hillel Foundations, 1980.

Rudavsky, Tamar M. *Time Matters: Time, Creation, and Cosmology in Medieval Jewish Philosophy.* Albany: State University of New York Press, 2000.

Russell, D. S. *The Method and Message of Jewish Apocalyptic: 200 BC–AD 100.* Old Testament Library. Philadelphia: Westminster Press, 1964.

Safrai, Shmuel, ed. *The Literature of the Sages, First Part: Oral Torah, Halakha, Mishna, Tosefta, Talmud, External Tractates.* CRINT II.3.1. Assen: Van Gorcum, 1987.

Saldarini, Anthony J. *Pharisees, Scribes and Sadducees in Palestinian Society: A Sociological Approach.* Wilmington, Del.: Michael Glazier, 1988.

Salles, Ricardo. *The Stoics on Determinism and Compatibilism.* Aldershot, England: Ashgate, 2005.

Sanders, E. P. "The Dead Sea Sect and Other Jews: Commonalities, Overlaps, and Differences." In *The Dead Sea Scrolls in Their Historical Context,* edited by Timothy H. Lim, with Larry W. Hurtado, A. Graeme Auld, and Alison Jack, 7–43. London: T. and T. Clark, 2004.

Sanders, E. P. *Jewish Law from Jesus to the Mishnah: Five Studies.* London: SCM Press, 1990.

Sanders, E. P. *Judaism: Practice and Belief, 63 BCE–66 CE.* London: SCM Press, 1992.

Sanders, E. P. *Paul and Palestinian Judaism: A Comparison of Patterns of Religion.* Minneapolis: Fortress, 1977.

Schäfer, Peter. "Bar Kokhba and the Rabbis." In *The Bar Kokhba War: New Perspectives on the Second Jewish Revolt against Rome,* edited by Peter Schäfer, 1–22. TSAJ 100. Tübingen: Mohr Siebeck 2003.

Schalit, Abraham, ed. and trans. *Flavii Josephi, Antiquitates Judaicae: In Linguam Hebraicam Vertit Annotationibus Amplissimis Illustravit et Prooemio Instruxit* [Hebrew]. 3 vols. Jerusalem: Bialik Institute, 1944–63.

Schechter, Solomon, ed. *Aboth de Rabbi Nathan*. Vienna: Ch. D. Lippe, 1887.

Schechter, Solomon. *Aspects of Rabbinic Theology: Major Concepts of the Talmud*. New York: Macmillan, 1909.

Schechter, Solomon. *Studies in Judaism: First Series*. Philadelphia: Jewish Publication Society, 1911.

Schiffman, Lawrence H. *From Text to Tradition: A History of Second Temple and Rabbinic Judaism*. Hoboken, N.J.: Ktav, 1991.

Schiffman, Lawrence H. *The Halakhah at Qumran*. SJLA 16. Leiden: Brill, 1975.

Schiffman, Lawrence H. "Pharisaic and Sadducean Halakhah in Light of the Dead Sea Scrolls: The Case of Tevul Yom." *DSD* 1.3 (1994): 285–299.

Schiffman, Lawrence H. *Qumran and Jerusalem: Studies in the Dead Sea Scrolls and the History of Judaism*. Grand Rapids, Mich.: Eerdmans, 2010.

Schofield, Alison, and James C. VanderKam. "Were the Hasmoneans Zadokites?" *JBL* 124.1 (2005): 73–87.

Schreckenberg, Heinz. "Josephus in Early Christian Literature and Medieval Christian Art." In *Jewish Historiography and Iconography in Early and Medieval Christianity*, by Heinz Schreckenberg and Kurt Schubert, 1–138. CRINT III.1. Assen: Van Gorcum 1992.

Schremer, Adiel. "'The Lord Has Forsaken the Land': Radical Explanations of the Military and Political Defeat of the Jews in Tannaitic Times." *JJS* 59.2 (2008): 183–200.

Schremer, Adiel. "'[T]he[y] Did Not Read in the Sealed Book': Qumran Halakhic Revolution and the Emergence of Torah Study in Second Temple Judaism." In *Historical Perspectives: From the Hasmoneans to Bar Kokhba in Light of the Dead Sea Scrolls; Proceedings of the Fourth International Symposium of the Orion Center for the Study of the Dead Sea Scrolls and Associated Literature, 27–31 January, 1999*, edited by David Goodblatt, Avital Pinnick, and Daniel R. Schwartz, 105–126. STDJ 37. Leiden: Brill, 2001.

Schröder, Bernd. *Die "väterlichen Gesetze": Flavius Josephus als Vermittler von Halachah an Greichen und Römer*. TSAJ 53. Tübingen: Mohr Siebeck, 1996.

Schuller, Eileen. "Petitionary Prayer and the Religion of Qumran." In *Religion in the Dead Sea Scrolls*, edited by John J. Collins and Robert A. Kugler, 29–45. Grand Rapids, Mich.: Eerdmans, 2000.

Schürer, Emil. *The History of the Jewish People in the Age of Jesus Christ*. Revised and edited by Geza Vermes, et al. 4 vols. Edinburgh: T. and T. Clark, 1973–87.

Schwartz, Daniel R. *Flavius Josephus, "Vita": Introduction, Hebrew Translation, and Commentary* [Hebrew]. Between Bible and Mishnah. Jerusalem: Yad Ben-Zvi, 2007.

Schwartz, Daniel R. "Josephus on the Jewish Constitutions and Community." *Scripta Classica Israelica* 7 (1983): 30–52.

Schwartz, Daniel R. "KATA TOYTON TON KAIPON: Josephus' Source on Agrippa II." *JQR* 72.4 (1982): 241–268.

Schwartz, Daniel R. "Law and Truth: On Qumranic-Sadducean and Rabbinic Views of Law." In *The Dead Sea Scrolls: Forty Years of Research*, edited by Devorah Dimant and Uriel Rappaport, 229–240. STDJ 10. Leiden: Brill, 1992.

Schwartz, Daniel R. "On Abraham Schalit, Herod, Josephus, the Holocaust, Horst R. Moehring, and the Study of Ancient Jewish History." *Jewish History* 2.2 (1987): 9–28.

Schwartz, Daniel R. Review of *Jewish Martyrs in the Pagan and Christian Worlds*, by Shmuel Shepkaru. *Review of Biblical Literature*, 2/2007. www.bookreviews.org/pdf/5198_5473.pdf.

Schwartz, Daniel R. *Studies in the Jewish Background of Christianity*. WUNT 1, 60. Tübingen: Mohr Siebeck, 1992.

Schwartz, Daniel R. *2 Maccabees*. Commentaries on Early Jewish Literature. Berlin: de Gruyter, 2008.

Schwartz, Seth. "The Composition and Publication of Josephus's *Bellum Iudaicum* Book 7." *HTR* 79.4 (1986): 373–386.

Schwartz, Seth. *Imperialism and Jewish Society, 200 B.C.E. to 640 C.E.* Princeton: Princeton University Press, 2001.

Schwartz, Seth. *Josephus and Judaean Politics*. Columbia Studies in the Classical Tradition 18. Leiden: Brill, 1990.

Schwartz, Seth. *Were the Jews a Mediterranean Society? Reciprocity and Solidarity in Ancient Judaism*. Princeton: Princeton University Press, 2010.

Sedley, David. "The School, from Zeno to Arius Didymus." In *The Cambridge Companion to the Stoics*, edited by Brad Inwood, 7–32. Cambridge: Cambridge University Press, 2003.

Seeskin, Kenneth. *Jewish Philosophy in a Secular Age*. Albany: State University of New York Press, 1990.

Segal, Alan F. *Life after Death: A History of the Afterlife in the Religions of the West*. New York: Doubleday, 2004.

Segal, Alan F. *Rebecca's Children: Judaism and Christianity in the Roman World*. Cambridge, Mass.: Harvard University Press, 1986.

Segal, Moshe Tzvi. *Sefer Ben Sira ha-Shalem*. 2nd corrected and expanded ed. Jerusalem: Bialik Institute, 1958.

Shapiro, Schubert. "In Defense of the Defenders of Masada." *Tradition* 11.1 (1970): 31–43.

Sharples, R. W. "Alexander of Aphrodisias, *De Fato*: Some Parallels." *Classical Quarterly* 28.2 (1978): 243–266.

Sharples, R. W., ed. and trans. *Cicero: On Fate (De Fato) and Boethius: The Consolation of Philosophy (Philosophiae Consolationis IV.5–7, V)*. Warminster, England: Aris and Phillips, 1991.

Sharples, R. W. "Soft Determinism and Freedom in Early Stoicism." *Phronesis* 31.3 (1986): 266–279.

Shemesh, Aharon. *Halakhah in the Making: The Development of Jewish Law from Qumran to the Rabbis.* Taubman Lectures in Jewish Studies. Berkeley: University of California Press, 2009.

Shemesh, Aharon, and Cana Werman. "Halakhah at Qumran: Genre and Authority." *DSD* 10.1 (2003): 104–129.

Shemesh, Aharon, and Cana Werman. "Hidden Things and Their Revelation." *RevQ* 71/18.3 (1998): 409–427.

Shepkaru, Shmuel. "From After Death to Afterlife: Martyrdom and Its Recompense." *AJSR* 24.1 (1999): 1–44.

Shepkaru, Shmuel. *Jewish Martyrs in the Pagan and Christian Worlds.* New York: Cambridge University Press, 2006.

Sievers, Joseph. "Josephus and the Afterlife." In *Understanding Josephus: Seven Perspectives*, edited by Steve Mason, 20–34. JSPSup 32. Sheffield, England: Sheffield Academic Press, 1998.

Sievers, Joseph. "Josephus, First Maccabees, Sparta, the Three *Haireseis*—and Cicero." *JSJ* 32.3 (2001): 241–251.

Sievers, Joseph. *Synopsis of the Greek Sources for the Study of the Hasmonean Period: 1–2 Maccabees and Josephus, "War" 1 and "Antiquities," 12–14.* Subsidia biblica 20. Rome: Pontifical Biblical Institute, 2001.

Sievers, Joseph. "Who Were the Pharisees?" In *Hillel and Jesus: Comparisons of Two Major Religious Leaders*, edited by James H. Charlesworth and Loren L. Johns, 137–155. Minneapolis: Fortress Press, 1997.

Simchoni, Jacob Naftali. *Flavii Josephus: Bellum Judaicum* [Hebrew]. 1923–28. Reprint, Jerusalem: Bialik Institute, 1968.

Simon, Marcel. *Jewish Sects at the Time of Jesus.* Philadelphia: Fortress, 1967.

Singer, Isidore, et al., eds. *The Jewish Encyclopedia.* 12 vols. New York: Funk and Wagnall's, 1901–6.

Sivan, Hagith. *Between Woman, Man, and God: A New Interpretation of the Ten Commandments.* London: T. and T. Clark, 2004.

Skehan, Patrick W., and Alexander A. Di Lella. *The Wisdom of Ben Sira: A New Translation with Notes, Introduction and Commentary.* AB 39. New York: Doubleday, 1987.

Smith, Jonathan Z. *Drudgery Divine: On the Comparison of Early Christians and the Religions of Late Antiquity.* Chicago: University of Chicago Press, 1990.

Smith, Jonathan Z. "Tillich['s] Remains . . ." *JAAR* 78.4 (2010): 1139–1170.

Smith, Morton. "The Dead Sea Sect in Relation to Ancient Judaism." *New Testament Studies* 7 (1961): 347–360.

Smith, Morton. "The Description of the Essenes in the Josephus and the Philosophumena." *HUCA* 29 (1958): 273–313.

Smith, Morton. "Helios in Palestine." *Eretz-Israel* 16 (1982): 199–214.

Smith, Morton. "'Transformation by Burial' (1 Cor 15:35–49; Rom 6:3–5 and 8.9–11)." *Eranos Jahrbuch* 52 (1983): 87–112.

Snaith, John G. "Ecclesiastics: A Tract for the Times." In *Wisdom in Ancient Israel: Essays in Honour of J. A. Emerton*, edited by John Day, Rorbert P. Gordon, and H. G. M. Williamson, 170181. Cambridge: Cambridge University Press, 1995.

Sokol, Moshe. "Maimonides on Freedom of the Will and Moral Responsibility." *HTR* 91.1 1998): 25–39.

Spilsbury, Paul. "*Contra Apionem* and *Antiquitates Judaicae:* Points of Contact." In *Josephus' "Contra Apionem": Studies in Its Character and Context with a Latin Concordance to the Portion Missing in Greek*, edited by Louis H. Feldman and John R. Levison, 348–368. AGJU 34. Leiden: Brill, 1996.

Spilsbury, Paul. "Flavius Josephus on the Rise and Fall of the Roman Empire." *JTS* 54.1 (2003): 1–24.

Spilsbury, Paul. "God and Israel in Josephus: A Patron-Client Relationship." In *Understanding Josephus: Seven Perspectives*, edited by Steve Mason, 172–191. JSPSup 32. Sheffield, England: Sheffield Academic Press, 1998.

Spilsbury, Paul. "Josephus on the Burning of the Temple, the Flavian Triumph, and the Providence of God." *Society of Biblical Literature Seminar Papers* 41 (2002): 306–327.

Stegemann, Hartmut, and Eileen Schuller. With translation of texts by Carol Newsom. In consultation with James VanderKam and Monica Brady. *Qumran Cave 1, III: 1QHodayot^a, with incorporation of 4QHodayot^{a-f} and 1QHodayot^b*. DJD 40. Oxford: Clarendon, 2009.

Stemberger, Günter. *Jewish Contemporaries of Jesus: Pharisees, Sadducees, Essenes.* Translated by Allan W. Mahnke. Minneapolis: Fortress, 1995.

Stemberger, Günter. "The Sadducees—Their History and Doctrines." In *The Cambridge History of Judaism*, vol. 3,*The Early Roman Period*, edited by William Horbury, W. D. Davies, and John Sturdy, 428–443. Cambridge: Cambridge University Press, 1999.

Stern, Menahem. *Greek and Latin Authors on Jews and Judaism: Edited with Introductions, Translations, and Commentary.* 3 vols. Jerusalem: Israel Academy of Sciences and Humanities, 1976–84.

Stern, Menahem. "Josephus and the Roman Empire as Reflected in *The Jewish War*." In *Josephus, Judaism and Christianity*, edited by Louis H. Feldman and Gohei Hata, 71–80. Detroit: Wayne State University Press, 1987.

Stern, Menahem. "The Suicide of Eleazar ben Jair and His Men at Masada, and the 'Fourth Philosophy'" [Hebrew]. *Zion* 47.4 (1982): 367–398.

Stern, Pnina. "*Life of Josephus:* The Autobiography of Flavius Josephus." *JSJ* 41.1 (2010): 63–93.

Stone, Michael, ed. *Jewish Writings of the Second Temple Period: Apocrypha, Pseudepigrapha, Qumran Sectarian Writings, Philo, Josephus.* CRINT II.2. Assen: Van Gorcum, 1984.

Stroumsa, Guy G. "From Anti-Judaism to Antisemitism in Ancient Christianity?" In Contra Iudaeos: *Ancient and Medieval Polemics Between Christians and Jews,* edited by Ora Limor and Guy G. Stroumsa, 1–26. Texts and Studies in Medieval and Early Modern Judaism 10. Tübingen, Mohr Siebeck, 1996.

Stuckrad, Kocku von. "Jewish and Christian Astrology in Late Antiquity: A New Approach." *Numen* 47.1 (2000): 1–40.

Sussmann, Yaakov. "Appendix 1: The History of the Halakha and the Dead Sea Scrolls." In *Qumran Cave 4, V (Miqsat Ma'aseh ha-Torah)*, by Elisha Qimron and John Strugnell, 179–200. DJD 10. Oxford: Clarendon, 1994.

Sussmann, Yaakov. "The History of the Halakha and the Dead Sea Scrolls: A Preliminary to the Publication of 4QMMT" [Hebrew]. *Tarbiz* 59.1–2 (1989): 11–76.

Tabor, James D. "Josephus's Portrayal of the Disappearances of Enoch, Elijah, and Moses." *JBL* 108.2 (1989): 225–238.

Talmon, Shemaryahu. "Was the Book of Esther Known at Qumran?" *DSD* 2.3 (1995): 249–267.

Taylor, Charles. *An Appendix to Sayings of the Jewish Fathers: Containing a Catalogue of Manuscripts and Notes on the Text of Aboth*. Cambridge: Cambridge University Press, 1900.

Taylor, Charles. *Sayings of the Jewish Fathers: Comprising Pirqe Aboth in Hebrew and English with Notes and Excurses*. 2nd ed. with additional notes. Cambridge: Cambridge University Press, 1897.

Taylor, Joan E. "Philo of Alexandria on the Essenes: A Case Study on the Use of Classical Sources in Discussions of the Qumran-Essene Hypothesis." *Studia Philonica Annual* 19 (2007): 1–28.

Tcherikover, Victor. *Hellenistic Civilization and the Jews*. Translated by S. Appelbaum. Philadelphia: Jewish Publication Society, 1959.

Thackeray, H. St. John. *Josephus: The Man and the Historian*. With a preface by George Foot Moore. New York: Jewish Institute of Religion, 1929.

Thackeray, H. St. John, Ralph Marcus, Allen Wilkgren, and L. H. Feldman, eds. and trans. *Josephus*. LCL. 9 vols. Cambridge, Mass.: Harvard University Press, 1926–65.

Theodor, Julius, and Chanoch Albeck, eds. *Midrash Bereshit Rabba: Critical Edition with Notes and Commentary* [Hebrew]. 2nd ed. with corrections. 3 vols. Jerusalem: Wahrmann, 1965.

Thoma, Clemens. "High Priesthood in the Judgment of Josephus." In *Josephus, the Bible, and History*, edited by Louis H. Feldman and Gohei Hata, 196–215. Detroit: Wayne State University Press, 1989.

Tomes, Roger. "Heroism in 1 and 2 Maccabees." *Biblical Interpretation* 15.2 (2007): 171–199.

Trever, John C. *The Dead Sea Scrolls: A Personal Account*. Rev. ed. Grand Rapids, Mich.: Eerdmans, 1977.

Tropper, Amram. "Yohanan ben Zakkai, *Amicus Caesaris*: A Jewish Hero in Rabbinic Eyes." *Jewish Studies: An Internet Journal* 4 (2005): 133–149. www.biu.ac.il/JS/JSIJ/4-2005/Tropper.pdf.

Tzoref, Shani (Berrin). "The 'Hidden' and the 'Revealed': Progressive Revelation of Law and Esoterica" [Hebrew]. In *Meghillot: Studies in the Dead Sea Scrolls VII*, edited by Moshe Bar-Asher and Devorah Dimant, 157–190. Jerusalem: Haifa University and Bialik Institute, 2009.

Ullmann-Margalit, Edna. *Out of the Cave: A Philosophical Inquiry into the Dead Sea Scrolls Research*. Cambridge, Mass.: Harvard University Press, 2006.

Ulrich, Eugene. *The Dead Sea Scrolls and the Origins of the Bible*. Grand Rapids, Mich.: Eerdmans, 1999.

Urbach, Ephraim E. "The Derashah as a Basis for the Halakhah and the Problem of the *Soferim*" [Hebrew]. *Tarbiz* 27.2–3 (1958): 166–182.

Urbach, Ephraim E. "Halakhah and Prophecy" [Hebrew]. *Tarbiz* 18.1 (1947): 1–27.

Urbach, Ephraim E. *The Halakhah: Its Sources and Development*. Translated by Raphael Posner. Jerusalem: Yad la-Talmud, 1986.

Urbach, Ephraim E. *The Sages: Their Concepts and Beliefs*. Translated by Israel Abrahams. Cambridge, Mass.: Harvard University Press, 1987.

VanderKam, James C. *From Joshua to Caiaphas: High Priests after the Exile*. Minneapolis: Fortress, 2004.

VanderKam, James C., and Peter Flint. *The Meaning of the Dead Sea Scrolls: Their Significance for Understanding the Bible, Judaism, Jesus, and Christianity*. New York: HarperSanFrancisco, 2002.

Vermes, Geza. *The Complete Dead Sea Scrolls in English*. Rev. ed. New York: Penguin, 2004.

Vermes, Geza. "Josephus' Treatment of the Book of Daniel." *JJS* 42.2 (1991): 149–166.

Vermes, Geza. *Providential Accidents: An Autobiography*. Lanham, Md.: Rowman and Littlefield, 1999.

Vermes, Geza. "A Summary of the Law by Flavius Josephus." *Novum Testamentum* 24.4 (1982): 289–303.

Vermes, Geza, and Marin D. Goodman, eds. *The Essenes: According to the Classical Sources*. Sheffield, England: JSOT Press (for Oxford Centre for Postgraduate Hebrew Study), 1989.

Von Rad, Gerhard. *Wisdom in Israel*. Translated by James D. Martin. Nashville: Abingdon Press, 1972.

Weber, Max. *The Sociology of Religion*. 1922. Reprint, Translated by Ephraim Fischoff. Boston: Beacon Press, 1963.

Weiss, Isaac H., ed. *Sifra D'Be Rab (Torat Kohanim)*. Vienna: Jacob Schlossberg, 1862.

Weitzman, Steven. "Josephus on How to Survive Martyrdom." *JJS* 55.2 (2004) 230–245.

Weitzman, Steven. *Surviving Sacrilege: Cultural Persistence in Jewish Antiquity*. Cambridge, Mass.: Harvard University Press, 2005.

Wellhausen, Julius. *The Pharisees and Sadducees*. 1874. Reprint, Translated by Mark E. Biddle. Macon, Ga.: Mercer University Press, 2001.

Wendland, Paul, ed. *Hippolytus Werke*. Vol. 3. *Refutatio omnium haeresium*. Die griechischen christlichen Schriftsteller der ersten drei Jahrhunderte, 26. Leipzig: J. C. Hinrichs, 1916.

Werman, Cana. "Oral Torah vs. Written Torah(s): Competing Claims to Authority." In *Rabbinic Perspectives: Rabbinic Literature and the Dead Sea Scrolls; Proceedings of the Eighth International Symposium of the Orient Center for the Study of the Dead Sea Scrolls and Associated Literature, 7–9 January, 2003*, edited by Steven D. Fraade, Aharon Shemesh, and Ruth A. Clements, 175–197. STJD 72. Leiden: Brill, 2006.

Whiston, William, trans. *The Works of Josephus: Complete and Unabridged*. 1736. Reprint, new updated ed., Peabody, Mass.: Hendrickson, 1995.

Wiebe, Donald. *The Politics of Religious Studies: The Continuing Conflict with Theology in the Academy*. New York: St. Martin's Press, 1999.

Wieder, Naphtali. *The Judean Scrolls and Karaism*. 1962. Reprint, with addenda, corrigenda, and supplementary articles, Jerusalem: Yad Ben-Zvi, 2005.

Wieder, Naphtali. "The 'Law-Interpreter' of the Sect of the Dead Sea Scrolls: The Second Moses." *JJS* 4.4 (1953): 158–175.

Williams, Frank, trans. *The Panarion of Epiphanius of Salamis: Book I (Sects. 1–46)*. Nag Hammadi Studies 35. Leiden: Brill, 1987.

Williams, Michael A. "Higher Providence, Lower Providences and Fate in Gnosticism and Middle Plantonism." In *Neoplatonism and Gnosticism*, edited by Richard T. Wallis and Jay Bregman, 483–507. Albany: State University of New York Press, 1992.

Williams, Michael A. *Rethinking "Gnosticism": An Argument for Dismantling a Dubious Category*. Princeton: Princeton University Press, 1996.

Williamson, H. G. M. "The Historical Value of Josephus' *Jewish Antiquities* XI. 197–301." *JTS* 28.1 (1977): 49–66.

Wilson, S. G. *Luke and the Law*. Cambridge: Cambridge University Press, 1983.

Winston, David. *The Ancestral Philosophy: Hellenistic Philosophy in Second Temple Judaism*. BJS 331. Providence: Brown Judaic Studies, 2001.

Winston, David. *The Wisdom of Solomon: A New Translation with Introduction and Commentary*. AB 43. New York: Doubleday, 1979.

Winter, Paul. "Ben Sira and the Teaching of 'Two Ways.'" *VT* 5.3 (1955): 315–318.

Wise, Michael O. "Dating the Teacher of Righteousness and the *Floruit* of His Movement." *JBL* 122.1 (2003): 53–87.

Wolfson, Harry Austryn. *Philo: Foundations of Religious Philosophy in Judaism, Christianity, and Islam*. 2 vols. Cambridge, Mass.: Harvard University Press, 1947.

Wright, R. B. "Psalms of Solomon." In *The Old Testament Pseudepigrapha*, edited by James H. Charlesworth, 2 vols., 2:639–670. Garden City, N.Y.: Doubleday, 1983.

Yadin, Azzan. "4QMMT, Rabbi Ishmael, and the Origins of Legal Midrash." *DSD* 10.1 (2003): 130–149.

Yadin, Yigael. *Masada: Herod's Fortress and the Zealots' Last Stand*. Translated by Moshe Pearlman. New York: Random House, 1966.

Yadin, Yigael. *The Temple Scroll*. 3 vols. Jerusalem: Israel Exploration Society, 1983.

Yerushalmi, Yosef Hayim. *Zakhor: Jewish History and Jewish Memory*. With a new preface and postscript by the author. New York: Schocken, 1989.

Yonge, Charles Duke, trans. *The Works of Philo Judaeus: The Contemporary of Josephus*. 1854–90. Reprint, new updated version with foreword by David M. Scholer, Peabody, Mass.: Hendrickson, 2004.

Zeitlin, Solomon. "The Account of the Essenes in Josephus and in the Philosophumena (a reply to M. Smith)." *JQR* 49.4 (1958–59): 292–299.

Zeitlin, Solomon. *The Rise and Fall of the Judaean State: A Political, Social and Religious History of the Second Commonwealth*. 3 vols. Philadelphia: Jewish Publication Society, 1962–78.

Zerubavel, Yael. *Recovered Roots: Collective Memory and the Making of Israeli National Tradition*. Chicago: University of Chicago Press, 1995.

General Index

Aaronides (priestly), 19–23, 218
   See also Zadokites
Abegg, Martin G., xv
Abraham, 61, 95, 97–98, 100–102, 155
   binding of Isaac, 98, 100, 155
accidents (unfated events), 61, 87–88, 215
afterlife (as catch-all term), 93
   beatific, 95–98, 102
   burial and, 98, 119
   origins of beliefs, 98–100, 105–106, 135
   social impact, 92, 97, 100, 116–119, 135–136, 215
   and wealth, 24, 104–105
   See also immortality, resurrection, Sheol
Agrippa I, 85
Agrippa II, 4, 7, 189, 284n.90, 288n.117, 289–290n.123, 290n.128
Akiba, 54, 56–57, 68, 72, 125, 250nn.41, 42, 273n.101
Albeck, Chanoch, 284n.80
Alexander and Aristobulus (sons of Herod), 54–56, 88
Alexander of Aphrodisias, 78
Alexander Jannaeus, 6, 140
Alexander, Philip S., 304n.116
Alexandra, 143
Alon, Gedaliah, 299n.61, 302n.96

Altshuler, David, 278n.6
Ananus, 6, 28, 86–87, 128, 132, 188, 189, 204, 239n.108, 263n.173, 289n.123
Angels, 93, 101–102, 109, 114, 226, 249n.33, 269n.71
apocalyptic literature
   after 70 CE, 185–187, 197–201, 208–209
   and determinism, 50
   and wisdom, 29–30
   See also Josephus, eschatology of
Appelbaum, Alan, 235n.57, 274n.122
Aristobulus I, 189, 261n.152
Aristobulus II, 127, 166
Aristobulus, brother of Mariamme, 165, 251n.47, 289n.122
Astren, Fred, 303n.110, 304n.111
astrology, 48, 253n.74, 259n.133
Atkinson, Kenneth, 244nn.155, 166
atonement, 57, 132, 172, 187, 194–200, 271n.88
   Day of, 285n.88, 299n.58
   without temple, 194–195, 198–200
   See also repentance
Attridge, Harold W. 5, 86, 230nn.10, 13, 235n.59, 247nn.16–18, 21, 260nn.139, 142, 261nn.145, 150, 151, 262n.153, 159, 160, 263n.170
Avery-Peck, Alan J., 243n.139, 264n.1

Ehrenkrook, Jason von, 231nn.18, 21,
290nn.131, 132
Ein Gedi (massacre), 129, 132, 188
Elbogen, Ismar, 302n.98
Eleazar (martyr), 122–123
Eleazar Avaran, 121–122
Eleazar son of Yair, 117–119, 133
no fear of Hell, 119, 133
See also Masada
Elijah, 82, 95, 97, 98
Elior, Rachel, 237n.89, 244n.154
Elledge, C. D., 107–108, 113, 224,
234n.47, 235n.56, 239n.114,
247n.11, 264nn.1, 3, 5, 265nn.19,
22, 24, 267n.40, 268nn.54, 55,
60, 62, 64, 269n.70, 72, 73, 77,
270nn.79, 81, 271nn.85, 86, 87,
88, 306nn.2, 4, 5, 13, 307n.25,
308n.30
Enoch, 97, 98
"Enochic" Judaism, 25
Epicureans, 12, 13, 47, 58, 63, 81–83,
227, 239n.109
Epstein, Isidore, xv
Epstein, Jacob N., 280n.32
Erder, Yoram, 303n.110, 304n.111
eruv, 143
Eshel, Hanan, 237n.88, 300n.64
Essene hypothesis, 19, 26–28, 35–41, 112
harder and softer forms, 36–37
Essenes
after 70 CE, 201–204
biases against, 201–204, 219–220
celibacy, 11, 22, 171–172
compared with Pythagoreans, 11, 63
compatibilism, 48, 57–58, 79–81
exempt from Herod's oath of
allegiance, 12, 142–143
fate, 10–11, 44–45, 49–52
free will, 57–58, 65–66
immortality beliefs of, 10–11, 111–112,
115–116, 118–119, 189

Josephus's affection for, 6–7, 12, 90,
120, 124, 133, 170–172
martyrdom, 115–116, 120, 124, 133, 175,
204
other-worldly stance, 111–112
in Philo, 41–42, 249n.36
prophecy among, 10, 12, 160–161,
177–178, 204
resurrection among (according to
Hippolytus), 223–228
spitting, 39
sun-worship among, 40–41
withdrawal from temple, 11, 171, 204
See also Qumran sectarians
Ezekiel, 19, 20, 22, 82, 95, 112, 160,
197–198, 208, 217–218

Falk, Daniel K., 303n.102
fate (*heimarmene*), 10–11, 20, 44–91, 192
and determinism, 46
and fortune, 46–47, 85–86
and free will. *See* compatibilism
and providence, 47–48, 81–89, 175
See also determinism, Essenes, fortune,
predestination, providence
Feinberg, John S., 248n.24, 258n.126,
259n.134
Feldman, Louis H., 5, 7, 107, 138, 230n.16,
231n.18, 232n.28, 233nn.31, 32,
35, 235n.56, 242n.133, 243n.145,
245n.177, 249n.33, 250n.40,
253nn.75, 76, 255nn.94, 103, 259–
260n.139, 260n.142, 261nn.143,
140, 262nn.159, 162, 266n.31,
267n.44, 270n.81, 275–276n.132,
277n.1, 277–278n.3, 279n.19,
280n.30, 281n.51, 282n.56,
286nn.85, 86, 287nn.103, 104,
291nn.135, 143, 292nn.146, 149,
153, 293n.157, 300nn.66, 68, 73,
300–301n.74
Fine, Steven, 265n.17, 272n.93

Index of Ancient Sources

6.1–7.42   94, 109, 115, 123, 227, 270n.79
6.11   155
6.12–17   123, 200
7.9   94, 98, 107
7.11   94, 108
7.14   98
7.22–23   94
7.28   94
7.32–38   123
8.1–4   123
8.25–26   155
10.1–8   159
14.37–46   123, 129–130
14.46   94, 108
15.1–50   155
15.36   159
17.1–36   123
1 Esdras
8.80   160
3 Maccabees
4.21   47
5.30   47
4 Ezra (2 Esdras 3–14)
3.1–4.52   199
7.32–37   75–103
8.19–36   199
9.27–37   201
10.25–27   197, 201
10.44–54   197
4 Maccabees
1.11   123, 269n.75
5.23   269n.75
6.9, 16   269n.75
6.28–29   123
7.4, 9, 14, 22   269n.75
7.19–20   95, 97, 116, 123
8.11, 13, 24   269n.75
9.17, 22   269n.75
9.24   47, 123
12.3, 11   269n.75

12.17   123
13.14–17   94–95
13.17   97, 116
13.19   47
14.1, 12   269n.75
15.14–30   269n.75
16.16   272n.95
16.17, 22   269n.75
16.25   95, 97, 116
17.4, 12, 17, 23   269n.75
17.5   95, 116
17.19–24   123
17.22   47, 123
18.4   123

NEW TESTAMENT
Matthew
3.1–17   172
3.6   173
5.16   226
5.44   226
13.3–12   172
15.1–20   143, 226
22.23–33   101, 148, 226
22.32   98
23.2–3   34
23.35   128
Mark
1.2–11   172
1.4   173
6.17–29   172
7.1–23   143, 226
12.18–27   101, 148, 226, 266n.29
12.25   109
12.26   98
13.1–2, 14   193
Luke
1.9   291n.142
3.1–22   172
3.3, 6   173
6.28   226

Printed in the USA/Agawam, MA
June 17, 2013

576562.068